In the Room With Men

In the
Room
With Men

A CASEBOOK OF THERAPEUTIC CHANGE

Edited by
Matt Englar-Carlson and
Mark A. Stevens

American Psychological Association • Washington, DC

Copyright © 2006 by the American Psychological Association. All rights reserved. Except
as permitted under the United States Copyright Act of 1976, no part of this publication
may be reproduced or distributed in any form or by any means, including, but not limited
to, the process of scanning and digitization, or stored in a database or retrieval system,
without the prior written permission of the publisher.

Published by
American Psychological Association
750 First Street, NE
Washington, DC 20002
www.apa.org

To order
APA Order Department
P.O. Box 92984
Washington, DC 20090-2984
Tel: (800) 374-2721; Direct: (202) 336-5510
Fax: (202) 336-5502; TDD/TTY: (202) 336-6123
Online: www.apa.org/books/
E-mail: order@apa.org

In the U.K., Europe, Africa, and the Middle East, copies may be ordered from
American Psychological Association
3 Henrietta Street
Covent Garden, London
WC2E 8LU England

Typeset in Goudy by Stephen McDougal, Mechanicsville, MD

Printer: Data Reproductions, Auburn Hills, MI
Cover Designer: Naylor Design, Washington, DC
Technical/Production Editor: Devon Bourexis

The opinions and statements published are the responsibility of the authors, and such
opinions and statements do not necessarily represent the policies of the American
Psychological Association.

Library of Congress Cataloging-in-Publication Data

In the room with men : a casebook of therapeutic change / edited by Matt Englar-Carlson
and Mark A. Stevens.— 1st ed.
        p. cm.
    Includes bibliographical references and indexes.
    ISBN 1-59147-332-2
    1. Men—Mental health—Case studies. 2. Psychotherapy—Case studies. I. Englar-
Carlson, Matt. II. Stevens, Mark A.

British Library Cataloguing-in-Publication Data
A CIP record is available from the British Library.

Printed in the United States of America
First Edition

In memory of my parents Raye and Jerry.
To my wife Jawai;
my kids Jamie, Jeremy, and Shawn;
my sister Laurie;
my aunt Dena;
and my uncle Eddie.
Thank you for your roots, branches, and leaves.
—*Mark*

To Alison, Jackson, Mom, and Dad,
Amor est vitae essentia.
—*Matt*

CONTENTS

Contributors xi

Foreword xv
Ronald F. Levant

Acknowledgments xxi

I. Exploring the Psychotherapy Process With Men 1

Chapter 1.   An Invitation: Bringing the Reader Into
              the Book 3
              Mark A. Stevens and Matt Englar-Carlson

Chapter 2.   Masculine Norms and the Therapy Process . . . 13
              Matt Englar-Carlson

II. Exploring Emotions: Awaking the Inner Worlds of Men . . 49

Chapter 3.   Paul's Journey to Find Calmness: From Sweat
              to Tears 51
              Mark A. Stevens

Chapter 4.   Finding the Person Behind the Persona:
              Engaging Men as a Female Therapist 69
              Holly Sweet

Chapter 5.   Struggling for Sadness: A Relational Approach
              to Healing Men's Grief 91
              Sam V. Cochran

Chapter 6.   Thawing the Ice Man: Coping With Grief
             and Loss 109
             Fredric E. Rabinowitz

Chapter 7.   Finding Joshua's Soul: Working With
             Religious Men 129
             John M. Robertson

Chapter 8.   Facing Fear Without Losing Face: Working
             With Asian American Men 151
             Samuel Park

III. **Exploring Connection: Building the Therapeutic Alliance
     With Men**.................................... **175**

Chapter 9.   The Case of the Angry Black Man 177
             Jay C. Wade

Chapter 10. A New Understanding of the Macho Male
             Image: Exploration of the Mexican
             American Man 197
             Joseph M. Cervantes

Chapter 11. Helping a Boy Become a Parent: Male-Sensitive
             Psychotherapy With a Teenage Father 225
             Mark S. Kiselica

Chapter 12. Counseling Men: Perspectives and Experiences
             of a Woman of Color.................... 241
             Melba J. T. Vasquez

IV. **Exploring Masculinity: Examining Gender Role
    Conflicts With Men** **257**

Chapter 13. Helping Jack Heal His Emotional Wounds:
             The Gender Role Conflict Diagnostic
             Schema 259
             James M. O'Neil

Chapter 14. Adam and the Pain of Divorce 285
             Roberta L. Nutt

Chapter 15. Queer Eye on the Straight Guy: A Case of
             Gay Male Heterophobia 301
             Douglas C. Haldeman

Chapter 16. A Man With a "Woman's Problem":
            Male Gender and Eating Disorders 319
            Rebekah Smart

Author Index 339

Subject Index 347

About the Editors 363

CONTRIBUTORS

Joseph M. Cervantes, PhD, ABPP, is professor in the Department of Counseling, California State University, Fullerton, and maintains an independent practice in child, adolescent, and family psychology. He is licensed in the states of California and Hawaii. Dr. Cervantes's research interests are in the relatedness of cultural diversity and indigenous spirituality.

Sam V. Cochran, PhD, is director of the University Counseling Service and clinical professor in counseling psychology at the University of Iowa. He has worked with men in therapy, written about men's issues, and researched depression in men.

Matt Englar-Carlson, PhD, is assistant professor of counseling at California State University, Fullerton. He received his doctorate in counseling psychology from Pennsylvania State University in 2001. His clinical and research interests focus on two aspects of diversity: men's issues and social class.

Douglas C. Haldeman, PhD, has been a counseling psychologist in independent practice in Seattle for over 20 years. He serves on the clinical faculty of the Department of Psychology at the University of Washington. His clinical and research interests focus on the ethical treatment of lesbian, gay, bisexual, and transgendered clients in psychotherapy.

Mark S. Kiselica, PhD, HSPP, NCC, LPC, is professor and chairperson of the Department of Counselor Education at the College of New Jersey. His research focuses on the science and practice of counseling and psychotherapy with boys.

Ronald F. Levant, EdD, MBA, ABPP, has been a clinician in solo independent practice, clinical supervisor in hospital settings, clinical and academic administrator, and academic faculty member, including serving on the faculties of Boston, Rutgers, Harvard, and Nova Southeastern Universities. He is currently dean and professor at the Buchtel College of Arts and Sciences, University of Akron, and is serving as president of the American Psychological Association. His career has focused on family psychology, gender psychology, and advancing professional psychology.

James M. O'Neil, PhD, is professor of family studies and educational psychology at the University of Connecticut and is a counseling psychologist in private practice. His research has focused on men's gender role conflict using the Gender Role Conflict Scale.

Roberta L. Nutt, PhD, ABPP, is professor of psychology and director and founder of the counseling psychology doctoral program at Texas Woman's University, which emphasizes family psychology and gender issues. She has written and presented extensively on gender issues in therapy with individuals, couples, and families.

Samuel Park, PhD, is a counseling psychologist at Psychological and Counseling Services, University of California, San Diego. His clinical and research interests include service and utilization patterns among Asian Americans, men's issues, shame and loss of face, ethnic identity development, multicultural counseling, and training and supervision.

Fredric E. Rabinowitz, PhD, is full professor of psychology at the University of Redlands, California. He has served several years as the chair of the Department of Psychology at Redlands and has also been the clinical director of the local community mental health center in Redlands. His private psychotherapy practice is primarily focused on individual and group work with men.

John M. Robertson, PhD, conducts a full-time private practice for adolescent boys and men in Lawrence, Kansas. Prior to that, he was at Kansas State University for 15 years, where he was senior staff psychologist and coordinator of research at University Counseling Services, lecturer in clinical psychology for the Department of Psychology, and member of the graduate faculty in the Department of Counseling and Educational Psychology.

Rebekah Smart, PhD, is assistant professor of counseling at the California State University, Fullerton. She has worked in university mental health, community mental health, and private practice, with an emphasis in the treatment of body image problems and eating disorders. Her clinical and research interests are primarily in gender issues across cultures.

Mark A. Stevens, PhD, is director of University Counseling Services at California State University, Northridge. Previously, he was the coordinator of training and assistant director at the University of Southern California Student Counseling Services. Dr. Stevens is a fellow of the American Psychological Association (APA) and the president elect of Division 51 (Society for the Psychological Study of Men and Masculinity). He is the featured therapist in the APA produced video *Psychotherapy With Men*.

Holly Sweet, PhD, is a psychologist in private practice in Brookline, Massachusetts, and lecturer at the Massachusetts Institute of Technology. She is also the cofounder of the Cambridge Center for Gender Relations, a consulting company specializing in workshops and training focused on finding ways to improve relationships between men and women in personal, academic, and professional settings.

Melba J. T. Vasquez, PhD, ABPP, is in full-time independent practice in Austin, Texas. Her research and professional interests include ethnic minority psychology, psychology of women, professional ethics, and supervision and training.

Jay C. Wade, PhD, is a professor at Fordham University in the doctoral program in clinical psychology. His research and scholarly interests include the psychology of men and masculinity; identity issues; multicultural issues in psychology, and, in particular, his theory and scale on male reference group identity dependence.

FOREWORD

RONALD F. LEVANT

I am delighted to have been asked to write this foreword to Matt Englar Carlson's and Mark Stevens's wonderful new casebook on psychotherapy with men because of the opportunity it affords to reflect on the field and look back on where we have come. The field of the new psychology of boys, men, and masculinity is quite young. Researchers still have much to learn, from a gender-aware perspective, about the unique socialization and developmental influences that shape the personalities of boys and men and how these influences affect their life experiences.

Those not familiar with the new work in this area sometimes ask, Why do we need to study boys and men? Isn't psychology in general the psychology of males? The answer is, Well, yes, of course, males have been the focal point of most psychological research. However, these were studies that viewed males as representative of humanity as a whole. Feminist scholars challenged this traditional viewpoint by arguing for a gender-specific approach and, over the past 4 decades, have developed a new psychology of women. In the same spirit, men's studies scholars over the past 25 years have examined masculinity not as a standard by which to measure humanity (both males and females) but rather as a complex and often problematic construct. In so doing, they have provided a framework for a perspective on men and masculinity that questions traditional norms of the male role, such as the emphasis on toughness, competition, status, and emotional stoicism, and views certain male problems (such as aggression and violence, devaluation of women, fear and hatred of homosexuals, neglect of health needs, and detached fathering) as unfortunate but predictable results of the male role socialization process (Levant & Pollack, 1995; Pleck, 1981). They have also provided a framework for creating positive new definitions of masculinity that support the optimal development of men, women, and children.

This new perspective on boys and men is both overdue and urgently needed. Boys and men are disproportionately represented among many problem populations. A new perspective might contribute to the understanding of, and solution to, some of these male problems that have long impacted women, men, boys, girls, and society in negative ways.

In addition, there is a "crisis of connection" between men and women resulting from major structural changes in women's roles over the past 40 years without compensatory changes in men's roles (Levant, 1996). This has resulted from women's dramatically increased participation in the labor market. There has been an almost 600% rise in the employment of mothers of small children since the 1950s: Twelve percent of mothers of children under the age of 6 were employed in 1950, whereas almost 70% were employed in 2000. Women have thus moved from having a sole emphasis on the family to combining career and family focuses. In making this shift, women have integrated traditional values such as love, family, and caring for others with newer values such as independence, career, and defining themselves through their own accomplishments. Men in general have been slow to make equivalent and corresponding changes. Although there has been an increase in some men's openness to relationships and greater participation in the emotional and domestic arenas, many men still cling to the older definitions of their roles and emphasize work and individual accomplishment over emotional intimacy and family involvement. As a result, the pressures on men to behave in ways that conflict with various aspects of traditional masculinity ideology have never been greater. These new pressures—pressures to commit to relationships, to communicate one's innermost feelings, to share in housework, to nurture children, to integrate sexuality with love, and to curb aggression and violence—have shaken traditional masculinity ideology to such an extent there is now a "masculinity crisis" in which many men feel bewildered and confused, and the pride associated with being a man is lower than at any time in the recent past (Levant, 1997).

Finally, there is the growing awareness of cultural diversity in all of its dimensions, including race, ethnicity, social class, age, religion, sexual orientation, gender identity, and disability status. Researchers now understand that definitions of *masculinity* are dimensional, are socially constructed, and can vary in complex ways in different cultures and social conditions. Hence, they speak of *masculinities* to denote this plurality. One prominent strength of this casebook is the attention to multicultural diversity in men and psychotherapeutic practice.

With regard to the matter of psychotherapy for males, the field has come quite a long way. Beginning more than 15 years ago, the Task Force on Men's Roles and Psychotherapy of the American Psychological Association's (APA's) Division 29, Psychotherapy, began sponsoring symposia at the annual conventions of the APA and published a special series in the journal *Psychotherapy: Theory, Research, Practice, Training* (Levant, 1990) on men and psychotherapy. Growing out of this effort, and requiring a tremendous effort on the part of many people, a new division of the APA was formed— Division 51, the Society for the Psychological Study of Men and Masculinity (see Brooks & Levant, 1999, for a history of this effort). From this and other quarters, a new body of work on the treatment of men has emerged (e.g., Andronico, 1996; Brooks, 1998; Brooks & Good, 2001a, 2001b; Kiselica, 1995; Lynch & Kilmartin, 1999; Pollack & Levant, 1998; Rabinowitz & Cochran, 2002; the present casebook). Three major developments have emerged from this work.

First, this new literature has shown that boys and men need psychotherapy. Researchers have known for a while that although women have more reported psychological distress, men are closing the gap. For example, Kessler and McRae (1981) analyzed five national surveys on mental health conducted between 1957 and 1976 and found that men's rates of symptoms of psychological distress increased three times as much as women's and that, as a result, the "gender gap" in symptoms was 38% smaller at the end of the 2-decade period. Kessler and McRae (1983) also found a similar process occurring with regard to attempted suicides. Generalizing across a group of studies, the investigators reported that the ratio of females to males attempting suicide dropped from 2.3:10 in 1960 to 1.3:10 in 1980. It should also be noted that men continue to have substantially higher rates of completed suicides than women. Further, a large scale National Institutes of Mental Health study found that although women have higher rates of affective, anxiety, and somatization disorders, men have higher rates of substance abuse and antisocial personality disorders (Landers, 1989). Finally, we know that boys and men are disproportionately represented among many problem populations— schoolchildren with learning or behavior problems as well as those diagnosed with attention-deficit/hyperactivity disorder; parents estranged from their children; the homeless; substance abusers; perpetrators of family and interpersonal violence; sex addicts and sex offenders; victims of lifestyle- and stress-related fatal illnesses; and victims of homicide, suicide, and fatal automobile accidents (Brooks & Silverstein, 1995).

Second, this new literature has shown that psychotherapy, as traditionally practiced, does not serve men well. In this context, it should be recognized that traditional therapy was designed by men to treat women, primarily; thus, it reflects male assumptions about female personality development. Feminist psychotherapists have long ago pointed out the flaws in these assumptions and offered correctives. The next step was to design psychotherapy for men.

The code of masculinity requires that men be aggressive, dominant, achievement oriented, self-sufficient, adventure seeking, and emotionally restricted and that they avoid all things feminine (David & Brannon, 1976;

Levant & Fischer, 1998), characteristics that both take a toll on men's mental health and make it difficult for them to use psychotherapy readily. Five factors appear to stand in the way:

1. difficulty in admitting the existence of a problem, which stems from the "sturdy oak" trait, in which the man feels he must conceal weakness, even from himself;
2. difficulty in asking for help, due to the requirement for extreme self-sufficiency and the related inability to tolerate dependence on others;
3. difficulty identifying and putting into words vulnerable and caring emotions, due to the ordeal of male emotion socialization which leaves many men at least mildly alexithymic (Levant & Kopecky, 1995);
4. difficulty with emotional intimacy, which as Bergman (1995) has pointed out, can never feel as good to men as it does to women; and
5. a tendency to sexualize close encounters with female therapists and experience homophobia in close encounters with male therapists.

Recently, Addis and Mahalik (2003) have argued that men's low rates of seeking psychological health care can best be understood as an interaction between traditional male socialization and the social psychology of giving and receiving help. Such a perspective opens the door to considering individual difference in men's propensity to receive psychological health care.

The task of designing psychotherapy for men can be conceptualized as a cross-cultural process, in which it is recognized that the culture of traditional psychotherapy requires behaviors that conflict with aspects of the male role (remember that psychotherapy was originally developed by male therapists to treat, primarily, female patients). Therapy is then modified to remove these conflicts.

Third, this new literature has taken that next step and has evolved new psychotherapeutic approaches for men on the basis of a more accurate understanding of male personality development and the male experience. This casebook is evidence that these efforts have matured.

I cannot conclude this brief foreword without also pointing out that the world has changed as we psychologists were busy at work developing this new psychology of men, particularly in regard to men's openness to emotional experience and to psychotherapy, thus removing some of the barriers to our work. A perspective on how much has changed can be gained by reflecting on the ease with which U.S. presidents such as Bill Clinton and George W. Bush, and military generals such as Norman Schwartzkopf, have publicly expressed their sadness and tears, whereas when former Maine Senator and presidential candidate Ed Muskie shed his tears on a wintry day in New Hampshire in 1968, it cost him his viability as a candidate. So too, athletes like St. Louis Cardinals and Oakland A's slugger Mark McGuire and Pittsburgh Steelers Hall of Fame Quarterback Terry Bradshaw have openly acknowledged treatment for their emotional problems, as have public figures like Mike Wallace and Howard Dean; whereas, in an earlier era, former Missouri Senator Thomas Eagelton was dropped from the No. 2 slot on the 1972 democratic ticket by former Senator and presidential candidate George McGovern following the media hullabaloo about his having been treated for depression.

Finally, I want to express my enthusiasm for the new multidivisional APA task force for developing guidelines for psychological practices for boys and men, which was inaugurated early in 2005. The goal of this task force is to develop psychological practice guidelines for working with boys and men, reflecting current research, theory, and practice in the fields of counseling psychology; clinical psychology; psychology of women; psychology of men; psychology of gay, lesbian, bisexual, and transgendered people; and the psychology of ethnic minorities. The very existence of such a task force bespeaks the emerging maturation of the field of the psychology of boys and men. This task force will play a major role in shaping the future of this field.

REFERENCES

Addis, M. E., & Mahalik, J. R. (2003). Men, masculinity, and the contexts of help seeking. *American Psychologist, 58*, 5–14.

Andronico, M. (Ed.). (1996). *Men in groups*. Washington, DC: American Psychological Association.

Bergman, S. J. (1995). Men's psychological development: A relational perspective. In R. F. Levant & W. S. Pollack (Eds.), *A new psychology of men* (pp. 68–90). New York: Basic Books.

Brooks, G. R. (1998). *A new psychotherapy for traditional men*. San Francisco: Jossey-Bass.

Brooks, G. R., & Good, G. E. (Eds.). (2001a). *The new handbook of psychotherapy and counseling with men: A comprehensive guide to settings, problems, and treatment approaches*. San Francisco: Jossey-Bass.

Brooks, G. R., & Good, G. E. (2001b). *The new handbook of psychotherapy and counseling with men: A comprehensive guide to settings, problems, and treatment approaches* (Vol. 2). San Francisco: Jossey-Bass.

Brooks, G. R., & Levant, R. F. (1999). A history of Division 51: The Society for the Psychological Study of Men and Masculinity. In D. A. Dewsbury (Ed.), *Unification through division: Histories of the divisions of the American Psychological Association* (Vol. 3, pp. 197–222). Washington, DC: American Psychological Association.

Brooks, G. R., & Silverstein, L. B. (1995). Understanding the dark side of masculinity: An interactive systems model. In R. F. Levant & W. S. Pollack (Eds.), *A new psychology of men* (pp. 280–333). New York: Basic Books.

David, D. S., & Brannon, R. (Eds.). (1976). *The forty-nine percent majority: The male sex role*. Reading, MA: Addison-Wesley.

Kessler, R., & McRae, J. (1981). Trends in the relationship between sex and psychological distress: 1957–1976. *American Sociological Review, 46*, 443–452.

Kessler, R., & McRae, J. (1983). Trends in the relationship between sex and attempted suicide. *Journal of Health and Social Behavior, 24*, 98–110.

Kiselica, M. S. (1995). *Multicultural counseling with teenage fathers*. Thousand Oaks, CA: Sage.

Landers, S. (1989, January). In U.S., mental disorders affect 15 percent of adults. *APA Monitor, 20*, 16.

Levant, R. F. (1990). Introduction to special series on men's roles and psychotherapy. *Psychotherapy: Theory, Research, Practice, Training, 27*, 307–308.

Levant, R. F. (1996). The crisis of connection between men and women. *Journal of Men's Studies, 5*, 1–12.

Levant, R. F. (1997). The masculinity crisis. *Journal of Men's Studies, 5*, 221–231.

Levant, R. F., & Fischer, J. (1998). The Male Role Norms Inventory. In C. Davis, W. Yarber, R. Bauserman, G. Schreer, & S. Davis (Eds.), *Sexuality-related measures: A compendium* (2nd ed., pp. 469–472). Newbury Park, CA: Sage.

Levant, R. F., & Kopecky, G. (1995). *Masculinity reconstructed: Changing the rules of manhood*. New York: Dutton/Plume.

Levant, R. F., & Pollack, W. S. (Eds.). (1995). *A new psychology of men*. New York: Basic Books.

Lynch, J., & Kilmartin, C. T. (1999). *The pain behind the mask: Overcoming masculine depression*. New York: Haworth Press.

Pleck, J. H. (1981). *The myth of masculinity*. Cambridge, MA: MIT Press.

Pollack, W. S., & Levant, R. F. (Eds.). (1998). *New psychotherapy for men*. New York: Wiley.

Rabinowitz, F. E., & Cochran, S. V. (2002). *Deepening psychotherapy with men*. Washington, DC: American Psychological Association.

ACKNOWLEDGMENTS

The delight of editing this book was developing a concept and then choosing the contributors we believed would be able to best deliver that concept to the reader. We hit the jackpot. First and foremost, we want to acknowledge all of the contributors to this book. They took risks, opened themselves up to the readers, and modeled a wonderful balance of professional expertise and personal sharing. We wanted the readers to feel like they were in the therapy room with the therapist and client, and the contributors accomplished this. We asked the contributors difficult questions and sometimes asked them to share more than they were comfortable sharing, and we thank them for putting up with our gentle, and sometimes not-so-gentle, nudging.

This book would not have gotten off the ground without the assistance of Susan Reynolds, Senior Acquisitions Editor at the American Psychological Association (APA) Books Department. Further, we thank the anonymous reviewers of the early versions of the book. Our development editor, Ed Meidenbauer, provided insightful ideas to help communicate our vision of this book. He was a true pleasure to work with on this project. His editorial comments helped us shape our ideas for this book.

We also want to acknowledge APA Division 51, the Society for the Psychological Study of Men and Masculinity, whose members have been great mentors and colleagues and wonderful friends. Their collective energy has been inspirational and supportive. So much of what we know about working with men has come from this dynamic group of men and women.

To our clients and students, who over the years have opened themselves up to us and taught us so much about struggles and change, we extend our gratitude and our thanks.

In addition, we would like to individually acknowledge support and help. I (Mark) am deeply appreciative of the evolving friendship with my coeditor, Matt Englar-Carlson. It has been so personally rewarding to be first his supervisor, then colleague, and now a great friend. I have so enjoyed being part of his life—whether it be climbing on our mountain bikes or just watching the joy on his face as he holds his son, Jackson. As a coeditor, his efficiency, creativity, openness, business acuity, and clinical knowledge has made this project one of the most enjoyable of my career. I also thank my colleagues and past and present interns at the University of Southern California Student Counseling Services. For 20 years, they have provided a dialogue and space for me to grow as a clinician. I look forward to the next chapter of my professional journey with my new colleagues at California State University, Northridge.

"All you need is love." I (Mark) am grateful for my lifelong friendship with my buddy and colleague Glenn Good. I also thank the following people: the wonderful men from the March Madness Vegas group and my biking soul mates Ralph Livingston and Matt Finders, who provide my life with balance and perspective; my dear and best friend Quinn Crosbie, who has generously given gifts of love and knowledge over the past 30 years; and finally, Jawai Nabau-Stevens, Jamie, Jeremy, and Shawn, the people who feed my purpose and love in ways that words cannot describe.

I (Matt) would like to give a big hug and an extra water bottle to my coeditor, Mark Stevens. Little did I know what was waiting for me in Southern California, but all of our time together has been so natural and meaningful. From the first phone interview to now, he has always helped me feel comfortable and supported as we navigated the roles of supervisor–supervisee into colleagues and friends. He continues to teach me so much about being a good friend, father, professional, and human being. All the while, he models integrity, positivity, balance, generosity, creativity, sensitivity, and the list goes on. Whatever we do together never feels like work (and most of the time it is not), but another adventure in play. Even all of the uphill grinds are enjoyable. Collaborating with him on this book has been personally and professionally rewarding, but most of all, it was enjoyable.

In the professional realm, I (Matt) thank all of my colleagues in the Department of Counseling, California State University, Fullerton, for the ongoing collegiality and creation of a healthy family atmosphere at work. It is an honor to be on this faculty. Specifically, I thank Jeffrey Kottler for offering me a home at Fullerton and for our friendship, which has developed out in the surf, the Himalayas, and over tea and coffee. Special appreciation goes to Donald Keat for his love and compassion as my mentor. I believe it is rare for a graduate school mentor to emphasize the importance of music, food, basketball, literature, love, and friendship over scholarly production, yet that is what he did, and it has transformed and helped me the most.

Because this is a book about men and relationships, I (Matt) would be remiss without mentioning the ongoing friendship of Caleb Banta-Green, Juan Cagampang, Chandler Dimberg, Chris Kane, and Bryan Marshall. Further, I am fortunate to have four talented, loving, and unique siblings—thanks to Kirstin, Karin, Ben, and Kali for continuing to enrich my life. Unconditional love and acceptance are concepts all psychotherapists learn about in books, yet not everyone is fortunate enough to experience it from birth into adulthood. Thanks to my parents, Jon and Laura, I have never known anything other than unconditional love and acceptance. They were the models who taught me how to surround myself with loving, sensitive, and supportive people throughout my life.

Finally, I (Matt) want to acknowledge my source of inspiration: my soul mate, Alison. I thank her for her passion, intelligence, playfulness, and caring, along with her ongoing support. To my son, Jackson: I can only dream about the man you will become.

I

EXPLORING THE PSYCHOTHERAPY PROCESS WITH MEN

1

AN INVITATION: BRINGING THE READER INTO THE BOOK

MARK A. STEVENS AND MATT ENGLAR-CARLSON

A client you have never met before sits down in the chair across from you. From his appearance, you can gather an idea about his racial background, height and weight, and his relative age. He is dressed casually, but not in a sloppy manner. Your client has a hardened look to his face; he seems to fidget in his chair, as if he cannot get comfortable, but soon firmly settles in his chair. His gaze darts around the room, taking in the pictures on the wall, book titles on the shelf, and the plants on the floor, before his stare is placed firmly on you. His voice says nothing, but his eyes are asking you to begin, and so you do. Innocently, without passing judgment, you ask, "What brings you in today?" The next 5 minutes feel like a game of poker in which your client is playing the role of the unwavering house dealer—you ask about the man's life and current concerns—in response you get short answers that seem to reflect some discomfort, yet an overall attitude that he can handle it and does not need your help. Each one of his statements feels like a little push or deflection. Your client keeps his cards close to his chest, revealing little of his inner world, yet more detail about those people around him who seem to be creating problems in his life (coworkers, family members, etc.). What is really happening with him? Is it a mistake for him to be here or is he bluffing? It is at that moment when you realize how truly uncomfortable your client seems to be feeling in your office. You notice his feet tapping on the floor, a little sweat on his brow, and he seems to be focused on the clock behind you. Although his statements that "this is just a phase, and there is just a lot of stress happening right now, but it will pass" seem to be meant to reassure you (and him?), you find that you are trying a little harder with each question to probe a little deeper. With each attempt to get the client to open up and build some rapport, it seems that a wall is being built. You begin to wonder how you will be able to connect with this man. Clearly something is happening in his life; after all, he is in your office, yet in the present moment he seems like he does not want to be here. You get the sense that unless something changes between now and the end of the session, he will soon be leaving your office, never to return.

Does the scenario above seem like a familiar situation? Can you image sitting with a male client and having this experience? For most psychotherapists who work with men, this scenario is not an altogether unique or foreign situation but captures the feeling of what it can initially be like to be in the therapy room with a male client. For many male clients, however, the scenario reflects the difficulty they experience entering and engaging in psychotherapy. Many male clients are not sure how to behave, are confused about how to enter into a relationship with a psychotherapist (or if they really want or need to), and question how psychotherapy can really make a difference in their life. For both client and psychotherapist, the backdrop for psychotherapy with men creates unique challenges that can be overcome. *In the Room With Men: A Casebook of Therapeutic Change* is a volume dedicated to chronicling the features of psychotherapy with men with an eye toward showcasing how psychotherapy can be a powerful, effective, and life-changing experience for both client and psychotherapist.

This book is about not only the experience of being engaged in psychotherapy with male clients but also the ways in which psychotherapists can adapt their practice to best meet the needs of men. As Scher (1990) astutely noted, most men do not see therapy as something for them but instead see it as the result of something or someone external who has pushed them to seek psychological help. A great deal has been written and discussed recently regarding therapy with men (see Brooks & Good, 2001a, 2001b; Levant & Pollack, 1995; Pollack & Levant, 1998) to help clinicians understand working with them. This book looks to take discussions about men, masculinity, and psychotherapy one step further by specifically targeting psychotherapy experiences with men from a case study perspective. The promise in this book for readers is the rare opportunity for an inside view of the experience of client and psychotherapist when men enter psychotherapy. Further, this book highlights the best practices of competent and effective psychotherapists who have worked effectively with men for many years.

A NEW PSYCHOTHERAPY WITH MEN: CONTEXT AND CREDIT

Over the past 30 years, there has been an increased awareness and attention given to men as clients in psychotherapy. This focus has highlighted that there is something unique about being a man (i.e., masculinity) that wholly influences how men experience the world both intrapersonally and interpersonally. It is the saliency of masculinity for men across all facets of life that has led researchers and clinicians alike to question the influence of masculinity on mental health, well-being, and ultimately, psychotherapy itself. One rationale for looking at masculinity and psychotherapy has been the understanding that little is known about psychotherapy with men (Brooks, 1998; Scher, 1990). That may seem like an odd statement, considering that historically most writers and researchers about psychotherapy, until more recently, were men. Males have traditionally been viewed as representative of humanity; thus, males and their characteristics have been the object of most psychological research (Levant, 1990). Further, ideas and theories of psychotherapy were created from a Western, male view of the world, despite the fact that the majority of clients were, and continue to be, women. In general, knowledge about psychotherapy appeared to be structured from a male perspective about treating women. Within this paradigm, specific information incorporating women's perspectives or worldviews was absent, yet at the same time attention about what it means to be a man in the broader culture and the specific culture as clients in psychotherapy was not considered. Hartman (1990) noted that psychological writing was both androcentric and gender blind, with an assumed male perspective that had "not really explored what it means to be a man any more than what it means to be a woman" (p. vii).

The women's movement created a needed critique of the practice of psychotherapy, highlighting how the roles of women and views about femininity influenced how women saw themselves and experienced the world. The resulting influence from the women's movement was the notion that women needed to be understood within the context of role restrictions and that they needed to be clinically treated with gender-appropriate models that acknowledged, considered, and adapted to the experience of women. One outcome of the women's movement within psychotherapy was the creation of specific therapies and treatments that acknowledged the experiences of women and outlined treatment tailored to women's ways of experiencing the world (Brown, 1986; Enns, 1997). The acknowledgment of the need for specific treatments has been further advanced by the American Psychological Association's (APA; 2005) development of *Guidelines for Psychological Practice With Girls and Women*. Building on these advances in conceptualizing both gender and psychotherapy, scholars and practitioners working with men began to acknowledge the need for conceptual paradigms to better understand the experiences of men and treatments that could be tailored to men's experiences of the world.

Another arena where the value of understanding gender roles and development has been appreciated is within multicultural counseling. Incorporating and considering multicultural factors is no longer viewed as a separate approach or type of treatment. All counseling at its core is multicultural counseling (Pedersen, 1990). In that context, a multitude of cultural variables, including sex and gender, are recognized as essential to understanding cultural identities. The generally accepted and promoted effective and ethical treatment of any one individual must consider cultural factors and diversity in the treatment process (APA, 2003). At the core of multicultural counseling is the direct and purposeful consideration and exploration of the cultural context and worldview that both a psychotherapist and client hold. Not so long ago, the idea that clients are embedded within a cultural context that dramatically influences clinical treatment would have been accepted only by a small group of psychotherapists. Currently, however, this very same idea is now a cornerstone and necessity to effective treatment planning. The women's movement, when paired with the multicultural counseling movement within psychology, has led to the acknowledgment in current clinical practice that cultural identity and memberships not only matter but are also considered an integral aspect of ethical and effective clinical practice.

These influential movements on the practice of psychotherapy helped practitioners of psychotherapy discover and begin to understand gender and gender roles. What began as an effort to appropriately understand and consider women specifically as women has broadened to include considering men as first and foremost men in the clinical setting. Thus the main shift was movement away from considering men as the model of humanity and instead understanding both men and women from a perspective that acknowledges the role of biological differences (sex) and social environment (gender roles) on the development of men and women. This area of scholarly research and writing has been labeled the "new psychology of men" and is represented within APA as a specific division: Society for the Psychological Study of Men and Masculinity (Division 51). The past 30 years have seen a remarkable change in understanding the role of sex and gender on the development of men and women.

For men, this concerted appreciation of masculinity in terms of mental health and well-being could not come at a better time. There have been vast changes in societal expectations for men. Scholars have documented changing gender roles for men (Bernard, 1981; Kilmartin, 2000), often highlighting the difficulties that men have experienced when their gender role appears outdated or out of line with current connotations of recent variations of masculinity. Many researchers (Clare, 2000; Kimmel, 1995; Kupers, 1993; Levant, 1997; Levant & Kopecky, 1996) have offered the observation that masculinity is in crisis and is in need of "redefinition," "revisioning," or "reconstruction." One example of the changing view of masculinity can be found in the classic Broverman, Vogel, Broverman, Clarkson, and Rosenkrantz (1972) study. This study, over 30 years ago, found that adjectives (e.g., *assertive, competitive, reasonable*) associated with healthy adults and healthy men were synonymous. Now words traditionally associated with femininity (e.g., *relational, intimate, connected*), and not the ones associated with masculinity, are equated with healthy adults (Jordan, Kaplan, Miller, Stiver, & Surrey, 1991). Levant (1996) suggested that masculinity has already collapsed, noting that this collapse could be positive for men, freeing them from restrictive gender role constraints. Clearly, it is a changing world for men.

In the clinical realm, however, incorporating advances in understanding about men and masculinity can be difficult. Working with men presents special challenges that are often contrary to the manner that most psychotherapists were trained to understand both the process of psychotherapy and client dynamics. Many men appear resistant or reluctant to be in therapy, appear skeptical about the value of disclosure, and seem evasive and uncertain about emotional expression. Further, many men come to psychotherapy viewing their presenting concerns as external and not related to their functioning or their responsibility. In addition, many presenting concerns of men (i.e., emotional restriction, interpersonal isolation and distance, anger and aggression, workaholism) appear closely tied to their enactment of masculinity and seem culturally sanctioned as appropriate. Within this context, it appears that masculinity plays a crucial role in a man's experience of psychotherapy and requires that psychotherapists understand how to incorporate men's experiences (i.e., their masculine selves) into therapeutic work. It is the goal of this book to clearly illuminate how men, masculinity, and psychotherapy can exist in the same healing space.

ABOUT THE CASEBOOK:
ORIGINS, INTENTIONS, AND INSPIRATIONS

This book was inspired and grew out of our passion and interest in working with men. At the University of Southern California, where we worked together as clinical supervisor (Mark) and predoctoral intern (Matt), we co-led a men's therapy group and spent numerous hours sharing our ideas and experiences of doing psychotherapy with male clients. Often we commented on how we wished we had audio- or videotaped our conversations. We wanted other clinicians to be in the room with us and join in our conversation. Our wish spoke to the perceived absence of hearing from other clinicians how they were integrating theory and practice and what it was "really like" working with male clients. *In the Room With Men: A Casebook of Therapeutic Change* attempts to fill part of that void and carry on the therapy conversations that we found so valuable. This book opens the discussion to include multiple voices about working with men.

In the Room With Men represents a unique moment in the psychological study of men and masculinity. Over the past 30 years, this field has grown by building a substantial base of research and theory about the psychological needs and experiences of men. A generation of psychotherapists has benefited from these advances in the field by learning about the distinct concerns of men and how to best meet their clinical needs. What has been largely absent from the attention given to the psychology of men has been the focus on clinical application that represents actual clinical practice. There appears to be little actual documentation of the experiences that psychotherapists have while counseling men, as well as how the research findings and scholarly recommendations are being used in these therapeutic encounters. This book integrates contemporary theory about psychotherapy and the psychology of men with current masculinity research, and it displays how these ideas and concepts come to life in the practice of psychotherapy with actual male clients.

It was our intention to bring the reader into the therapy room in order to know the client, the therapist, and their clinical work together. We did this by specifically asking the contributors to share critical dialogue and conceptualizations, as well as their own reactions and pushes and pulls that they may or may not have shared with their clients. It is our hope that the professional and personal reflections of the contributors will motivate readers to do the same in regards to the psychotherapy work they are doing with men. Finally, we hope the readers, especially the less experienced clinicians, will recognize and find comfort from the humbleness, openness, and uncertainty that these experienced clinicians shared in regard to the work with their clients.

We selected contributors (both men and women) from across the country who have distinguished themselves in terms of their innovative research and national presentations about masculinity and psychotherapy with men. Additionally, and perhaps most important, these contributors are all practicing and excellent clinicians who have the ability to examine and reflect on their real-life case experiences with selected male clients.

THEORETICAL ORIENTATION AND THERAPEUTIC THEMES

Because we have drawn from a wide range of practitioners from various theoretical perspectives, the theoretical basis of this book is integrative. Throughout the chapters, contributors draw from a range of theoretical perspectives—psychodynamic, relational, interpersonal, cognitive–behavioral, feminist, and multicultural—yet all integrate a gender-aware approach to their work, with an emphasis on understanding masculinity. The range of theoretical perspectives is perhaps most reflective of current practices of psychotherapy with men. Currently, there is no one theoretical orientation that appears to be more effective than others in conceptualizing and doing psychotherapy with men. Instead, scholars and practitioners have looked to tailor existing theoretical views in accordance with perspectives on male socialization (chap. 2 further addresses the role of theory in treating men).

The integrative nature of this book allowed room for other types of themes to emerge that do not necessarily have a theoretical home. For example, most of the contributors highlighted and recognized the importance of having compassion and patience with their male clients. Another themed therapeutic stance acknowledged by the contributors was the importance of creating a safe therapeutic environment in which the male clients could save "masculine face" in the context of therapy while exploring and feeling their more "vulnerable" (some may say "feminine") aspects of their personhood. The paradox of men feeling their strength through their vulnerability, while cocreating a safe enough therapeutic environment, was a powerful learning opportunity provided for many of the male clients in this book. Additionally, the relational nature of the therapy, although not said in so many words, seemed to be an integral part of the healing and learning process for both the client and author. Is this aspect of the therapy process more unique and salient to counseling men than counseling women? It is our hope that the clinical cases described in *In the Room With Men* are models of clinical expertise with men that will stimulate questions for further therapy research.

TURNING THE PAGES: AN OVERVIEW

Ron Levant, President of the APA and cofounder of the Society for the Psychological Study of Men and Masculinity (Division 51), provides a foreword to this book. He calls the reader's attention to both the history of the "new psychology of men" and future directions, including the development of the *Guidelines for Psychological Practice With Boys and Men*. The second chapter of this book is a literature review by Matt Englar-Carlson, which summarizes the current knowledge base about psychotherapy with men, in terms of research and theory. Fourteen case study chapters covering a variety of client demographics, concerns, symptoms, and treatment settings are then presented. The case study chapters are divided into three discreet, yet not mutually exclusive, parts (beginning with Part II) that highlight the major themes and approaches to working with the particular clients.

Exploring Emotions: Awaking the Inner Worlds of Men offers powerful clinical stories of how men learn more fully to experience, communicate, and understand their feelings and how those feelings can also serve as a map for getting to better know themselves. Part III, Exploring Connection: Building the Therapeutic Alliance With Men, highlights how the humanity and sincerity of the therapist opens the door for his or her male clients to feel wanted and understood. Some of these men seemed disconnected from themselves and society yet were able to bond with the humanness and care shown by the therapist. Part IV, Exploring Masculinity: Examining Gender Role Conflicts With Men, speaks beautifully to the intersection of gender role socialization issues and psychological distress, as a window to provide self-understanding and openness to being in the world in a different way.

In each case study chapter, the contributor first provides a context about his or her own personal and professional path into the world of understanding and working with male clients. Some of the contributors concentrate on influential readings and mentors, whereas others lean more toward sharing salient personal experiences. Each contributor also provides the reader with a framework of how he or she conceptualized the issues of men and masculinity and how he or she tends to work with male clients. The reader will notice both overlap and uniqueness amongst the contributors. The contributor then shares with the reader his or her work with a particular client. Infused in the text of the work are actual dialogue and professional–personal reactions and reflections about the nature of the session. At the end of each chapter, the contributor answers a series of questions from the editors regarding the work with the client. Along with standard questions that were asked to each contributor, the editors also asked questions that were unique to the contributor and their particular case study. Finally, each contributor provides a list of favorite resources for counseling men. It is important to note that each chapter is a reflection of an actual clinical case. Following APA guidelines, the contributors masked demographic and identifying details to ensure confidentiality of their clients.

It is our hope that a wide range of audiences can use *In the Room With Men: A Casebook of Therapeutic Change*. Although we originally viewed this book as being focused on men and masculinity, we are struck by how much of this book is about the actual process of psychotherapy. It could be used as a textbook for counseling skills classes, as it provides excellent role modeling of how important the therapist's process is to the therapy experience. This book also provides the most current research on the study of men and masculinity. For more seasoned mental health practitioners, bringing the reader into the counseling room, as described by informed practitioners, will help practitioners develop a better appreciation for the complexities and nuances of doing therapy with men. This book, we hope, offers a mirror to reflect on one's own personal reactions and clinical practice with male clients.

REFERENCES

American Psychological Association. (2003). Guidelines on multicultural education, training, research, practice, and organizational change for psychologists. *American Psychologist, 58*, 377–402.

American Psychological Association. (2005). *Guidelines for psychological practice with girls and women.* Draft from the Joint Task Force of APA Divisions 17 and 35, June, 2005.

Bernard, J. (1981). The good-provider role: Its rise and fall. *American Psychologist, 36*, 1–12.

Brooks, G. R. (1998). *A new psychotherapy for traditional men.* San Francisco: Jossey-Bass.

Brooks, G. R., & Good, G. E. (Eds.). (2001a). *The new handbook of psychotherapy and counseling with men: A comprehensive guide to settings, problems, and treatment approaches* (Vol. 1). San Francisco: Jossey-Bass.

Brooks, G. R., & Good, G. E. (Eds.). (2001b). *The new handbook of psychotherapy and counseling with men: A comprehensive guide to settings, problems, and treatment approaches* (Vol. 2). San Francisco: Jossey-Bass.

Broverman, I. K., Vogel, S. R., Broverman, D. M., Clarkson, E. E., & Rosenkrantz, D. S. (1972). Sex role stereotypes: A current appraisal. *Journal of Social Issues, 28*, 59–78.

Brown, L. S. (1986). Gender role analysis: A neglected component of psychological assessment. *Psychotherapy, 23*, 243–248.

Clare, A. (2000). *On men: Masculinity in crisis.* London: Chatto & Windus.

Enns, C. Z. (1997). *Feminist theories and feminist psychotherapies: Origins, themes, and variations.* New York: The Harrington Park Press.

Hartman, A. (1990). Foreword. In R. Meth & R. Pasick (Eds.), *Men in therapy: The challenge of change* (pp. vii–viii). New York: Guilford Press.

Jordan, J. V., Kaplan, A. G., Miller, J. B., Stiver, I. P., & Surrey, J. L. (1991). *Woman's growth in connection.* New York: Guilford Press.

Kilmartin, C. T. (2000). *The masculine self* (2nd ed.). Boston: McGraw-Hill.

Kimmel, M. (1995). *Manhood in America: A cultural history.* New York: Free Press.

Kupers, T. A. (1993). *Revisioning men's lives: Gender, intimacy, and power.* New York: Guilford Press.

Levant, R. F. (1990). Introduction to the special series on men's roles and psychotherapy. *Psychotherapy, 27*, 307–308.

Levant, R. F. (1996). Masculinity reconsidered. *Independent Practitioner, 16*, 36–39.

Levant, R. F. (1997). The masculinity crisis. *Journal of Men's Studies, 5*, 221–231.

Levant, R. F., & Kopecky, G. (1996). *Masculinity reconstructed: Changing the rules of manhood.* New York: Dutton/Plume.

Levant, R. F., & Pollack, W. S. (Eds.). (1995). *A new psychology of men.* New York: Basic Books.

Pedersen, P. B. (1990). The multicultural perspective as a fourth force in counseling. *Journal of Mental Health Counseling, 12*, 93–95.

Pollack, W. S., & Levant, R. F. (1998). *New psychotherapy for men.* New York: Wiley.

Scher, M. (1990). Effect of gender role incongruence on men's experience as clients in psychotherapy. *Psychotherapy, 27*, 322–326.

2

MASCULINE NORMS AND THE THERAPY PROCESS

MATT ENGLAR-CARLSON

For many years, an obvious but historically overlooked aspect of conducting psychotherapy with men was the fact that male clients were first and foremost men. The development of the scholarly discipline of the new psychology of men has drawn needed attention to the notion that being a man matters to the extent that masculinity is a focal organizing principle for all aspects of a man's life (see Brooks & Good, 2001a, 2001b; Levant & Pollack, 1995; Pollack & Levant, 1998). Masculinity, therefore, can be an influential contributor to not only why (or why not) a man is in psychotherapy but also how therapy is ultimately enacted. This casebook is a testament to the ways that men "do" therapy as clients, but it is also an observation as to how male-sensitive psychotherapists "do" therapy with men. This chapter is a deviation from the remaining chapters in this book in that it does not contain a case study. Essentially, this chapter is a review of the existing scholarly literature that provides foundational material to explore psychotherapy with men. To begin this exploration into men and psychotherapy, one needs a base knowledge of research, theory, and practice about men, masculinity, psychology, and psychotherapy. This chapter provides an introduction to masculinity and gender socialization, models of masculinities, how masculine socialization influences the well-being of men, and how there has been an integration of the new psychology of men research findings into the practice of psychotherapy with men. Suggestions and observations about ways to create male-sensitive clinical practice are presented. A good place to begin understanding men is to develop a deeper appreciation and understanding of masculinity itself.

TOWARD AN UNDERSTANDING OF MASCULINITY

It is difficult to outline a definition of *masculinity*. Amid the growing research on men and masculinity, definitional and conceptual ambiguity exists (Good, Wallace, & Borst, 1994). A commonly misguided assumption in gender role research has been the equating of biologically determined, sex-based characteristics (maleness, or sex roles) with social psychologically based gender role behaviors and conceptions of masculinity when the research is specifically concerned with socialized male gender roles (Mintz & O'Neil, 1990). The terms *sex* and *gender* have different meanings. *Sex* refers to whether one is born male or female, whereas *gender* refers to the psychological, social, and cultural features and characteristics that have been strongly associated with the biological categories of "female" and "male" (Gilbert & Scher, 1999). Some scholars have taken a pure sex differences approach to understanding the differences between men and women. From this perspective, research has pointed out that compared with women, men seek psychological help at lower rates (Vessey & Howard, 1993); have higher rates of substance abuse (Kessler et al., 1994); die, on average, close to 7 years younger than women and have higher rates of the 15 leading causes of death (see Courtenay, 2000); are less likely to be diagnosed with anxiety- and depression-related disorders (e.g., Sachs-Ericsson & Ciarlo, 2000), and have significantly less healthy lifestyles (Courtenay, 1998). The fact that men and women differ across the spectrum of physical and mental health behaviors and conditions reveals little, however, about the nature of these differences. It is unclear what psychological, sociological, biological, or cultural processes are responsible for differences between men and women (Addis & Mahalik, 2003). A further and potentially more damaging limitation of a sex differences approach is the endorsement of an essentialist position of standard differences between men and women. An essentialist position views differences between men and women as static attributes and can lead to stereotyping and constraint in regard to the roles of men and women.

An alternative to the sex differences approach understands men and masculinity through the lens of gender role socialization. Drawing on a social learning paradigm, this approach is more commonly found in the psychological literature (Addis & Cohane, 2005). Gender role socialization paradigms are based on the assumption that men and women learn gendered attitudes and behaviors from social environments in which cultural values, norms, and ideologies about what it means to be men and women are reinforced and modeled. In the following sections, a variety of perspectives is reviewed to better understand different conceptualizations of masculinity.

Sex Roles Versus Gender Roles

Sex roles are specific behaviors related to human biology, such as reproductive functioning and hormone production (Meth, 1990). Whereas the disciplines of evolutionary biology and sociobiology have attributed biological sex with specific gender behaviors (Sapolsky, 1997), the majority of research on men in psychology has focused on male socialization and gender roles (Levant & Pollack, 1995). Gender roles have an enormous influence on how individuals function both intra- and interpersonally (Jakupcak, Lisak, & Roemer, 2002). *Gender roles* are behaviors that are enacted congruent with the socially constructed ideas of masculinity and femininity. A person's biological sex may be male, but masculine gender role identity is less prescriptive and is based on societal standards in regard to what it means to be male in a society or culture (Kimmel & Messner, 2004). As de Beauvoir (1970) observed, unlike biological sex, people are not born with a gender. Instead, a man learns what is considered to be a man congruent with a particular society at a particular time. To explain how gender ideals are internalized, Bem (1981) proposed a cognitive theory based on schema to explain the development of gender roles in which cultural forces shape an individual's gender role schema of "maleness" and "femaleness." Specifically, men and women develop their identity and gender role schemas through an interactive process with their culture, in which they learn gender-appropriate scripts and behavior and attempt to modify those scripts to make life more palatable (Brooks, 1998; Kimmel & Messner, 2004; Pollack, 1998). Thus, biological sex does not determine gender roles, but the social forces of peers, parents, teachers, and the media reinforce the current gender paradigm that determines gender roles and the norms of masculinity (Gergan, 1991; Pleck, 1995). Through socialization, men are taught and ingrained with societal standards, norms, and expectations about gender-specific behavior (Pleck, 1995).

Eisler (1995) derived from Bem's (1981) gender role schema model three inferences regarding men's gender role development. First, men learn to evaluate their adequacy on the basis of their ability to regulate their behavior in accord with their learned masculinity gender schema. Second, this process, although developmental, becomes stable at an early age. Third, some men become more highly committed than others in regulating their behavior according to socially prescribed masculine schemas as a way to affirm their worth. On the basis of these inferences, Eisler concluded that men's internalization of specific gender role schemas might affect their behaviors and feelings of well-being. Men inevitably experience some harmful effects trying to live up to these roles. Pleck (1981) referred to this process as "gender role strain."

The Dimensionality of Gender Roles

Early conceptualizations of gender socialization that implied that men were socialized into a single gender role have since been deemed highly questionable (Gibbons, Hamby, & Dennis, 1997; Smiler, 2004; Thompson & Pleck, 1995). In 1946, Green theorized that multiple conceptions of masculinity could exist. Adding to this inquiry, other researchers began using the term *masculinities* rather than *masculinity* to reflect the various conceptions of male gender roles that may exist by sexual orientation and geographic regions (Blazina, 1997); among different racial, ethnic, religious, age, and socioeconomic groups (Gibbons et al., 1997); and across developmental periods (Kimmel & Messner, 2004; O'Neil & Egan, 1992). This view is captured by the social constructivist perspective of masculinity that focuses on how men "do gender" across various settings, highlighting the ways in which masculinity is continuously being constructed and contested (Addis & Cohane, 2005). It is the concept of "masculinities" that accounts for the differing definitions and variations of masculinity that exist among men representing various cultures (e.g., rural White masculinities may take a different form than urban African American masculinities).

The new psychology of men primarily relies on the gender role socialization paradigm, a social constructivist perspective, to account for the formation of gender roles and understanding masculinities (Addis & Mahalik, 2003; Levant et al., 2003). The paradigm recognizes biological differences between men and women but argues that "masculinity" and "femininity" are not constructed by biology or fixed (Levant & Pollack, 1995). From this perspective, individuals are informed by society and their culture that they are part of particular groups and thus adopt masculine or feminine identities consistent with their group identification and contextual surroundings (Imms, 2000; Toerien & Durrheim, 2001). Prevailing gender ideologies (e.g., conceptions of what it "means" to be a man), which vary according to psychological, historical, social, cultural, and political contexts, influence parents, teachers, and peers in how children are socialized.

Reviewers (Good et al., 1994; Smiler, 2004; Thompson & Pleck, 1995) of masculinity research have suggested the need to empirically examine multiple conceptions of masculinity and to identify particular masculine constructs. Specifically, researchers were directed to compare groups of men on masculinity-related instruments (Thompson & Pleck, 1995) and to identify patterns of responses that typify gender role clusters (Good et al., 1994). Scholarly literature on the new psychology of men identified two major overlapping clusters in theory and research on masculine role socialization: masculine ideology and masculine gender role strain (Betz & Fitzgerald, 1993; Good et al., 1994). These two areas have formed the basis of most recent research with psychology about men and masculinity.

Masculine Ideology

An overarching conceptualization of gender roles is *masculine ideology*, which is defined as the "endorsement and internalization of cultural belief systems about masculinity and male gender, rooted in the structural relationship between the two sexes" (Pleck, Sonenstein, & Ku, 1993, p. 88). Masculine ideology develops as growing boys internalize cultural norms and expectations about gender-appropriate behavior (Thompson & Pleck, 1995). Whereas various masculine ideologies are purported to exist and assume different forms (e.g., traditional, men in transition, male liberationists; Skovholt, 1978; Thompson & Pleck, 1995), the majority of research on specific masculine gender role clusters has focused on identifying and measuring "traditional" masculinity (Good et al., 1994). During the past 30 years, scholars and researchers (Brannon, 1976; Doyle, 1995; Eisler & Skidmore, 1987; O'Neil, 1982) have identified a number of gender roles associated with traditional masculinity. Within the United States and other Western countries, traditional masculinity can be viewed as the dominant (referred to as "hegemonic") form of masculinity and thus has been viewed as more powerful than others in determining what members of a culture take to be normative (e.g., White, middle-class, heterosexual definitions of masculinity in the United States). Connell (1990) defined *hegemonic masculinity* as the "culturally idealized form of masculine character" (p. 83) that emphasizes "the connecting of masculinity to toughness and competitiveness" as well as "the subordination of women" and the "marginalization of gay men" (p. 94). Traditional masculinity serves to uphold patriarchal codes by requiring that males adopt dominant and aggressive behaviors and function in the public sphere while requiring that females adopt adaptive and nurturing behaviors and function in the private sphere of the family (Levant, 1996).

There is considerable evidence that traditional gender role socialization for men in Western countries discourages feelings of sadness and vulnerability and promotes aggression when anger is aroused (Lytton & Romney, 1991). Two of the most often cited models of traditional masculinity are the "blueprint for manhood" (Brannon, 1976) and the masculinity mystique model (O'Neil, 1982). One of the benchmarks in masculine ideology theorizing, Brannon's (1976) blueprint for manhood outlined four guidelines for men within the United States. These guidelines describe how a man should act and suggest that men are socialized to avoid appearing feminine ("no sissy stuff"), to gain status and respect ("the big wheel"), to appear invulnerable ("the sturdy oak"), and to seek violence and adventure ("give 'em hell").

The masculine mystique model delineates the kind of stereotyped masculinity that could produce dysfunction and distress. According to O'Neil (1982), men are typically socialized toward independence and achievement (instrumentality), avoidance of characteristics associated with femininity and homosexuality (interpersonal dominance), and restriction or suppression of emotional expression (rationality). Masculine values and norms, learned during early socialization, are specifically based on rigid stereotypes and beliefs about men, masculinity, and femininity. For men to be accepted as adequately masculine, O'Neil posited that men must adhere to these norms. Thus, the process of masculine socialization influences men to internalize ideals that encourage emotional disconnection, achievement and status seeking, and interpersonal dominance (Good et al., 1994). Internalizing these ideals produces problems in living for men, what Pleck (1981, 1995) described as "gender role strain."

Gender Role Strain

The second major focus of the masculine gender role approach identifies the negative consequences for men's well-being of adopting particular masculinity ideologies. The terms *gender role strain* (Pleck, 1981) and a later extension, *gender role conflict* (O'Neil, Helms, Gable, David, & Wrightsman, 1986), have been coined to depict the detrimental consequences of men's endorsement of various aspects of masculinity (Mintz & O'Neil, 1990).

The basic premise of the gender role strain paradigm is that gender roles are defined by socially determined gender role stereotypes (i.e., what a "man" should do); however, these gender roles are naturally contradictory and inconsistent, and the number of individuals (both male and female) who cross and violate gender roles is high (Pleck, 1995). When a man fails to live up to the rigid standards, norms, and expectations of the traditional gender role and violates it, gender role strain occurs. These violations can lead to psychological distress because a man fails to live up to internalized notions of what it means to be a man. This is referred to as *discrepancy strain* (Pleck, 1995). This turmoil does not occur because men are unable to exhibit nontraditional gender roles but because of the negative psychological consequences and social condemnation when the actual or imagined gender roles are violated. Further, because of these negative consequences, many men overconform to traditional roles to be more consistent with the stereotypical traditional male role (O'Neil, 1990). However, certain characteristics associated with the traditional male role are psychologically dysfunctional and may cause harm if the individual rigidly adheres to expected traditional male roles; this is known as *dysfunction strain* (Pleck, 1995). The dysfunction is not due to being necessarily overly masculine but is more due to being overly rigid in one's adoption and enactment of masculinity (Smiler, 2004).

Masculine Gender Role Conflict

The stressful experience of male gender role discrepancies has been identified in the literature as *gender role conflict*. Gender role conflict has been a focal point of masculinity research for the past 25 years. O'Neil (1990) defined *gender role conflict* as "rigid, sexist, or restrictive gender roles, learned during socialization, that result in personal restriction, devaluation, or violation of others or self" (p. 25). As a result, traditional male socialization produces unrealistic and contradictory messages that lead to a fear of femininity in men (O'Neil, 1981). The result is that men engage in gender role conflict patterns that restrict their roles and behaviors to stereotypical masculine roles to avoid being, or appearing to be, feminine. *Gender role conflict* implies cognitive, emotional, unconscious, or behavioral problems caused by gender roles learned in sexist and patriarchal societies. Boys and men experience gender role conflict in the following situational contexts: When they (a) deviate from or violate gender role norms (Pleck, 1981); (b) try to meet or fail to meet gender role norms of masculinity; (c) experience discrepancies between their real and ideal self-concepts, based on gender role stereotypes (Garnets & Pleck, 1979); (d) personally devalue, restrict, or violate themselves (O'Neil, Good, & Holmes, 1995); (e) experience personal devaluations, restrictions, or violations from others; and (f) personally devalue, restrict, or violate others because of gender role stereotypes (O'Neil et al., 1995).

In his original conception of the masculine gender role conflict construct, O'Neil (1981) identified six patterns of masculine gender role conflict: restrictive emotionality; health care problems; obsession with achievement and success, restrictive sexual and affectionate behavior between men; socialized control, power, and competition issues; and homophobia. These gender role conflict patterns were the basis for the Gender Role Conflict Scale (GRCS; O'Neil et al., 1986). Factor analysis of the GRCS supported four of the six gender role patterns (the gender role patterns of health care problems and homophobia were not supported): Success, Power, and Competition; Restrictive Emotionality; Restrictive Affection Behavior Between Men; and Conflicts Between Work and Family Relations. *Success, Power, and Competition* measures the emphasis that a man places on achievement, authority and control over others, and the struggle for personal gain. *Restrictive Emotionality* refers to a man's difficulty with his own emotional self-disclosure as well as his comfort level with the emotional expression of others. *Restrictive Affection Behavior Between Men* is a measure of discomfort with expressions of caring between men. *Conflicts Between Work and Family Relations* assesses the level of discomfort experienced by men due to the impact of work or school on personal or family life (O'Neil et al., 1986). To date, over 200 empirical studies addressing men and masculinity have been conducted on the gender role conflict construct (O'Neil, 2005).

Masculinity and Diversity

For the most part, early scholarship on gender roles, socialization, and masculinity focused primarily on White–European American men and women, particularly those in the middle class. In many ways, research about masculinity in the United States discusses men's experiences in general terms, as if all men have similar reactions to dominant male paradigms (Casas, Wagenheim, Banchero, & Mendoza-Romero, 1994; Levant & Pollack, 1995; Liu, 2005; Moore & Gillette, 1991). Liu (2002a) suggested that even though the literature on men and masculinity has grown, the understanding of masculinity among men of color has remained limited. In particular, it is unclear how men of color navigate expectations of hegemonic masculinity. From a contextual perspective, the idea of "masculinities" reflects the intersection of masculinity with other culturally salient variables such as race, ethnicity, social class, sexual orientation, ability, and age. It is important to recognize the wide variation within male cultures when multiple identities are considered (Smiler, 2004). From this intersection, new forms of masculinity are constantly formed. For many men and boys, learning what it means to be a man is difficult, with competing notions of masculinity among cultural forms of masculinity and hegemonic masculinity. Lee (1998) noted that some African American boys might wrestle with the dilemma of adopting an African American versus a White model of masculinity. For some gay men, conflict may exist between feeling forced to outwardly project a heterosexual model of masculinity while privately experiencing a gay identity as a man.

Several empirical studies about men and diversity have found that masculine ideology does vary in theoretically meaningful ways, which supports the proposition that gender roles are socially enacted in relation to one's culture and context. Pleck et al. (1993) and Levant et al. (1992) found several variables were significantly associated with the endorsement of traditional masculinity (i.e., hegemonic masculinity), including being male, being younger, being single, having lower expectations of educational attainment, having greater church participation, being sexually active, being African American (as compared with being European American), and not living in the North, Midwest, or West (as compared with the South). In a diverse sample of U.S. college students, Levant and Majors (1997) found that African American men endorsed traditional masculinity (i.e., hegemonic masculinity) to the greatest extent, followed by European American men. Other research (Levant, Majors, & Kelley, 1998) found that geographic residency (i.e., which part of the United States a person lived) moderated the effect of race on masculine ideology, suggesting that variations within groups (e.g., metropolitan northeastern and mid-Atlantic United States vs. rural southern United States) may be more relevant than race itself.

In an investigation of manhood meaning among African American men, Hammond and Mattis (2005) suggested that responsibility and accountability for one's actions, thoughts, and behaviors are emerging themes that define African American masculinity. Furthermore, Franklin (1999) outlined that understanding African American men requires an appreciation for the influence of racism that persistently marginalizes the status of African American men. He detailed the *invisibility syndrome* as a conceptual model for understanding the inner evaluative processes and adaptive behavior of African Americans in managing experiences of racism. Invisibility is considered a psychological experience wherein the person feels that his personal identity and ability is undermined by racism in a myriad of interpersonal circumstances. For African American men, the encountering of repeated racial slights can create a feeling of being not seen as a person of worth.

The literature addressing masculine ideology among Latino men is conflicting. Male Mexican Americans have been traditionally socialized to be the authority or dominant figure in the family (Baruth & Manning, 1999; Paniagua, 2005). Mexican American men are expected to be strong, dominant, and the provider for the family (Sue & Sue, 2002). Supporting this, Abreu, Goodyear, Campos, and Newcomb (2000) found that Latinos endorsed higher degrees of traditional masculine ideology than did European Americans and African Americans. Pleck et al. (1993), however, did not find that being Latino led to an endorsement of traditional masculinity. Further, Torres, Solberg, and Carlstrom (2002) noted that among Mexican American and Puerto Rican men, traditional definitions of machismo (authoritarian, emotionally restrictive, and controlling) represented only 10% of the participants. Most of the participants identified with more emotionally responsive, collaborative, and flexible enactments of masculinity. In terms of Asian American men, Liu (2002a) found that Asian men endorsed traditional masculine ideology, with no significant differences between ethnically different Asian men. For Native American men, there has been virtually no research conducted to understand their endorsement of masculinity.

Limited research has been conducted on gender role conflict and men of color. The detrimental aspects of masculinity have been theoretically examined for African American men (Majors & Billson, 1992; Parham & McDavis, 1987) and Hispanic men (Valdez, Baron, & Ponce, 1987). Wade (1996) studied gender role conflict and the relationship with racial identity, finding that African American men do experience gender role conflict. Kim, O'Neil, and Owen (1996) examined gender role conflict with Asian American (Japanese American, Chinese American, and Korean American) college men. Chinese American men reported more conflict with success, power, and competition and between work and family relations than did Japanese American men. Asian American men with higher levels of acculturation reported more conflict with success, power, and competition and less restricted emotionality.

For gay and bisexual men, Haldeman (2001) noted the wide range of diversity due to race and culture, social experience, generation, and ability status. Therefore, gay and bisexual men can appear very different from one another. It is important to note that gay and bisexual men are socialized in the same cultural environment as heterosexual men, thus influence of hegemonic masculinity is often present yet often in conflict with emerging notions of one's identity as a gay or bisexual man. Research indicates that gay men experience gender role conflicts that can influence psychological well-being (Simonsen, Blazina, & Watkins, 2000). Yet, as Kilianski (2003) and O'Neil (1982) outlined, negative attitudes toward gay men and homophobia seem to compose core notions of traditional masculine ideology. Further, some gay and bisexual men struggle with internalized homophobia as they develop an identity as a gay or bisexual man (Haldeman, 2001).

Liu (2002b) discussed the social class dimensions of the masculine experience and noted how admonitions to compete and achieve economic success may be particularly salient for men of certain social classes. In particular, Liu suggested that normative masculinity inherently contains class variables such as status ideals and expectations. *Hegemonic masculinity* refers to being in control, being a self-made man, and being the "breadwinner" or "good provider," all of which relate to social class and status. In effect, *normative masculinity*, or "being a man," refers to providing for one's family and achieving success in the workplace (O'Neil, 1982)..

In summary, for psychotherapists working with all men, it is crucial to note that existing models of masculinity do not account for all men in terms of who they are and how they behave. Traditional and rigid models do not speak to or necessarily account for invisible populations and groups of men. For example, transgendered men may not associate any aspects of masculine ideology with their identity. Furthermore, remaining myopically fixed on traditional notions of masculinity can lead to overlooking the emotionally strong and available, involved and connected, compassionate and nurturing man that exists but is often ignored and marginalized, not only among groups of men, but within society as a whole.

MASCULINITY AND MENTAL HEALTH

Various perspectives exist regarding the influence of male gender role socialization on the mental health of men (Kelly & Hall, 1994; Mahalik, Good, & Englar-Carlson, 2003). At face value, the male gender role seems to have some benefits. Societal prescriptions dictate that men are to behave in a certain manner (i.e., traditionally masculine), and this behavior carries the expectation that men be seen as having positive qualities (i.e., confident, assertive, independent; Gilbert & Scher, 1999). Traditional masculinity has been associated with characteristics such as the willingness to sacrifice personal needs to provide for dependents; the tendency to think logically and calmly in the face of danger; the willingness to shoulder and try to solve other people's problems; expressing love by doing things; and valuing integrity, steadfastness, and loyalty to commitments (Levant, 1996). One would assume that on the basis of traditional masculine ideology, men may have strengths in areas such as problem solving, logical thinking, appropriate risk-taking, and assertive behavior (Levant, 1995). Most men are thought to function well and positively within their environments (Kelly & Hall, 1992). The masculine gender role has been viewed as fostering psychological well-being as well as positive qualities of self-esteem, assertiveness, confidence, and independence (Bem, 1974; Whitley, 1985). Mahalik et al. (2003) pointed out, however, that many studies reporting masculinity to be related to better psychological functioning are relating an instrumental personality trait, rather than being masculine, with greater psychological well-being.

On further review, it appears that many positive psychological qualities tend to be related to feelings of being masculine, not to the adherence to traditional masculine gender norms. The positive feelings associated with masculinity, however, may also be indicative of interpersonal, intrapersonal, and physical difficulties. Research (Blazina & Watkins, 1996; Cournoyer & Mahalik, 1995; Good, Dell, & Mintz, 1989) on the male gender role has indicated that major psychological difficulties may result from adherence to the traditional male gender role. These difficulties include risk-taking and self-destructive behaviors (Meth, 1990), poorer self-esteem (Cournoyer & Mahalik, 1995), problems with interpersonal intimacy (Fischer & Good, 1997; Sharpe & Heppner, 1991), greater depression and anxiety (Cournoyer & Mahalik, 1995; Good & Mintz, 1990; Sharpe & Heppner, 1991), greater biomedical concerns (Watkins, Eisler, Carpenter, Schechtman, & Fischer, 1991), emotional inexpressiveness (Pleck, 1981), high rates of "Type A" behavior patterns (Thompson, Grisanti, & Pleck, 1986), negative attitudes toward seeking professional psychological help (Good et al., 1989), abuse of substances (Blazina & Watkins, 1996), problems with interpersonal violence (Franchina, Eisler, & Moore, 2001), as well as greater overall psychological distress (Good, Robertson, Fitzgerald, Stevens, & Bartels, 1996; Hayes & Mahalik, 2000). (For a further review of the relationship between masculine ideology and mental health, see Mahalik et al., 2003.)

Recently, there has been increased attention to depression as a serious, yet often undiagnosed, condition in men. Depression in men is likely to be underdiagnosed because of the expression of symptoms that differ from the *Diagnostic and Statistical Manual of Mental Disorders* (4th ed., text rev.; American Psychiatric Association, 2000) criteria (Real, 1997). The term *covert depression* has been used to refer to the male experience of depression. Cochran and Rabinowitz (2003) noted the influence of gender role socialization, which encourages stoicism and suppression of emotion, as one of several factors that obscure the expression of depressed mood in many men. Hegemonic masculinity prohibitions placed on men against the experience of mood states of depression (e.g., sadness) and the behavioral expression of these mood states (e.g., crying) make clear and simple descriptions of male depression difficult (Cochran & Rabinowitz, 2000). Thus, the true expression of depression for many men creates a conflict. Because men experience many problems related to depression, such as alcohol and drug abuse (Hanna & Grant, 1997), and because suicide rates in men continue to be high (Moscicki, 1997), depression in many men remains unidentified, undiagnosed, and untreated.

Reviews (Courtenay, 2000; Eisler & Blalock, 1991; Good, Sherrod, & Dillon, 2000; Lemle & Mishkind, 1989) on the health of men highlighted the likely contribution of masculinity-related issues to the physical health of men. Pollack and Levant (1998) reported that in comparison to women, men suffer from lower life expectancies (by 7 years), higher levels of stress, and higher rates of completed suicides (4 times more). Conceptions of masculinity have been cited as a contributing factor to higher mortality rates for men from lung cancer, cirrhosis of the liver, coronary heart disease, motor vehicle accidents, suicide, and homicide (Eisler & Blalock, 1991). Moreover, men may not be aware of the effect that gender role socialization may have or is having on their mental health (Betz & Fitzgerald, 1993; Good, Robertson, Fitzgerald, Stevens, & Bartels, 1996).

Contradictory assumptions bring into question the ability of men to live psychologically and socially healthy lives within mainstream American culture. On the one hand, Caucasian men, the primary developers of traditional psychological theories, used man as the model of humanity (Sue, Ivey, & Pedersen, 1996), which made the concept of "masculinity" equivalent to the positive view of mental health (Broverman, Vogel, Broverman, Clarkson, & Rosenkrantz, 1972). In that sense, the endorsement of masculine traits and enactment of traditional masculinity is viewed as healthy, despite the research suggesting otherwise. From this perspective, some men who are successful in meeting the cultural expectations of masculinity may actually be harming themselves in the process because of the restrictive range of cognitive, affective, and behavioral coping repertoires. On the other hand, the failure to meet the cultural expectations of masculinity also appears to be detrimental, as others may evaluate men harshly for not living up to societal expectations of what it means to be a man. In essence, a double bind exists for men assuming one masculine role over another.

Help Seeking and Fears About Psychotherapy

Betz and Fitzgerald (1993) noted that one of the major themes in the psychology of men is the influence of male socialization on men's willingness to seek and participate in therapy:

> As far back as the original *Counseling Psychologist* collection on counseling men, the consensus in the literature has been that the requirements

of the male role appear antithetical to the requirements of a "good" client, i.e., psychological mindedness, willingness to self-disclose, and a capacity for emotional intimacy. (pp. 358–359)

Researchers (Mahalik et al., 2003) identified the lack of fit between conceptualizations of masculinity and the popular perception of counseling and mental health services as a likely reason for the lack of mental health utilization by men. Scher (1990) stated,

The man who comes into the consulting room is usually there because he believes there is no alternative. Very few men come for therapy because they subscribe to its life-enhancing qualities. Even if they did they would likely not see it as something for them anyway. Men are in therapy because something, internal or external, has driven them to it. (p. 323)

Some research has compared differences in help seeking between men and women, and other research has explored these differences in reference to gender role socialization.

From a gender role socialization perspective, many of the tasks associated with help seeking, such as relying on others, admitting that one needs help, or recognizing and labeling an emotional problem, are at odds with hegemonic notions of masculinity. Supportive of this thinking, research (Blazina & Watkins, 1996; Good et al., 1989; Good & Wood, 1995; Komiya, Good, & Sherrod, 2000; Robertson & Fitzgerald, 1992; Rochlen & O'Brien, 2002; Wisch, Mahalik, Hayes, & Nutt, 1995) indicated that masculine gender role conflict is consistently inversely related to men's willingness to seek psychological help or career-related assistance. Examining specific elements of gender role conflict, Good et al. (1989) reported that men who endorse restrictive emotionality and restrictive affectionate behavior between men were reluctant to seek psychological help. Similarly, Robertson and Fitzgerald (1992) reported that success, power, competition, and restrictive emotionality were correlated with negative attitudes toward psychological help seeking. Komiya et al. (2000) linked emotional restriction with a reluctance to seek psychological help, with greater emotional openness predictive of more favorable attitudes toward psychological help seeking.

These results suggest that internalized gender roles may create barriers to help seeking for men, particularly if help seeking involves violating important masculine gender roles. For example, if masculine gender socialization includes an emphasis on seeking power, control, and self-reliance (Nadler, Maler, & Friedman, 1984), men may be reluctant to seek psychological treatment and likely to terminate treatment early, as seeking help implies need of assistance and potential loss of control. Of particular importance to beginning the therapeutic process are male clients' reactions to emotional expression. Men may believe that feelings are unnecessary, time-consuming baggage. Men may believe they will experience social sanctions, such as rejection and condemnation from expressing emotions, and may be motivated to conceal feelings of sadness and not seek treatment because of an attributable fear of intimacy or emotional closeness and fear of appearing feminine (Hammen & Peters, 1977). Thus, men who are fearful of disclosing affectionate emotions or behavior toward other men may be more likely to avoid counseling. Specifically, male clients may expect that they will be encouraged, or even demanded, to use affective language and explore the emotional context of their life experiences in psychotherapy. The inhibition of strong emotional expression has typically been valued in North American culture (Bronstein, 1984) and represents a core component of the norms for masculinity (David & Brannon, 1976; Levant & Pollack, 1995). Men may believe that feelings are unnecessary and better left unexplored, particularly if they feel comfortable and more skilled in rational problem solving. Thus, men who are ambivalent about experiencing or expressing emotions may be more likely to avoid or terminate counseling as the work becomes focused on feelings.

Treatment fears appear to be different from negative attitudes toward seeking help (Englar-Carlson & Vandiver, 2001) and therefore should additionally be understood in relation to men. Kushner and Sher (1991) considered the decision to seek help to be motivated in part by a conflict between approach tendencies (e.g., mental distress, transition in life, pressures from others) and avoidance tendencies (e.g., fear of stigma, cost, time commitments, access to services). From this perspective, although men experience mental distress, they may also experience specific treatment fears around image concerns (i.e., fears of being judged negatively by oneself or others for seeking treatment; Deane & Chamberlain, 1994; Komiya et al., 2000) and coercion concerns (i.e., fears about being pushed to think, do, or say things related to their problems in a new way).

Related to image concerns, men may perceive a "gender specific" stigma associated with breaching the dictates of the masculine gender role that goes beyond the general negative societal reaction toward those who seek psychological help (Sibicky & Dovidio, 1986). In this case, the stigma of not living up to a masculine image likely interferes with asking for psychological help, particularly when it is around a salient (i.e., ego-central) masculine ideology (Addis & Mahalik, 2003). Men who obey the so-called sturdy oak dictate follow the injunction that men "should" never show weakness and "should" endure difficulties without relying on others for help; therefore, going to counseling is admitting that a man is not sturdy, but rather shaky (Mahalik, 1999). If asking for and receiving help is viewed by some men as "unmasculine," it would be logical to assume that men would be fearful of being stigmatized for receiving any assistance, particularly assistance of a psychological nature. Further, psychotherapy requires clients to acknowledge that they cannot control or manage their problems and need help. Amato and Bradshaw (1985) found that the most important cluster of reasons for avoiding or delaying seeking mental health services involved fears linked to exposing, facing, and treating problems.

Coercion addresses the fear of being pushed to think, do, or say things against one's will (Kushner & Sher, 1989). Men are taught to be tough, self-sufficient, and invulnerable to protect themselves from those who would take advantage of them and their weaknesses. Yet in therapy, clients are expected to present their concerns, expose vulnerability, and ask for assistance. The behavior that men may engage in during therapy may seem to be against societal expectations for them (i.e., men may be encouraged to cry or to express emotions in therapy, whereas the dictates of the male gender role encourage the restriction of affect) and contrary to the rigid manner in which men limit their behavior. When men imagine being clients and in a vulnerable position, they may fear being taken advantage of and coerced to behave and think differently. Simply put, some men may hold the belief that psychotherapy is a feminizing process that threatens their masculine identity (Englar-Carlson & Shepard, 2005). Those men who project an image of toughness and restrict their expression of affect may fear being coerced to be vulnerable and emotional in therapy. Men who feel threatened by affection between men for fear of appearing gay themselves may fear appearing passive in therapy, and when working with a male therapist or in group therapy with other men, they may fear being coerced into intimacy with other men.

Addressing Attitudes About Help Seeking and Fears About Psychotherapy

Given the concerns about seeking psychological help that some men may have, psychotherapists need to actively consider the process of help seeking as a salient clinical variable. Psychotherapists can expect some concerns about psychological help seeking and the process of therapy, and they can anticipate that men may fear being stigmatized for being in psychotherapy, may fear being coerced or changed against their will, may fear not being understood, and may be confused about how psychotherapy actually works. Consider how these fears may be related to their model of masculinity and gender roles. It may be best to acknowledge these concerns up front with clients to show awareness of these fears and to reflect the normality of being ambivalent about psychotherapy. One recommendation is to examine how male clients found their way into therapy and ask from the onset if there are any initial questions about what takes place in psychotherapy. For example, ask the male client about his thoughts about being in psychotherapy. Further, discuss what treatment could entail (i.e., tasks and goals) while giving the client a chance to be involved in the process, thus modeling an egalitarian relationship between the client and the psychotherapist as opposed to putting the male client in a "one-down" position from the onset.

Mahalik et al. (2003) recommended that psychotherapists first work to identify the expectations that male clients may have about the psychotherapy process and either correct those that are erroneous or change the structure of therapy to be more congruent for a given male client. For example, if a man expresses the concern that he will be forced or "made" to change his behavior, the psychotherapist can explain the collaborative nature of the working alliance and that the client will ultimately set treatment goals. To limit the male client's fear that psychotherapy will be unbalanced against him, the psychotherapist can bring these fears out in the open and discuss them, as well as be extra-careful in initial sessions about not appearing to take sides (Englar-Carlson & Shepard, 2005).

To promote more adaptive ways of help seeking for men, Addis and Mahalik (2003) proposed a model of men's help seeking grounded in social psychological theory. They recommended changes to help-seeking environments such as providing greater opportunities for reciprocity for men (e.g., with other group members or the community), increasing the perception of normativeness for particular problems, training psychotherapists to recognize the ego-centrality of certain problems (e.g., is this problem part of me?) to be more sensitive to how a man may be perceiving the relevance of the concern, reducing stigma of seeking help and of experiencing mental health problems, and creating alternative nontraditional forms of assistance more congruent with masculine socialization. All of these changes could help men feel more comfortable in seeking help. There are many ways psychotherapists can anticipate stigma, treatment fearfulness, and ambivalence about therapy and can then take concrete steps to help male clients feel more comfortable. By doing so, psychotherapists have a greater chance to engage clients in the therapy process, which may allow critical work on difficult issues to begin.

PSYCHOTHERAPY WITH MEN: CLINICAL CONSIDERATIONS

The previous sections have outlined theory and research pertaining to the new psychology of men. Men's socialization into masculine roles contributes to (a) gender identity and ways of thinking, feeling, behaving, and presenting problems and (b) attitudes and potential fears about psychotherapy. It is not possible to effectively work with men without viewing them within the context of their gender roles (Good, Gilbert, & Scher, 1990; Scher, 1990). As a whole, it appears that the psychotherapy community is becoming more sensitive to cultural diversity issues in psychotherapy, including the influence of gender roles (Sue & Sue, 2002). Gender is now recognized as a salient organizing variable of clients' lives and experiences. The guidelines developed for multicultural counseling competency (American Psychological Association [APA], 2003) and for practice with girls and women (APA, 2005) offer some direction and considerations in regard to helping psychotherapists work with men. These guidelines and principles highlight the importance of the sociocultural context in tailoring psychotherapy. Liu (2005) further provided a rationale for including the study of men and masculinity as a critical component of multicultural competency.

When it comes to theoretical perspectives on treating men, there is no one theoretical orientation that appears to be more effective than others in conceptualizing distress or treating men. Within the existing scholarly literature are treatment suggestions from various theoretical perspectives, including psychodynamic (Pollack, 1995, 2001; Rabinowitz & Cochran, 2002; Shepard, 2005), cognitive–behavioral (Mahalik, 2001a), interpersonal (Mahalik, 2001b), multicultural (Caldwell & White, 2001; Casas, Turner, & Ruiz de Esparza, 2001), integrative (Good & Mintz, 2001), family therapy (Philpot, 2001), and feminist (Walker, 2001). The range of theoretical perspectives is perhaps most reflective of current practices of psychotherapy with men. Many scholars and practitioners have looked to tailor existing theoretical views in accordance with perspectives on male socialization. The consideration of gender role socialization and a client's "masculinity" in each step of the therapy process is in line with what Good et al. (1990) referred to as "gender-aware therapy." In this approach, knowledge and understanding of a client's gender role orientation is placed alongside and in conjunction with a psychotherapist's theoretical orientation.

Cochran (2005) noted the adoption of evidence-based practice as a dominant treatment paradigm for many psychotherapists. In an age of theoretical integration, evidence-based practice is guided by the use of research-based evidence for diagnosis and treatment, the use of clinical expertise to guide judgment, and the consideration of client values and preferences. Cochran noted that although the psychology of men is recognized as a distinct area of clinical practice, there have yet to be controlled studies that demonstrate the effectiveness of specific treatments with men. Thus the field is guided by integrating clinical expertise with masculinity ideologies and values. The following sections specifically address areas of attention for tailoring psychotherapy to meet the needs of men.

Understanding and Assessing Masculine Socialization

Psychotherapists must begin by being knowledgeable about masculine socialization. This requires knowledge and appreciation of the full range of "masculinities" and how masculinity is influenced by cultural, racial, political, historical, and economic contexts. Mahalik et al. (2003) noted that given the vast research about men's socialization, psychotherapists who develop awareness of how socialization experiences may constrain men's lives and affect their well-being are likely to be more effective in working clinically with men. One of the early assessments made in psychotherapy can address traditionality and rigidity of masculine role beliefs. From the first point of contact, psychotherapists can note and observe whether male clients seem highly competitive and success oriented, appear reluctant to admit any psychological distress, and appear to gauge their level of emotionality (e.g., monitor the use of the words *think* and *feel* and determine whether clients are actually matching thoughts with thinking and affect with feeling).

For example, in psychotherapy, the so-called big wheel can emerge in a man's complaints about working long hours and the urge to provide for one's family; it may be seen in the pressure a man puts on himself to compete and succeed across multiple settings (e.g., workplace, sporting events); and it can emerge in a man's complaints about not being appreciated by others for how hard he works and how stressed he is by his efforts to succeed. Reluctance to admit psychological distress often is apparent in the male client telling a psychotherapist that there is no real reason to be in psychotherapy, and he is coming to please someone else (e.g., partner, spouse, boss, legal system). Level of emotionality can be assessed by asking a client for reactions to an emotionally charged situation and by checking whether he responds with *thinking* or *feeling* terms.

Building on the information presented in the previous section about help seeking and treatment fears, a psychotherapist can examine and explore the relationship between masculine socialization and thoughts, behaviors, and feelings regarding getting help. Addressing this early in therapy can help a man reassess his understanding about therapy. As Scher (1990) stated,

> Psychotherapy is traditionally viewed as the refuge of the weak—those who cannot handle their own situations and therefore must submit to the help of another. Therefore, the man who comes for therapy feels at a disadvantage and must compensate for that. He feels powerless and exposed. These feelings cause him to behave less than ideally as a client because he struggles to stay hidden and have control over the situation. This behavior is compounded by the typical qualities of men that are contrary to the qualities necessary for therapy. These necessary qualities include openness and willingness to examine oneself in the presence of and with the aid of another person. (p. 323)

Therapists would do well to assess and understand the help-seeking process (i.e., thoughts, feelings, and behaviors) that male clients experience in terms of their gender role and expectations and concerns about seeking psychological help to offset the scenario that Scher (1990) suggested. For example, a psychotherapist can ask the client a variety of questions about help seeking, such as, "Can you tell me how you came to see someone like me?" or "What do you think about coming to see a therapist?" Understanding and anticipating how masculinity issues interact with experiences of seeking help may lead to initial psychotherapy experiences that respect the experiences of men while exploring what may be unrealistic fears and expectations male clients may be holding (Mahalik et al., 2003). It may also be useful to begin to reframe the notion of seeing a psychotherapist as a weakness into the idea of it being courageous to take the path of trying to create change and being responsible for one's life. This can affirm the positive value of seeking help (Cochran, 2005).

Incorporating a Gender Role Analysis

One of the most important aspects of working effectively with men is incorporating a gender role analysis into conceptualization and treatment. Having an understanding of masculine socialization provides psychotherapists with a keen insight into the inner lives of most male clients. When the influence of masculine socialization is examined and explored in the open dialogue between client and therapist, a bridge can be built that links a man's lifelong experience with his presenting problem. Talking about masculine socialization experiences in the open is a rare event for most men. Masculine socialization is often experienced in silence and not overtly explored or examined, particularly between two men. Some male clients may look to see if the psychotherapist will take the first risk and break the silence about socialization. If the psychotherapist is male, talking about male socialization may be an opportunity to model openness and appropriate self-disclosure. A male psychotherapist may first disclose some of his own male socialization experiences in an effort to make a connection. This disclosure can show that the psychotherapist is willing to work cooperatively rather than giving all responsibility in the session to reveal and disclose to the male client (Englar-Carlson & Shepard, 2005).

Psychotherapists can invite clients to examine their socialization experiences by linking content that comes up in therapy (e.g., emotional stoicism, or having a man talk about sacrificing or forgoing his needs for another's) with dictates or messages of masculine socialization (e.g., men are supposed to be tough and support others, or men do not cry) with specific examples from the past (e.g., "What are some experiences you remember that taught you to think and be this way?"). Such questions help men gain insight to why they may be experiencing current stressors and can provide an opportunity to examine the restrictive nature of masculine socialization (e.g., gender role conflicts). When men have the insight and awareness to explore masculine socialization and feel safe and secure enough in psychotherapy to question past experiences, they can begin to consider becoming less restrictive in their gender roles to allow unfettered expression of some thoughts, feelings, and behavior.

Relationship Considerations

This chapter has outlined many ways in which male gender socialization seems to be inherently antithetical to the therapeutic process. At the core of these observations is the apparent conflict between the conceptualization of psychotherapy as relationally driven and the socialization of men as emotionally stoic, instrumental, and interpersonally dominant (Addis & Mahalik, 2003; Brooks, 1998). Many men learn to hide vulnerabilities and restrict their emotional world to be accepted as men and to avoid shame and ridicule. Further, many men have difficulties creating and maintaining intimate relationships that require self-disclosure and emotional expressiveness. Yet it is widely recognized that at the core of any effective psychotherapy experience is an intimate therapeutic relationship signified by trust, empathy, and positive regard. Further, the quality of the therapeutic alliance has been noted as the single best predictor of therapeutic outcome (Bachelor & Horvath, 1999; Messer & Wampold, 2002). Whereas it appears clear that a positive psychotherapy experience for men would have a collaborative and caring psychotherapy relationship as its foundation (Scher, 2001), creating such a relationship can be difficult (Good, Thomson, & Brathwaite, 2005). Good et al. noted that one way to build relationships with men in therapy is to clearly acknowledge and accept the differences that may exist between the culture of psychotherapy and masculine socialization. Building on this awareness, psychotherapists can then begin by tailoring the developing therapy relationship in a more male-friendly manner.

Although the psychotherapy relationship is a unique type of relationship, research about male friendships offers some clues about how men seek, and ultimately "do," intimacy. When it comes to relationships, emotional boundaries seem to characterize male friendships, especially when compared with female relationships. According to Gilligan (1982), men develop more "positional" identities, fearing intimacy, whereas women tend to develop "relational" identities, fearing separation. Rubin (1985) characterized male friendships as "bonding without intimacy," whereas female friendships were described as more talkative and sharing of intimate feelings. Male friendships are predicated on external activities ("doing"), through which men can share the same emotional experience without having to reveal any details about their personal lives. Swain (1989) noted that male friendships may be characterized by a "covert style of intimacy" that is clearly different from women, but intimate nonetheless. A man's masculine gender role orientation often provides the context for much of the discussion concerning the nature of men's relationships with other men and also with women. It is important to note that men can create intimate interpersonal relationships; however, how this is accomplished and what these relationships look like may be different from the popular connotations of intimacy and closeness.

Research and knowledge of male friendships provide some direction for ways to connect with male clients. From the first session, psychotherapy must first be about making a connection with a man, rather than giving all the responsibility for the session to the client. The therapeutic relationship can be strengthened by action empathy (Pollack, 1998). This involves using active or action-oriented words (e.g., "What should we do [or accomplish] today?") or engaging in more give-and-take interactions with the client. In contrast to a therapeutic style in which the psychotherapist reflects or responds only to the client, the give and take facilitates a face-to-face interaction that is less threatening and may be more familiar to men. Further, with the emphasis on action, the therapy parallels instrumentality of many men, with an emphasis on using therapy to "fix" something with a tangible outcome. Therapists may also find themselves using more humor and self-disclosure as a way of talking with men in their language in a manner conducive to the types of things that men naturally do as a means of establishing friendships (Kiselica, 1999).

Further, psychotherapists can take an active role to facilitate an egalitarian relationship with men. Some men will be "trying on" new parts of themselves in session and are helped by seeing the therapist try skills or interventions first. Thus, psychotherapists should be prepared to model openness and self-disclosure about themselves, as some men may look to see if their therapist will take the first risk. Further, psychotherapists can respond honestly to questions that may require some self-disclosure, as this may be a form of testing and even "asking" for a model. At times, therapy may feel like regular conversation, much like the Latino concept of *personalismo* (Cervantes, chap. 10, this volume; Paniagua, 2005), in which men are more oriented toward people than relationships. As Paniagua (2005) noted, Latino clients may select a psychotherapist more on the basis of their ability to self-disclose personal information (e.g., hobbies, food preferences, sports team preferences) than on the basis of professional credentials.

As therapy progresses, the development of a connected psychotherapy relationship can create the opportunity to reconnect men with their lost talent for intimacy and intimacy's requirements: self-disclosure, emotional expressiveness, and empathy for others' emotional states (Shepard, 2005). As male clients become more relationally connected in psychotherapy, a parallel process can occur in which men can begin to be more connected with those outside of therapy.

Working With Emotions

One of the more controversial and discussed topics in the new psychology of men concerns men's ability to express emotions. (For a comprehensive review on men's emotional behavior, see Wong & Rochlen, 2005.) Emotional inexpressiveness in men has been viewed as having negative consequences for men, including contributing to psychological distress (Brooks, 1998; Levant, 1998). It is frequently asserted that men find it difficult to talk about emotions, and in particular, vulnerable emotions (e.g., fear, sadness, shame, helplessness). Some researchers have suggested that emotional inexpressiveness is a pervasive problem for men because of masculine gender role socialization (Brooks, 1998; Good & Sherrod, 2001; Pollack & Levant, 1998). Whereas the empirical evidence on sex difference in emotionality concludes that men's and women's emotional behavior is more similar than different (Wester, Vogel, Pressly, & Heesacker, 2002), men may experience more difficulty in expressing emotions because they have been socialized to say less or because they have a more limited capacity to express themselves, not because there is a lack of emotional arousal in men (Robertson, Lin, Woodford, Danos, & Hurst, 2001). Further, it appears that the degree to which men have internalized traditional masculine beliefs and roles may speak more to a man's willingness to express emotions rather than his ability to do so (Fischer & Good, 1997). It seems that the connection between emotional inexpressiveness and psychological distress may have more to do with whether a man is conflicted about his own emotional-related values or is conflicted between these values and those of important people in his life. Consequently, men who are not internally or externally conflicted about emotions may be psychologically healthy (Wong & Rochlen, 2005). For example, Heesacker and Prichard (1992) reminded psychotherapists to consider that a man's emotional inexpressiveness and the ability to remain calm and focused could be a strength used to help him deal with his problems.

As Wong and Rochlen (2005) observed, being unaware of one's emotions and being unwilling to disclose one's emotions are two crucial factors that help explain men and emotional inexpressiveness. Therefore, a particular challenge for the psychotherapist is facilitating emotional expressiveness with emotionally restricted men (Englar-Carlson & Shepard, 2005). A hallmark of the masculine gender role conflict paradigm (O'Neil, 1982), restrictive emotionality is beginning to be understood as a complex phenomenon, influenced by intrapsychic, socialization, and contextual factors. Addressing restrictive emotionality in treatment needs to begin with an assessment of why the male client is inexpressive. Wong and Rochlen summarized that men may unconsciously repress emotions, experience emotions but have difficulty labeling the feeling experience, withhold emotions because of internalized associations between vulnerable emotions and weakness, or consciously withhold them because of appraisal of the social context as being unsafe for expression.

One possibility is that the male client is unable to identify and label emotional experiences, may virtually not be conscious of his feelings, and even if slightly aware, is unable to find the words to describe his inner experience. The term *alexithymia* has been used to describe an inability to identify and verbalize feelings, yet this term was originally used to describe a more pathological condition of hospitalized patients with mental illness, whose emotional capacity was markedly restricted. Levant (1995) suggested that many psychologically healthy men may experience a "normative alexithymia" due to socialization experiences in which boys are actively discouraged from expressing emotions, resulting in a failure to develop the capacity to recognize and articulate the emotions they may be experiencing. Normative alexithymia stemming from male socialization helps explain some men's difficulty identifying more subtle negative affective states such as sadness, shame, or disappointment. It must be stressed that the normative alexithymia construct does not imply that men are innately less emotional than women, but,

for a variety of reasons, some men struggle with the identification and labeling
t is essential if one is to accurately report one's feelings to others.
nportant to add that the very act of expressing emotions may not
be healthy for men (Wong & Rochlen, 2005). Whereas express-
ns to another can often reduce distress if the feelings are validated
as in psychotherapy), men can also feel vulnerable and threatened
Moore & Watson, 2001). A crucial assessment with male clients
are a client's perception of the importance of experiencing and
emotions, as well as gaining an understanding of how, when, and
whom emotions can be expressed or withheld (Wong & Rochlen,
iseful metaphor to use with male clients is to compare their emo-
ression appraisal process as a stoplight with green, yellow, and red
: clients to talk about who in their lives, as well as what times and
s of emotions, are green lighted as okay, red lighted as restricted,
v lighted as proceeding with caution or confusion. The stoplight
/ help men talk about the aspects of their emotional world and how
rience the expression of emotions in their life.

rms of psychotherapy, Wong and Rochlen (2005) pointed out that
psychotherapists who primarily use their male clients' degree of emotional
expressiveness or inexpressiveness as a measuring stick for psychological health
may be oversimplifying a client's experience. A deeper analysis of a man's
emotion-related values and how these values influence his psychological functioning may be more accurate to understand his emotional world. Thus a
psychotherapist can explore potential conflicts about the value of emotional
expression between a man and significant others. It is important for psychotherapists to consider the modes of emotional expression that are healthy
and appropriate for male clients (Wester et al., 2002). There are multiple
ways to facilitate emotional expression in psychotherapy. Emotions can be
expressed verbally, nonverbally (writing), linguistically (using language), and
through physiological means (facial expressions and body movements; Wong
& Rochlen, 2005). Changing the mode of expression can be a helpful intervention to provide expressive outlets for men. Robertson, Lin, Woodford,
Danos, & Hurst (2001) noted success using a structured scale as a means of
helping emotionally restricted men chart and record emotions. Further,
Robertson and Freeman (1995) outlined a structured program of masculine-
congruent ways of emotional expression that focused on framing emotions as
tools to help men assess, adapt, and ultimately be successful in their surroundings. Rabinowitz and Cochran (2002) outlined a series of bodywork
techniques to facilitate emotional expression through physiological means.

A Final Clinical Note: Positive Attributes of Male Socialization

One of the least discussed aspects of masculine socialization within the
new psychology of men concerns the positive aspects of male socialization.

The majority of research on men and masculinity has examined problems in living and collateral damage inflicted by men to the self and others (including other men). Although this evidence and research is striking in terms of the influence of masculinity and its contribution to pain, grief, and suffering, it must be remembered that many men function well in society and contribute to the welfare of others. Levant (1996) noted many of the positive attributions of traditional masculinity such as providing to others, courage and bravery in the eye of danger, a willingness to carry other's burdens, and expressing love by doing things rather than by direct emotional or intimate expression. Whereas much attention has been directed at the problems associated with emotional expressiveness, psychotherapists must also question how emotional inexpressiveness can be a strength that helps men solve problems by remaining calm and focused in times of crisis (Mahalik et al., 2003). Whereas some of these qualities, when taken to extreme, can create problems for men, these attributions also highlight some strengths and positive qualities. Psychotherapists can tap into these positive qualities (and the corresponding tools that promote them) and harness them as an adjunct to psychotherapy and at times as a vehicle to promote change.

A hallmark of brief therapies, a strengths-based approach, invites a fuller appreciation of human potential by focusing on the strengths and resources that clients bring into psychotherapy rather than by exclusively looking at weaknesses or deficits (Hoyt, 1998). For men, a strengths-based approach would acknowledge positive attributes of being a man by enlisting these resources into service toward reaching client goals. Some strengths can be suggested by clients and defined early in therapy. Men can speak to the things they do well and the qualities that they value and view as enriching to their life. Collaboratively, a male client and psychotherapist can also discover hidden strengths by deconstructing how the client is successful in life. As an example, the psychotherapist can acknowledge a client's help seeking and entry into therapy both as taking responsibility for creating change and also by noting the ability to use available resources.

As highlighted earlier, many of the attributes associated with men and masculinity can be enhancing or destructive, depending on the degree and application in a man's life. Psychotherapy can teach men to evaluate the extent to which some attributes, such as independence, dedication to a task or cause, or emotional stoicism both help and hurt depending on the context. As Wong and Rochlen (2005) pointed out, emotional inexpressiveness is not inherently harmful if men are not experiencing conflicts over it, and in some settings, the benefit of emotional expressiveness is directly tied to whether the emotion will be validated.

Some lessons from research on fathering can also be useful to tap in psychotherapy with men. Pollack (1998) noted the unique relationship between fathers and sons, noting the adaptive contributions that fathers add to the healthy development of boys. He noted that fathers often have the ability to draw out an infant's emotional expression across a wider scale of intensity that helps a child learn to tolerate the range of people and situations. This is often achieved through playing games (often physical games) in which both father and son become enthralled in the intensity of the experience. This is a powerful reciprocal moment of action intimacy for both father and son in which the father shows love through action. Therefore, some men can create and experience intimacy in their life, yet they may not recognize the potential, because action empathy is often overlooked. A psychotherapist can help men understand how they achieve intimacy through action in other relationships and use this as a reflective tool to explore not only the affect associated with intimacy but also as a base for building other intimacy skills. Further, the role of fatherly love and acceptance with children has been indicated as a buffer against psychological adjustment problems whereas the withdrawal of fatherly love has been indicated in a myriad of adjustment problems including anxiety, social and emotional withdrawal, and issues of negative self-concept and self-esteem (Rohner & Veneziano, 2001). The awareness that fathers have something critical to contribute to the development of children can serve as a powerful reminder and encouraging point for some men.

The Adlerian concept of social interest (Adler, 1931/1992) seems particularly relevant for many men. *Social interest* is the development of a feeling of being part of the larger whole, a sense of belonging to and participating with others for the common good. Adlerians view one's social interest as the true measure of mental health (Carlson, Watts, & Maniacci, 2006). As social interest grows, so does the capacity for empathy and altruism. A way to tap social interest that parallels with male socialization is to encourage men to be involved in their respective communities by doing something for others. This can be volunteer work; donations of time, money, or effort; or involvement with youth through coaching or mentoring.

Another way in which men can tap their personal strengths can be seen in the use of men's psychotherapy groups. As Addis and Mahalik (2003) suggested, many men look for ways to reciprocate assistance or aid that was given to them. One of the powerful aspects of men's group psychotherapy is seeing men help each other. Building on the idea of "intimacy by doing," being supportive of another man just by being in the room can be helpful for both parties. Group psychotherapy is a way in which men feel they can support others by "carrying their burden" through testimonial experiences but also by commitment to stick by others. Further, psychotherapists can explore the role of work with heroic men (first responders such as police, fire, and emergency services personnel and those serving in the armed forces) to address the awareness and importance of being in a position that puts the lives of others before the life of oneself.

SUMMARY

The world of psychotherapy can provide men with a unique space in which they can be effectively treated despite masculine gender role socialization restrictions. The more psychotherapists understand masculine socialization, the better equipped they become about the private and intimate lives of their male clients. This chapter has reviewed the emerging scholarly literature based on the integration of the new psychology of men within the clinical realm. This review of literature provides the empirical and theoretical base to better conceptualize the cases presented within this casebook. The cases in this book serve as clear examples of effective gender-aware treatment that capture the variation of masculinities while highlighting the complexities associated with treating men.

REFERENCES

Abreu, J. M., Goodyear, R. K., Campos, A., & Newcomb, M. D. (2000). Ethnic belonging and traditional masculine ideology among African Americans, European Americans, and Latinos. *Psychology of Men and Masculinity, 1,* 75–86.

Addis, M. E., & Cohane, G. H. (2005). Social scientific paradigms of masculinity and their implications for research and practice in men's mental health. *Journal of Clinical Psychology, 6,* 633–647.

Addis, M. E., & Mahalik, J. R. (2003). Men, masculinity, and the contexts of help seeking. *American Psychologist, 58,* 5–14.

Adler, A. (1992). *What life could mean to you.* Oxford, England: Oneworld. (Original work published 1931)

Amato, P. R., & Bradshaw, R. (1985). An exploratory study of people's reasons for delaying or avoiding help seeking. *Australian Psychologist, 20,* 21–31.

American Psychiatric Association. (2000). *Diagnostic and statistical manual of mental disorders* (4th ed., text rev.). Washington, DC: Author.

American Psychological Association. (2003). Guidelines on multicultural education, training, research, practice, and organizational change for psychologists. *American Psychologist, 58,* 377–402.

American Psychological Association. (2005). *Guidelines for psychological practice with girls and women.* Draft from the Joint Task Force of APA Divisions 17 and 35, June, 2005.

Bachelor, A., & Horvath, A. (1999). The therapeutic relationship. In M. Hubble, B. Duncan, & S. Miller (Eds.), *The heart and soul of change* (pp. 133–178). Washington, DC: American Psychological Association.

Baruth, L. G., & Manning, M. L. (1999). *Multicultural counseling and psychotherapy: A lifespan perspective.* Upper Saddle River, NJ: Prentice Hall.

Bem, S. L. (1974). The measurement of psychological androgyny. *Journal of Consulting and Clinical Psychology, 42,* 155–162.

Bem, S. L. (1981). Gender schema theory: A cognitive account of sex typing. *Psychological Review*, 88, 354–364.

Betz, N. E., & Fitzgerald, L. F. (1993). Individuality and diversity: Theory and research in counseling psychology. *Annual Review of Psychology*, 44, 343–381.

Blazina, C. (1997). Mythos and men: Toward new paradigms of masculinity. *The Journal of Men's Studies*, 5, 285–294.

Blazina, C., & Watkins, C. E., Jr. (1996). Masculine gender role conflict: Effects on college men's psychological well-being, chemical substance usage, and attitudes towards help-seeking. *Journal of Counseling Psychology*, 43, 461–465.

Brannon, R. (1976). The male sex role: Our culture's blueprint of manhood and what it's done for us lately. In D. S. David & R. Brannon (Eds.), *The forty-nine percent majority: The male sex role* (pp. 1–45). Reading, MA: Addison-Wesley.

Bronstein, P. (1984). Promoting healthy emotional development in children. *Journal of Primary Prevention*, 5, 110.

Brooks, G. R. (1998). *A new psychotherapy for traditional men*. San Francisco: Jossey-Bass.

Brooks, G. R., & Good, G. E. (Eds.). (2001a). *The new handbook of psychotherapy and counseling with men: A comprehensive guide to settings, problems, and treatment approaches* (Vol. 1). San Francisco: Jossey-Bass.

Brooks, G. R., & Good, G. E. (Eds.). (2001b). *The new handbook of psychotherapy and counseling with men: A comprehensive guide to settings, problems, and treatment approaches* (Vol. 2). San Francisco: Jossey-Bass.

Broverman, I. K., Vogel, S. R., Broverman, D. M., Clarkson, E. E., & Rosenkrantz, D. S. (1972). Sex role stereotypes: A current appraisal. *Journal of Social Issues*, 28, 59–78.

Caldwell, L. D., & White, J. L. (2001). African-centered therapeutic and counseling interventions for African American males. In G. R. Brooks & G. E. Good (Eds.), *The new handbook of psychotherapy and counseling with men: A comprehensive guide to settings, problems, and treatment approaches* (Vol. 2, pp. 737–753). San Francisco: Jossey-Bass.

Carlson, J., Watts, R. E., & Maniacci, M. (2006). *Adlerian therapy: Theory and practice*. Washington, DC: American Psychological Association.

Casas, J. M., Turner, J. A., & Ruiz de Esparza, C. A. (2001). Machismo revisited in a time of crisis: Implications for understanding and counseling Hispanic men. In G. R. Brooks & G. E. Good (Eds.), *The new handbook of psychotherapy and counseling with men: A comprehensive guide to settings, problems, and treatment approaches* (Vol. 2, pp. 754–779). San Francisco: Jossey-Bass.

Casas, J. M., Wagenheim, B. R., Banchero, R., & Mendoza-Romero, J. (1994). Hispanic masculinity: Myth or psychological schema meriting clinical considerations. *Hispanic Journal of Behavioral Sciences*, 16, 315–331.

Cochran, S. V. (2005). Evidence-based assessment with men. *Journal of Clinical Psychology*, 6, 649–660.

Cochran, S. V., & Rabinowitz, F. E. (2000). *Men and depression: Clinical and empirical perspectives*. San Diego, CA: Academic Press.

Cochran, S. V., & Rabinowitz, F. E. (2003). Gender-sensitive recommendations for assessment and treatment of depression in men. *Professional Psychology: Research and Practice, 34*, 132–140.

Connell, R. W. (1990). An iron man: The body and some contradictions of hegemonic masculinity. In M. A. Messner & D. F. Sabo (Eds.), *Sport, men, and the gender order* (pp. 83–95). Champaign, IL: Human Kinetics.

Cournoyer, R. J., & Mahalik, J. R. (1995). Cross-sectional study of gender role conflict examining college-aged and middle-aged men. *Journal of Counseling Psychology, 42*, 11–19.

Courtenay, W. H. (1998). College men's health: An overview and a call to action. *Journal of American College Health, 46*, 279–290.

Courtenay, W. H. (2000). Engendering health: A social constructionist examination of men's health beliefs and behaviors. *Psychology of Men and Masculinity, 1*, 4–15.

David, D. S., & Brannon, R. (1976). *The forty-nine percent majority: The male sex role.* Reading, MA: Addison-Wesley.

Deane, F. P., & Chamberlain, K. (1994). Treatment fearfulness and distress as predictors of professional psychological help seeking. *British Journal of Guidance and Counselling, 22*, 207–217.

de Beauvoir, S. (1970). *The second sex.* New York: Bantam Books.

Doyle, J. A. (1995). *The male experience* (3rd ed.). Dubuque, IA: W. C. Brown.

Eisler, R. M. (1995). The relationship between masculine gender role stress and men's health risk: The validation of a construct. In R. F. Levant & W. S. Pollack (Eds.), *A new psychology of men* (pp. 164–206). New York: Basic Books.

Eisler, R. M., & Blalock, J. A. (1991). Masculine gender role stress: Implications for the assessment of men. *Clinical Psychology Review, 11*, 45–60.

Eisler, R. M., & Skidmore, J. R. (1987). Masculine gender role stress: Scale development and component factors in appraisal of stressful situations. *Behavior Modification, 11*, 123–126.

Englar-Carlson, M., & Shepard, D. S. (2005). Engaging men in couples counseling: Strategies for overcoming ambivalence and inexpressiveness. *The Family Journal, 13*, 383–391.

Englar-Carlson, M., & Vandiver, B. J. (2001, August). Gender-role conflict, help-seeking attitudes, and psychological treatment fearfulness. In J. M. O'Neil & G. E. Good (Cochairs), *Gender role conflict research: Testing new constructs and dimensions empirically.* Symposium at the 109th Annual Convention of the American Psychological Association, San Francisco.

Fischer, A. F., & Good, G. E. (1997). Men and psychotherapy: An investigation of alexithymia, intimacy, and masculine gender role beliefs. *Psychotherapy, 34*, 160–170.

Franchina, J. J., Eisler, R. M., & Moore, T. M. (2001). Masculine gender role stress and intimate abuse: Effects of masculine gender relevance of dating situations and female threat on men's attributions and affective responses. *Psychology of Men and Masculinity, 2*, 34–41.

Franklin, A. J. (1999). Invisibility syndrome and racial identity development in psychotherapy and counseling African American men. *The Counseling Psychologist, 27*, 761–793.

Garnets, L., & Pleck, J. H. (1979). Sex role identity, androgyny, and sex role transcendence: A sex role strain analysis. *Psychology of Women Quarterly, 3*, 270–283.

Gergan, K. J. (1991). *The saturated self.* New York: Basic Books.

Gibbons, J. L., Hamby, B. A., & Dennis, W. D. (1997). Researching gender-role ideologies internationally and cross-culturally. *Psychology of Women Quarterly, 21*, 151–170.

Gilbert, L. A., & Scher, M. (1999). *Gender and sex in counseling and psychotherapy.* Boston: Allyn & Bacon.

Gilligan, C. (1982). *In a different voice: Psychological theory and women's development.* Cambridge, MA: Harvard University Press.

Good, G. E., Dell, D. M., & Mintz, L. B. (1989). Male role and gender role conflict: Relations to help seeking in men. *Journal of Counseling Psychology, 36*, 295–300.

Good, G. E., Gilbert, L. A., & Scher, M. (1990). Gender-aware therapy: A synthesis of feminist therapy and knowledge about gender. *Journal of Counseling and Development, 68*, 376–380.

Good, G. E., & Mintz, L. B. (1990). Gender role conflict and depression in college men: Evidence for compounded risk. *Journal of Counseling and Development, 69*, 17–21.

Good, G. E., & Mintz, L. B. (2001). Gender-aware integrative psychotherapy for men. In G. R. Brooks & G. E. Good (Eds.), *The new handbook of psychotherapy and counseling with men: A comprehensive guide to settings, problems, and treatment approaches* (Vol. 2, pp. 582–602). San Francisco: Jossey-Bass.

Good, G. E., Robertson, J. M., Fitzgerald, L. F., Stevens, M., & Bartels, K. M. (1996). The relation between masculine role conflict and psychological distress in male university counseling center clients. *Journal of Counseling and Development, 75*, 44–49.

Good, G. E., & Sherrod, N. (2001). The psychology of men and masculinity: Research status and future directions. In R. Unger (Ed.), *Handbook of the psychology of women and gender* (pp. 201–214). New York: Wiley.

Good, G. E., Sherrod, N., & Dillon, M. (2000). Masculine gender role stressors and men's health. In R. Eisler & M. Hersen (Eds.), *Handbook of gender, culture, and health* (pp. 63–81). Mahwah, NJ: Erlbaum.

Good, G. E., Thomson, D. A., & Brathwaite, A. (2005). Men and therapy: Critical concepts, theoretical frameworks, and research recommendations. *Journal of Clinical Psychology, 61*, 699–711.

Good, G. E., Wallace, D. L., & Borst, T. S. (1994). Masculinity research: A review and critique. *Applied and Preventive Psychology, 3*, 3–14.

Good, G. E., & Wood, P. K. (1995). Male gender role conflict, depression, and help seeking: Do college men face double jeopardy? *Journal of Counseling and Development, 74*, 70–75.

Green, A. (1946). The male middle-class child and neurosis. *American Sociological Review, 11*, 31–41.

Haldeman, D. C. (2001). Psychotherapy with gay and bisexual men. In G. R. Brooks & G. E. Good (Eds.), *The new handbook of psychotherapy and counseling with men: A comprehensive guide to settings, problems, and treatment approaches* (Vol. 2, pp. 796–815). San Francisco: Jossey-Bass.

Hammond, W. P., & Mattis, J. S. (2005). Being a man about it: Manhood meaning among African American men. *Psychology of Men and Masculinity. 6*, 114–126.

Hammen, C. L., & Peters, S. D. (1977). Differential responses to male and female depressive reactions. *Journal of Consulting and Clinical Psychology, 35*, 79–90.

Hanna, E., & Grant, B. (1997). Gender differences in *DSM–IV* alcohol use disorders and major depression as distributed in the general population: Clinical implications. *Comprehensive Psychiatry, 38*, 202–212.

Hayes, J. A., & Mahalik, J. R. (2000). Gender role conflict and psychological distress in male counseling center clients. *Psychology of Men and Masculinity, 1*, 116–125.

Heesacker, M., & Prichard, S. (1992). In a different voice, revisited: Men, women, and emotion. *Journal of Mental Health Counseling, 14*, 274–290.

Hoyt, M. F. (1998). *The handbook of constructive therapies.* San Francisco: Jossey-Bass.

Imms, W. D. (2000). Multiple masculinities and the schooling of boys. *Canadian Journal of Education, 25*, 152–165.

Jakupcak, M., Lisak, D., & Roemer, L. (2002). The role of masculine ideology and masculine gender role stress in men's perpetration of relationship violence. *Psychology of Men and Masculinity, 3*, 97–106

Kelly, K. R., & Hall, A. S. (1992). Mental health counseling for men: A special issue. *Journal of Mental Health Counseling, 14*, 255–256.

Kelly, K. R., & Hall, A. S. (1994). Affirming the assumptions of the developmental model for counseling men. *Journal of Mental Health Counseling, 16*, 475–482.

Kennedy-Moore, E., & Watson, J. C. (2001). How and when does emotional expression help? *Review of General Psychology, 5*, 187–212.

Kessler, R. C., McGonagle, K. A., Zhao, S., Nelson, C. B., Hughes, M., Eshelman, S., et al. (1994). Lifetime and 12-month prevalence of *DSM–III–R* psychiatric disorders in the United States: Results from the National Comorbidity Survey. *Archives of General Psychiatry, 51*, 8–19.

Kilianski, S. E. (2003). Explaining heterosexual men's attitudes toward women and gay men: The theory of exclusively masculine identity. *Psychology of Men and Masculinity, 4*, 37–56.

Kim, E. J., O'Neil, J. M., & Owen, S. V. (1996). Asian American men's acculturation and gender role conflict. *Psychological Reports, 79*, 95–104.

Kimmel, M., & Messner, M. A. (Eds.). (2004). *Men's lives* (6th ed.). New York: Macmillan.

Kiselica, M. S. (1999). Counseling teenage fathers. In A. M. Horne & M. S. Kiselica (Eds.), *Handbook of counseling boys and adolescent males: A practitioner's guide* (pp. 179–198). Thousand Oaks, CA: Sage.

Komiya, N., Good, G. E., & Sherrod, N. B. (2000). Emotional openness as a predictor of college students' attitudes toward seeking psychological help. *Journal of Counseling Psychology, 33*, 148–154.

Kushner, M. G., & Sher, K. J. (1989). Fear of psychological treatment and its relation to mental health service avoidance. *Professional Psychology: Research and Practice, 20*, 251–257.

Kushner, M. G., & Sher, K. J. (1991). The relation of treatment fearfulness and psychological service utilization: An overview. *Professional Psychology: Research and Practice, 22*, 196–203.

Lee, C. C. (1998). Counseling African American men. In L. E. Davis (Ed.), *Working with African American males: A guide to practice* (pp. 39–53). Thousand Oaks, CA: Sage.

Lemle, E., & Mishkind, M. E. (1989). Alcohol and masculinity. *Journal of Substance Abuse Treatment, 6*, 213–222.

Levant, R. F. (1995). Toward the reconstruction of masculinity. In R. F. Levant & W. S. Pollack (Eds.), *A new psychology of men* (pp. 229–251). New York: Basic Books.

Levant, R. F. (1996). Masculinity reconsidered. *Independent Practitioner, 16*, 36–39.

Levant, R. F. (1998). Desperately seeking language: Understanding, assessing, and treating normative male alexithymia. In W. S. Pollack & R. F. Levant (Eds.), *New psychotherapy for men* (pp. 35–56). New York: Wiley.

Levant, R. F., Hirsch, L., Celentano, E., Cozza, T., Hill, S., & MacEachern, M. (1992). The male role: An investigation of contemporary norms. *Journal of Mental Health Counseling, 14*, 325–337.

Levant, R. F., & Majors, R. G. (1997). An investigation into variations in the construction of the male gender role among young African American and European American women and men. *Journal of Gender, Culture, and Health, 2*, 33–43.

Levant, R. F., Majors, R. G., & Kelley, M. L. (1998). Masculinity ideology among young African American and European American women and men in different regions of the United States. *Cultural Diversity and Mental Health, 4*, 227–236.

Levant, R. F., & Pollack, W. S. (Eds.). (1995). *A new psychology of men*. New York: Basic Books.

Levant, R. F., Richmond, K., Majors, R. G., Inclan, J. E., Rossello, J., Heesacker, M., et al. (2003). A multicultural investigation of masculinity ideology and alexithymia. *Psychology of Men and Masculinity, 4*, 91–99.

Liu, W. M. (2002a). Exploring the lives of Asian American men: Racial identity, male role norms, gender role conflict, and prejudicial attitudes. *Psychology of Men and Masculinity, 3*, 107–118.

Liu, W. M. (2002b). The social class-related experiences of men: Integrating theory and practice. *Professional Psychology, 33*, 355–360.

Liu, W. M. (2005). The study of men and masculinity as an important multicultural competency consideration. *Journal of Clinical Psychology, 6*, 685–697.

Lytton, H., & Romney, D. M. (1991). Parents' differential socialization of boys and girls: A meta-analysis. *Psychological Bulletin, 109,* 267–296.

Mahalik, J. R. (1999). Men's gender role socialization: Effect on presenting problems and experiences in psychotherapy. *Progress: Family Systems Research and Therapy, 3,* 13–18.

Mahalik, J. R. (2001a). Cognitive therapy for men. In G. R. Brooks & G. E. Good (Eds.), *The new handbook of psychotherapy and counseling with men: A comprehensive guide to settings, problems, and treatment approaches* (Vol. 2., pp. 544–564). San Francisco: Jossey-Bass.

Mahalik, J. R. (2001b). Interpersonal therapy for men. In G. R. Brooks & G. E. Good (Eds.), *The new handbook of psychotherapy and counseling with men: A comprehensive guide to settings, problems, and treatment approaches* (Vol. 2, pp. 565–581). San Francisco: Jossey-Bass.

Mahalik, J. R., Good, G. E., & Englar-Carlson, M. (2003). Masculinity scripts, presenting concerns, and help seeking: Implications for practice and training. *Professional Psychology: Research and Practice, 34,* 123–131.

Majors, R. G., & Billson, J. M. (1992). *Cool pose: The dilemmas of Black manhood in America.* New York: Lexington Books.

Messer, S. B., & Wampold, B. E. (2002). Let's face facts: Common factors are more potent than specific therapy ingredients. *Clinical Psychology: Science and Practice, 9,* 21–25.

Meth, R. L. (1990). The road to masculinity. In R. L. Meth & R. S. Pasick (Eds.), *Men in therapy: The challenge of change* (pp. 3–34). New York: Guilford Press.

Mintz, L. B., & O'Neil, J. M. (1990). Gender roles, sex, and the process of psychotherapy: Many questions and few answers. *Journal of Counseling and Development, 68,* 381–387.

Moore, R., & Gillette, D. (1991). *King, warrior, magician, lover: Rediscovering the archetypes of the mature masculine.* San Francisco: Harper.

Moscicki, E. (1997). Identification of suicide risk factors using epidemiologic studies. *Psychiatric Clinics of North America, 20,* 499–517.

Nadler, A., Maler, S., & Friedman, A. (1984). Effects of helper's sex, subject's androgyny, and self-evaluation on males' and females' willingness to seek and receive help. *Sex Roles, 10,* 327–339.

O'Neil, J. M. (1981). Patterns of gender role conflict and strain: Sexism and fear of femininity in men's lives. *Personnel and Guidance Journal, 60,* 203–210.

O'Neil, J. M. (1982). Gender role conflict and strain in men's lives: Implications for psychiatrists, psychologists, and other human service providers. In K. Solomon & N. B. Levy (Eds.), *Men in transition: Changing male roles, theory, and therapy* (pp. 5–44). New York: Plenum Press.

O'Neil, J. M. (1990). Assessing men's gender role conflict. In D. Moore & F. Leafgren (Eds.), *Problem-solving strategies and interventions for men in conflict* (pp. 23–38). Alexandria, VA: American Association for Counseling and Development.

O'Neil, J. M. (2005). *Introduction and content of the gender role conflict research program*. Retrieved May 8, 2005, from http://web.uconn.edu/joneil/GenderHome.html

O'Neil, J. M., & Egan, J. (1992). Men's gender role transitions over the life span: Transformations and fears of femininity. *Journal of Mental Health Counseling, 14,* 305–324.

O'Neil, J. M., Good, G. E., & Holmes, S. (1995). Fifteen years of theory and research of men's gender role conflict: New paradigms for empirical research. In R. F. Levant & W. S. Pollack (Eds.), *A new psychology of men* (pp. 164–206). New York: Basic Books.

O'Neil, J. M., Helms, B. J., Gable, R. K., David, L., & Wrightsman, L. S. (1986). Gender Role Conflict Scale: College men's fear of femininity. *Sex Roles, 14,* 335–350.

Paniagua, F. A. (2005). *Assessing and treating culturally diverse clients: A practical guide* (2nd ed.). Thousand Oaks, CA: Sage.

Parham, T., & McDavis, R. (1987). Black men, an endangered species: Who's pulling the trigger? *Journal of Counseling and Development, 66,* 24–27.

Philpot, C. L. (2001). Family therapy for men. In G. R. Brooks & G. E. Good (Eds.), *The new handbook of psychotherapy and counseling with men: A comprehensive guide to settings, problems, and treatment approaches* (Vol. 2, pp. 622–636). San Francisco: Jossey-Bass.

Pleck, J. H. (1981). *The myth of masculinity*. Cambridge, MA: MIT Press.

Pleck, J. H. (1995). The gender role strain paradigm: An update. In R. F. Levant & W. S. Pollack (Eds.), *A new psychology of men* (pp. 11–32). New York: Basic Books.

Pleck, J. H., Sonenstein, F. L., & Ku, L. C. (1993). Masculinity ideology and its correlates. In S. Oskamp & M. Costanzo (Eds.), *Gender issues in social psychology* (pp. 85–110). Newbury Park, CA: Sage.

Pollack, W. S. (1995). No man is an island: Toward a new psychoanalytic psychology of men. In R. F. Levant & W. S. Pollack (Eds.), *A new psychology of men* (pp. 33–67). New York: Basic Books.

Pollack, W. S. (1998). *Real boys: Rescuing our sons from the myths of boyhood*. New York: Random House.

Pollack, W. S. (2001). "Masked men": New psychoanalytically oriented treatment models for adult and young adult men. In G. R. Brooks & G. E. Good (Eds.), *The new handbook of psychotherapy and counseling with men: A comprehensive guide to settings, problems, and treatment approaches* (Vol. 2, pp. 527–543). San Francisco: Jossey-Bass.

Pollack, W. S., & Levant, R. F. (1998). *New psychotherapy for men*. New York: Wiley.

Rabinowitz, F. E., & Cochran, S. V. (2002). *Deepening psychotherapy with men*. Washington, DC: American Psychological Association.

Real, T. (1997). *I don't want to talk about it: Overcoming the secret legacy of male depression*. New York: Fireside.

Robertson, J. M., & Fitzgerald, L. F. (1992). Overcoming the masculine mystique: Preferences for alternative forms of assistance among men who avoid counseling. *Journal of Counseling Psychology, 39,* 240–246.

Robertson, J. M., & Freeman, R. (1995). Men and emotions: Developing masculine-congruent views of affective expressiveness. *Journal of College Student Development, 36,* 606–607.

Robertson, J. M., Lin, C., Woodford, J., Danos, K. K., & Hurst, M. A. (2001). The (un)emotional male: Physiological, verbal, and written correlates of expressiveness. *Journal of Men's Studies, 9,* 393–412.

Rochlen, A. B., & O'Brien, K. M. (2002). The relation of male gender role conflict and attitudes toward career counseling to interest and preferences for different career counseling styles. *Psychology of Men and Masculinity, 3,* 9–21.

Rohner, R., & Veneziano, R. (2001). The importance of fatherly love: History and contemporary evidence. *Review of General Psychology, 5,* 382–405.

Rubin, L. B. (1985). *Just friends: The role of relationships in our lives.* New York: Harper & Row.

Sachs-Ericsson, N., & Ciarlo, J. A. (2000). Gender, social roles, and mental health: An epidemiological perspective. *Sex Roles, 43,* 605–628.

Sapolsky, R. M. (1997). *The problem with testosterone.* New York: Simon & Schuster.

Scher, M. (1990). Effect of gender role incongruence on men's experience as clients in psychotherapy. *Psychotherapy, 27,* 322–326.

Scher, M. (2001). Male therapist, male client: Reflections on critical dynamics. In G. R. Brooks & G. E. Good (Eds.), *The new handbook of psychotherapy and counseling with men: A comprehensive guide to settings, problems, and treatment approaches* (Vol. 2, pp. 719–733). San Francisco: Jossey-Bass.

Sharpe, M. J., & Heppner, P. P. (1991). Gender role, gender-role conflict, and psychological well-being in men. *Journal of Counseling Psychology, 39,* 240–246.

Shepard, D. S. (2005). Male development and the journey toward disconnection. In D. Comstock (Ed.), *Diversity and development: Critical contexts that shape our lives and relationships* (pp. 133–160). Belmont, CA: Brooks/Cole.

Sibicky, M., & Dovidio, J. F. (1986). Stigma of psychological therapy: Stereotypes, interpersonal reactions, and the self-fulfilling prophecy. *Journal of Counseling Psychology, 47,* 138–143.

Simonsen, G., Blazina, C., & Watkins, C. E. (2000). Gender role conflict and psychological well-being among gay men. *Journal of Counseling Psychology, 47,* 85–89.

Skovholt, T. M. (1978). Feminism and men's lives. *The Counseling Psychologist, 7,* 3–10.

Smiler, A. P. (2004). Thirty years after the discovery of gender: Psychological concepts and measures of masculinity. *Sex Roles, 50,* 15–26.

Sue, D. W., Ivey, A. E., & Pedersen, P. B. (Eds.). (1996). *A theory of multicultural counseling and therapy.* Pacific Grove, CA: Brooks/Cole.

Sue, D. W., & Sue, D. (2002). *Counseling the culturally different: Theory and practice* (4th ed.). New York: Wiley.

Swain, S. (1989). Covert intimacy: Closeness in men's friendships. In B. J. Risman & P. Schwartz (Eds.), *Gender in intimate relationships: A microstructural approach* (pp. 71–86). Belmont, CA: Wadsworth.

Thompson, E. H., Grisanti, C., & Pleck, J. H. (1986). The masculine role as a moderator of stress–distress relationships. *Sex Roles, 15,* 359–366.

Thompson, E. H., & Pleck, J. H. (1995). Masculine ideologies: A review of research instrumentation on men and masculinities. In R. F. Levant & W. S. Pollack (Eds.), *A new psychology of men* (pp. 129–163). New York: Basic Books.

Toerien, M., & Durrheim, K. (2001). Power through knowledge: Ignorance and the "real man." *Feminism & Psychology, 11,* 35–54.

Torres, J. B., Solberg, S. H., & Carlstrom, A. H. (2002). The myth of sameness among Latino men and their machismo. *American Journal of Orthopsychiatry, 72,* 163–181.

Valdez, L. F., Baron, A., & Ponce, F. Q. (1987). Counseling Hispanic men. In M. Scher, M. Stevens, G. Good., & M. Eichenfield (Eds.), *The handbook of counseling and psychotherapy with men* (pp. 372–387). Newbury Park, CA: Sage.

Vessey, J. T., & Howard, K. I. (1993). Who seeks psychotherapy? *Psychotherapy, 30,* 546–553.

Wade, J. C. (1996). African American men's gender role conflict: The significance of racial identity. *Sex Roles, 34,* 17–33.

Walker, L. E. A. (2001). A feminist perspective on men in emotional pain. In G. R. Brooks & G. E. Good (Eds.), *The new handbook of psychotherapy and counseling with men: A comprehensive guide to settings, problems, and treatment approaches* (Vol. 2, pp. 683–695). San Francisco: Jossey-Bass.

Watkins, P. L., Eisler, R. M., Carpenter, L., Schechtman, K. B., & Fischer, E. B. (1991). Psychosocial and physiological correlates of male gender role stress among employed adults. *Behavioral Medicine, 17,* 86–90.

Wester, S. R., Vogel, D. L., Pressly, P. K., & Heesacker, M. (2002). Sex differences in emotion: A critical review of the literature and implications for counseling psychology. *The Counseling Psychologist, 30,* 630–652.

Whitley, B. E. (1985). Sex role orientation and psychological well-being: Two meta-analyses. *Sex Roles, 12,* 207–225.

Wisch, A. F., Mahalik, J. R., Hayes, J. A., & Nutt, E. A. (1995). The impact of gender role conflict and counseling technique on psychological help seeking in men. *Sex Roles, 33,* 77–89.

Wong, J. Y., & Rochlen, A. B. (2005). Demystifying men's emotional behavior: New directions and implications for counseling and research. *Psychology of Men and Masculinity, 6,* 62–72.

II

EXPLORING EMOTIONS: AWAKING THE INNER WORLDS OF MEN

3

PAUL'S JOURNEY TO FIND CALMNESS: FROM SWEAT TO TEARS

MARK A. STEVENS

I've been studying men and masculinity as long as I can remember. Looking for male role models and heroes was an essential part of my early research efforts. Television, the movies, the ballpark, the playground, and my home provided ample data for me to collect and qualitatively analyze. I knew there was something very meaningful and powerful about the information that I was collecting. Yet, I did not know how, nor had the courage, to voice my questions or hypotheses about the impact of growing up male. I believe like most (if not all) young boys, I had many observations and questions about why I was supposed to act a certain way, yet felt it was inappropriate to question the rules of masculinity.

In graduate school, reading feminist literature and talking with my female cohorts both gave me a type of permission and encouraged me to look at how masculinity socialization had shaped my beliefs and behaviors. In many ways, I needed the legitimacy of science and psychology to ask the questions about male socialization that I had wanted to ask since I was a young boy.

Finding other men to talk about growing up male was an essential part of my "me-search." I discovered how terrifying and rewarding it can be to feel safe enough to be vulnerable around other men. When my friend Quin and I proclaimed to each other (nonalcohol induced) that we were best friends and loved each other and wanted to be in each other's lives forever, the tension of homophobia and joy coexisted. When I cofacilitated my first men's group in 1981, with my training director, Dr. Sam Gange, I discovered how our openness with one another outside of the therapy room facilitated increased openness of our group members. When Dr. Good and I started facilitating "men can stop rape" prevention workshops for all-male audiences, I discovered how close men could become by talking about real fears and stories about male sexuality.

The me-search findings of being a *son* (who lost his father at an early age), a *father* who was a stay-home dad with his first child in 1981 (and now a dad to an adult daughter and two late-adolescent boys), and a *man* who strives to find the courage to question and bend the rules of masculinity, have all provided an essential context for my clinical work with my male clients.

ABOUT THE CLINICIAN–PERSON

There are three guiding principles that set a context for the work I do with men:

1. Men have an (often unstated) strong desire and longing for deeper, more intimate, satisfying, trusting, safe, noncompetitive, heartfelt connections, yet they are often too scared or lack the knowledge of how to attain such connections.
2. Men do have a full range of feelings and are often able to sort out what the feelings are and how they may impact their relationships, although this may take some extra time and coaching.
3. Men ought to be viewed as being in pain and wanting relief while not wanting to be vulnerable.

Gender role conflict (O'Neil, 1981), gender role strain (Pleck, 1981), male norms (Brannon, 1985), and models of masculinity offer a backdrop to understanding the rules of masculinity and the fears associated with breaking these rules. The rules of masculinity are along the lines of the following: Be in charge and strong, avoid emotional intimacy with other men, don't engage in sissy stuff, don't back down from a fight, avoid showing vulnerability, view women as sexual conquests, be the breadwinner, and significantly impact the physical and emotional lives of all men and boys. I view these rules as a recipe for dissatisfaction associated with interpersonal connections. And it is within that context that I view my counseling work with men as an interpersonal journey. The psychotherapy room can be a unique environment for male–male interaction and feedback. A room where the rules of masculinity can be bent—by both my client and myself. A room where the little boy (inside of all adult men) can feel and remember the fears of growing up (Scher, 1979). A room where accessing vulnerability can feel like strength. A room where issues of homophobia can be processed. A room where my clients can explore and come to better understand their inner world. A room where interpersonal connection can be felt and appreciated. A room that eventually has no walls, where my clients can be in the world as they are in the room with me.

MEET MY CLIENT, PAUL

Paul is a biracial man in his early 20s. His mother is from Asia and his father is Caucasian. Paul is a junior, studying electrical engineering at a small liberal arts college in the Los Angeles, California, area. Paul identified as heterosexual and with no religious affiliation. At the time of our initial sessions, he was living alone with his mother near his college. Paul's parents divorced when he was in grammar school. He grew up primarily in his father's home. He has both older (full) and younger (half) siblings. Paul reported no history of sexual or physical abuse. He was physically healthy and reported minimal use of alcohol. Paul smoked marijuana in high school, but down the road he found it uncomfortable, as it made him mildly paranoid, and he subsequently stopped using upon entering college. He drank two to three cups of coffee per day during the school year and exercised infrequently. Paul had not dated since high school and reported not being sexually active. Academically he was doing fine (2.7 grade point average), but he thought he could do better. Paul had a set of friends from high school with whom he socialized, but he had not made any really close friends during college. I saw Paul in my private practice for a total of 31 sessions over an 18-month time span. A counselor referred him from his college after he had sought help with study and test-taking strategies. This was his first time in psychological counseling.

OUR WORK TOGETHER

Paul became extremely nervous in situations that involved other people. Paul said, "I only feel comfortable around people I have known for awhile, and even then, I am usually in the background of conversation." He was afraid that he would start to sweat (which he often did) and would feel awkward and embarrassed. He avoided talking in class and meeting new people. Paul said, "I have lots of ideas to share in class, but when I imagine even raising my hand to speak, I start to sweat."

Initial Sessions: Building Rapport and Finding the Relaxation Response

I met Paul in the waiting room. I did not have much information about him, except that he wanted to feel more comfortable in the classroom and in social situations. As we made eye contact, I could see his anxiety quite clearly. His eyes had difficulty meeting mine, and his face looked frightened, without much expression. We shook hands, and I immediately noticed how moist they were. I noticed that he looked older than I expected, although he appeared physically healthy and fit. His appearance did not match the sweat and the nervousness I saw on his face and in his eyes. I felt a pull to help him relax, and I was mildly uncomfortable with how uncomfortable he appeared to be. Initially, I felt too much of a power imbalance in the room: the in-control, calm therapist and the out-of-control, extremely nervous client. My mannerisms were more casual than usual, hoping they would help Paul relax. I remember sitting casually, not crossing my legs, putting aside the intake chart and my pen. Although my voice and speech style is typically not filled with psychological jargon, I did notice an even more "person-styled" approach and response with Paul. In retrospect, I believe shifting the power balance, even so slightly, helped to create an atmosphere of respect and "saving face."

Sitting across from Paul, I noticed there was perspiration on his forehead and upper lip. He looked like a deer in headlights. Paul apologized for sweating as he wiped his perspiration with tissues from the box on my table. I subtly registered that this was the first time a client had used my tissues for that purpose. I replied back to Paul that it must be difficult not being able to hide how nervous you get in certain situations. He nodded back to me with agreement, and I noticed a small smile on his face. I immediately started to feel paternal with Paul. I wondered how he felt in the presence of other men, authority figures, and his father. On some level, I identified with Paul. As a boy and now a man, I fear being and appearing as fearful as Paul. And subsequently, this paternal pull was in part my not wanting Paul to be and appear so fearful, so I would not have to face my own issues of losing control.

The initial session progressed with information gathering and building rapport. Paul had a concrete style of asking and responding to my questions. He was in a tremendous amount of pain and worry and wanted both relief from the pain and some kind of reassurance that he was not "crazy." Paul shared with me that he was afraid of accidentally killing his mother while he was sleepwalking. He asked me if I had ever heard of someone doing such a thing. I was somewhat caught off guard by his directness. Although I could have processed what he had hoped to hear from me or the significance of my response, I decided to be direct and told him I had not. He seemed to be relieved by my answer. I let Paul know that I appreciated his willingness to ask me such a direct question and that I thought his question to me signified how he was trying to take care of himself. Paul seemed to respond well to the nurturing, noncritical, and understanding stance that I took with him. He let me know more details about his fears of what he might do while sleep-walking and also elaborated on other behaviors that concerned him, such as double-checking to make certain the gas was turned off in his house and the front door was locked. Later in the session, he abruptly changed topics and told me he had one more worry to share that he was quite embarrassed about. It became immediately clear to me that he, for some time, had been sitting on his discomfort about bringing up the new worry, yet had been very polite in following and answering my intake assessment questions. I could not tell by his facial expressions or answers to my questions that he was preoccupied and was waiting for the right moment to change directions. Again I responded that I was appreciative of how he was trying to take care of himself. He was bringing himself into the room, and there was a type of assertiveness or back-bone to his presence that was contrasting his nervous sweat. I asked him how long he had been holding onto his question.

He let me know that it was on his mind since he came into the room but that he was not ready to ask the question. He felt the pressure of time and did not want to wait until next week. Paul stated that he often felt conflict about asking for what he wanted and needed and usually kept his wishes on the back burner with his family and friends. Being quiet and silent was a pervasive theme throughout his life.

Paul reported to me, with visible discomfort, that for the past year he was concerned that he might sexually molest a female child. He found those thoughts disturbing and was afraid that he might act on them even though he had not done so in the past. He told me he does not visualize or fantasize about molesting children but rather fears losing control and becoming a child molester. He says his fears have been reinforced and intensified by the media coverage of molestation by clergy in recent months. Paul again asked me if I had ever read in my psychology books or heard of anyone losing control and molesting someone without intention. I wanted to soothe his worry and an-swered honestly: "No." I was uncomfortable with the content of his fear. Paul reported that he did not recollect any experiences or memories of being mo-lested, which offered me a temporary yet vulnerable sense of relief. I was aware of my own fears of losing control, as I wondered and worried if Paul would molest a child. Who was this man in front of me that I felt so nurtur-ing and paternal toward? In reality, he was a complete stranger to me, and I had only to rely on my intuitive and clinical judgment to comfort myself about the likelihood of his future harming actions. I wanted to know for certain that Paul would not molest a young girl. I felt scared about not abso-lutely knowing, and in this way, I identified with Paul about not being in absolute control of outcomes.

Although I was getting a pretty good picture of Paul's fear of losing control, I wanted to better understand the content or objects of his fears. I knew this would take plenty of time to unfold. As our initial session was nearing the end, I decided to take a psychoeducational approach with Paul and offer him some of my initial impressions and suggestions. Although I do not do this with all of my male clients, I felt pulled to put some type of closure to our session. I intuited that Paul was craving information. I wanted to offer him some hope without guarantee. I also believe I was trying to soothe myself by putting some type of clinical frame around a complex yet limited amount of developmental information. In summary of our session, I explained to Paul that I thought his worries about losing control were indicative of his high level of anxiety. His body and mind were on constant alert. I suggested that he eliminate caffeine use and start a regular cardiovascular exercise program. I applauded him for coming in to seek treatment, and I told him that I looked forward to getting to know him better. I asked him how he felt about the session, and he responded that it was much easier than he thought it would be. We ended with a handshake, and the clamminess of his palm let me know the session was not too easy for him. After the first session, I wrote in my case notes that I thought Paul seemed motivated and ready to change and he was genuinely tired of the amount of pain he was experiencing.

My head and heart were activated. I felt nervous, hopeful, and excited about working with Paul. I found talking with a colleague to be extremely helpful. I did not want to keep in the secret of my fears about Paul losing control and molesting a young girl. My relief in talking with a colleague, I believe, paralleled Paul's relief in sharing his secret fears with me.

Toward the end of the first session, we mapped out a tentative plan to help with Paul's high and consistent level of anxiety. Subsequently, the next several sessions focused on helping Paul remember and establishing a better relaxation response. In reviewing Paul's history and difficulty to relax in his body and feel comfortable with himself and others, I saw that Paul had a long history and tolerance for feeling anxiety. Although I knew there was a complicated and remarkable story that would unfold about Paul's developmental history, initially I (we) chose to focus on relaxation and comfort. As I have seen in many men I work with who struggle with interpersonal and physical discomfort, I assumed that there were past environments or circumstances in which relaxation and comfort were present. Paul shared with me how he loved to surf when he was younger. He had not been surfing for many years. Surfing was energizing, somewhat social, and he felt a sense of comfort and confidence while in the ocean. He no longer had a surfboard, but he decided to ask an old friend if he could borrow one. Surfing became a mainstay metaphor during our time together. Words and concepts like "timing," "finding your balance," "having a relaxed focus," "sharing a wave with another," and "not worrying about falling" all became ways to access how he wanted his mind and body to feel (like he knew it could) in situations that were anxiety provoking. As a person who likes the outdoors and mountain biking, I was pleased and found an unexpected connection when I heard about Paul's history and enthusiasm for surfing. Although I am not a surfer, many of the metaphors he found about surfing were parallel to my experiences mountain biking. I felt an aspect of healthy masculinity in the room and sensed how much he appreciated my listening to his stories about surfing. Having this sense of healthy masculinity in the room felt like a bonding experience. We both knew, without mention, that there was risk and both physical and mental challenges involved in surfing. His stories about surfing allowed him to save face with me and show a side of himself that overcame his fears. I mentioned how interesting and enthusiastic he was when he shared his surfing adventures. It appeared to me that Paul was "surfing" in the therapy room.

I also like to offer a type of guided imagery and full mind–body relaxation experience (which usually takes 30–35 minutes) for my clients who have difficulty relaxing. Paul stated he was very much interested in trying, although he looked nervous. I let Paul know that there was no "right way" to experience the guided relaxation experience. Paul stated he was worried he might laugh or be too fidgety. I reminded Paul that whatever he experienced would be useful information that could help him understand himself more. He seemed to find comfort in my statement, and I remember registering how Paul melted with my permission to be himself. As I do with all of my clients, I participated in the relaxation and guided imagery with Paul. Certain cognitive messages are given to the client, such as "there is nothing to do and this is your time to take a minivacation and slow down your body and mind." In this type of therapy, images such as "melting into your chair" and "allowing gravity to take over" are suggested to the client. Paying attention to one's breathing also helps facilitate relaxation with instructions, such as "notice how your whole body changes with each inhale and exhale." After increasing the physical relaxation, Paul was asked to think back in his mind to a place and time when he felt really calm and relaxed. He was asked to picture that place with detail, remember the smells and sounds, and imagine he was there.

Paul responded extremely well to the guided imagery. When we finished, I looked at Paul and noticed a gentle calmness, no perspiration, and a glow of confidence in his eyes. He was able to gaze back at me with no fear on his face. He looked like a new man. I asked Paul how he experienced the guided imagery. He described how paying attention to his breathing helped him relax. He felt proud and stated he enjoyed feeling so relaxed. It had been some time since he experienced such a deep calmness. I shared with Paul that I noticed the calm on his face and the serenity in his eyes. He did not flinch, and a small smile came onto his face. He struggled to find words for a few moments and finally said in a concise and unapologetic manner, "That felt really good."

Paul reported that he had cut out caffeine, was exercising three or four times a week, and got back into the ocean on his board. I also made a guided imagery–relaxation tape for Paul, and he was listening to the tape several times a week. He reported feeling more relaxed and that his obsessive thinking was dramatically reduced. As his therapist, I was feeling quite pleased with the progress of our meetings. A positive transference usually feels good and often makes me feel more powerful and useful than I really deserve to feel. I remember feeling optimistic about our treatment, yet I knew there was a lot of territory yet to be explored and understood by both Paul and myself.

Paul also reported that his obsessive thoughts about molesting a young girl had not surfaced. He was feeling more certain and hopeful that by reducing his level of anxiety, his fears about losing control would be reduced or eliminated. I cautiously enjoyed his increased sense of hope. I found that as Paul's hope increased, my fears about losing control as a therapist decreased.

The Second Phase: Being With People

The area of social anxiety and confidence was brought to the foreground during this phase. Brought by whom, I am not certain. Although Paul was reporting having more enjoyable moments of relaxation, particularly after surfing and exercise, when we were in the therapy room, he appeared tense. Moments of silence were excruciatingly painful for Paul. His eyes darted slightly and the expression on his face was like he had been drugged with Novocaine. Perspiration could be seen on his forehead. Not knowing what to say was a gigantic concern and theme in Paul's life. In the initial sessions, I had taken a rather active role and avoided the discomfort of silence. My active approach with Paul felt more intuitive than calculated. In many ways, I thought if I helped provide an environment in which Paul would feel less anxious, our power differential would be reduced.

I was also wondering how Paul was viewing and experiencing me. Was he experiencing me as an older brother, a father figure, or a teacher? Although I was not too much younger than his father, I felt more like the interested, "hip" uncle. And how was I experiencing Paul? Initially his biracial ethnicity did not catch my attention. His facial features did not stand out as particularly Asian. Yet as I got to know Paul, his Asian heritage subtly entered the room. He was extremely polite and deferential to me. When he listened to me, he showed very little facial expression and never interrupted me. I wondered how others experienced Paul's Asian ethnicity. He grew up in a predominantly White neighborhood and could easily pass for Caucasian. We did not explore enough about his Asian roots, and I carry some regrets about that. He had spent several summers living in Japan, and in retrospect, I wonder how much of his interpersonal discomfort was related to some cultural confusion and identity issues. Nonetheless, silence was something that we both agreed needed to be talked about.

The discomfort of the silence could not be avoided. We started to process the silence and the fears of the silence. Paul described, much like in social situations, that he did not know how to carry on a conversation. When the ball was in his court, he did not know what to do or how to throw it back. He became consumed with negative thoughts and paralyzing self-absorption.

In social situations, Paul would often start to sweat, which only added to his worry and desire to flee. In terms of what was happening in the therapy room, I gave Paul permission and invited him to notice our silence without evaluation. I asked Paul to describe how he was experiencing our silence and any thoughts he wanted to share with me. Paul first stated that he was afraid I would think less of him if he did not have anything to say. He described his mind going blank and not feeling very interesting. Paul also described difficulty listening to others because he was so consumed with his own physiological anxiety.

Our interactions over the next several sessions slowed down considerably. We did a lot of noticing, role playing, and processing what was going on in the room. One of my working hypotheses was how difficult it must be for Paul to find others interesting if he did not find himself very interesting. Subsequently, his difficulty finding himself and others interesting was a contributing factor in his inability to be more socially fluid. I shared my hypothesis with Paul. He quickly agreed and started to share stories about feeling like an outsider most of his life. He was again catching a wave in the room. I asked Paul to slow down and elaborate on the details. I was quite interested in his stories. There were so many snapshots of his life that had gone unexamined by himself and others. It became apparent that Paul was not used to talking about himself and sharing the details of his journey. He would listen to others, hoping he did not have to say much. He had gone along with others, not wanting to stir up any tension or bring any unnecessary attention to his wishes. Paul at times flowed with details and other times staggered and looked at me as if there was a correct answer. I responded with much interest and let him know how much I appreciated his stories. I told him I found him a very interesting person. He sort of smiled with a wonderful glimmer in his eyes. He seemed to soak in quite quickly how I noticed him. I understood more clearly than ever that Paul needed a lot of encouragement and that he must have lived in environments that were scarce of praise. Because of the nature of Paul's symptoms and his severe social anxiety and self-consciousness, I wanted to give Paul an opportunity for our relationship to become more interpersonal within the confines of the therapy room. I was feeling safer, less fearful, and more appreciative of Paul. I started to think of him differently than just the guy with fears of losing control

There were still plenty of moments of silence and discomfort. I wondered what Paul was noticing about our work and about me. I was aware he had not asked me any questions about myself, even though there was plenty of stimulus material he could have noticed and responded too. There are an assortment of pictures and knickknacks around my office, which oftentimes clients notice and ask me about. I had also shared with Paul some information about my interest in mountain biking and where I went on a summer vacation. Why did Paul not ask me any follow-up questions? Did he not notice? Did he not know how to ask?

I also noticed that Paul had not thanked me after our sessions. He appeared to leave our sessions in a mild state of disorganization. When I said our time was winding down and I would see him next week at the same hour, Paul became mechanical and compliant. He would get up from his chair abruptly, nod his head, gently yet nervously smile, and leave the room. How was I going to bring what I noticed, about him and us, into the therapy room? I did not want to shame him or discourage him. I wanted him to be curious about how I experienced him and invite me or give me permission to share my awareness about him and us. Paul came into therapy complaining of intense social anxiety. At this point in the therapy, I felt we had enough of a connection and level of trust that a more directive interpersonal intervention could possibly take place.

In one of our middle-phase sessions, I said to Paul, "Would you be interested in trying an experiment in our therapy meeting?" I went on to describe the experiment and get his permission. The experiment involved imagining the two of us in a social situation in which we temporarily suspended (as much as possible) our roles as client and therapist. I went on to explain that either of us could stop the experiment anytime during the session and that I would most likely stop the process at different times to offer some "coaching" or feedback. From my perspective, the experiment would help shed some light as to how Paul stayed engaged or became disengaged in interpersonal conversation. The therapy room would be a place to practice, make mistakes, have some successes, and get immediate feedback. As is discussed later in the chapter, the process of the experiment also stimulated some unexpected changes in the way Paul utilized therapy and the material he brought into the room.

Paul agreed, with reluctance and enthusiasm, to participate in the interpersonal experiment. I saw the familiar look of anxiety and awkwardness in his eyes and on his forehead. I asked him to share his reactions to my suggestion. Knowing that Paul was rather compliant, I wanted us to move as slowly as we needed in order for Paul to be "grounded" with the idea and his decision to participate. He said to me that he thought it was a really good idea. He was looking for guidance. He said that nobody had ever taken the time to help him with his social anxiety in a teaching type of way. I had the sense that father-loss issues were in the room. Paul wanted to be taught in a safe environment. After he shared with me about never having someone teach him about social interactions, he looked much more relaxed and appeared grounded in his body. I took a mental note that what appeared to relax Paul was his sharing of what he missed in his childhood and young adulthood. Why did that type of sharing offer so much, and rather immediate, relief? A working hypothesis was that Paul had much to ask for and much that went unsaid. He found relief in acknowledging his needs without shame. How did this dynamic come about? Was it cultural? I started to get a picture of how Paul must have interacted with his father as a young boy and adolescent. I wondered what was being played out and healed in the therapy room.

I gave permission to Paul to ask me anything he would like. I let him know if there was something I was uncomfortable answering, I would explain to him my reluctance. Everything that occurred between us was grist for the mill. My attitude going into the experiment was to provide an atmosphere of acceptance, process, and safety to speak up: "So, Paul, what would you like to know about me? Is there anything you have been particularly curious about?" Paul took a few moments, and with a small smile on his face, said to me, "You wear unusual-looking socks, where do you get them from?" Casually I replied that they are really comfortable socks and that I started wearing them first when I bike and now wear them most of the time. He replied, "Cool." The conversation seemed to end. We waited in silence. I suggested he stay curious. Moments later he asked me where I mountain bike and how long I have been doing it for. I answered him rather directly with the facts. Again we waited and he looked stuck. With a feeling of warmth toward Paul, I asked him if he would like some coaching. He immediately said, "Yes." In my mind, I was wondering if I was rescuing Paul too soon. Nonetheless, I asked Paul to share with me his reactions to my answers. I suggested that he pay attention to his subtle internal responses and said that there was no right answer or question. Paul relaxed. He told me he imagined how beautiful it must be mountain biking. I felt engaged by his response. I let him know how much I appreciated his paying attention to a really important aspect of my experience of mountain biking: the beauty of the mountains. I asked him more about where that question came from, and he let me know how important and relaxed he feels in nature. We continued to talk with one another for 5 or so more minutes. We were both engaged in a delightful conversation.

There was much ease to our dialogue, and I noticed a comfort in his eyes and face, much like he looked after our guided imagery. With a smile on my face I said, "Wow, what just happened here? You seem so comfortable." Paul let me know that my self-disclosure, particularly when I shared how much I appreciated him for bringing up the beauty of the mountains, helped him feel calm on the inside. He liked that I gave him permission not to have to think about coming up with the right question. He reported that oftentimes he had a lot of reactions to what people were saying to him, but he was afraid to share and risk looking "stupid." The deflating tone he used to say the word *stupid* caught my attention. I imagined him shrinking and wondered how he would internally and externally respond if he thought I did not like his answer or reaction. I asked him to imagine my not liking one of his responses to me: How would he know? What would he imagine me saying or looking like? How would he most likely react?

We practiced Paul reacting and sharing his observations with me. It became quite clear that Paul had difficulty standing up for himself and was petrified of being deflated; he stayed deflated with those he interacted with.

The concept of staying engaged and inflated during conversation became quite useful. Paul did not remember a time in his life when he stayed inflated under fear of appearing stupid. He did not remember a time when he externalized his fears and communicated his perception that the other was not valuing what he was saying. I asked Paul specifically what he might do to elicit a nonvaluing response from me. Paul told me he thought he might be too intrusive with a question. I avoided asking him at this point what question he thought might be too intrusive. Instead I asked him a process question, "What would you say or do if you sensed that you had been too intrusive?" Paul did not have an immediate response. I waited and then thought to ask him how he would know I was disappointed. Paul had quick access to that information and shared that he would see it in my facial expression. When I asked Paul what he would say to me if he noticed something on my face that implied negative judgment, he replied, "Nothing."

I was moving too fast with Paul. I needed to slow down and allow him to let me know more about his experience. My agenda of wanting to hear what he might "say or do" when he felt uncomfortable was intrusive to his process. Instead, I became more curious and asked Paul to describe how I would look and what he would imagine noticing on my face if I were disappointed. He described a face that did not show much expression, eyes that closed slightly and were hard rather than soft. I registered, without comment, that he was describing what I saw on his face when I thought he was anxious.

I complimented Paul for communicating, with such clarity and nuance, his description of my potential negative reaction. The mechanical nature of Paul's responses had been something I noticed. They were often dry and constricted. I noticed I was more "flowery" in the room with Paul than I am with other male clients. I thought that perhaps my less mechanical way of description was giving him permission to be more expressive and less mechanical. Paul seemed to absorb my compliment with ease. With most of my male clients, I attend to how the client is absorbing my nurturing and engagement. I try to be aware of both my own and my client's homophobia and realize that two men in the room sharing appreciation with one another can be threatening.

We continued in a role play. He appeared to be more inflated with my compliments. Paul tried on new ways that he could stay inflated by sharing his observations. I coached him and he found words and phrases he had rarely used before, such as "You look disappointed with me now"; "Did I say something to upset you?"; "What do you think about what I just said?" Our interpersonal work continued. We spent many sessions role playing and in experimental conversation. Although we both knew we were in the therapy room, there was a connection going on between two human beings, even though we had different titles. Paul's comfort with me and his ability to be appropriately curious became quite noticeable. He started to ask questions of me that showed interest in my inner world and process. I remember Paul asking me if I enjoyed being a psychologist and what the best and worst part of my job was. With some reluctance, he asked me about my family and told me that was the question he was afraid to ask in fears he would be too intrusive. I replied by letting him know I thought he was courageous and taking good care of himself by communicating to me his fears about being too intrusive.

Paul reported that he was starting to feel more comfortable speaking up in class and that he was experimenting outside of our room engaging in conversation. He let me know that he still had some anxieties that he wanted to talk more about.

The Third Phase: Remembering and Challenging His Family

A type of courage was growing inside of Paul. He was better equipped to ask some of the questions he had asked earlier in our session, particularly those involving his sleepwalking and fears of killing his mother. Although he did want the symptoms to go away, he also wanted to understand the meaning of the symptoms. Paul had woken up on the inside and had much better access to unanswered questions and unsaid conversations. What became clear to Paul during this last part of our time together was that his family survived on silence and he had a lot of anger stored up because of the silence.

Why would he want to hurt his mother? Where was his father in the picture? When I asked Paul how he could better understand himself and how he responded to his surroundings, he replied by saying that there were many unanswered questions about his parents' divorce. I was not surprised, even though initially during our history taking phase, when asked about his parents' divorce and his relationship with them, he replied that it was unremarkable.

During this last phase of treatment, Paul realized he knew very little about the nature of the divorce. It did not take much encouraging on my part for Paul to start to question and remember the nuances of his experience of being a young boy when his parents divorced. His onset of extreme shyness coincided with his parents' divorce and his moving away from his mother and into a different neighborhood (and school) with his father and his father's new wife. When I questioned Paul and commented that it was quite unusual for a young child to be taken out of his mother's home after a divorce, Paul initially replied he did not know why. I had a lot of questions. More important, though, I wondered what type of questions Paul had and whether he could access those questions and feelings about having to leave his mother. Paul shared that his father had left his mother for another woman. Paul started to recall how upset his mother was before the divorce. He often found her crying alone and did not know what to say to her or how to comfort her. Paul voiced for the first time his curiosity of why his mother would allow his father to have full custody of him. When I asked Paul if he thought he could ask his mother (he was currently living with her) about the circumstances of the custody decision, he replied he did not think he could. I was curious about his hesitancy, and he stated he felt protective of his mother and was afraid of hurting her.

We both experienced the silence of the moment. I reflected back on him saying he was "afraid of hurting her." The fears of sleepwalking and killing his mother came to light. Paul started to remember more details about the divorce. He started to recollect his mother being in the hospital and being sick, and he wondered if his mother had tried to commit suicide. Was he taken away from his mother, or did his mother give him up? Paul let me know that he thought he could talk with his mother about the divorce. He stated he thought it would be easier for him to get some of the details from his father, whom he usually met for dinner once a month.

Much to my surprise, Paul came into the next session reporting that he had talked with his mother about the circumstances around the divorce. He reported the discussion to be much easier than he had imagined. His mother apologized to Paul for keeping the details of the divorce such a secret and not preparing Paul for the move to a new neighborhood and school. She reported to Paul being afraid of creating too much worry for her young son. Paul's suspicion about his mother's illness and reason for going to live with his father was primarily correct. His mother was quite distraught and sought psychiatric attention and decided she was not in a well enough state of mind to raise her son. Paul reported that he got many of his questions answered by his mother but still wanted to talk with his father.

Some sessions later, after Paul met his father for dinner, he reported not talking with his father about the divorce. Although he initially thought it would be easier to talk with his father, he soon faced the realization it would not be so easy. As we talked more about his relationship with his father, I asked Paul how his father helped him, when he was just 8 years old, adjust to moving into a new neighborhood and school. Paul started to cry. He tried to hold himself back, as his lower lip quivered. I felt moved. I felt nervous. There was a part of me that wanted to cry with him. Paul was missing his father at that moment. He felt the pain and sadness of not being comforted by his father. I think I was reacting to both Paul's sadness and my own sadness and loss issues with my father.

Even after all these years of doing therapy, there is something quite moving and intimate about witnessing another man's tears. Perhaps it is my discomfort and hesitancy to cry in front of another man that brings a special meaning to these moments.

At first Paul was quite embarrassed to cry in front of me, and he apologized. I asked Paul how long it had been since he cried, and he let me know he could not remember the last time. He thought it was even before his parent's divorce. I let Paul know how much I appreciated his willingness to feel safe enough to cry in front of me. And without any hesitation, I said to him, "I think if you cried more, you would sweat less." I am not certain why I said what I said. I surprised myself. I noticed that Paul allowed his tears to flow. He let me know how good it felt to cry and did not want to leave the room. I felt good for Paul. I saw how relief was on his face. Although he was struggling with some embarrassment, he also had calmness on his face and in his eyes. I mentioned to Paul that I saw the same look on his face now that I saw after our guided imagery and relaxation session. He smiled and his eyes glowed. He gave himself permission to express himself with very little shame. He looked proud, and I felt proud for him. I imagine that my face looked peaceful and nonjudgmental, although I did not ask Paul to comment.

What touched Paul so deeply was just the tip of the iceberg concerning an unexamined relationship with his father. Further sessions explored his relationship with his father—the disappointment of his father's lack of expression and their lack of conversations. By the time our sessions ended, Paul had not found the right energy or time to talk about these issues with his father. I trusted that when Paul was ready, he would find the right energy. I was not really clear, nor was Paul, on what was holding him back from talking with his father. At one session, Paul let me know he thought I might be disappointed that he had not talked with his father, after feeling confident that he would during the previous session. I was delighted that Paul shared his fears with me.

The Fourth Phase: Our Ending

Paul graduated from college and moved out of town. We both knew several months ahead of time when our last session would be. Paul reported most of his anxiety symptoms were reduced significantly or eliminated. His fears about molesting a young girl and killing his mother in his sleep were nonexistent. He was considerably more socially comfortable, yet with an understanding that being with people, particularly if he did not know them, was going to be somewhat anxiety provoking. He felt better about himself and was viewing himself as someone who was comfortable enough to start dating.

We spent our last few sessions saying goodbye and putting some closure to this part of our therapy relationship. The permanence of our goodbye remains a question, as it does with many clients I see in private practice. I enjoyed my work with Paul. I felt and appreciated his desire and drive to blossom and find ways to enjoy his life. His suffering had gone unexamined and our therapy had given him an opportunity to find his voice.

We talked about the future. He did not want to continue therapy. Because of my interest and belief in the efficacy of men's groups, we talked about finding a men's support or therapy group in his new community. We discussed unfinished business, mainly with his father. We said goodbye.

Paul wanted to let me know how much he appreciated me and how helpful counseling had been. I knew it was important for Paul to share those feelings with me. Although intellectually I understood that the locus of responsibility for the benefit that Paul received from counseling had more to do with him than me, I did not want to diminish Paul's opportunity to feel and express his gratefulness. He really shined. He was grounded and calm. I shared how much I would miss him and thanked him for his sincerity. The awkwardness of the goodbye was present as we looked into each other's eyes. We shook hands and then hugged, and I noticed that both of our hands were a little clammy. I guess we both have some more crying to do.

QUESTIONS FROM THE EDITOR (MATT ENGLAR-CARLSON)

1. *How did your own gender role issues influence your work with this client?*

You are assuming by this question that I have some awareness of my own gender role issues. Even though I have studied gender role conflict and strain models of masculinity for many years, I still find the question difficult to answer on a personal level. That being said, what comes to mind first is Paul's sense of vulnerability and the strong personal messages I received as a man about how not to appear vulnerable. I am aware that I don't have access to the precise words I would like to use to describe the experience of being in the room with another man who is exhibiting his vulnerability. I have some sense that because of my own fears of vulnerability, I was also fearful of Paul's vulnerability. I am not certain how this played out in the therapy room with Paul, yet I am convinced that it was part of our relationship. In thinking about this question, I do have recollections of feeling comfortable being nurturing toward Paul. Sometimes this nurturing may have come at the expense of allowing Paul to feel more of his sense of being out of control and vulnerable. I felt protective of Paul, yet I also realize I was being protective of myself as well.

2. *There is a point in the therapy when you open yourself up to Paul. This was self-disclosure of personal information. What is the role of self-disclosure with men and how does it assist the process of therapy?*

I view part of my role, as a male therapist with a male client, as that of a quasi-mentor. Our sex and gender is in the room. As the relationship builds, so does the transference and possible idealization of the therapist. The client's attention is captured through this positive transference and idealization. They are noticing our interactions and what is on the walls of our offices and wanting to learn from us. That being said, I believe we have an opportunity (perhaps responsibility) to let our male clients know of our humanness. In doing so, we give them implicit permission and perhaps confidence to show more of their humanness.

3. Why is this so important with male clients?

I believe many male clients are starving for information about how to navigate life as a male. There is not a lot of good information out there, particularly if there are codes of silence and false information with or from their male peers, brothers, and fathers.

4. How does father transference appear in the therapy room with this client?

With Paul, his face lighted up when I talked about myself. I believe not only that he wanted to get to know me but also that he wished to get to know his father. And through our interactions, his craving for getting to know his father increased. So did his fears: Would his father be as understanding as I was with him? Paul gave me too much power in our relationship, I believe, similar to the power he gave his father. I intimidated him and he wanted to please me. At first he appeared very small in the room and grew taller as our relationship developed. His ability and confidence to ask me about who I am was critically important to the transference process. He had so many questions to ask his father, yet did not have the confidence to do so. Our relationship was one step in the process of Paul learning how to get to know his father.

5. Looking back on the case, knowing what you know now, how would you change the way you worked with this client?

I think I may have been a little less protective and more curious about Paul's pain and fear of being out of control. After writing this chapter, I've thought more about Paul's fear of being out of control and reconceptualizing my understanding of that dynamic. More specifically, Paul not knowing too much about his childhood was a way for him to try to maintain a sense of control, albeit a false sense of control. His inner world in many ways had gone unexplored, yet it was desperately wanting to be explored and understood (hence, all of his symptoms). Looking back on this case, I wish I had allowed myself to feel even more lost and more scared and sought more supervision to talk about my process with Paul.

REFERENCES

Brannon, R. (1985). A scale for measuring attitudes about masculinity. In A. Sargent (Ed.), *Beyond sex roles* (pp. 110–116). St. Paul, MN: West.

O'Neil, J. M. (1981). Patterns of gender role conflict and strain: Sexism and fears of femininity in men's lives. *Personnel and Guidance Journal, 60,* 203–210.

Pleck, J. H. (1981). *The myth of masculinity.* Cambridge, MA: MIT Press.

Scher, M. (1979). The little boy in the adult male client. *Personnel and Guidance Journal, 57,* 537–539.

4

FINDING THE PERSON BEHIND THE PERSONA: ENGAGING MEN AS A FEMALE THERAPIST

HOLLY SWEET

Traditional talk therapy encourages clients to rely on others for help and to be emotionally expressive about vulnerable feelings. These actions are based more on feminine norms of connection and emotional expression than on male norms of autonomy and emotional stoicism. Many men grow up in a world in which men who lean on others for emotional assistance or openly express vulnerable feelings are scorned. As a result, men often grow up shut down, hardened to feelings, or having difficulty being intimately connected with others. Men entering the world of therapy, in which affect and intimacy are expected, are therefore at a disadvantage. A number of books about men in therapy (Cochran & Rabinowitz, 2000; Erickson, 1993; Good & Brooks, 2005; Meth & Pasick, 1990) have discussed the obstacles that men face in working successfully in a setting in which talking about emotions is expected and valued.

THERAPY IS NOT A LEVEL PLAYING FIELD FOR MEN

Female clinicians, like male clinicians, need to understand how sex role norms affect their male clients. Training about men's issues is often lim-

69

ited in graduate school, and women may come to their work with men unprepared. In fact, many women may come to their work with men expecting that men are in a position of power and privilege in the world at large and that they have relatively few problems with which to contend. It is important that female clinicians have a solid background knowledge of men's issues, especially the concept of "sex role strain" (O'Neil, 1995; Pleck, 1981), which makes men's lives difficult, particularly in the areas of intimacy. Reading in the area of women's studies is another way in which women can better understand the impact of gender roles on themselves and their male clients and how their sex role norms and experiences as women may have shaped them into being unaware of, or less sympathetic to, the problems of men.

Given the fact that men are not socialized to engage in a traditional therapeutic setting, how can female clinicians help men participate in a therapeutic world in which gender plays a large part in what transpires? How can women allow men to find a safe and respectful space to make changes when necessary, yet help them hold on to a positive masculine identity? What changes may female therapists need to make in their therapeutic style and personal beliefs to better help men? If therapy is a difficult environment for most men, then female clinicians need to be cognizant of that fact in the way they do therapy with men, making sure men feel as comfortable, respected, and hopeful as possible. Therapy begins only when a client feels that his clinician is on his side and can help him.

A CASE STUDY: THE STORY OF JIM

My initial connection to Jim was an unusual one, as referrals go. I was taking a vacation from my counseling job on the West Coast and ended up sitting next to a woman on the plane ride with whom I started chatting. When she asked what I did for a living, I said I was a specialist in men's studies. I often find this is a good conversation starter—most people do not know that men's studies exists, and everyone wants to know why a woman would want to specialize in this area. Sure enough, she asked about why I was in the field. I told her about the importance of understanding the problems that men face in living up to rigid and unrealistic norms that often impair their ability to lead a healthy life and how this understanding can help both men and women relate to one another better. She grew intrigued and said she had a friend, a fellow software engineer, who was going through marital problems and could use a therapist sympathetic to the issues of men. I gave her my business card and thought that was the last of it. A month later, much to my surprise, I got a call from Jim, who said his friend had mentioned meeting me recently. He said that he understood I was an expert on men's studies and wanted to set up an appointment with me to work on issues relating to his desire to get divorced from his wife. I was a little apprehensive because I had already revealed to his friend a fair amount about my personal background. I decided, however, that this could work to my advantage because Jim might view me as a human being first and a therapist second. This might help him feel more at ease in entering a situation that can have a one-up, one-down feel to it, especially for men.

We set up an initial appointment for the following week. As I prepared for our first meeting, I became aware that the magazines on top of the table in our waiting room were *Martha Stewart* and *Oprah*. I asked myself how I would feel if the magazines in my male therapist's office were *Guns and Ammo* and *Automotive Weekly*. I had not noticed this before, but I wondered whether this might have a negative effect on him, that he would think the space was feminized by their presence, and that he did not belong there, as a man. I had a premonition that Jim might be easily scared off by therapy and that any excuse would do. I am not quite sure why I felt this way: I knew only that his friend had mentioned that Jim had been considering therapy for some time but had been unable to act on it. I quickly rearranged the magazines so that *National Geographic* and *Sports Illustrated* were the ones visible. At our agreed-upon time, I opened my door, saw a man sitting next to my door, said "you must be Jim," and welcomed him in with a handshake. I usually shake hands with new clients—it is one way of making them feel welcomed in what is culturally viewed as a normal greeting. I remember being aware that my handshake was particularly firm, as a way of saying, "I'm sure of what I'm doing." As he entered my office, I noted that he was Caucasian, was about 6 feet tall, had blond hair, was casually but neatly dressed, and appeared to be in his mid-40s. I also noticed that he was attractive, seemed self-assured, and to my consternation, looked and acted a great deal like an ex-boyfriend of mine. The thought occurred to me that I might be headed for some interesting countertransference. I was curious about what effect it might have on our interaction. As it would later turn out, my countertransference was a very useful tool in telling me about the parts of Jim that he could not tell me about himself.

After our initial conversation about how he got my name, I asked him what brought him to my office. "I'm stuck" he said, "I really want to leave my marriage, but I cannot seem to do so. Can you help?" We talked for a while about the background of the problem (a 10-year marriage, an affair in the middle of it, and general dissatisfaction with what he found in his relationship with his wife). I said I would try to help and that we would work together in a collaborative fashion to try to find a solution to his presenting problem. I am not so specific and directive with female clients, but I have found that at least initially, male clients respond more favorably to the more cognitive–behavioral, solution-oriented approach of two equals working together to solve a problem. The first session is crucial in setting a safe tone for any client and establishing a working therapeutic alliance. I felt that too much emphasis initially on painful emotions that do not have a readily accessible framework in which to fit them (or a way to quickly resolve them) might turn Jim away. When I look back on this, I realize that I was not completely honest with myself. In my own life, I had been on the fence for a long time about a relationship that I could not seem to break off. I struggled for many years and got very little therapeutic help with it (although we saw a number of therapists in the process). I think somewhere in my subconscious, I was determined that I would help Jim the way I had not been helped.

In our first few sessions, I worked with Jim to find out more about his goals and his history. He quickly gave me a list of reasons why he should leave the marriage—she was not his intellectual equal; she was too needy; their modes of communication were totally different; her values were at opposite ends of the spectrum from his, and so on. He seemed sure that he wanted a divorce and was quite convincing in his persistence that he simply needed a clear way out that would save face for everyone and would not hurt his wife and adopted daughter too much. As he discussed what he was looking for in therapy, I noticed that he was articulate and poised throughout our first sessions. I began to think that this might be a relatively short-term case, one in which through judicious use of homework assignments and supportive therapy, he would be able to leave a marriage that he had clearly outlined as one that he wanted to end. When I asked him about couples counseling, he said they had tried it, it had simply amplified their differences, and that he was really ready to move on with his life and get divorced.

Although I noted some sadness in his voice and affect, I believed Jim was a man ready to move forward with his life and find someone who would be a better match for him. I made the mistaken assumption that because he looked good, he was in fact doing well, and that his controlled affect was a sign of strength, not a cover-up for his pain and fear. I should have known better, of course, but I was drawn into his persona, the person he wanted to be and wanted me to see. I colluded with Jim in identifying the problem as lying with his partner, not with his long-standing patterns of difficulty with intimacy. Despite my familiarity with men's issues, it was still hard for me to see the "covert depression" (Real, 1997), "the pain behind the mask" (Lynch & Kilmartin, 1999), and to understand that many men can look good on the outside but feel bad on the inside. Perhaps I had spent too much of my life working with depressed woman to really see that depression in men does not always show itself as visibly or in the same ways. Perhaps I wanted Jim to not be depressed because I liked him and wanted him to be healthier than he was so he could get better more quickly. Or it is possible that I just could not see it at first because he did not show it: Like so many men, he has been trained to look good at all costs.

The Lonely Golden Boy

In our history taking, I found out Jim had indeed been trained to be a success. He grew up on the West Coast and described himself as the golden boy of the family, the one with a good sense of humor, a clear sense of direction, and a clear future in front of him. He was the middle child of seven from an intact family, which he described as close but not overtly affectionate. His father was the primary breadwinner of the family and worked unusually long hours. Jim saw his father as living for his family, although he was not emotionally expressive about it and did not show much affection to either his wife or his children. He described his mother as being a super-mom, working full time but always involved in activities like the parent–teacher association and baking cookies for his friends but not someone he felt he could talk with, because she was so busy. Jim said that although he had a lot of friends, there was no one he could really speak with about his feelings. "I'm not a communicator," he would say on numerous occasions, "I like to keep things private." When asked why he did this, Jim could only say that he preferred it this way. Jim dated in high school and finally fell in love with a woman who then started dating someone else—Jim was hurt but did not show it and again was not clear about why he did not share his feelings. In college, he dated a second woman, with whom he got more serious, but she too left him, a situation Jim described this time as "crushing." After that, Jim totally clammed up and blamed himself but did not want to talk with others about it, because "I don't dump my problems on others." At that point, I noted to myself the fact that given Jim's history of difficulty with intimacy, it was amazing he was in my office at all, because therapy is by its very nature an exercise in intimacy. I foresaw problems looming on the horizon. It seemed that if Jim continued to open up to me, it could be at odds with his self-image and also might stir up memories of being rejected by women with whom he had been close. I chose not to share this with him because I felt it was too soon in our therapy to make an interpretation that might be shameful or exposing.

After college, Jim met his wife-to-be (Mary) and dated her for 6 years before they decided to get married. At the time, Mary had a young daughter by a former husband. Jim was attracted to Mary because he said she was simple, accepting, and not demanding of his time, and he said he eventually married her because it felt like a natural progression for him after dating her for so long. A few years after they got married, Jim grew dissatisfied with those traits and began to date Susan, someone he met through friends. Jim became attracted to his affair partner because she was the opposite of his wife. Susan was complex, intellectually stimulating, and needed a lot from him, making him the focus of her life. According to Jim, neither Susan nor Mary knew of the existence of the other in Jim's life. At the beginning of our therapy, Susan was in the process of leaving him because she felt (correctly, as it turns out) that he was not available enough. I found myself uncomfortable with the deception, especially the length of it, and the fact that neither party knew about the other. I explored with Jim his feelings about it. Jim felt relieved because he was not comfortable with the life of deception he had led for 4 years. I wondered whether he had a tendency to compartmentalize, to keep one part of his life quite separate from another part of his life. I have noticed that compartmentalization is a defense often used by men who are afraid to have the full story be known by all. The consequence of this defense is that it can leave the man safe from judgment but not really known by anyone at all—a lonely position for most people. If this was true for Jim, then he might well be at cross-purposes with himself—hungry for intimacy, yet threatened by what would happen if the truth were known.

The Therapeutic Impasse

Our sessions initially focused on helping Jim clarify his relationship with Mary: why he had married her and what his dissatisfactions were. I would routinely assign him homework, including reading chapters from books such as *Getting the Love You Want* (Hendrix, 1988), making lists of what he wanted out of a relationship, writing a short autobiography, talking to his mother about his childhood, and watching movies that dealt with intimacy issues such as the film *Shadowlands* (Attenborough & Eastman, 1993). With male clients, I have had luck with such assignments, in part because it makes therapy seem more like education. Jim invariably did not do the homework, saying the time was not right, he was too busy at work, or he did not want to do a mediocre job of it. After about 12 sessions, Jim said he was feeling too pressured by the homework assignments and the thought of taking practical steps to leave Mary and wanted to take a break from therapy. We discussed why he felt this way and decided that he would not focus on leaving Mary but would rather stay with her and explore in a more neutral fashion why he was with her and what might be worth saving in the relationship. I felt like my own impatience with Jim had been getting in the way of making good clinical decisions. Jim was telling me consistently that he wanted out of an unhappy marriage, a marriage he described as a total mistake, and I felt that my job was to help him along rather than sit with his frustration and explore it. I also felt uncomfortable with the degree of denial and dishonesty in Jim's life. Although I sensed he was sad, he did not identify himself that way and he always looked in charge of things.

As our sessions continued, I realized that Jim had a side that was hidden to him and to others, hidden behind his professional competence and hidden behind his articulate and humorous speech. This side seemed to be a sad and lonely young boy who had grown up without enough attention. When he said that one of the reasons he stayed with Mary was because he felt comfort with her, I knew this was much more than a home-cooked meal and a warm body in bed at night. It was a sense of companionship and a sense of home in a world in which home seemed elusive. I began to see that my task as a therapist was not to help him get a divorce but rather to help him get in touch with the sad boy inside of himself, to make friends with this boy, and to respect his unmet needs. How could I do this without accessing his vulnerability? If he was vulnerable in front of someone else, how could I prevent the sense of shame he might feel? I was aware that as a woman, I was unlikely to intuitively grasp what it might feel like to show feelings of vulnerability for a man. When I cry or need to ask for help, my behavior does not make me feel unfeminine and it does not go against female norms. Male norms often dictate that men rely on themselves, do not get too close to others, do not show feelings, and do not ask for help. If they do, they often feel shame for acting unmanly. In my desire to help Jim not suffer, I had unconsciously adopted the male strategy of pushing Jim to act rather than to sit and feel uncomfortable emotions.

Changing the Focus: Going Fishing

In response to Jim's feelings of being pushed, I decided to make a change in our strategy and described it to Jim as "going on a fishing expedition." Our job together would be to look at different areas of his life (including his childhood) to see what we might find that would be relevant to the problem he was presenting—being stuck in an unfulfilling relationship—with no expectation that he would have to do anything at all for the time being. We agreed to reevaluate this fishing expedition in a few months time and see whether he was ready to take some action, based on what we had caught. Jim seemed relieved by this change in strategy. Therapy became more about feeling than about doing. He was not responsible for making a decision but rather for exploring the environment involving that decision. Jim became more articulate about his fears of being truly intimate with someone else and running the risk of her leaving him. Mary was safe because she was not the leaving kind; he knew she was in it for the long haul. We looked at how his past history might have contributed to his fears. It was slow going as Jim wanted to blame Mary and revert back to thinking that he needed to get out of the relationship rather than just observe it. As I encouraged him to look more at himself, he began to understand that being stuck in his marriage was not as much about Mary being the wrong partner (although she might be) but was more about his own conflicting and at times overwhelming feelings, feelings he had not shared with many others in his life. We looked at his fears—fears of being close, of being left, of not being a good father or husband, and overall a fear of being ignored, something that he did not present at all during his first few sessions with me.

In addition to switching the focus of our work together, I mentioned the possibility of antidepressant medication. I put this suggestion in the form of an experiment, saying, "I'm not sure you are depressed but you are showing some of the classic signs of depression, including indecisiveness and hopelessness. If you try the medication and you feel less indecisive and more hopeful, then you probably were depressed." Jim was initially resistant to this idea. Like many men, he felt that he was not depressed, he just had to get on with things that he was sure he could do. However, he agreed that after a year of being in therapy and still feeling stuck, it was time to "get out the big guns." He understood that it was his decision, that it was an experiment, and that he did not have to take the medication. All of these factors helped him feel more in control of the decision and less pathologized. After taking antidepressant medication for about 1 month, he said he found it helpful to him in terms of allowing him to have more energy to understand his situation and agreed to keep taking it. We agreed that we would continue to explore "what makes Jim tick" instead of forcing him to make a decision about a situation in which he had been mired for a long time.

As Jim was able to articulate that he might be depressed, he was able to communicate his true feelings without shame. Jim began talking about what it felt like to be the middle child who was both ignored in terms of his emotional needs and expected to be the good boy who never got into trouble and did not need guidance or help. Jim started doing some homework (reading some from Beck's book on couples [1988]) and saw how negative he felt about everything and how this might be related to his depression. He began to seem sad in sessions, and occasionally his eyes would fill with tears. But he was unable to target quite why he felt sad, saying, "I really don't know what I feel." I found myself feeling impatient at this remark: It triggered memories of men who had, it seemed, deliberately withheld their feelings from me. How could he not understand his feelings? I assumed, like many women, that men actively choose not to share with others the feelings they have, rather than not even knowing what they feel or how to name the feelings that flood them.

Involving the Partner

We began to discuss strategies that would involve making a more concrete plan to see whether Jim's marriage could work, including having Mary join us for a session as a prelude to finding a couples therapist. When we started our joint session, I explained that Mary was a consultant to Jim and myself, not my client. Mary was not my client, but she could help me understand the nature of their marital relationship, which would help me work with Jim more effectively. If Jim tended to compartmentalize his life, then this would be a way of bringing different parts of his life together. Mary was an attractive woman with a good deal of affect. She spent most of the session crying, saying she felt that Jim's depression was the reason their marriage was failing and that Jim seemed detached and angry. Right on cue, Jim sat through most of the session with his arms folded, looking away from Mary, and making angry and negative remarks. They said that they loved each other, but both felt the situation was getting close to hopeless. I said that it looked like their marriage was in trouble, and I asked whether they were willing to see a couples counselor. They said they would think about it. I found out in later sessions with Jim that they had begun seeing someone (picked out by Mary) a few weeks later.

I found this session to be a turning point, as it showed me clearly what each person was up against and how each person might misunderstand the other's feelings on the basis of sex role differences. When Jim looked angry, I believed him to be sad; when Mary looked sad, I believed her to be angry. I found myself siding with Mary at the time. While she was crying, Jim looked away with an annoyed, irritated expression on his face. It reminded me of men I had known who distanced themselves from me when I cried. I had a hard time not allying with Mary, but I tried to use my feelings and my knowledge of men's issues for therapeutic benefit, saying, "If I were Mary, I might feel like you were annoyed and irritated with me—Is that what you were feeling? Is there anything else you might have been feeling that she didn't see?" Jim admitted that underneath his irritation lay sadness that Mary did not seem capable of listening to him and paying attention to him. I said this somewhat reminded me of his relationship with his mother as Jim was trying to get attention from a busy woman. Jim did not say much to that interpretation, and so I let it go, believing that the interpretation might be true but too painful for Jim to look at closely at that moment.

Shortly after they started couples therapy, I got Jim's permission to speak with the counselor. The couples counselor indicated that Jim had not said a word about our counseling work together. When she said, "I had no idea Jim was seeing someone," I had two instantaneous and related thoughts—that Jim was seeing another woman romantically (possibly a realistic conclusion) and that I was the person he was seeing romantically. I was taken aback by the latter thought, but the association also intrigued me. Was there something in Jim's style that sexualized relationships with women or in mine that sexualized relationships with men? Was Jim in fact "seeing me" in some basic sense of the term—being intimate with me in a way he could not be with others? Instead of being afraid of my association, could I understand it in a therapeutic context, that is, that our relationship could have a positive modeling effect on him?

It did not surprise me that Jim had not told his couples counselor about me, because it was in character for Jim to keep his life compartmentalized. In further conversation with her, however, I was surprised and disturbed to have her describe him as brutal, rigid, and sarcastic, and possibly character disordered with an obsessive–compulsive flavor. I questioned whether she saw his sadness. "I do," she said, "but he's so hostile." I thought once again of how hard it is for men to show sadness, how quickly it can turn to anger, and how men's anger can be frightening to women. I spoke to her about the importance of seeing Jim's sadness beneath his mask of irritation. I also felt protective of Jim and wondered whether other people in his life, particularly women (and perhaps most of all Mary) reacted to him this way. Did I react this way?

Did I see him as hostile or rigid? Wasn't I a little peeved that he did not follow up on my homework suggestions?

Getting to the Heart of the Matter

About a month after couples counseling started, we began to look at the real distress Jim was feeling in the relationship—not that Mary was too simple or too accepting but that she did not pay enough attention to him and his needs and that all of her attention seemed focused on her daughter. We began to look at ways in which Jim might be contributing to this triangulation (by withdrawing from Mary) and ways in which he indirectly expressed core feelings of sadness and disappointment (primarily through distancing himself or getting angry). One day, sensing Jim's underlying sadness, I mentioned a line from the film *Shadowlands* (Attenborough & Eastman, 1993) in which C. S. Lewis, having just lost his wife to a terminal illness, turns to his stepson and says, "For the first part of my life, I chose safety over love, now I have chosen love over safety." Jim's eyes filled with tears and he said, "I got goose bumps when you said that, that really hits home." After a moment or two, I gently asked, "What hits home the most about that line?" to which he replied,

> I feel like I've played it safe for my whole life but in the process, have not been able to really feel close to another person, I mean really close. I, too, have chosen safety over love and it makes me very sad.

After over 1 year of therapy, Jim is still in therapy with me—I do not know what will happen in his marriage or his couples counseling. I do know that he is still struggling to be honest in both arenas. I do not know whether he will stay married or leave. I only know that he has begun to show the person behind the persona, to know once again his lost boy, and to be willing to share his feelings with me as we continue our work together. He says that therapy is indeed therapeutic for him—when I ask him what it does, he says that it allows him to talk about his feelings in an open and honest way that he has not been able to do before. I know that he has been depressed for some time, perhaps for years, but has not been able to show it or even understand it as depression. Real (1997) talked about this as "covert depression" and said that men may be inwardly depressed but often do not show it outwardly. Like many depressed men, Jim has had a difficult time accepting an emotional state that is at odds with normative male behavior (Cochran & Rabinowitz, 2000). For men like Jim, being able to be intimate in a safe setting is indeed therapeutic—to trust that he will not be judged or made light of and to know that I will listen to him no matter what. As a woman, being open with others comes as second nature, so it has taken me some time to realize how hard this can be for men.

I am still coming to terms with my own impatience that Jim has not made the decision to stay in the marriage or leave it and that he is violating the male norm that says "take action." He is asking for space to tell his story and figure out who he is, and I am still struggling with "getting him fixed"—an odd reversal of gender roles. I worry somewhat about the feelings of intimacy I have with him. I understand that he is using me as a surrogate partner, a safe partner who listens well to him, who does not ask anything of him, perhaps the only partner he can risk having at the moment. I question at times my feelings toward him—does that warm, cozy feeling of intimacy I have with him (and with other clients as well, both male and female) ever get in my way of seeing him for who he is? However, I believe that questioning myself is healthy and that it is important that I continue to explore the ramifications of our gender role norms as they impact treatment.

Above all, Jim and I are engaged in a process that allows him to have the space to be the things he has not been able to be and to feel the feelings he has not been able to feel. If Jim can begin to see that feelings are an essential part of what helps people get close to others, then he may be able to open up and honor those feelings in himself rather than running away from them. It seems his training as a man has done the opposite: teaching him to not open up and to not be close with others, with negative personal consequences for him. As a therapist, especially as a female therapist, I can serve as a companion for him when he enters that place of loneliness, powerlessness, and helplessness; I can witness his feelings without judgment; and I continue to encourage him to see that a life worth living is about love and connection, despite their risks.

The Ongoing Journey

Jim has tried hard to be a man in his life by being a combination of the "sturdy oak" and someone who shows "no sissy stuff" (David & Brannon, 1976). These phrases refer to norms of being in control of feelings and the situation at hand, taking care of others (often at the expense of oneself), and not asking for help or attention. As a result, Jim, like so many men in our culture, has led a life of emotional restriction and personal detachment, in which he has had to deny his needs for intimacy, compassion, and attention. He was the good son who did not bother his parents, the good boyfriend who did not complain when women left him, and the good husband who provided for his wife and stepdaughter without asking much for himself. He was the loner who did not open up to others and did not ask for help. Jim's sadness and depression are particularly hard to see because those traits are seen as normatively positive in our culture—we value men who are strong, independent, and stoic. They are our role models, our heroes. What makes it even harder for someone like Jim is that men are not supposed to talk about the fact that they may be suffering (and may not even know it on a conscious level), and women may only see the mask of a man and not his pain (Lynch

& Kilmartin, 1999). Women may in fact assume that men are actively choosing to withhold feelings from them, whereas men believe that they either do not know how to share the feelings, do not know what they are feeling, do not know how to name the feelings they are having, or are afraid to show their feelings for fear of being seen by themselves and others as weak and unmanly (Sweet, 1995). When a man is not allowed by cultural norms to express his true feelings and internalizes that restriction, he is trapped in a potentially devastating way.

This is Jim's story, one in which the ending is not yet written. Doors have been opened for him to see himself in a new light, to experience a new kind of relationship with himself and his history, and to take risks to move beyond norms that have unknowingly held him prisoner. It is also a story in which I am learning about myself as a female therapist working with a male client. We are both on journeys that are pushing us to break through some of the gender role barriers that keep us stuck personally and professionally. It has been exciting, exasperating, and humbling work that has challenged my conceptions on many different levels. Above all, I have tried to keep in mind two key thoughts about working with men: It takes time and compassion to truly see the person behind the persona, and the journey of therapy itself can be curative, especially when therapy is about openness and involves a man who has never been able to open up to others.

WORKING WITH MEN: THE FEMALE THERAPIST'S JOURNEY

As female therapists working with male clients, we come into the sessions with our own views (conscious or otherwise) on men. It is important, therefore, that we be honest with ourselves about how we understand who men are and how we see them. My own introduction to men's studies actually started in the 1960s with the advent of feminism. I read *Sisterhood Is Powerful* (Morgan, 1970) and *The Feminine Mystique* (Friedan, 1962), I attended women's groups and consciousness-raising groups, and I became determined to help women become equals with men and have the same rights, status, and opportunities. Although I believed at the time that women were victims of a patriarchal society in which men had all the power and privilege, something felt one-sided and did not ring true to my own experience. Some part of the equation was missing, but I could not put my finger on it because everyone around was telling me that the "system" was great for men and terrible for women. However, the men I knew did not seem all that happy or even healthy. These men seemed caught up in a race for achievement that seemed never ending. They also did not seem to have many intimate relationships, and the ones they did have seemed to be limited to sexual, romantic relationships with women, which often ended badly. The women I knew, however, might not have the power or prestige of men, but they knew how to make good friends and rely on them for support and love, and balance their lives in a healthier fashion.

It was not until I stumbled upon *The Hazards of Being Male* (Goldberg, 1976) in the mid-1970s that I truly began to understand what was missing. I read and reread this book and underlined half of each page with references to men I knew who seemed to be burdened with expectations and restrictions that described the "men in harness" in Goldberg's (1976) book. I finally began to understand what was missing from the equation: Men's problems seemed to stem from trying to live up to standards that were unattainable and inhuman in many ways. I began to see that men and women were part of a system of reinforcing and interlocking gender roles that ultimately benefited neither. It just seemed that the women's roles were visible in terms of their negative implications, and men's roles were not. I continued to explore the field of men's studies, feeling like I was wandering in uncharted land. I read *The Forty-Nine Percent Majority* (David & Brannon, 1976) and *The Myth of Masculinity* (Pleck, 1981). Everything I read made sense to me, especially the nature of the problems that men faced (especially with engaging in healthy intimacy, expressing vulnerable emotions, and striving for realistic achievement), the invisibility of those problems, and the ramifications of those problems for relationships between men and women.

Over the years, I have stayed committed to the idea that by understanding more about the consequences of sex role strain in men, both men and women are helped. In particular, I believe that knowledge of men's difficulties can allow women to be less likely to get drawn into negative feedback loops with men and unhealthy internalizations of men's distress and more likely to listen without judgment and understand more clearly the pressures that men face. By learning more about the impact of gender on treatment, female therapists will be better able to practice compassionate knowledge, and thus be more effective clinicians with men.

I have found it helpful in my own practice to take time to answer the following questions, keeping in mind the current male clients with whom I am working as well as past experiences I have had with significant men in my life. As both male and female therapists know, we are all susceptible to countertransference. In fact, countertransference is one of the tools of our trade. We can use it wisely in the clinical process if we are aware of it. However, if we do not examine ourselves honestly and openly, we run the danger of having our own issues interfere with effective therapy with clients.

Do we welcome men into our offices? Many male clients initially come to therapy because their female partners, employers, or doctors have asked them to come, not because they initiated the visit. Men may feel uncomfortable and out of place in an environment traditionally identified with female norms. It is important that we help men feel as comfortable as possible, be aware of how they might be responding to the process of therapy, and be willing to make changes if necessary. This can include changing the decor of our offices or waiting rooms, the way we greet men on the telephone or at our door, and how we conduct the first session. If men do not feel welcome or have hope that therapy can help them, they may not come back for a second session.

Are we knowledgeable about the reasons behind many men's resistance to understanding and feeling their emotions? Men often either do not know what they feel or do not feel comfortable showing it. When they are depressed, it is particularly hard for them to express this feeling because talking about depression violates two key male norms (i.e., "do not show feelings" and "do not ask others for help"). Because women have a different socialization process than men, one in which expression of emotions is not seen as unfeminine, women may end up blaming the individual man for having a hard time expressing emotions. Too often, women may assume that because men do not share feelings, they do not want to share their feelings, and not that men do not know how to or are afraid to show their emotions (Sweet, 1995). Whereas women may be able to identify themselves as depressed, men may deny that they are depressed and turn to substance abuse, outbursts of anger, social withdrawal, workaholism, or somatic complaints as a way of handling their pain (Cochran & Rabinowitz, 2000). One way to really gain understanding of men's experiences is to take a course, class, or workshop in men's issues or do reading in the area of men's studies (Erickson, 1993).

Do we explore our own countertransference? Men's defenses can trigger reactions in women that may be based on the therapist's past experiences with significant men in their lives. Women may feel disconnected from men when they do not share feelings or pathologized by men when men put down emotions or therapy in general. When heterosexual men discuss their relationships with female clinicians, the clinician may unconsciously side with the female partner of the male client. Women may try to get men to express vulnerable affect when they are not ready because they want to get things moving or handle men's anger in a defensive or blaming manner because they feel threatened by it. Female therapists may be attracted to male clients and end up blaming them for the attraction or feeling uncomfortable about it and withdrawing from them on some level. If sexual countertransference proves to be a problem, consultation should be sought about how to understand it and use it constructively instead of being afraid of it.

Can we understand and be compassionate to the transference of our male clients? Women need to deal effectively with the transference male clients have to us as women. Women may be seen as their mother figures who can both give and withhold essential love and nurturing. With heterosexual male clients, women may be seen as potential lovers, because men are socialized to sexualize intimacy. If the sexual transference on the client's part becomes enacted, women need to find nonshaming ways to work with it. For some men, the relationship with their female therapist may be the first intimate relationship they have ever had, thereby increasing the intensity of the transference. Discomfort with being seen as a mother or lover can prevent women from working positively with this transference.

Can we talk with men in their own language? It is helpful to observe how men communicate and use language and metaphors (such as therapy being seen as coaching or consulting), which are relevant and nonthreatening to them. Deborah Tannen's (1990) book *You Just Don't Understand* is useful in understanding the different ways in which men and women have been socialized to communicate. In general, I have found it helpful to try to match the language of my clients as much as possible, at least at the beginning of treatment.

Do we consider using different kinds of techniques in our work with men? Many clinicians are trained in the more traditional psychodynamic, talk therapy approaches. Women may need to learn about new techniques and approaches that might work better for men. For example, cognitive–behavioral therapy may be more likely to be seen as psychoeducation rather than therapy, making it more palatable to many men. Bibliotherapy and videotherapy (referring male clients to books and movies of relevance to them) can be helpful in getting men to understand more about themselves in an educative way. In addition to individual psychotherapy for male clients, it is useful to consider referring them to a men's group when appropriate (Andronico, 1996). Men's support or therapy groups can allow them to participate in a safe and nurturing environment that can provide a corrective emotional experience for those who lacked warm and loving male role models.

Are we afraid of men, or do we dislike men on some level? Men often can only show their feelings of sadness through anger at first. If women are afraid of angry men, their offices are not safe places for angry men to vent their feelings and learn how to understand and better control them. Sometimes male clients transfer the general cultural devaluation of women into therapy. This devaluation can be subtle or overt, but if it incurs a hostile or defensive reaction, the therapeutic connection suffers (Erickson, 1993). I have found that one of the biggest stumbling blocks for female therapists is a male client who shows anger or lack of respect for women (especially female therapists). A detached yet compassionate stance that allows the male client to explore his feelings is what is needed, not the tendency to withdraw or strike back at men who may remind us of men in our lives who have gotten angry with us or whom we felt were disrespectful.

How do we view masculinity? Do we subscribe to an approach that sees maleness as a sickness to be cured, or more as a set of roles, some of which have value and some of which are too rigid or overemphasized? If we see masculinity as negative, then we do a disservice to our male clients who are struggling to be good men. Most of the male sex role norms have a positive side that men need to learn how to judiciously incorporate, balancing the positive parts of male norms with the positive parts of female norms, rather than discarding them outright (Heesacker & Prichard, 1992).

Do we really like men? Finally, do we have a solid history of good personal and professional relationships with men? If we do not, our negative experiences and feelings may leak into the therapeutic relationship in a nonproductive way. It is important to be honest with oneself about one's relationships with men and, when necessary, seek therapy about why we do not really like or feel comfortable with men. Because of the history of sexism in our culture, some women have been victims of men and men's pathologizing of women. It can be a hard road out of this history, but it must be taken for the sake of our male clients and us.

CONCLUSION

Female therapists have an obligation to be educated about the world of men—how men were raised and what it is like to be a man in this culture. This education should also include understanding how our socialization as women and our own personal history might interfere with working most effectively with our male clients. It is helpful to be open to different methods of working with men that may challenge our particular preference for doing therapy. Psychologists need to do more research, writing, and teaching in the area of men's studies, particularly how men view therapy and what may work best with them. Perhaps the biggest error female clinicians may make is to underestimate the degree of sadness and frustration that so many men experience. Female therapists need to appreciate how men struggle to acknowledge and show feelings that are antithetical to the values of being a strong male in this culture. We stand the best chance of engaging men in therapy when we truly understand the experiences of men, are compassionate about their struggles, can monitor our own reactions to their defenses and transferences, and are continually willing to try new therapeutic techniques and approaches that might better suit men.

QUESTIONS FROM THE EDITORS

1. *What gender-based stereotypes were you aware of in counseling this client? How did that impact your therapy with this client?*

Jim entered therapy looking like a combination of the "sturdy oak" (dependable, able to take care of others) and "the big wheel" (successful, in charge of his life). I made the mistake of thinking that because he looked okay on the outside, he was okay on the inside. Because Jim presented his problem as one in which he just needed some help in following through on a decision he had already made (and he felt was the correct one), I did not question his presentation as readily as I might have with someone who looked a little less put together. As a woman, I am used to men wanting to fix things and get them right and being problem solvers. Jim said he had a problem that needed to be solved. I believed that the way he presented the problem was accurate. We went down the road of trying to fix the problem without taking more time to analyze what the problem really was. I was also hesitant about having him experience feelings of sadness, hurt, vulnerability, and fear too soon in therapy. These feelings are very much at odds with the male norm of emotional inexpressivity. If he got in touch with feelings of vulnerability too quickly, I was afraid it would feel shaming for him and he would leave therapy. One way I had of softening some of the hard part of our work was to use humor with Jim. I have found humor to be an effective tool in working with male clients. It helps make therapy seem less intense by giving them a little detachment from difficult feelings. Humor also helps bond us as equals. If a man is coming to me for help, he may already view himself in a one-down position, so acting in ways that make us feel more like colleagues and equal partners may be important as a way of redressing the perceived imbalance of our roles.

So I stayed on the safe side with Jim for quite a while. As we worked together side by side to solve a problem, we formed a solid therapeutic alliance. This has been crucial in helping Jim feel safe and respected enough to get in touch with parts of him such as his sadness and need, which challenged traditional male norms. However, he may have suffered longer than he needed to because we were both hesitant to go to the places of pain in him. I am reminded of an old Sufi parable about a man who falls down a hole and cannot get back out. He tries putting a pile of rocks on top of each other but cannot reach the opening. In despair, he wanders into the darkest corner of the cave to die. There he finds a tunnel, through which he crawls until he reaches the light he had given up ever finding. With men, I find that I am a little less willing to sit in the cave with them and a little more timid about helping them crawl through that tunnel of darkness. Their fear becomes my fear, unless I am careful to remember that feelings are our guides into wholeness and health. With female clients, I am less likely to worry about the impact of feelings of dependency or vulnerability in terms of our relationship or the challenge it presents to their femininity.

2. How did your own gender role issues influence your work with this client?

First and foremost, my gender role socialization says I should nurture others. This is in some ways the meta-norm of accepted feminine behavior—to take care of others. As a therapist, of course, a large part of my role is to help others. But I think that my relationship with Jim had a particular flavor to it based on my being a woman. I felt like I was acting in two different roles: as Jim's mother and as his intimate partner. I think that I am socialized to act those roles with men because taking care of men is a large part of the feminine norm. But because I am heterosexual, the quality of that intimacy holds a special value to therapist and client, one that at times can have a romantic tinge to it. My experience as a woman being intimate with men outside of a therapeutic situation has sometimes involved a romantic or sexual component. Being intimate within the therapy hour can trigger memories of what intimacy means in my personal life. If I am afraid of those feelings, I can shut myself off to some valuable information about what is going on between my male client and myself. If I act on those feelings, I muddy the waters of therapy and I violate the ethical principles of my profession. What I am learning to do is to accept and learn from the feelings—to use them as a guide to help me better understand my client and what he feels about being close to women.

Another female sex role norm that I carry into therapy is to value emotional expressivity. Because this has been relatively easy for me, I have not always had the empathy for Jim that I would like to. Sometimes I get frustrated with his difficulty opening up, and I have to remind myself that it is not easy for men to do so. I try to remember that patience and kindness are crucial in helping any client but especially men, who have to act and feel in ways in therapy that directly challenge traditional male norms (e.g., being the stoic "Marlboro Man"). I also try to remember that men open up more easily to women than to men in general and that as a female therapist, I am of special importance to male clients in helping them explore painful feelings in a safe environment. The value I put on emotions will help the men I work with also value their own emotions.

A third female sex role norm that influenced my work with Jim is the importance of close connection with others. As a woman, I do not have the experience of finding close connection as difficult as I suspect many men might. It does not threaten my sense of femininity to depend on someone else, to open up to them, or to let them know what I am feeling. I implicitly trust that others will not think me unfeminine for wanting to be connected to others. I felt it was very important for Jim to understand how lonely he really is because he has not been able to really articulate it to himself until recently, yet he has suffered from the consequences of disconnection. His tendency to compartmentalize his life and to keep important things hidden from people to whom he has ostensibly been close is sometimes difficult for me to accept or even understand. I have a hard time not being judgmental about his dishonesty with himself, his wife, his affair partner, and his couples therapist (and perhaps me as well). I do not think I truly understand what it must be like for him to risk putting it out on the table for everyone to see. Like so many women, I underestimate how vulnerable men really are to other people's feelings about them and misunderstand how they protect themselves (often by looking as if nothing is wrong) to avoid being hurt.

3. Looking back on the case, knowing what you know now, would you change the way you worked with this client?

I would have taken more time for both of us to explore the context of his presenting problem rather than focus on trying to solve the problem. The saying that "you can never solve a problem on the level on which it is presented" is often true in therapy but is particularly true in working with men, who often cannot articulate clearly what they are feeling or what their real problems are. I think that by accepting his presenting problem in his terms, I allowed the focus of therapy to stay away from looking at Jim's history and what issues he brought into the marriage, especially his difficulty in getting close to others. I would therefore have taken a more extended history than the two sessions we spent doing so in the beginning of therapy, or I would have returned to it in more detail later in therapy. I would certainly have raised the issue of depression earlier in our treatment, especially as it related to his relationship with Mary and feeling ignored by her. I would have taken more of a systems approach to Jim's depression, locating it more explicitly in what happened in his family of origin and in the dynamics playing out between Mary, her daughter, and himself. I would also have explored more the relationship that Jim and I had. I shied away from this at first because I was afraid I might frighten him off. Perhaps I was also a little cautious about talking too soon about our relationship when I was not quite clear about my own feelings about it. But I think a more direct approach to understanding our relationship would have helped Jim to better understand his issues with intimacy and to be able to feel safe acknowledging what was happening in the therapy hour and how this could be of use to him in general.

4. How did the triangulation of you, Jim, and Mary get processed in the session?

After a few months of therapy, I began to feel uncomfortable with the fact that Jim's wife had never met me, and I felt a bit like an affair partner in that Jim was sharing material with me that he was not sharing with his wife. I felt that the windows were more open and the walls were less present between the two of us than they were with his wife (Glass, 2003). At that point, I felt it would be helpful to have Mary join us for one session, to bring the different parts of Jim's life together. Once Mary and Jim began seeing a couples therapist, I made sure that I communicated regularly with that therapist. However, I began to be in the odd position of being the only woman in Jim's life to defend him—his couples counselor felt he was a difficult person, and his wife found him detached and angry. My interaction with Jim presented me with a very different Jim: someone who was connected, humorous, warm, and open. I was curious with him about the difference—Why was he one way with me and such a different way with Mary? He said that he was pushed away by her and was annoyed with her for her spaciness, disorganization, and overinvolvement with her daughter. When he consistently described her this way, I often felt that Mary was really who he described her as being. I then recognized that I was colluding with Jim in seeing Mary as the problem. It was at that point that I made an effort to see her point of view and to look at the ways that he pushed her away. I would often say,

> Jim, this therapy is about you, not about Mary—when you spend time complaining about her, you're not doing the work you need to do to look at yourself. Maybe you and Mary aren't right for each other, but I think it would be more helpful to you in the long run if you understood more about your own issues with intimacy.

5. *How did this client see you? Were you protected? Devalued? Sexualized?*

I think that Jim saw me as a surrogate partner of great value—neither mother nor lover, but someone who was safe precisely because I was neither. I was detached from his life; there were clear boundaries between us; I did not ask anything of him for my own needs; he could always depend on me to be there for him; I spent most of the session listening intently to him; and his cares and concerns came first in our sessions. It is possible that for Jim, there was some sexual feeling involved in our relationship. Because of the intimate setting of therapy and how men view intimacy, it is easy for men to connect emotional intimacy with sexual intimacy. If there was attraction on his part, it was not obvious to me (e.g., he did not make remarks about me of a sexual nature, and he did not act seductively toward me). Intimacy for Jim has been threatening—he easily feels suffocated on the one hand and abandoned on the other. Our relationship allowed him to open up about painful material in a way that felt safe for him, which was an important step in the direction of understanding himself more and facing his fears. He said on several occasions that he valued our sessions because he felt heard and could talk about everything without being judged. In some ways, this might be one of the most important roles a female therapist can play with a male client—creating a safe space in which he can express his feelings and explore intimacy within the context of a respectful, egalitarian relationship with a woman. We can role model what intimacy can be without overwhelming the client with fears about expectations or rejection. We can be a warm, nurturing presence to support him in challenging long-held beliefs about what men should be that have proved to be damaging to developing healthy connection with others.

SUGGESTED RESOURCES

Barton, E. (Ed.). (2000). *Mythopoetic perspectives of men's healing work: An anthology for therapists and others.* New York: Bergin & Garvey.

Beck, A. (1988). *Love is never enough.* New York: Harper & Row.

Cochran, S. V., & Rabinowitz, F. E. (2000). *Men and depression: Clinical and empirical perspectives.* Boston: Academic Press.

Erickson, B. M. (1993). *Helping men change: The role of the female therapist.* Newbury Park, CA: Sage.

Glass, S. (2003). *Not "just friends."* New York: Free Press.

Goldberg, H. (1976). *The hazards of being male.* New York: Signet.

Good, G. E., & Brooks, G. R. (Eds.). (2005). *The new handbook of psychotherapy and counseling with men: A comprehensive guide to settings, problems, and treatment approaches* (Rev. and abridged). San Francisco: Jossey-Bass.

Gray, J. (1992). *Men are from Mars, women are from Venus.* New York: HarperCollins.

Hendrix, H. (1988). *Getting the love you want.* New York: Harper-Perennial.

Johnson, N. (2005). Women helping men: Strengths of and barriers to women therapists working with male clients. In G. E. Good & G. R. Brooks (Eds.), *The new handbook of psychotherapy and counseling with men: A comprehensive guide to settings, problems, and treatment approaches* (Rev. and abridged, pp. 696–718). San Francisco: Jossey-Bass.

Levant, R. F. (1995). *Masculinity reconstructed.* New York: Plume.

Levant, R. F., & Pollack, W. S. (Eds.). (1995). *A new psychology of men.* New York: Basic Books.

Lynch, J., & Kilmartin, C. T. (1999). *The pain behind the mask: Overcoming masculine depression.* Haworth Press.

Meth, R. L., & Pasick, R. S. (1990). *Men in therapy: The challenge of change.* New York: Guilford Press.

Osherson, S. (1992). *Wrestling with love.* New York: Fawcett-Columbine.

Philpot, C., Brooks, G. R., Lusterman, D., & Nutt, R. (1997). *Bridging separate gender worlds.* Washington, DC: American Psychological Association.

Rabinowitz, F., & Cochran, S. (2002). *Deepening psychotherapy with men.* Washington, DC: American Psychological Association.

Real, T. (1997). *I don't want to talk about it: Overcoming the legacy of male depression.* New York: Fireside Books.

Schwartz, P. (1994). *Love between equals.* New York: Free Press.

Shem, S., & Surrey, J. L. (1998). *We have to talk.* New York: Basic Books.

Tannen, D. (1990). *You just don't understand: Women and men in conversation.* New York: Morrow/Ballantine.

REFERENCES

Andronico, M. (1996). *Men in groups.* Washington, DC: American Psychological Association.

Attenborough, R. (Producer/Director), & Eastman, B. (Producer). (1993). *Shadowlands* [Motion picture]. England: Savoy Pictures.

Beck, A. (1988). *Love is never enough*. New York: Harper & Row.

Cochran, S. V., & Rabinowitz, F. E. (2000). *Men and depression: Clinical and empirical perspectives*. Boston: Academic Press.

David, D. S., & Brannon, R. (1976). *The forty-nine percent majority: The male sex role*. Reading, MA: Addison-Wesley.

Erickson, B. M. (1993). *Helping men change: The role of the female therapist*. Newbury Park, CA: Sage.

Friedan, B. (1962). *The feminine mystique*. New York: Norton.

Glass, S. (2003). *Not "just friends."* New York: Free Press.

Goldberg, H. (1976). *The hazards of being male*. New York: Signet.

Good, G. E. , & Brooks, G. R. (2005). *The new handbook of psychotherapy and counseling with men: A comprehensive guide to settings, problems, and treatment approaches* (Rev. and abridged). San Francisco: Jossey-Bass.

Heesacker, M., & Prichard, S. (1992). In a different voice, revisited: Men, women, and emotion. *Journal of Mental Health Counseling, 14*, 274–290.

Hendrix, H. (1988). *Getting the love you want*. New York: Harper-Perennial.

Levant, R. F., & Pollack, W. S. (Eds.). (1995). *A new psychology of men*. New York: Basic Books.

Lynch, J., & Kilmartin, C. T. (1999). *The pain behind the mask: Overcoming masculine depression*. Haworth Press.

Meth, R. L., & Pasick, R. S. (1990). *Men in therapy: The challenge of change*. New York: Guilford Press.

Morgan, R. (Ed.). (1970). *Sisterhood is powerful*. New York: Vintage.

O'Neil, J. (1995). Fifteen years of theory and research in men's gender role conflict: New paradigms for empirical research. In R. F. Levant & W. S. Pollack (Eds.), *A new psychology of men* (pp. 164–208). New York: Basic Books.

Pleck, J. H. (1981). *The myth of masculinity*. Cambridge, MA: MIT Press.

Real, T. (1997). *I don't want to talk about it: Overcoming the legacy of male depression*. New York: Fireside Books.

Sweet, H. (1995). *Perceptions of undergraduate male experiences in heterosexual romantic relationships: A sex role norms analysis*. PhD dissertation, Department of Counseling, Developmental Psychology, and Research Methods, Boston College.

Tannen, D. (1990). *You just don't understand: Women and men in conversation*. New York: Morrow/Ballantine.

5

STRUGGLING FOR SADNESS: A RELATIONAL APPROACH TO HEALING MEN'S GRIEF

SAM V. COCHRAN

From birth, little boys and, later, adult men in the United States are hamstrung with negative, restrictive admonitions that mirror the culture's prevailing attitudes about masculinity. The maxim "big boys don't cry" is potentially one of the most emotionally damaging of these cultural admonitions. This admonition requires boys and men to hide their tears and to suppress their sadness. When internalized by boys and men, such a prohibition on sadness and crying deprives them of the full depth of the universal human experience of loss.

Helping men embrace sadness has been a prime motivating force for me. Early in my career, I noticed that many of the men I was treating sought therapy after experiencing some kind of loss. Often, this was a real loss such as a rejection in an intimate relationship, a loss of employment, or the death of someone close. This loss could also be a symbolic loss such as a loss on the sports field or failure to achieve some coveted goal. These men had almost universally repressed the sadness associated with this experience and in doing so had dissociated themselves from both the actual memory of the loss and the emotional component of that memory.

Encountering these men in therapy was a moving experience for me. As I worked with them to explore and define their goals, we would almost always encounter a hidden, protected reservoir of sadness that remained unfelt and unexpressed. As I struggled to understand what I was learning from these men, it became clear to me that our Western, American culture affords men few sanctions to experience, in a healthy manner, the experience of loss and the accompanying sadness. My therapy with these men was a process of moving toward this sadness and unlocking its healing potential. This process of discovery was, and continues to be, a central force that has energized my ongoing interest in psychotherapy with men. Sitting with my male clients and helping them encounter loss and sadness is the foundation to my conceptual and practical approach to working with men in therapy.

Lerner (1980) observed that women internalize powerful prohibitions against the full expression of anger. She argued that anger was a force of distance and disconnection, one that is fundamentally at odds with many women's value systems and one that threatens a woman's sense of self. The relational model of psychotherapy with men I describe here is based on the assumption that men, mirroring the process that Lerner described for women, internalize a powerful prohibition against sadness. Sadness is a force for connection, a bid for solace and comfort from another. Yet this force is at odds with the prevailing values associated with masculinity in our culture. Pulls for connection and solace threaten the importance of independence, of "going it alone" and of "taking the bull by the horns" to solve one's problems without assistance from anyone else. Hence, the experience of sadness threatens the very sense of masculinity that men learn in our culture.

The men I have worked with in therapy told stories about being taught to deny or avoid experiencing loss and sadness. Beginning with what Pollack (1995, p. 41) described as the "traumatic abrogation of the early holding environment"—that disconnection forced on little boys at an early age as we ask them to be strong, to not cry, to not be a sissy—and continuing through adolescence, young adulthood, middle adulthood, and old age, men must come to terms with myriad physical and psychological losses (Cochran & Rabinowitz, 1996). This accrual of loss experiences, the accompanying retreat from emotional connection, and the need to undo this disconnection are key therapy issues in the approach to psychotherapy with men I describe in this chapter.

Because the personal, affectively charged prohibitions against sadness that many men have learned are taught in the context of close interpersonal relationships, these admonitions can be unlearned in the context of a close therapy relationship. The therapy relationship becomes a vessel for reclaiming, holding, and learning to contain the lost sadness and grief that a man has carried throughout his life. At termination, many of my male clients are left with a sadness that reflects the recognition of their losses and the acknowledgment of these losses' emotional impact (see Stiver & Miller, 1997).

INITIAL SESSIONS: UNCOVERING THE SADNESS

Brent was a 26-year-old Caucasian man who had grown up in an upper-middle-class urban environment in Northeastern United States.[1] He had just moved to Iowa City from New York City to begin a graduate program in comparative literature. During his first semester, he scheduled an initial consultation appointment with me at the University Counseling Service to discuss "concerns with my career choice and my relationships with women." At this initial consultation session, he indicated that he was interested in looking at how a career would meet his "needs." He also mentioned that he was concerned about his relationships with women and about his "anger." He said he had "learned a lot" about himself since graduating from college and in previous therapy but was concerned that he would not be able to sustain a close relationship with a woman.

Brent indicated in his application for services that he had a preference for working with a male therapist. I found this unusual because most men, when they express a sex preference for a therapist, usually state a preference for working with a female. I asked him about this in our initial encounter. He replied that there were a number of aspects of his concerns about his work and career and his relationships with women that he just did not think a woman would be able to fully appreciate. And, he noted, most of his relationships with women recently had been "troubled" and he was not sure whether he would be able to really trust and open up to a female therapist.

I liked Brent right away. He was bright, engaging, and conveyed a good deal of psychological mindedness in our initial conversation. Because Brent had requested to work with a male therapist, I asked him toward the close of our initial consultation session how he felt our conversation had gone and how he might feel about continuing to meet with me a few more sessions. He thought that would be fine, as he had felt comfortable and respected by me, and we agreed to meet to explore his concerns more fully.

In our second and third sessions, Brent elaborated more on his doubts about his graduate program, which were a source of a good deal of his current discomfort. One element of this doubt was related to what he called being "misperceived" by his peers in his program. He thought his peers attributed sexist, conservative, and aggressive attitudes to him. As he described his concern, I wondered to myself how much of his perception of his peers' attitudes was a projection of his own sentiment. Sensing a good deal of grist for the mill here, I told him that we would need to "unpack" the meaning of these terms—*sexist, conservative, aggressive*—together. I also shared with him my own experience of having felt misperceived and out of place in my initial

---

[1]Some unique features of this case have been altered, masked, or deleted to conceal the identity of the client. The essential features of the case are preserved to accurately reflect the therapy process. Quotation marks signify material taken from case notes and denote or nearly denote words and phrases used in session.

attempt at a graduate program in drosophila genetics. We shared a laugh from this, and I think Brent felt understood and accepted by me about having doubts over his choice of programs.

We talked more about his concern of being misperceived. He related this to an experience of having been accused of sexual misconduct when he was a senior in high school. He had been dating a woman who, one night after having had sex with Brent, "turned on him" (as he put it) and screamed for him to leave her house. The next day she told her parents that he had forced her to have sex with him. He was picked up and questioned, but ultimately no charges were filed. Nonetheless, he felt ashamed and humiliated at the attention this drew to his sexual behavior. After word spread around school about the reason for his breakup with his girlfriend, he was shunned by mutual friends and treated with anger by his now ex-girlfriend and her friends. He said he felt "naked" when he walked down the school corridors and felt that everyone in his school "misperceived" him and did not fully understand what had happened.

As Brent conveyed this story to me, I could tell he was experiencing a great deal of discomfort. His pace of speech had slowed, and he would pause at times to take deep breaths, rocking slowly back and forth in the chair as he inhaled and exhaled deeply. He would put his hands behind his head, as if getting ready to do a sit-up, and arch his back as he stretched his head back and looked up at the ceiling.

I made a mental note that his reaction was more than he could easily contain. I wondered to myself about the pain and vulnerability he must have felt as he described this situation. Although the incident sounded to me like some kind of sexual misconduct, I chose to simply take it in without jumping to conclusions or passing judgment. I said to him that it looked to me like he still "carried a lot of feeling" for this, even though it had happened 8 years before we met. Brent appeared shaken as we ended the session and planned our next meeting.

Our next few sessions proved to be even more eventful. We talked about relationship difficulties he experienced during his college years. These difficulties usually involved misunderstandings with his partner about the level of intimacy desired or about expectations concerning the number of sexual partners he was permitted. He openly acknowledged concern about this pattern of "problems" in his relationships with women and conveyed his wish to develop a happy, mutually fulfilling relationship.

Continuing with the theme of conflict in his relationships with women, Brent segued into a discussion of his relationships with his mother and his older sister. He told me he felt disadvantaged and "victimized" growing up. Because his father was often gone and was usually intoxicated when home, Brent felt alone and at the "mercy" of his mother and sister, who were openly critical and disapproving of him. He expressed dismay and confusion when discussing his relationship with his sister, lamenting that they were hopelessly estranged in spite of rather frequent phone contact. As I had done when hearing his story about the incident with his ex-girlfriend in high school, I simply took in this material, asked a question here and there for clarification, and supported Brent as he struggled to tell his story.

Then, at the beginning of our sixth session, he told me that he had something difficult to discuss but that he felt he needed to "get it out on the table." He then proceeded to tell me that he had had a sexual relationship with his sister for a short period of time when they were young adolescents. He was 12 years old at the time it began, and his sister was 14. He discussed this revelation with considerable emotion, as he had when discussing the episode of sexual misconduct with his ex-girlfriend. He again took deep breaths and rocked back and forth in his chair as we talked about his sexual experiences with his sister (which amounted to mutual masturbation and petting over a several-month period).

As before, I simply listened attentively to his disclosure and tried not to pass judgment on what I was hearing. I also noted to myself the emotion that accompanied this revelation and decided to venture a relationally oriented process observation by commenting on how difficult it must have been for him to share these things with another person. ("Whew! I can see that there is a lot of emotion still connected to this situation. It must be hard to be so open about it with me.")

In our next session, Brent told me he had felt "lighter" after our last meeting, and he appreciated what he perceived to be my acceptance of these disclosures without moralizing or being "judgmental." I again told him how I thought it took courage to share this "man to man" and acknowledged his being able to be so vulnerable in our session. Brent appeared relieved by this comment. In light of his having requested a male therapist, it seemed to me that he was happy to find a man with whom he could confide these experiences and feel accepted and safe.

After these disclosures concerning his sexual behavior, we returned to his concern about his choice of a graduate program and his fear that becoming a professor of comparative literature would not be a satisfying or fulfilling career for him. He told me he saw himself as a "caring person" and that he did not see how "studying the study of literature" would allow him to express this "caring side" of himself. We identified this idea of him as a "caring person" as an integral component of his core value system, one that he wanted to be sure held a central place in his choice of a career.

I wondered where the sexual issues had gone all of a sudden, but I opted to follow his lead. I asked him whether he had other ideas about work or careers. He said that he had fantasized about medicine since he was a little boy but that he just never really took that direction. He was immensely talented academically and had graduated with a perfect grade point average from a competitive and prestigious college. I decided to press him on why he had not pursued medicine. ("I don't get it, Brent. Obviously, you could make it academically. Why give up the fantasy if it sounds so meaningful to you?") He replied that he was afraid, deep down, that he really was not a "caring person" and that if that were the case, he should not become a physician, because a physician's job is to care for others. He wanted to "do the right thing" and did not want to exploit or abuse others by virtue of his role as a healer if he was, in fact, not a "caring person." I shared with Brent how I could understand his concern, particularly in the context of his feelings about his sexual experiences that he had described earlier. After all, how can someone who is a "caring person" be accused of sexual assault and engage in forbidden sexual activity with his sister?

This conversation added a new perspective to his concern about his career choice. Brent was a sincere, sensitive, and deeply introspective young man who took all his choices and actions quite seriously. We agreed that we needed to discuss this issue further. What made him think he was not a "caring person"? How was he so sure he would not be able to handle this work if it really "fit" him? What careers would afford him the opportunity to be a "caring person"?

We had covered 12 sessions now and were approaching a semester break. In our next session Brent inquired about what I thought of his issues and what we were doing together. I jumped at this opportunity to discuss my impressions and to share with him my perspective on the role masculine gender role socialization played in our work together.

I told him that on the basis of what we had discussed so far, I thought a central theme for him would involve coming to terms with the many losses he had experienced—in his family and in his relationships. I noted to him the lack of supportive, understanding connection in his family, his father's unavailability as a source of support, and a continuing replay of disconnection in his relationships after he left home for college. I told him that I thought these traumatic experiences had significantly impacted how he viewed himself and how our upbringing as males in our culture makes coming to terms with these kinds of losses a unique challenge.

Brent resonated with this conceptualization and picked up on the themes of pain and loss. He commented that he did not feel as if he "belonged" anywhere and that his pain and loss only reinforced this. The one place he said he did feel as if he did belong, where he felt safe, was "in the mountains." He loved to hike, and he would sometimes go by himself for 1 or 2 days and camp all alone. Together, we formulated an image of him carrying a heavy pack on his back through the mountains and at times having to "redistribute" the weight of this load but of never being able to simply cast off the load.

He said that the "load" metaphor represented suffering and that he believed coming to terms with his own suffering—finding a new way to carry it—was important for him at this time in his life. We connected his feeling of "not belonging" to his family experience and noted how this theme had played out at various times in his life, from high school through college and

96   SAM V. COCHRAN

now into graduate school, where he did not feel like he "belonged" in his program or that it would afford him a fulfilling career in which he would "belong." We also noted that although the hiker felt that he "belonged" on the path in the mountains, he was also alone, not connected to anyone. Why was that?

As we talked in this session about my impressions of him and about the challenges that lie ahead, I felt a strong sense of connection to Brent. I noted how our relationship had developed quickly and had deepened to where we were able to talk openly about his struggles, pain, goals, and hopes. I hoped he felt he "belonged" in the room with me. I could see as we openly acknowledged his losses in this session that Brent was again having a hard time containing his own emotional response. He drew a deep breath, widened his eyes, and rocked back in his chair. I could barely detect that his eyes appeared to be tearing up, and I chose to simply comment on how he really "struggled with his sadness."

COMMENTARY ON INITIAL SESSIONS

This early phase of therapy was characterized by a relatively rapid engagement and the early establishment of a strong therapeutic bond. My goal in these sessions was to secure a safe and respectful space in which Brent felt he "belonged." Brent quickly disclosed difficult material to me early in our work together. Although this was difficult for him, as evidenced by his deep breathing and rocking in his chair as he discussed the material, he pushed himself hard to break through his shame about his experiences and share them with me.

The process of working through the shame he felt about his sexual experiences was notable. Brent was very articulate and was able to name his discomfort and acknowledge the strength of his level of trust and safety with me in our sessions together. This safety aided his capacity to push himself in disclosing this difficult material with little guarantee of my response at such an early time in the therapy. Being aware of this, I decided to adopt a relatively neutral stance to these disclosures (I do not assume that my interpretation of the meaning of these events was the same as the meaning for him) while affirming the strength, honesty, and courage it took to tell me of these experiences.

After hearing Brent describe these experiences, I thought that a key aspect of our longer therapy work would be recovering and experiencing the emotional impact of these events. I viewed much of our work through the lens of loss and sadness and envisioned helping him "struggle" to accept his losses and sadness and, through this, to come to terms with his painful life experiences.

It was evident to me that he had endured traumatic loss after loss from an early age, including a cold and uncaring family environment, a shameful sexual relationship with his sister, accusations of sexual assault, and the absence of a positive male figure in his life. These losses had impinged upon his nascent masculine identity and left him feeling inadequate as a man, ashamed of his needs and his feelings, and disempowered in terms of his capacity to create meaningful relationships and participate in a meaningful career. To disentangle the meaning he had made for himself of these events and their impact on his life, we would need to address the anger, grief, and sadness that accompanied them head on.

MIDDLE SESSIONS: SHARING THE SADNESS

After the rather quick and intense engagement over our first 12 sessions, we then settled into what felt to me like a quieter and more relaxed pace. Brent had decided over the semester break to take a leave from his graduate program and work while he pursued emergency medical technician (EMT) training as a means to test out his desire and commitment to a career in medicine. He began the EMT training and was fully engaged in this work. He felt the training provided him a real, "hands-on," practical means by which he could demonstrate that he was truly a "caring person."

In one session, he described how he felt challenged by the opportunity to deal with trauma situations. He discussed this in terms of his masculinity—he wanted a career in which he could really help others in a concrete way in challenging, dangerous situations. He described his desire to master his emotional response to the trauma and how he found this both challenging as well as disturbing. He did not want to disconnect too much from the side of himself that was sensitive and empathic to others' suffering, because he could relate quite well to that experience on the basis of his own life experiences. However, he was well aware of the potential for burnout and for vicarious traumatization for the helper in the role for which he was training. By and large, the EMT training was providing him with the real-life engagement and opportunity to be a "caring person" that he felt was sorely lacking in his graduate program.

I noticed that Brent was becoming more comfortable with me and with our sessions. He was on time for every session, and I could tell from his mood and energy level as we walked to my office that he was also becoming more comfortable with himself. He was eager to share his experiences from his EMT training, and we continued to discuss his career concerns, his work issues, and his relationship struggles through a lens that was critical of traditional masculine socialization norms.

Brent resonated to this perspective as a scholar who was well versed in critical social theory and gender theory. At times, he would impress me with his sensitive analysis of his situation. At other times, he would wonder aloud whether some nuance in our interaction was "the transference" coming out and whether we should discuss this. (My typical response was a "What do you think?" delivered in a playful and inviting manner.) Occasionally, he would describe a book that he was reading that pertained to our discussions about the meaning of manhood and share his discovery with me. I gratefully accepted his book recommendations (without interpretation or comment) and have found that they frequently became personal favorites of mine.

During this middle phase of therapy, Brent also enrolled in a martial arts class, which he had been meaning to do since he arrived in town. This led to discussions of how he felt it was important for him to "honor" his "aggressive" side and to find ways to focus and channel this energy and not disavow it. This, too, was discussed through a gender lens, as we noted how important it was for men to fully embrace all aspects of themselves but to also recognize the importance of restraining the destructive nature of aggression. Brent told stories of how he was the recipient of much verbal and, at times, physical, aggression in his own family and how important it was for him to find other ways to express his anger and frustrations. He felt that his Kung Fu class provided him an opportunity to do this.

This class and his experiences in it provided the springboard for our next major therapeutic passage. As Brent discussed his concern about his difficulty accepting what he called the "aggressive side" of himself, he discovered how painful it was for him to fully embrace this part of himself. At the same time, he noted how important it was for him to produce what he called "acts of kindness" that were concrete evidence that he was, indeed, a kind and caring person. How could he contain and honor both of these seemingly contradictory aspects of himself?

He again wondered aloud what I thought of him, particularly how I saw this aggressive side of him. I was not quite sure how to reply. Was he asking me to affirm his aggressive side? Did he just want reassurance that it was acceptable to harbor aggressive impulses? Not knowing quite what he was asking, I simply said that I was just "soaking up" what he was saying and did not want to pass judgment in any way that would make him feel bad about himself. I said that I thought both sides—the aggressive and the compassionate—were important and that we could work to affirm both.

He returned the following session and told me how he had felt ashamed and embarrassed and wanted to "retract" what he had said and "take back" the session: Was it possible to "erase" that session? He went on to lament that he feared his expectations for me were too high and that he had hoped that by disclosing his aggressiveness to me, it would somehow relieve him of the need to "hone" that side of himself in his day-to-day life. He was afraid of what would happen in our work, now that he revealed what he felt was a deeply shameful aspect of himself. Then, seemingly out of nowhere, he blurted out that he had been engaged in a series of one-night stands with both men and women over the past month or so and that this, too, made him feel defective, ashamed, and afraid. What did I think of him now?

I was quite surprised by these new disclosures ("Brent, I have to say, I'm surprised and not quite sure what to say here!"). Initially, I thought he had been scolding me for an empathic disconnect in the previous session, in which I had fumbled my response to his question about how I saw him and his aggressiveness. We had not been devoting much air time to sexual issues in our recent sessions, so I was somewhat taken aback at these new revelations.

I was also deeply concerned for his well-being. Had he been safe? Had he been taking precautions to avoid contracting a sexually transmitted disease? I did not want to jump to conclusions, but I wanted to let the meaning of this disclosure about his sexual activities unfold naturally. In response to these revelations, I attempted to simply keep the focus on how he felt in sharing these things with me—vulnerable, ashamed, and frightened. We acknowledged these feelings, and I made it a point to maintain what I considered neutrality with regard to his revelations about his sexual activity as I had with regard to his previous disclosures about his sexual activity with his sister and his sexual assault.

It was apparent to me that Brent was extremely uncomfortable with the turn he had taken with our therapy in this session. He looked visibly frightened and uneasy. For the first time since our earlier sessions he strained as he struggled to contain his emotions in the session, resorting to his characteristic rocking and breathing deeply. Having thought we had worked through a good deal of his sadness about his earlier disclosures, I wondered what sadness he struggled with now.

Brent openly acknowledged the self-destructive nature of these anonymous sexual contacts and how ashamed he felt about them. I made a conscious point of not minimizing or ignoring this discomfort or the seriousness of the disclosures. Attempting to stay empathically connected, I commented that it must have been hard to talk about this and hoped he felt some relief at having gotten this out on the table now so we could openly discuss it.

It was at this point in our therapy that I recognized how important it was to continue to shake hands at the beginning and end of each of our sessions. We had developed a ritual of shaking hands as we greeted one another in the waiting room when I went to pick him up for our sessions. Then, at the end of each session after we agreed on our meeting time and day for the next week, we again shook hands as he left my office. In retrospect, this was a direct enactment of our connection. I sensed it was important to continue to demonstrate this connection during a time that Brent probably feared that our connection might be overwhelmed by his disclosures.

I chose not to focus too explicitly on how these revelations were shaped or influenced by our growing intimacy and how they might affect our relationship. I noted to myself that Brent had been a dutiful participant in the therapy for some 20 sessions now and must have been internalizing my interest and caring in order to feel comfortable enough to share these things.

I think this particular interlude in our therapy illustrates the importance of not evoking shame by being too explicit with certain relational aspects of treatment. Pollack (1990), discussing the importance of Kohut's (1977) contributions to our understanding of the treatment of narcissistic disorders, noted

> The appropriate [therapeutic] response is an "empathic" or "experience near" understanding of the individual's needs to take in and utilize the other, that is, the self-object [therapist], in a manner that silently performs missing functions within the self without necessarily acknowledging these significant external contributions. In other words, Kohut accepts that certain people may need to be highly dependent on others in order to fulfill deficits or tolerate conflicts and traumas in their earlier lines of narcissistic development, *while never consciously acknowledging such dependency.* (p. 318, emphasis added)

COMMENTARY ON MIDDLE SESSIONS

This middle phase of therapy built on our emotionally charged opening sessions. Brent had developed a feeling of trust and safety as he continued to come to our sessions. I wondered sometimes whether his early disclosures of such sensitive material were not a way of quickly establishing a safe environment in which he could then explore more fully his career and his relationship concerns.

We discovered that his interest in exploring an alternative career path was actually a return to a more central, core motivation in him—namely his desire to connect to others in a wholesome, giving, positive way. He fully understood the roots of this motivation—both his family-of-origin experiences of disconnection as well as his wish to be perceived as a "caring person" by others. We discussed this in terms of his drive to connect in positive ways with others (Bergman, 1995) and how this relational value was a core aspect of his identity.

It was during this middle phase of therapy that we explicitly named a part of our process as being devoted to exploring what it means to be a man in our culture. As Brent discussed his struggle with being a "caring person," I shared with Brent my own struggles with balancing being a "caring" therapist with wanting to also be perceived as strong, competent, sometimes powerful, and in control. I also talked about how this played out in relationships for me, and my belief that we (he, I, and everyone) were engaged in a continuous process of "doing gender" (see Gilbert & Scher, 1999) as we invented and re-invented both masculine and feminine aspects of ourselves on the basis of a number of considerations, including family values, cultural injunction, situational demands, and sometimes just plain random experimentation.

To minimize the intrusion of shame-based defenses into our therapy process, I was conservative in my interventions that made our therapy process transparent by naming or commenting on it. I always followed Brent's lead in taking us to that level of in-session intimacy. As I observed Brent's growing confidence, I found myself trusting more and more the Kohutian (1977, as cited by Pollack, 1990) maxim of simply accepting the client's use of the therapist and the therapy relationship for a possibly un-named and unspoken reparative resource (see Chessick, 1993).

TERMINATION PROCESS: CONTAINING THE SADNESS

After the disclosures about his recent sexual activity, Brent told me that he thought he should get tested for HIV. He said that he felt "relieved" that he had shared the details of his "sexual escapades" with me but also that he now felt like he could no longer deny or avoid the "reality" of the risks that accompanied his behaviors. In our next session, his mood was notably sad, and we discussed the potential irony in his "getting better" on the one hand and the potential for him to have contracted a life-threatening disease, on the other. He simply reiterated the mixture of relief he felt to be finally fully known to someone ("I'm so relieved that I finally got this all out") and the sense of "sadness" he felt at having acknowledged this "unhealthy and self-destructive" part of himself to me. I followed his use of the word *sad* and noted that the sadness was more accessible and less difficult for him to feel.

In the session after he got tested for HIV, he told me about his office visit and how it made him feel. He said he could not help but laugh as he walked out of the office thinking "here I was, someone who had taken on this therapy to learn more about my own psychology, and now my own psychology will probably wind up killing me in the end before I really get it figured out." We both had an uneasy laugh about this and acknowledged how sad it would be if that were to happen. We sat in silence for a short time, nodded at each other, and then ended the session.

In our next meeting, Brent told me that his test was negative and that again he was both relieved and yet challenged by the inescapable conclusion that he held within himself a deeply self-destructive dynamic that he did not yet fully understand. I told him I had worried about the outcome and was extremely happy that the test was negative. We each expressed relief that he had "survived."

After the intensity of the HIV testing and the waiting for the results subsided, Brent returned to a consideration of one of his main presenting problems for our work together—his career choice. He had moved away from preparing for what he considered to be a rather isolating and self-absorbed career as an academic and had plunged into pursuit of a medical career. He was now questioning this choice, questioning his need to "help" others and to "be a caring person." He wondered aloud whether this was truly a valid motivation for choosing a career.

Although he continued to excel in the training he was obtaining and was enjoying it a great deal, the actual work of the EMT in particular and the medical professionals in general triggered an insight into his own family dynamics. In playing the rescuer role as an EMT, he told me he recognized how the "abuser–victim–rescuer" patterns were playing out for him in this work. He now doubted the validity of his motivations and wondered whether there could be a self-destructive component to his choice of work and the role he was playing, just as there had been a self-destructive component to his sexual acting out.

I told him that I thought all career choices contained an element of individual psychology that reflected a person's motivations, values, and personal and interpersonal needs. I told Brent that as long as he had awareness of the role his own family upbringing played in his choice of work, he would be able to channel his energy into being a "caring" and "helpful" person and would not replay one of the roles of the victim–abuser–rescuer triad. Brent appeared relieved by this reassurance, and we continued discussing his work experiences.

Our next few sessions were relatively quiet. Brent reported with pride that he had finished up his first EMT course and was now planning on enrolling for some premedical courses to prepare his applications for medical school. He had started dating a woman he had met at a local coffeehouse, and he felt this was going very well. He began to voice his thought that maybe we were winding up our sessions and that maybe he did not need to come back. After a total of 45 sessions, we agreed that we could probably take a break and planned to have 2 more sessions in order to "wrap up."

These last two sessions felt anticlimactic to me. Anticipating the end of our therapy relationship, I found myself wondering how Brent would handle this loss. How would he and I manage to bring closure to what felt to me like an undeniable, but largely unspoken, emotional connection? As we moved into these last two sessions, Brent and I discussed what had happened in his therapy. He recalled the image of carrying a pack on his back, and how he felt the weight had been redistributed and was now easier to bear.

This image of a young man carrying a loaded pack on his back as he makes his way down the path of life gave me a great deal of satisfaction. There is a masculine element to the image that we both acknowledged—a solitary journey, at times painful and difficult, and requiring the journeyman to occasionally stop and shift the weight in his load before he can continue. We agreed that our therapy had represented this process and that Brent was ready to carry on by himself now. I thought to myself he had "used" our relationship as he needed at this time in his life and was now ready to venture forth. I restrained my impulse to seek my own gratification by querying him about the importance of our therapy relationship and what it had meant to him. His growth and the confidence he now carried spoke for itself.

Our goodbye was warm and affectionate, a testament to the strength of our connection. I looked Brent in the eye and said "Well, I guess we don't need to schedule another meeting, do we?" We looked at each other and shook hands for the last time and then embraced somewhat awkwardly. We patted each other on the back a few times and then broke our embrace and said goodbye. After he departed my office, I felt sadness at ending our work but a great feeling of satisfaction and accomplishment knowing that he was ready to go it alone now.

About 3 years after our sessions ended, I received an unexpected e-mail from Brent giving me an update on his activities. He had gained entrance to a medical school in New England and had just started classes. He said he now felt enthusiastic about this career choice and that he had been able to manage the preparatory science classes with ease once he had resolved his doubts about being a "caring person." He had become engaged to the woman he had met at a coffeehouse and thanked me for the time we had spent together. I sent him an e-mail reply that I was happy for him and congratulated him on his successes, wished him well, and invited him to contact me anytime he was in town again.

COMMENTARY ON FINAL SESSIONS

This final phase of treatment afforded Brent an opportunity to delve deeper into his own psychological dynamics and to explore them as they related to his initial concerns about his career choice. The sessions during which we encountered Brent's continuing sexual misadventures and, later, his decision to get tested for HIV provided material that was rich in existential meaning. The encounter with death (through the prospect of having contracted HIV), the owning of responsibility for the behaviors that led to these dilemmas, and the opportunity to sift down to the least common denominator of what gives life value were all very meaningful discussions for us in our therapy journey.

Navigating the terrain of grief and loss was a central theme in Brent's therapy. Although not always the manifest text of our sessions, I always viewed Brent's struggles as designed to offset what we came to understand as a damaging, unsupportive upbringing. His desire to be a "caring person" and his willingness to work hard at doing the right thing in spite of his fears and anxieties were powerful forces against a self-destructive, regressive pull that threatened to engulf him and drag him down into repeating the dysfunctional patterns to which he was exposed as a young boy. At times, his grief and sadness were palatable, and at other times, they were a mere shadow in our conversations.

Stiver and Miller (1997) noted that it is important to move from depression—that state of powerless, hopeless, lethargic inactivity—to sadness in treating depression in women. Sadness signifies a loss—loss of connection, loss of an object, loss of status, loss of esteem. I think that in this therapy with Brent, we navigated a pathway through loss that contained anger, his deep self-loathing and "depression," his recognition of the losses and disconnections he experienced through his life, and his deeply held wish for connection through being a "caring person" and finding a career in which he could realize this wish. Throughout this process, Brent struggled with the sadness he felt at recognizing these disavowals and disconnections. At first, his struggle was nonverbal, manifest in his characteristic deep breathing and rocking in his chair. Later, this struggle was verbalized in our discussions about carrying the pack of suffering on his back and of having to rearrange the weight in the pack while moving ahead. At the end of our work together, we were able to acknowledge sadness openly in our conversations.

REFLECTIONS ON STRUGGLING FOR SADNESS

All humans experience loss. How a person copes with loss is probably determined by multiple forces. Culturally derived gender role norms play an important part in determining how a man copes with loss and how he comes to manage the emotions associated with loss. To the extent that a man has adopted what might be considered traditional masculine gender role norms, he will experience discomfort with the sadness associated with loss.

This discomfort may compel a man to truncate or abort the necessary psychological processes associated with mourning. This discomfort also may help propel a man to seek help with this process. A relational, loss-focused psychotherapy for men that is empathic to the losses and works toward uncovering the grief and sadness associated with these losses will help complete a natural grief process and prevent some men from resorting to less healthy coping mechanisms such as workaholism, substance abuse, or violence.

QUESTIONS FROM THE EDITORS

1. *What types of gender-based stereotypes were you aware of in counseling this client? How did that impact your therapy with this client?*

Probably one of the most compelling stereotypes I was aware of in working with Brent was the stereotype that a male client who was taking Kung Fu and honing his "aggression," and training in a profession (EMT) that I (incorrectly) perceived to be preferred by "real men" would find little of value in therapy or in the therapy process. Over our sessions, as I got to know Brent and to appreciate his complex psychological makeup and his sensitivity, I learned that this was, indeed, a stereotype that was unfounded. I simply "hung in" with him as he used the therapy relationship as he needed at the time.

Our therapy sessions were not devoted to a great deal of "processing" our relationship. We were more focused on Brent's goals and what kept him from achieving his goals. I liked this aspect of our work, and think that it reinforces the sentiment that Pollack (1990) describes in the quote I used in the text of the chapter about how clients silently (nonverbally) use the therapist and the therapy relationship in service of their own reparative process. I think this happened with Brent.

2. How did your own gender role issues influence your work with this client?

As noted, I think I held some gender role stereotypes about what kinds of men could make use of therapy, namely those that were more like me than not like me. Although Brent and I forged a very intimate connection, he is not a man I would probably be friends with outside the therapy room. Again, I think that my own process of breaking down this gender-based stereotype was an important aspect I have taken from our therapy.

3. Looking back on the case, knowing what you know now, would you change the way you worked with this client?

In retrospect, it could not have come out any better. The only thing I might have changed would be to have stated more directly how the therapy had changed me as we terminated. But then, the termination felt to me like it fully reflected what our therapy had been—not explicitly personal, yet very intimate and transformative for each of us.

4. How did you address his sexual behavior without shaming him? Do you have a paradigm about male sexuality that you work from?

As I noted in the chapter, I tried to stay "neutral." This does not mean detached or disengaged but rather it means that I did not attribute any particular meaning or significance to his revelations about his sexual behavior. I worked with him to put words on the meaning of these experiences for him. I think that by working with Brent to verbalize what his sexual misadventures meant to him I found a way to address the behavior without shaming him. If there is a paradigm about male sexuality that I work from, it would be that men experience and express themselves sexually in myriad ways. Stereotypes and culturally derived expectations reflect only one part of a man's sexual learning and experience. Sexuality and sexual behavior are a microcosm of individual psychology and psychodynamics and reflect the value of relationships in the individual's life as they are played out in a man's sexual values and behavior.

SUGGESTED RESOURCES

Bergman, S. (1995). Men's psychological development: A relational perspective. In R. F. Levant & W. S. Pollack (Eds.), *A new psychology of men* (pp. 68–90). New York: Basic Books.

Chodorow, N. (1999). *The power of feelings.* New Haven, CT: Yale University Press.

Rabinowitz, F., & Cochran, S. (2002). *Deepening psychotherapy with men.* Washington, DC: American Psychological Association.

Yalom, I. D. (1980). *Existential psychotherapy.* New York: Basic Books.

REFERENCES

Bergman, S. J. (1995). Men's psychological development: A relational perspective. In R. F. Levant & W. S. Pollack (Eds.), *A new psychology of men* (pp. 68–90). New York: Basic Books.

Chessick, R. (1993). *Psychology of the self and the treatment of narcissism.* Northvale, NJ: Jason Aronson.

Cochran, S., & Rabinowitz, F. (1996). Men, loss, and psychotherapy. *Psychotherapy, 33,* 593–600.

Gilbert, L. A., & Scher, M. (1999). *Gender and sex in counseling and psychotherapy.* Needham Heights, MA: Allyn & Bacon.

Lerner, H. (1980). Internal prohibitions against female anger. *American Journal of Psychoanalysis, 40,* 137–147.

Pollack, W. S. (1990). Men's development and psychotherapy: A psychoanalytic perspective. *Psychotherapy, 27,* 316–321.

Pollack, W. S. (1995). No man is an island: Toward a new psychoanalytic psychology of men. In R. F. Levant & W. S. Pollack (Eds.), *A new psychology of men* (pp. 33–67). New York: Basic Books.

Stiver, I., & Miller, J. B. (1997). From depression to sadness in women's psychotherapy. In J. Jordan (Ed.), *Women's growth in diversity* (pp. 217–238). New York: Guilford Press.

6

THAWING THE ICE MAN: COPING WITH GRIEF AND LOSS

FREDRIC E. RABINOWITZ

"Up against the wall" is how most of my male clients come into their first therapy sessions, regardless of the specific problem they are encountering. Although some may act cool, together, or rational, I know that they would not be in my office if something "big" had not happened to them. Externalizing and distracting tactics that normally keep a man in equilibrium are stymied. Work, sex, exercise, television, religion, drugs, or alcohol is not effective. Rational problem-solving methods that normally contain and fix dilemmas in the external world do not seem to apply. Men who are not feeling successful, upbeat, strong, attractive, or interpersonally savvy feel shame about not meeting the socially accepted ideals of manhood. Instead of expressing openly their conflicts to a therapist, many men revert to a frozen, emotionally paralyzed version of themselves, what I call the "Ice Man."

The Ice Man often has its origins in traditional male socialization. O'Neil (1981), Pleck (1995), and others described a male culture that emphasizes power, control, strength, and stoicism that are so powerful, pervasive, and blinding that men have little awareness about how or why their lives seem so strained and emotionally frozen. Many men vaguely recall a life of childhood exuberance in which there was a strong and wide-ranging movement of passion and interest in the world. As adults, they find it difficult to recapture this flow of experience except temporarily, and often through addictive behavior. It is not uncommon in my practice to find men with little vocabulary to describe their inner world except for phrases like "I'm not happy with my life or the people in it." When I ask how long this has been going on, most reply that it seems to have always been there but that they thought they could beat it or wait it out. When I ask how they tried to beat it, most refer to ignoring it through sheer willpower, changing jobs, or changing partners, or through drinking, drugs, or sex (see Cooper, Frone, Russell, & Muldar, 1995; Real, 1997).

Ironically, seeking help or talking about one's discomfort, depression, or desperation is usually a very last resort. The "rules of manhood" remind men that it is wrong to ask for help because it implies weakness and a failure of the self-sufficient ideal (Keen, 1991). A partner or spouse may have been a man's "sounding board," yet when an inner conflict is so entwined with one's primary relationship, it seems to shut off this avenue of expression. An extramarital affair might temporarily provide the outlet a man seeks, but it is not too long before this relationship begins to mirror the problematic ones in his life. Before psychotherapy is considered an option, some men in conflict consult a family physician or psychiatrist, who prescribes antidepressants or antianxiety medication to balance mood. This does not address the psychological elements contributing to inner conflict. It seems that most often a partner's urging, a separation or divorce, legal troubles stemming from violence or addiction, or a traumatic loss are what finally push men reluctantly into my office.

MELTING THE ICE THROUGH A DEEPENING THERAPY APPROACH

I know the Ice Man personally. It has taken many years of reversing my male training to rediscover the emotional self that lay trapped under a thick layer of cultural ice. I tried alcohol and drugs to break through and found glimpses of a self that was just barely out of reach. I attached myself to emotionally intense women in the hopes of having them pull me out of my numbness. It was not until I encountered my fears through various forms of psychotherapy that I started to deal with what I was running from. My neediness, dependency, vulnerability, and aloneness were my demons. Only by engaging in a process of embracing and feeling these very real aspects of myself in a safe environment could I regain the energy, spontaneity, and aliveness that came when I was not putting all my energy into defending against the fears.

Sam Cochran and I (Rabinowitz & Cochran, 2002) developed a deepening therapy approach with men to "melt the ice" and reconnect them with their inner experience. I am indebted to the work of many master theorists and clinicians who provided both theory and technique, including but not limited to Freud's (1917/1961) framework of the unconscious, Kohut's (1977) description of the narcissistic wounds of self, Rogers's (1961) unconditional positive regard and acceptance, Perls's (1969) creativity in working with clients, Pollack's (1995) ideas about the impact of early loss and trauma on boys, O'Neil's (1981) pioneering work with masculine gender role conflict, Yalom's (1980) existential perspective, and Lowen's (1975) emphasis on engaging the body in therapy. I have also been influenced by my own individual and group therapy experiences as a client in Gestalt, psychodynamic, Jungian, existential, and bioenergetic therapies. These therapeutic encounters have demonstrated to me the power of psychotherapy in its many forms and left me with a creative and flexible approach to working with men.

The deepening approach itself uses a wide range of techniques to explore the trauma or wound that brings a man to treatment. The realms of interpersonal dependence, the management of grief and loss experiences, the shaping of masculine specific self-structures, and a man's preference for doing as opposed to being are major themes that are addressed throughout the therapy process (Rabinowitz & Cochran, 2002).

Any man who has crossed the unconscious obstacle course into my office deserves my appreciation for making it this far. I might say, "I know this feels like you have failed, but honestly I see you being here as an act of courage. Most men are too afraid to look at themselves in any depth." I want my clients to know that I understand how difficult and shameful it must feel to have to seek help. I listen to the nuances of his words and nonverbal actions, I try to speak his language, self-disclose relevant information about myself, and normalize the interaction so it does not feel so sterile and clinical.

Recently, while my office building was going through remodeling, the most wonderful opportunities arose to normalize my initial encounters with male clients. Before proceeding to the consulting room, I would take them on a brief tour of the construction site in its unfinished, raw state. Torn down walls, exposed framing, and broken-off plaster were apt metaphors for the reconstruction project each man was going through in his own life. Not only did most of my clients use the imagery in describing themselves later in our sessions, it also gave us a chance to have "normal" conversations about 2 × 4 boards, drywall, and building plans that more closely matched traditional male interaction norms. It also seemed to lower my clients' and my initial anxiety level about being intimate and vulnerable in a relationship with another man. It felt like it made me more "real" and the therapy process more tangible.

It does not take long for me to learn how a man expresses himself emotionally and, in particular, how he handles grief and sadness. Male prohibition on expressing sadness leaves many men repressing these emotions, even when they have encountered significant losses. Many of the symptoms that men bring to therapy, including depression, anxiety, anger, and frustration, can be tied to loss experiences that have never been talked about or consciously acknowledged as being important.

Before proceeding to the central case, I would like to give an example of how a deepening approach to psychotherapy can "melt" some of the core issues for a man. Len, a 48-year-old man, presented his main concern as his worry that he was being non-empathic to his third wife, who had given him this feedback over the course of several years. When I probed for signs of his not having empathy, I instead found a man who was perceptive and very "in tune" with his wife's emotions, maybe too much so. He was in therapy to show her that he was working on himself as she wished he would. As we talked about his past, Len revealed that he had grown up in a family without overt verbal or physical affection. He had never learned to gauge if he was accurate in his perceptions, leaving him vulnerable to the criticism that brought him into treatment and that had cost him his two earlier marriages. What was more revealing was that Len grew sad when I asked him to talk about his ex-wives, his children from previous marriages, and his early childhood memories. For Len, therapy was really about "not losing" another relationship. He had been wounded badly in the interpersonal realm.

How a male client defines himself as a man almost always emerges in our sessions. I wanted to know how he has incorporated the values of his family, religion, culture, and media into his self-definition of masculinity. Each man is different in these elements, but it is important to understand what he faces internally and externally when he enters the realms that ask him to act in the proscribed ways of manhood. In a later session, Len revealed that he was feeling unhappy with other aspects of his life as well. He had been "downsized" from his job as an executive at a large corporation and was now working as a "paper pusher" for a small company, earning less than half of his former salary. He acknowledged that he felt he had been emasculated at work and at home and was not sure how he could go on living this way. Apart from the loss of prestige and income, Len also was dealing with his internalized judgment about manhood. By exploring how he perceived himself as a man, he was more open to redefining his self-concept and throwing out that which no longer worked for him.

I also look at how a man handles his life situations in terms of being and doing. Traditional masculine socialization teaches men to act, problem solve, and do something when there is a problem. Men are less likely to "be" with a problem than are women. Being requires a more process-oriented, contemplative, inward focus (Rabinowitz & Cochran, 2002). It seems important in my therapy with men to incorporate "doing" in the form of physical exercises and active interventions to help with learning how to attend and be aware of how one is in a "being" sense. As a part of our therapy, I encouraged Len to hit the punching bag to express his frustration about his job. His anger changed to sadness and eventually to an insight that he might have had some responsibility in losing his position at his former work. By holding back and worrying about how he was doing, Len realized that he had let others take advantage of him. He felt more like a victim than a person in charge of his own life. Therapy eventually moved from discovering how he was feeling to what options he had foreclosed and finally to how he could take a more creative approach to his life.

THE ICE MAN COMETH TO PSYCHOTHERAPY: THE CASE OF BILL

Bill, a ruggedly handsome, 60-year-old man, arrived 10 minutes early for his therapy session. This was not his first-ever session, but it was his first appointment with me in 10 years. I was feeling a bit unsettled, knowing that the last time I had seen Bill, he seemed content in life. I like happy endings and something told me that he was not here to tell me about his joy. Fifteen years ago, Bill and his wife Maureen consulted me. They were having marital problems in the aftermath of their 11-year-old son Andrew's horrific death at the hands of a drunk driver. As a parent myself, this was a worst-case scenario of what life could dish up.

For 2 years, Bill and Maureen had tried to keep life "normal" for their daughter Christy, who was 8 years old at the time of Andrew's death. For the family, *normal* was defined as having a consistent and rigidly followed daily schedule with little free time to float into their grief. Christy was involved in several extracurricular activities beyond school. Maureen maintained her job as a teacher, waking up early and working late into the night on lesson planning and homework. Bill owned an auto and truck specialty supply store in town. He arrived at work at 6:30 a.m. and came home at 7:00 p.m. each night. Outside of work, the family plans revolved around Christy's soccer, softball, and swimming schedules after school and on weekends. In the months before Bill and Maureen came to therapy, Christy started having academic problems at school and began to see a child therapist. The therapist picked up on the conflict in the household and referred Bill and Maureen for marital counseling.

In that first session 15 years ago, my initial impression of Bill was that he was an Ice Man. Despite his strong, fit, suntanned exterior, Bill was stiff and inarticulate. His eyes darted to his wife whenever I asked him a question. He only spoke when asked a direct question, and even then, his answers were short two- or three-word sentences. I recall asking him, "How are you handling your grief?" "Okay, I guess," he replied. Maureen, who was hot, angry, and expressive, then shot him a disgusted look: "Tell the therapist how you avoid me and never want to talk about anything real." The tension when the two of them were in the consulting room was palpable. I consciously braced myself against her hostile accusations toward Bill, who looked like he was going to splinter and break. I understood from my own experience with emotionally intense partners the desire to lay low and avoid as much conflict as possible. Bill did not feel safe in his marriage, and I could see why. Maureen was ready to blowtorch anyone who got in her way. Before the tragedy, Bill relied on her assertiveness and emotional intensity to guide him. Now it was being turned toward him.

In one exchange after Bill had spoken about his desire to ride his mountain bike or go surfing, I said, "Bill, it seems like your grief is more internal and only comes out when you are alone." Before Bill could respond, Maureen interjected, "That is such bullshit. You men are just afraid to express yourselves. Quit supporting his ineptitude, Fred." I liked her emotional energy but was disturbed by how shut down Bill became in her fiery presence. I felt like arguing with her and tried to get her to listen to Bill's pain, but she was quite caught up in her own. I knew she felt betrayed by God and wanted a place to vent at what a cruel and unfair world this was. I hardly knew what Bill was thinking and feeling. After 12 sessions, Maureen decided that she would rather be in individual therapy with a female therapist. She was angry at her husband, at me, and at men in general. She did not want to work on her marriage when she felt she was getting so little back from her husband. I felt a sense of relief in referring her to a colleague who worked well with women.

Because he was so emotionally dependent on his wife, I was afraid Bill would walk away from therapy and the possibility of working through his grief. I offered to see him individually.

"I know there has been a lot of pressure on you to express yourself in here. I know you are feeling a lot. It might be easier to talk if we go at your own pace," I said.

Bill hesitated but then said, "I have more to say."

"I know. Let's give it a try," I replied.

I felt relieved when he showed up at his first individual session. I was fearful that his ambivalence would keep him away. Our individual session felt entirely different than the couples work we had done. I asked Bill to talk to me about his daughter, about his business, and about his mountain biking and surfing. I wanted to give him a chance to tell me how he was dealing with his life. Unlike his wife in her current state, I was nonjudgmental and supportive. He had a lot to say. Although it was not deep emotional sharing at first, it was a good description of how he coped with his life. He appreciated his daughter, who was probably his biggest emotional support. He was happy with his business. He enjoyed solving the daily problems and had good relationships with his employees and customers. His favorite activity was to take his mountain bike into the local hills and become physically exhausted. He also liked to go to the beach and surf, an activity he had done since he was a teenager to get away from the conflicts and demands of his life. When I asked him to talk about his wife, he grew restless and had little to say.

"You met her. You see how she is. I honestly can't stand to look her in the eyes. She is just mean."

I asked him if she had always been like this, and he replied, "She has always been assertive and a control freak, but Andrew's death really threw her over the edge."

"What about you? How did Andrew's death change you?" I asked.

"I used to be pretty happy-go-lucky. I thought I was the luckiest man in the world. I had two beautiful kids, my own business and then bam, it all goes to hell. How have I changed? I guess I'm quieter and more humble. I get paranoid really easy. I'm suspicious for no reason at all. I want to escape more than ever."

"Escape from what?" I asked, knowing that his description of a perfect world had been permanently shattered.

"I can't put it into words. It's like a huge empty hole in me that seems to never go away. It's like I am paper thin and could be sucked away by a gust of wind."

Bill's description chilled me. To feel so insubstantial and lost made me lose my own bearings in that moment. Intellectually, I knew it was important for him to feel this emptiness, but on an emotional level, I felt like I was on a cruise into the underworld. Bill and I met individually every week for 6 months. I worked with him on identifying where in his body he was feeling sensations related to his life's circumstances. Bill began to speak about his own childhood. His father had been verbally and physically abusive toward him, leaving him quiet, powerless, and damaged. He connected Maureen's tirades at him to the paralysis he felt when his father would yell and hit him and his brothers. I noted to Bill that his silence was really masking a cauldron of smoldering anger he was afraid to express. Maureen had the rage for both of them. He smashed a tennis racquet I keep in the office on pillows while expressing his anger at his father and wife for their lack of support and hostility toward him. He twisted a towel I handed him as he was talking about his memories of his son to release tension, frustration, and his deep sadness. Bill was encouraged to speak with Andrew, using the Gestalt empty chair technique.

Bill also discussed his relationship with his mother, who had been unreliable, ditzy, and yet verbally loving. Bill cried for the first time since he was a boy after recalling a dream in which he and his son spent time together in the mountains. He wept for most of the session. His huge body heaved and convulsed. Huge tears flooded his face. I felt my own heaviness as he cried. My own repressed feelings of sadness around lost time with my own father were activated by his grief. My eyes watered as his poured. We hardly talked during this session, communing in a deep sadness. The following week he reported feeling more energy and an easier time sleeping.

Although Bill was thriving in individual therapy, I believed that group support from other men could be incredibly powerful for him. To be with other men who were working to recover their emotional selves might facilitate his journey. I mentioned the possibility of Bill joining the men's group that I co-led with two other therapists (see Rabinowitz, 2001). Bill perked up with interest. He was ready to talk on a deeper level with other men about life. Although he enjoyed his work relationships, they tended to be more superficial and focused on the tasks that needed to be done. Bill was interviewed and admitted to the group. He tapered off on his individual sessions while he attended the weekly group. Initially, Bill just listened to the other men. When he felt safe enough, he shared his story of losing his son. Another man in the group had also lost a child, which led to a strong emotional connection between the two. When the group explored their families of origin, Bill seemed to expand his understanding of his own childhood. He expressed anger not only at his father but also at his mother for not being reliable. He was able to role play several childhood scenarios. Men from the group played psychodramatic parts in his life, gave him support, and helped him work through the issues that were unresolved. Bill cried when talking about his older brother, who abandoned him and the family during his early teen years. He also felt the humiliation and fear in a more intense way than he had previously allowed himself before around his father's abusive behavior.

Over time, Bill became one of the senior members of the men's group. For 5 years, he took part in the group and was looked upon as a veteran by the cadre of new members that entered the group each fall. It was not uncommon for the ex–Ice Man to confront incoming Ice Men on their lack of emotion when sharing. He did this is in a loving and gentle way, understanding fully the fear and shame these men brought with them. I enjoyed his role as the emotional leader of the group. His survival and working through of his loss gave him credibility. As a man reclaiming his inner self, he facilitated others to take emotional risks within the group setting.

In the second year of the group, Maureen filed for divorce. He spent much of that year expressing his fear, anger, and hope about being on his own. The theme of taking care of himself and being there for his daughter dominated his input in the group. Other men in the group supported Bill through his custody battle with his wife. He was appreciated and honored as a single father by the group members.

By his 5th year of the group, Bill seemed to be less of an initiator and more of a reactor to other men's issues. He was supportive but brought up less of his own material. This paralleled him entering a new love relationship. He was swept away by Lauren, a woman 10 years younger than he, who seemed to be everything Maureen was not. As I have observed with other men who find "love," there often is less motivation for emotional work. Being in love replaces the existential angst that pushes us toward creative living and deep awareness. The emotional high leaves many men with an illusion of eternal bliss and a sense that they no longer need intimate relationships with others (Yalom, 1980). Bill let the group know 2 months before it was ending for the year that he and Lauren were getting married. He missed four of the last eight groups before the usual summer hiatus, but he was still supported and admired by his peers. He let everyone know that he would not be coming back to group next year. "I think I've pretty much worked through my issues and I have found someone who I can be myself with," he declared on the last night. I was choked up to see Bill leave but rationalized to myself that he deserved some joy in his life after so much sadness. I wished him the best and told him to be in touch if he ever felt the need to come back to therapy.

10 YEARS LATER

So 10 years later, at age 60, Bill was back. As he took his chair, I could see that he had aged. He was still quite handsome and in good shape, but I could see sadness in the wrinkle lines on his face. I felt an immediate closeness with Bill, like it had been a few months, not 10 years, since we had last talked. Instantly, the story of his life flashed back into my consciousness. I could feel a heaviness in the room that was not there before he arrived. I was curious about his return and knew in my gut it was something big.

"I didn't think I'd be seeing you again in this way," he started.

"You mean in therapy?" I asked.

"Yes. I thought I had dealt pretty well with Andrew's death all those years ago, but . . . " (he hesitated).

"But what?" I asked, wondering whether there had been another tragedy in his life.

"I've been thinking about him again and . . ."

"And . . . "

"It makes me feel like life is just one bad thing after another and it isn't likely to get any better." He said this with a glazed, frozen expression reminiscent of his Ice Man persona.

"You sound pretty down," I replied, noticing the flatness in myself as he spoke.

"I'm getting by. My daughter Christy is doing well. She just graduated from the university and is going out of state for physical therapy graduate school. I wish she was closer, but you can't have everything." Bill had a monotone voice. The absence of warmth and emotion told me something must be terribly wrong.

"Are you feeling sad about something else Bill?

"I'm not sure I can stay strong right now. When I saw you before I really learned to accept things the way they were. Life just was the way it was. You do the best you can everyday."

"And now?"

"Everything seems so out of control. I've never felt this close to giving up."

"What is it? Can you say?" I was impatient and not used to Bill being so emotionally constipated. It was as if his inner world was again covered by an icy layer of fear.

"I feel embarrassed even to tell you. Lauren is leaving me. I never thought I'd have to go through another divorce. She's not happy, and I haven't helped her enough."

"I'm sorry to hear this. You really loved her. What do you mean you haven't helped her enough?" So this was his shameful secret, a recapitulation of his emotional abandonment. I felt really bad for him.

"I feel so damn stupid. Why didn't I learn something from my first marriage? I was just fooling myself."

"Fooling yourself about what?" I asked. I was genuinely baffled by his self-deprecation. Why had he become so unraveled? Why was he referring back to his first marriage? What happened to his emotional strength? How had that critical self found its way into the executive mansion of his psyche?

"That I could be in a relationship, and I would be accepted for who I was," he said in a tone of anger.

"What's so foolish about wanting that? We all want that."

"I trusted her with my heart, and she put a hole in it."

His words made me feel like I had witnessed an assassination or an emotional goring.

"She betrayed you?"

"She told me I was too much for her. I had too many problems, too much crap in my life. She didn't want to deal with it, especially now that I have cancer."

"You have cancer? Oh wow. What kind? How long have you had it?" Now I was unraveled. This new information about cancer overwhelmed me and added a new level of emotional complexity to the situation. Now we were talking life and death. I didn't know what to say except to ask questions.

"It's prostate cancer. I've known for a few months now."

"You must be overwhelmed," I said, feeling overwhelmed myself.

"I could probably handle the cancer if I had some support right now. Lauren is the only one who knows. I haven't told my daughter or anyone else. Lauren and I were fighting before this so it just added gasoline on the fire. I didn't tell her at first. I thought, Why worry her? If you catch it early enough then it shouldn't be that big a deal."

"But you started to act differently?"

"That's why I am here. I started to pull away. I've been off by myself again. Lauren seems pissed off when I am around her, and so I've been out on my bike alone, a lot."

"You want to be pushing her away? I would have thought the cancer might have brought you closer together." I was being rational and, of course, relationships are not usually rational. I was still trying to get a bearing on Bill's situation to make sense of it.

"Her father and brother died of cancer. I thought it would make it worse. I thought, She won't handle this very well."

"So you were protecting her and hoping it wouldn't affect the relationship." I think I was starting to understand Bill's actions.

"Bingo. I was wrong. I made it worse. I don't know why I went back to being the Ice Man.'"

"We used to talk about the Ice Man appearing whenever you were protecting yourself. What are you protecting yourself from right now?" I asked.

This was an important connection to make for Bill. In the past, the Ice Man persona was a trigger for him to pay attention to what was bothering him that he did not want to deal with. Bill used to escape into his work and exercise to meet the rising tide of uncomfortable emotion. Even though he intellectually knew it was important to express himself to those close to him, he hesitated. He would rather find ways to distract himself than to deal directly with the emotional consequences of his life predicament. Instead of reaching out, he withdrew. Instead of stopping to be with his feelings, he felt compelled to run away as far as he could.

"My anger?" he asked, sheepishly.

"Say more about your anger. Here is a rolled up towel to squeeze."

Bill took the towel and squeezed it with all his energy. All I could hear were grunts coming from him.

"Bill, put some words on it."

"I don't deserve this crap!" he shouted.

"What don't you deserve?"

"To be treated like a friggin' leper."

"Who is treating you like a leper?"

"Lauren is. My father did. My mother did. Friggin' Maureen. God did. What is so wrong with me?" Bill's chest began to heave and finally tears appeared, which turned to large sobs.

"It's okay Bill. It's okay to feel your pain. Let it out. You've been really hurt."

"I thought I was stronger than this."

"This is strong, Bill. Most men don't let themselves feel the pain. Most men don't cry. You are letting yourself feel what's real for you right now. Nothing wrong with that." I felt relief as Bill's tears rolled down his face. He had been holding back so much. I felt good that he had returned to therapy to deal with his pain rather than withdrawing even further.

Although Bill challenged his stoicism during his time in therapy before, he, like many men, still felt the pressure in his everyday life to appear strong and not complain about his pain. The traditional male gender role and the introjected critic he inherited from his father exerted a tremendous influence on how Bill judged himself in his handling of his life situation. To return to therapy was to re-enter the world of vulnerability and to admit that he was not all powerful and in control.

There was still shame for Bill in his return. He believed that he was finished with the painful part of his life when he left the group 10 years earlier. At the time, he thought he did not need the support of other men. Although some of the men in the group tried to convince Bill to be a lifetime group member, he was convinced that his new relationship could take care of his emotional needs. His socialized ambivalence about emotional dependency was split between the group and his new relationship. He believed that the relationship could resolve his long-standing life issues, especially because he was "high" on the love he was receiving.

With Bill's illness, he also began to feel insecure with his identity as a man. Identified as a healthy, strong man, he believed at some level that he was not worthy or lovable if he was weak, dependent, or scared. The cancer served as another wounding, reminding him of his own mortality and stirring up the grief from the multiple losses he had experienced in his life. These included the loss of safety with his mother, a father he could not trust, his brother's abandonment, the loss of Andrew, the divorce from Maureen, his daughter moving away, the loss of support from the men's group, and now the possibility of losing his current relationship. Bill's cancer was the wound that opened the portal to his inner life. It led to the losses, disappointments, and pain, but it also left open the possibility of working through the emotional intensity of his life experiences. The cancer was a catalyst for him to acknowledge his humanness and accept his full view of himself as a mortal man. He believed that Lauren would not accept him with cancer, but this was likely his own projection of self-hate and shame that re-emerged when he did not live up to the masculine ideal.

In the ensuing sessions, Bill's icy exterior started to thaw again. It was much quicker this time. He seemed to pick up where he was when he had left group 10 years earlier, talking with passion and beginning to reexperience himself as whole, despite his cancer and the rift in his relationship. In the sixth session, he recalled another dream about his son, which seemed to drop him into a more emotionally integrated place within himself: "I was mountain biking with Andrew. It was beautiful. I knew it was special that he was with me, but in the dream I didn't know why. He was asking me how I'd been and how I was handling the cancer. He told me not to be afraid. He was watching over me. I began to cry tears of joy and reached out and hugged him. I can feel tears coming right now as I tell you this."

"Stay with your tears. What are they telling you?" I asked.

"It's okay to feel. That's what popped into my head."

"What a wonderful message your son has sent you." I was amazed at his clarity. It resonated with me.

"Yes. It's okay to feel sad about missing him. It's okay to feel joy at being with him in my dreams. It's just okay to be alive and just be real. I don't want to run away or hide anymore."

"How does this feel in your body?" I asked.

"I feel relaxed. I'm not so tight right now."

"Stay with the feeling and enjoy it. It is how you can be when you aren't trying to defend yourself from your pain."

"I'm ready to be more real with Lauren too. She didn't seem so frightening when I looked over at her this morning. I could feel love toward her instead of fear."

"Sounds significant. Did you let her know?"

"Not yet. She was asleep when I left the house, but I want to talk to her when I get back. She's put up with a lot of shit from me and has hung in there. I thought she'd be gone by now, like Maureen."

"You underestimated how much she cares about you?"

"I assumed she wouldn't want to be with me because I was such an emotional burden. Maybe I'm not that bad."

"Maybe you felt like an emotional burden to your parents, but you've worked real hard to know that it is acceptable to have emotional needs. You don't need to be the Ice Man to be accepted."

"I know. It's just such an ingrained part of me to follow the rules of manhood even when I know they make no sense."

"Seems like you've incorporated some of Andrew's advice from your dream to not be so afraid."

"I don't like who I am when I get scared. It's just a shell, not really me. I understand how Lauren would feel turned off by having the shell. When I met her, I was fully me and that is who she loves. It's been a long road back."

By accessing his internalized image of his son, Bill was able to incorporate the message that it was okay to just be. Even though his son, Andrew, had been dead for 17 years, Bill made a psychic space for him that acknowledged Bill's own innocence, as well as a kind and accepting self. Bill's loss had become a psychic gain. Andrew began to replace Bill's parents as introjected keepers of his emotional life. I was also impressed that Bill did not blame or project his harsh, critical self onto Lauren. When he owned his own feelings and psychological dynamics, he no longer had the need to see her as the judge of his badness. It was likely now that she would be able to move toward him without encountering as much of his defensiveness. Finally, I was struck by Bill's awareness of his gender role socialization and the part it has played in preventing him from feeling acceptance of his strong emotional needs. In this session, he had confronted the rules and acknowledged their power in his life. By naming it, he had taken another step to be free from it.

Bill's return to the therapy journey was powerful for me. As a man and as his therapist, I could identify with his pain, his fear, and his desire to pull away. It is often easier to form ice than to swim into what feels like a hot, churning sea of inner madness. Even though no one in the outside world can see the chaotic inner storm, it feels like it might surface into my external life at any moment. As a man, this feels dangerous and out of control, contradicting my masculine training to be calm, rational, and strong. Fortunately, over time I have learned to take the dive into my underworld, trusting that I will re-emerge a more whole and free individual. I believe that Bill thought he could come to me and share his inner anarchy because he sensed I knew what that hot, crazy place felt like inside.

Bill spent 12 sessions with me individually before opting to go back into the men's group for ongoing support. Although the individual focus seemed to help him identify his issues and bring to conscious awareness how his fears were binding him emotionally, Bill realized that it was important to have male friends and confidants who were also working on their inner lives. The group again gave Bill another outlet to get some of his psychological needs met, his frustrations vented, and his emotional wholeness supported. It also seemed to take some of the pressure off his primary relationship to supply him with all of the emotional intimacy he wants in his life. Currently, Bill continues to move fluidly into his grief, his fear, and his pain in the group, as well as the joy, freedom, and openness that comes with being aware and in touch with his inner depth.

WHY I LIKE TO MELT ICE MEN

The case of Bill is a good representation of the kind of work I do with male clients. I enjoy the process of reconnecting a man to his inner world because I know from firsthand experience how invigorating and opening it can be. I know a man would not be in my office if he had not been wounded in a personally significant way. For Bill, the wound of loss was a portal to his emotional depth. It was like an ice-fishing hole that gave him and me access to what churned below.

Although each man has a different configuration of defenses, the therapy process is relatively similar, in my experience. At first, it is important to make an interpersonal connection. This means I must be as real as I can be and not hide behind my therapeutic role and power. I must exude openness and help my male client know that it is not shameful to ask for assistance. My own aliveness and lack of defensiveness serves as a way to subtly debunk the cultural myths of what it means to be a man. Once his story has been told, it is important for me as a therapist to relate to it on a personal level and help him explore the emotional elements that have not been directly stated. I try to encourage each man to develop an emotional vocabulary with words and metaphors that are meaningful to him. At each step, I must show my trustworthiness and acceptance.

Next, I have to be willing to use the "action" mode to ask my male client to take a risk, whether it be squeezing a towel or using a punching bag to express the anger or frustration that has accumulated from his avoidance of his inner world. This usually leads to a sense of freedom and access to sadness and fear that lie beneath the surface. By being fully present and willing to go with each man to the scary and confusing waters of the emotional self, we are able to capture rare and exotic visions and insights not visible from the surface. With Bill, it meant seeing his son in his dreams or finding his voice with his abusive father or wife. Returning to these visions makes them less frightening and eventually leads to a transformation of the self.

I encourage men in this process to find a group of other men who are "fishing" in these waters of emotional depth. Bill found support for his journey in the men's group. There he can be joined on his inner expedition and also serve as a crewmember for others' voyages.

In the end, my life is enriched by each man I meet. His issues trigger my issues. I face not only my inner critic, my frightened self, and my depression but also my courageous hero groping his way through a rich and exhilarating adventure in this life as we work together.

QUESTIONS FROM THE EDITORS

1. What types of gender-based stereotypes were you aware of in counseling this client? How did that impact your therapy with this client?

The most obvious stereotype I encountered initially was of the strong, stoic man who kept himself busy both mentally and physically to avoid dealing with conflict. Bill was very athletic and nearly convinced me that by biking, surfing, and staying in top physical shape, he could rise above his inner conflicts. Once he lost his son and then had cancer, this physical way of handling stress was not sufficient. He also initially relied on his partner to be the "emotional" one in the relationship while he stayed rational and often silent.

In approaching Bill, I made sure that I was genuine, up front, but not too pushy. I went slowly in terms of asking him to self-disclose. The most important aspect of my approach with Bill was to listen nonjudgmentally and to let him know through my actions and words that I would accept and welcome anything he had to say about himself.

2. How did your own gender role issues influence your work with this client?

I have worked hard to look at my own male socialization and overcome the negative elements of withholding emotional expression and always needing to be in control. I grew up playing competitive sports and saw achievement as a way of validating my own masculinity, especially as defined by my father. My dad was very competitive and intense. He taught me that the road to success was paved with hard work and staying ahead of the competition.

My own coping mechanisms mirrored some of Bill's. I like to be athletic, active, and engaged in my environment. When I first met Bill, I did a
little comparison in terms of our levels of physical fitness and attractiveness, but when I saw how hard it was for Bill to express himself, I flashed to
my own past. When I was younger, I was quiet and took few risks in the
emotional realm. Instead of competing with Bill, I identified with him and
wanted to help him break through the ice that had formed over his emotional self.

3. *Looking back on the case, knowing what you know now, would you
change the way you worked with this client?*

My biggest mistake probably came in the couples work I did with Bill
and his wife Maureen. I was ambivalent about confronting Maureen and
stopping her from speaking for Bill. I was paralyzed by her intense emotionality and was hoping that Bill would come to life at some point. Instead she saw
me as colluding with him whenever I focused on his perspective and slowed
down the sessions to include him. If I was to do it again, I might have structured the session so that each of them had a turn and the other had to just
listen and repeat back what he or she had just heard. This would have given
Bill more of a chance to express himself, and it would have been perceived by
Maureen as fair. To be honest, I believe that the trauma that they both had
suffered was so powerful that each of them did need individual therapy to
help work through the grief in their own way. Bill needed unconditional
regard and encouragement. Maureen needed to jump into her anger and rage
in a safe environment.

4. *How do you approach men about working with their bodies? What is
your understanding of how bodywork can help men?*

I believe that the body is integrally connected to the psychological realm.
The body flinches, tenses, and contorts when it has been physically or psychologically impacted by trauma. Muscular armoring occurs much like psychological defenses. A rigid neck or jaw, a tense lower back, fatigue, impo-
tence, and pain sensitivity often are connected to emotional conflict.

Because many men are well-defended intellectually, bodywork can serve
as a powerful shortcut to the emotional self. Many men I see have a limited
vocabulary to describe the inner world of emotion. Some are barely aware of
what they are feeling in reaction to events that have impacted them. Often a
logical, rational explanation overlies the emotional wound. I like to have a
man use his body in some way to express himself. A man need not have the
intellectual vocabulary to "act out" a situation with his body. All he needs to
do is to be encouraged to play out his reaction. For instance, hitting pillows
with a tennis racquet while visualizing a person or situation that stresses him
often results in a release of tension, frustration, and anger. It is not uncommon for a man to then feel his sadness or grief after intensive hitting. This

sadness gives us a way to talk about that which has been lost in his life, whether it be a person, an opportunity, or his innocence.

5. *How do you carry off being a nontraditional man with traditional men?*

Even though I have much to critique about the traditional male role, I admit that I also have a love for many aspects of it. I like to see how traditional men have courageously endured difficult life situations. I admire their toughness and strength. I enjoy competition and the energy it brings into the life of a traditional man. When I first encounter a man, I make sure that I see his strengths before I zero in on his weaknesses. I want to know about his life journey and how he has survived in a world that has not always been kind or supportive to him.

By identifying with his coping and survival skills, I am able to show empathy with who he is. I know what it is like to not be able to express oneself in the way others might like. I listen and try to speak the language of the man I am seeing and make him feel more at ease. Although I am always genuine, I might hold back a bit on my own expressiveness at the start of our time together to give this particular man the space he needs to express himself in his own unique way. The bottom line is that I have an appreciation and curiosity about men. Once we begin to speak personally, the traditional stereotypes usually fall away for me. When I talk to the man behind the fortress walls, I usually feel very connected and linked through our common struggles with relationships, loss, and finding meaning in life.

6. *How do you conceptualize and work with male resistance?*

I perceive male resistance as a trust issue. So much of our male socialization is designed to protect us from being taken advantage of emotionally. To be embarrassed or shamed in front of other boys or men is to be humiliated as "less than" a man. Although many men are extremely emotional and sensitive, they are often prohibited from showing this side of themselves except in a few select situations. The price one pays for crying or expressing one's affection for a male friend is often too high. These vigilant defenses are brought into the therapy room.

It is our job as therapists to help men feel that their inner worlds will not be violated if they are open and honest about how they really think and feel. This means that there will be a testing period in therapy to see whether we are trustworthy. How we react to minor disclosures of conflict and discomfort will determine how fast and how deep our male clients share with us what is real for them. I need to be patient and understanding of the walls they have erected if I am going to be let inside. I must disclose some of myself to let them know it is acceptable to show vulnerability. Regardless of how resistant a man is at the start of treatment, it is important for me to remember that there is often an energetic, emotional, and innocent boy wanting to be heard and accepted for who he is.

SUGGESTED RESOURCES

Brooks, G. R., & Good, G. E. (2001). *The new handbook of psychotherapy and counseling with men*. San Francisco: Jossey-Bass.

Chodorow, N. J. (1999). *The power of feelings*. New Haven, CT: Yale University Press.

Cochran, S. V., & Rabinowitz, F. E. (2000). *Men and depression: Clinical and empirical perspectives*. San Diego, CA: Academic Press.

Conroy, P. (2003). *My losing season*. New York: Bantam Books.

Pollack, W. S., & Levant, R. F. (1998). *New psychotherapy for men*. New York: Wiley.

Rabinowitz, F. E., & Cochran, S. V. (1994). *Man alive: A primer of men's issues*. Pacific Grove, CA: Brooks/Cole.

Reich, W. (1976). *Character analysis*. New York: Pocket Books.

REFERENCES

Cooper, M., Frone, M., Russell, M., & Muldar, P. (1995). Drinking to regulate positive and negative emotions: A motivational model of alcohol use. *Journal of Personality and Social Psychology, 69*, 990–1005.

Freud, S. (1961). Introductory lectures on psychoanalysis. In J. Strachey (Ed. & Trans.), *The standard edition of the complete psychological works of Sigmund Freud* (Vol. 16, pp. 243–448). London: Hogarth Press. (Original work published 1917)

Levant, R. F. (1998). Desperately seeking language: Understanding, assessing, and treating normative male alexithymia. In W. S. Pollack & R. F. Levant (Eds.), *New psychotherapy for men* (pp. 35–56). New York: Wiley.

Keen, S. (1991). *Fire in the belly: On being a man*. New York: Bantam Books.

Kohut, H. (1977). *The restoration of the self*. New York: International Universities Press.

Lowen, A. (1975). *Bioenergetics*. New York: Penguin Books.

O'Neil, J. M. (1981). Patterns of gender role conflict and strain: Sexism and fear of femininity in men's lives. *Personnel and Guidance Journal, 60*, 203–210.

Perls, F. (1969). *Gestalt therapy verbatim*. Moab, UT: Real People Press.

Pleck, J. H. (1995). The gender role strain paradigm: An update. In R. F. Levant & W. S. Pollack (Eds.), *A new psychology of men* (pp. 11–32). New York: Basic Books.

Pollack, W. S. (1995). Deconstructing disidentification: Rethinking psychoanalytic concepts of male development. *Psychoanalysis and Psychotherapy, 12*, 30–45.

Rabinowitz, F. E. (2001). Group therapy for men. In G. R. Brooks & G. E. Good (Eds.), *The new handbook of psychotherapy and counseling with men: A comprehensive guide to settings, problems, and treatment approaches* (Vol. 2, pp. 603–621). San Francisco: Jossey-Bass.

Rabinowitz, F. E., & Cochran, S. V. (2002). *Deepening psychotherapy with men.* Washington, DC: American Psychological Association.

Real, T. (1997). *I don't want to talk about it: Overcoming the secret legacy of male depression.* New York: Fireside Books.

Rogers, C. R. (1961). *On becoming a person.* Boston: Houghton Mifflin.

Yalom, I. D. (1980). *Existential psychotherapy.* New York: Basic Books.

7

FINDING JOSHUA'S SOUL:
WORKING WITH RELIGIOUS MEN

JOHN M. ROBERTSON

How do I conduct therapy with men? Let me count some ways.

First, I tend to avoid using the word *psychotherapy* when talking to men about our work together, especially at the beginning. I prefer to talk about a session as a "consultation," a "meeting," or even a "discussion." My reason is that many men seem to define their value by their successes. They see participating in something called *psychotherapy* as evidence of a failure. So the idea of planning a series of meetings to address a problem seems more acceptable to many men and also seems to free clients earlier to begin talking openly. I use this language even on the phone as we talk about a first appointment.

Second, I look for strengths in a man's approach to life, and I name them when they are evident (e.g., *responsible, clear-thinking, successful, conscientious*). Again, the purpose is to counter the common perception among many men that only the weak call for help. This approach seems to offer considerable relief to some men and allows them to begin addressing an issue with a feeling of confidence and respect. When therapeutically appropriate, I look for ways to redefine a perceived weakness as a strength. For example, "being afraid to commit" can become "patient," "discriminating," or "careful"; "bottle it up" can become "reserved," "still thinking about it," or "concerned about the feelings of others." These strategies are only temporary; I have found that eventually, men want to understand their difficulties with commitment or expressiveness.

Third, I am slow to use confrontive strategies. If a session drifts into a discussion about two competing ideas (mine and his), then I am not being helpful. I would prefer to offer alternative thoughts in a tentative way, thus reducing the possibility that he will think that I am "one-upping" him. If my idea is useful, it will be accepted; if not, it won't. Many men slam their emotional doors shut if I use confrontation too early in our work. I have rarely found it helpful to challenge directly a rationalization that has been in place for many years; the result seems to be resistance and entrenchment.

Fourth, I try to talk about emotions in a masculine-congruent way. I describe emotions as "tools" that can be used to better understand a situation or as "information" that can be used to increase the likelihood of reaching a goal. Conceptually, it makes sense to many men to think of emotions as having a purpose, a function. That is, emotions direct attention to a situation in life that needs to be addressed, and they provide motivation and energy to resolve it. In addition, emotions seem to be more easily acknowledged by traditional men when they are made tangible by emphasizing the bodily sensations that announce their arrival. This suggests to men that emotions are not something to avoid; they are realities that help people adapt more effectively to their worlds. In this way, a man does not have to think he must become "all emotional" or that he must "cry like my wife" to work effectively with me.

Fifth, I take the question, "What can I do about this?" seriously. When a man asks for an action plan, he generally is ready to act. So I talk about creating "an experiment" to "see what might happen" if he were to change his approach. We might develop a plan and practice the new behavior in the consultation room itself (e.g., a stress-management exercise, a behavioral rehearsal). My role is to provide a "menu" of strategies that he might try and then to let him choose and shape his own experiment.

These five approaches represent some of the ways I work with men whose views about gender roles are more traditional. When I think about the development of these ideas, I feel indebted to two persons who first emphasized to me the importance of explicitly acknowledging gender in psychotherapy. Louise Fitzgerald (my first academic mentor) demonstrated to me that a gender-aware career in psychology can combine both research and direct service. Glenn Good (who guided the development of my research skills) has lived a model of masculinity that influences all his roles: He is a deeply involved parent and husband, a generous professor, a careful researcher, an assertive professional, an insightful psychotherapist, and an emotionally available friend. I am forever grateful to both of these pioneering scholars–practitioners in gender role studies.

My theoretical orientation is organized around developmental and constructivist themes. My central assumption about the human experience is that people move through lifelong processes of change. They are constantly adapting to the world around them—biologically, socially, emotionally, and cognitively. Although people are given genetic blueprints that function as a template for many elements of development, life experiences (especially the early ones) strongly influence how they view and interpret the world. Each person moves through this progression with possibilities for flexibility, adaptability, and individuality. From this perspective, it seems appropriate to assume that much of what is described as "gender role" attitudes and behavior is learned. That is to say, men can construct their views of what it means to be masculine, on the basis of their individual developmental trajectories.

Psychological distress (e.g., mood problems, behavioral or interactive difficulties, cognitive confusions) occurs when ordinary developmental processes no longer seem effective in interpreting events or responding to them. In time, these processes can become unproductive or maladaptive (e.g., overly withdrawn, aggressive, or dependent). The result can create bewilderment and emotional pain. But these struggles can also generate an interest in finding new ways of thinking or acting. Again, the implications for gender role behavior are direct: When particular gender role demands contribute to high levels of distress, they can lead to perplexity and a willingness to consider other ways of thinking and being. And that is where psychotherapy can become helpful.

Especially helpful to me in my thinking about human development and constructivism have been Donald Ford (1987), Michael Mahoney (1991, 1995), William Lyddon and John Jones (2001), and Leslie Greenberg and Sandra Paivio (1997). The Dalai Lama with Howard Cutler (1998) has influenced my understanding of human suffering, the value of personal awareness or "being present" in life, and the enduring influence that individual choices have on development. My gender awareness in psychotherapy has been immeasurably enhanced by the work of Gary Brooks, Glenn Good, and Laurie Mintz (Brooks, 1998; Brooks & Good, 2001a, 2001b; Good & Mintz, 2000), and my appreciation for doing therapy with men has been deepened by Fred Rabinowitz and Sam Cochran (2002). Chris Kilmartin (2001) has shown me how the creative arts can widen the understanding of gender.

JOSHUA'S FUNDAMENTAL(IST) PROBLEM

"My father always said that arriving late for an appointment is stealing—the stealing of someone's time." With that comment, Joshua settled into his chair on time for the intake. He stood 2 or 3 inches above 6 feet tall, and appeared to weigh well over 200 pounds. He would have checked "White" from a list of boxes that asked about his ethnic heritage. His shirt was white. His hair, suit, and shoes were black. His presence filled the room, and he immediately took charge of our conversation. He said that he had been thinking about our "initial consultation" and that he wanted to introduce himself. He pulled out a 4 × 6-inch card from his briefcase, saying that he had prepared some notes to give me "some background," and he wanted to make sure he didn't forget something.

Some men begin their first sessions feeling uncomfortable, uncertain. If Joshua felt uneasy, he was not acknowledging it. He gazed at me intently, as though sizing me up. I found myself being the uneasy one, and I noticed that my hands were gripping the arms of my chair. It felt like Joshua wanted to take me on a ride and that my therapy chair was going to be the passenger's seat. From this vantage point, I wondered how I was going to be helpful in ways that kept him in the driver's seat. How could I define his need for control as a strength that he might use in addressing his presenting problems?

He started at the beginning. He reported that he was born into a highly religious home in the rural mountains of one of the southern states. Both of his parents grew up in the same religion. He described his father as a "mountain man" and an "old-time Christian preacher" and his mother as a "housewife" who believed she should not work for pay because she must support her husband's work.

The church, he reported, was known for its conservative beliefs and had established a list of about 30 formal statements of belief that members must accept to belong to the church and "go to heaven." He again reached for his briefcase, pulled out a two-page pamphlet that summarized these beliefs, and handed it to me.

I glanced briefly at the list. Included were such ideas as the return of Jesus Christ to the earth from his current location in a galaxy that was specified by name; a requirement that members pay a certain percentage of their income to the group; the acceptance of a modern-day prophetic leader who had produced a set of rules defining appropriate behavior for members; and prohibitions against certain social behavior, such as playing cards, gambling, dancing, smoking, drinking alcohol, or "doing your own pleasure" on the Lord's Day.

As I looked at this list, my thoughts drifted, and I took a slow, deep breath. Here was another person with "fundamentalist" views of the world. (Even though the word *fundamentalist* has become a pejorative term because of its association with intolerance and even terrorism, I use the term here in its more generic sense to refer to a personal and strict adherence to a set of fundamental beliefs about religious matters.)

How does it happen that people with stories somewhat similar to my own appear in my office? Having been raised in a highly sectarian group that I left as an adult, I knew firsthand how much power this set of beliefs might have for Joshua. Could I be neutral and compassionate? Would my own history get in the way? My reverie was brief. Bracing myself somewhat, I looked up and he continued.

Joshua suggested that I keep the leaflet because we would be referring to it later. For now, at least, we were not going to devote any time to a detailed discussion of ideas in this list. But it was clear—abundantly clear—that he wanted me to understand from the outset that his religious beliefs were central in his life. It was also clear that I would not fully understand him unless I spent some time trying to understand the propositions in the pamphlet, and that I would be reviewing my own history if he actually started therapy.

At this point, I was still unclear about the presenting problem. Why had he come? Most people are ready to start their initial psychotherapy session by describing the reason they made the appointment. Not Joshua. He started by inviting me on board so that he could move through terrain that was important to him. But this was such an unusual start to a session that I did not know what he had come to address. Was he going to present a primarily personal problem? A family problem? A mood problem? A religious problem? I was not sure.

Next, Joshua noted that it was not easy to schedule his first appointment: "I've come here because my wife suggested it." This was much more familiar turf for me. I know that it is very difficult for some men to make a first appointment. But before I could respond to this opening, Joshua pressed onward with his story and returned to religious themes. His presentation, however, softened slightly.

He said that his decision to phone me had been complicated by his belief in God's "chain of command" for the family: Children submit to the mother; the mother submits to the father; the father deferred to Jesus Christ; and Jesus deferred to God the Father. When his wife made a suggestion, therefore, it was heard in this context. As her superior, he was faced with accepting a suggestion from someone lower in the chain of command. And that represented a failure on his part to meet his own responsibility to accurately identify a family problem and solve it himself. "I should have figured this out myself," he said ruefully. "It's my responsibility, not my wife's."

It is difficult to convey the intensity with which this idea was presented. Although it was a religious idea, it was conveyed as a military metaphor. A fleeting image of Joshua as a boot camp sergeant floated by. He spoke with deep conviction, but there was also a barely contained sense of regret. I wondered briefly how I might respond to this ambivalence, but he was not ready to hear me. There was no conversational pause. My hands remained on the arms of my passenger seat.

Joshua continued to explain. The chain-of-command approach had been introduced to him when he was a small boy. His father had described himself as the family's priest, in charge of all aspects of family life, from clothing selection and diet to entertainment and friendship approval. Any disagreement was viewed as insubordination and was subject to various forms of corporal punishment. While recalling these events, he stopped rather abruptly. He looked past me out the window.

"It looks like you are remembering some things." I said.

"I am." Joshua then offered several other reflections about his father, who he described as authoritarian, distant, and demanding. His father was often away from the family in the evenings, spending time with parishioners, who seemed to need him more than his family. Joshua was the oldest of three children and felt pressure to conform and to represent the family well. For example, he would be punished for any grade lower than an A or for playing nonreligious music on Sunday. Frequent comments were "When you sin, you let the entire family down" or "You have hurt the family's reputation in the church."

These memories of his father appeared to be quite vivid. He paused, as though lost in thought. Finally, he looked at me, but he did not say anything. I decided on a reflection: "It sounds like you have some very significant memories about those early years and that some of them are still quite present with you." I wondered whether we were closing in on the presenting problem—a father–son rift of some sort.

"Yes, I suppose so. I can remember them pretty well."

I paused for a moment. "Maybe some pain in those memories, as well?"

"Maybe. A little."

"Is that why you've come?" I asked.

"No, and I'll get to that in a moment. But I first want to tell you some more about . . ." And here he paused. "This is very difficult. I've never told anyone about this."

Joshua's tone became confessional. He leaned forward in his seat and rested his chin in the palms of his hands. He talked quietly, but steadily: "I wet my bed until I was 10. And I also . . . I soiled myself. Is that how you say it in polite company?"

Perhaps this is the presenting problem, I thought to myself—an anxiety that has troubled him his entire life, an anxiety that expressed itself in both enuresis and encopresis—with roots in mistreatment at home. "You had some pretty distressing experiences, huh? Most boys would feel quite shamed, I would think."

"Yeah. It wasn't easy, I'll tell you that."

"Have you talked about any of these experiences with someone over the years—family members, someone in the church, friends?"

"No. Nobody, really."

"Not even at the time it was happening? Your parents must have known about this."

"Nope. My mother simply cleaned up after me when I soiled myself. Nothing was said."

None of this was shared easily. Joshua's take-charge style had become quieter, more halting. And he looked very sad.

"I'm not really sure why I'm telling you this," he said.

"Well, I'm not either," I responded. At this point, I faced a dilemma. Sometimes men dump a whole series of painful stories all at once but do not want to talk about any of them. Should I continue to encourage him to talk about these painful memories, or would it be better to back away and return to them when our rapport was established, after he'd had a chance to develop a sense of safety with me? I thought it better to wait, but I felt cautious about taking the wheel from this man. I decided to let him decide. "Are these the reasons you called?" I asked, trying to give him an opportunity to drive us in either direction: to talk further about his memories or to tell more of his story. He returned to the story.

"No. But I'm getting to that. I want to tell you about the rest of my life, just briefly—high school, college, my marriage, and so forth."

For the rest of his intake and most of his second session, Joshua provided a highlight reel of stories about his life: He had two younger sisters, and he often felt pressure to set an example for them. He had extensive contact with his grandparents, who were members of the same church. In high school, Joshua's father cautioned him about making friends with "worldly" students, but Joshua did so anyway. Church members prayed for him and asked God to make him a "witness" to others at the public high school. Although he remembered having internal doubts about his faith, Joshua became a preacher like his father, and got his ministerial training from a sectarian seminary. He married a woman he met at a church social event while attending the seminary, and they had three children. At the time of his first appointment, Joshua was 35. His congregation of about 150 members supported him financially, yet his income placed him near poverty.

THE PRESENTING PROBLEM

Although Joshua noted that his father believed that psychologists "played on the devil's playground," Joshua had acceded to his wife's request and made an appointment. He said that she was concerned about the way he had been acting around the house. "She thinks I might be depressed," he said somewhat tentatively.

Indeed, he appeared depressed. He reported experiencing high levels of fatigue, sleeping nearly 10 hours a night (rather than his customary 7), gaining weight, losing his interest in his work, becoming more irritable with their three sons (who were under 10 years of age), finding it more and more difficult to concentrate on reading or conversations, and struggling with feelings of guilt that he was not functioning effectively at home or in his church. His mood was often depressed, although he preferred to use the word "numb" to describe his outlook. The symptoms were pronounced enough that I wondered about suicidal ideation.

"Many people who feel this way have thoughts about dying," I ventured. "They may think that it wouldn't matter much if they didn't wake up one morning, or if they were to die in some way."

"Well, that's not me. Goodness, no." He seemed offended at the question.

Finally, Joshua was ready to identify his reasons for making an appointment. He had come to address two problems in his life. The first he reported with great difficulty. The words came slowly and quietly. "I, uh, have been having some, uh, doubts about my faith and my church." He glanced quickly at me to see how I might react. I waited.

"I'm not sure if I believe every single statement on that summary I gave you, at least not in the way they are worded. And if I don't believe those teachings—I mean every single one of them—then my career is over."

"Oh?" I asked.

"Yes. And not only that. All my friends are in the church. If I say that I have some doubts, then they're going to shun me."

"I see."

"And my parents would treat me like a lost sinner the rest of my life, lost in hell."

"And your wife?"

"I don't know. Things would sure change at home. But I don't know how."

Putting these thoughts into words was excruciating for Joshua. He bent forward in his chair, lowered his voice, and talked in hushed tones as though someone might overhear him. It no longer felt like Joshua was driving. He had stopped the car and we had parked under a shady tree. My heart was moved by Joshua's story. Everything that was important to him—his wife and sons, his parents, his career, his friends—everything was at stake. He might lose it all. I felt sad with him.

This was going to be a process that must move slowly, I thought. He was contemplating making major changes in his life—his identity, his spiritual realities, his values, and his attachments. These had been his core definitions for many years. It seemed at this point that my role in the change process was going to be making sure therapy did not move too rapidly. Joshua needed to find ways of maintaining a sense of continuity with his past, even though he was having doubts about the beliefs he had been taught. This was going to be hard work.

"Doc, I want to ask you a question. Are you a religious man?"

I had been expecting this question, and I was ready to respond. I was aware that therapist disclosures could be powerful in therapy but that disclosures needed to be infrequent and brief: "I am quite willing to talk to you about that, but before I do, I wonder if you could tell me how my answer might be helpful to you."

"I don't know, really. I just think that you might not understand how hard it is to be asking questions like this. If I knew something about your beliefs, I don't know . . . maybe it would help in some way."

Typically, I do not think it is particularly helpful to talk about my religious history or values with my clients. But this case seemed different. I had traveled a somewhat similar road. Maybe a succinct comment would allow him to feel safer.

Well, here goes, I thought. "Okay, Joshua. I grew up in a very conservative and fundamentalist home. I left the tradition as a young adult, and it was extremely difficult for me. At this point in my life, I am no longer connected to that tradition, but I regard myself as deeply spiritual." I waited for a moment. "I'm concerned that telling you this might make you feel cautious about sharing your uncertainties with me."

A long pause followed. "No, I think it might be just the opposite. You might be less likely to think badly of me." This question came up only this once. He never asked me about it again, and I made no further references to it.

Joshua's second presenting problem was easier for him to report, but no less frightening. He indicated that his wife was unhappy with his style of "leadership" in the family. She thought him to be "too authoritarian" with the children and dismissive of her contributions to parenting and house care. It seemed to me that this issue precipitated his willingness to call. It was an immediate concern, and he had her encouragement to address it in therapy. This problem seemed familiar to me, yet in many ways, it seemed to rest on his religious concerns. His role in his family was defined by his pamphlet of beliefs. Although it seemed more straightforward to address, his marital concerns seemed secondary to his religious questions.

These two issues became the focus of his therapy. What would happen to him if he continued to doubt his faith and his church? And what would happen to his marriage if he didn't make some changes?

Religious Uncertainty

Joshua reported that he had always found certain aspects of his religion to be difficult to understand. He illustrated this by pulling his Bible from his briefcase (which he continued to bring to every session for several weeks) and quoting some lines. In one early session, he read what sounded like a metaphorical passage that included references to various numbers. He said that these passages were interpreted as predictions of dates about events in our time. But Joshua wasn't so sure about these teachings.

> How can I believe these things? If I just told someone in the street, "The Bible has predicted the rise of the AIDS epidemic," or "the outcome of

the conflict in the Middle East," they would think I'm crazy. If I met someone who told me that, I would write them off in a moment. And yet, I am supposed to preach these ideas to people.

It is not unusual for someone to put something into words for the very first time in my office. In Joshua's case, it was the first time he had heard his own voice expressing doubts so that someone else could hear and (more or less) understand them. He had not been able to discuss these questions with anyone. Not even his wife. He was afraid that he would lose control of the information and that, ultimately, members of his church executive board would discover his doubtfulness and relieve him of his duties. And he did not want to lose his job over his doubts. He wanted to be completely sure that he no longer believed before he said anything to anyone else—anyone except a psychologist, that is.

I recalled that Joshua had asked me about confidentiality on the phone when he had first called to make an appointment. Now I understood. Joshua's dilemma underlined for me the awesome responsibility that comes with being a therapist. He was sharing information with me that would utterly destroy his life if revealed.

It is difficult for me now to summarize this process in ways that adequately communicate the level of distress these doubts created for Joshua. The entire scaffolding of his life was threatened. He had used his church schemas to interpret everything in the world. Now I could read with more understanding the pamphlet that summarized his beliefs. No significant area of life was untouched by the assertions of his church: geology (the earth was created in six 24-hour days, just 6,000 years ago); astronomy (God lives in an actual mansion in a constellation in the sky); politics (vote for candidates that support family values and oppose abortion); marriage (wife and children must be submissive); diversity (opposition to gay rights, affirmative action, and school busing); and so much more, including views about the Middle East, Africa, and Islam.

If Joshua gave up his church's teachings on these topics, the entire cognitive structure of his life would have to be rebuilt. For a man who was used to having all the answers and who felt drawn to take charge of every conversation, this was a frightening undertaking to contemplate. All this left me feeling more than a little responsible not to lead him astray. I reminded myself that he was in charge of this process and that he might take some turns very different from the ones I had taken.

I felt compelled to acknowledge for him that many of his own personal strengths could help him in this rebuilding process—courage, curiosity, a growing open-mindedness, a willingness to change, self-control, and an ability to trust someone else. I did not want him to lose confidence in his own ability to undertake such a far-reaching project. From time to time over the next several months, I would return to this theme when he struggled with ambivalence or uncertainty.

Marital Distress

Joshua had been married for 11 years at the time of the intake. At first, the marriage was idyllic, as he saw it. There was no conflict between them. They belonged to the same church and viewed the world in the same way, and the church's chain of command determined the decision-making process. She was to provide input, but he was to make the major decisions. This process had been applied to all the significant areas of their marriage: buying a home, deciding how many children to have and when, disciplining the children, even deciding how to vote. For several years, this had worked rather well. There was no overt conflict because his wife accepted her role as an advisor rather than a partner in their family decision making.

But this system had not been working as well over the past few years. His wife had started complaining that he was treating her like one of the children; that sometimes her ideas were better than his; and that she felt unimportant, undervalued, and insignificant. He had responded defensively at first but gradually began to see that she was feeling stifled and restricted in the marriage. By the time of the intake, he had come to realize that her discontent might lead to irreparable emotional distancing, or even a separation—"but never a divorce, we don't believe in divorce."

He further noted that he would not have come to therapy if his wife had not seemed so unhappy. He could not imagine life without her, and he was shaken to realize that his religious views of marriage (that God had ordained him to be the head of his household) might in fact be making his wife unhappy. Yet it seemed that these views were making him unhappy as well. His religious beliefs gave him lot of responsibility to carry, both as a man and as a preacher—to find the right answers, to make the right decisions, and to live with the consequences.

I found Joshua's agenda daunting. This proud but troubled man had defined two problems for himself: clarifying his religious views and addressing his marriage. But it seemed so much more complex to me. Many strands were woven together—his isolation from friends, his traditional views about masculine roles, his relationship with his father, the strong possibility of some abuse, painful memories of shame, some obsessive–compulsive personality tendencies, and a backlog of unexpressed emotionality. I remember smiling to myself as I looked at the insurance forms, which require such definitive diagnoses. How could the complexity of Joshua's story be adequately summarized using the traditional multiaxial categories?

From Holy to Whole

Therapy was organized around two broad tasks. First, Joshua wanted to restructure his thinking to reflect his own views, ideas, and experiences. Using language familiar to him, he wanted to move from being *holy* (i.e., set apart from the "world" for religious purposes defined by others) to being *whole* (i.e., being part of the world in ways that were inclusive, interactive, and genuinely his own). Second, he wanted to redefine his marriage to convey more respect for the opinions, ideals, and observations of his wife.

To accomplish these tasks, the treatment plan included the following elements.

Providing Emotional Support

The first task was to offer nonjudgmental support as Joshua struggled in session to sort out his ideas. At times, he would bring his thoughts in outline form and just want to talk about the problems he saw in some church teaching. His cards and outlines seemed to represent his struggle to manage his own responses with all his troubles. At other times, Joshua just wanted to hear himself express his doubts without fear of being rejected or ridiculed. He would make a comment about some religious view and glance quickly at me, as though I might express some opinion. He would bring an alternative idea he had found elsewhere in his reading and ask whether this sounded "crazy" to me.

In some sessions, it did not feel like I was conducting therapy; instead, it seemed that I was simply providing him with time and space to think out loud about some religious teaching. But I knew that he had nobody else with whom he could talk about these ideas. After all, the number of people in our city who might have a strong interest in discussing biblical numerology was probably small. I hoped "just listening" was more supportive than it sometimes seemed to me.

My other supportive role was to continue affirming the importance of the questions he was asking and to encourage him to make connections between these questions and the way he was living his life. This process for him was highly cognitive. Throughout this process, Joshua seemed to desperately look for a new schematic structure to use in understanding the world. This was central in therapy—providing him a sort of drafting board on which he could redesign or remodel his religious structures. These types of metaphors were used frequently in our discussions, in part because of his interest in woodworking.

To assist in this reconstruction, I supported his idea that he might read English translations of writings found in some of the world's oldest religions—Hinduism, Judaism, Islam, Buddhism, and so forth. We called this his "grand experiment." He reported that he was not looking for "truth," so much as wanting to see how major traditions in human history had addressed the questions that were interesting to him—questions about origins, the purpose of life, ethical behavior, death, and so forth. He seemed to find comfort in this reading. He reported feeling less alone in his quest as he read the reflections of others over the centuries who had wrestled with the same questions that he was asking. This task was an ongoing thread in our work, and he would report on his findings from time to time. He developed an "action plan" that allowed him to keep track of what appealed to him in his reading. What began as an "experiment" in reading became a much more personal project of trying to compose a set of guiding principles about life. It was interesting to note that these beliefs were much more about ethics than about theological dogma. At the time of our termination, he indicated that he planned to continue reading and writing along these lines.

Treating the Depressed Mood

A second therapeutic task was to offer early in therapy a menu of ideas designed to lessen his symptoms of depression and anxiety. Given his high interest in cognitive formulations of "truth," he responded well to cognitive approaches to his depression: identifying automatic negative thoughts ("How can I have been so stupid for so long?"); reframing ("Maybe I was doing the best I could as a child, trying to live in a very demanding home"); and examining core beliefs ("Maybe this current crisis will actually end, and life can get better").

Joshua was uncomfortable considering medications, because that would be the ultimate indication that he could not handle his problems. As long as he continued to function in meeting the routine responsibilities of his life, that seemed reasonable.

Addressing Personality Variables

A third theme was the introduction of broader ways of thinking about Joshua's struggle. It seemed that Joshua's struggles were made more difficult by some of his basic personality tendencies. Because he liked writing in connection with his work (bringing notes to session or writing on a dry erase board during sessions) and because he liked "checking" his depression levels every couple of weeks with a written inventory, it seemed reasonable to respond to his request by giving him a personality inventory. We used the 16 Personality Factors (i.e., 16PF) inventory to help with this process (Cattell, Eber, & Tatsuoka, 1970). Results showed that he was high on reasoning ability, dominance, rule consciousness, self-reliance, and perfectionism.

When I first laid out the results of the 16PF for him, he frowned. "I don't like this picture," he said. "People who are perfectionistic have always bothered me. To think I might be that way is not good news." However, this profile led to him wondering whether the expression of these tendencies could be modified in some way. Could he learn to be more expressive of warmth, or learn to be more open to change?

Eventually, the 16PF provided Joshua with another way to think about his religious struggle. Maybe it was not exclusively his religion that he was trying to understand. Perhaps his basic personality tendencies made him more susceptible to certain types of religious teachings. If so, this could give him a way of thinking about his dilemma that was broader than it had been at the beginning. From this perspective, the issue was not simply accepting or rejecting a set of religious propositions, it was how he approached any major question in life.

Exploring Gender Roles

A fourth theme was to explore with him explicit ways in which gender was important to his scaffolding. Success, for example, was central. For a long time, he believed that if he were to leave his church, it would be an admission of failure. "Men aren't supposed to make mistakes like that," he said ruefully at one point. Therapy focused on finding new ways of thinking about his struggles—not as failure but as a new and exciting journey that he was creating for himself.

Gender issues were especially apparent in his family life and created significant stress for him. Given Joshua's comfort with structure, I gave him the Gender Role Conflict Scale (O'Neil, Helms, Gable, David, & Wrightsman, 1986), which identifies levels of stress in four areas: conflict between work and family; success, power, and competition; restrictive emotionality; and restrictive affectionate behavior between men. The purpose of using this research instrument was to give him some data regarding the level of gender-related stress he was feeling. He scored high on all four scales, which seemed to comfort him, as it allowed him to think about his struggles in a language that was not exclusively religious. At times, he wanted to expand his views to include fewer religious terms, and thinking about gender variables (as well as personality variables) enabled him to do this.

The therapeutic challenge was delicate. On the one hand, he clearly wanted support as he carved out his own religious pathway, but on the other hand, some of his views about that journey were strongly influenced by a traditionally masculine ideology that seemed to be making that journey more difficult. I felt cautious about challenging too directly the relevant gender role expectations (e.g., that he must avoid failure, solve problems on his own, or be a model of perfection for his sons) because those masculine expectations were deeply rooted in the very religious culture that was the focus of his own struggles in the first place. To challenge them would be to challenge his faith, and that was his task, not mine.

Two examples illustrate how gender role issues were addressed. The first involved his relationship with his wife. For a long time, he thought that his role in the family was something God wanted him to play. But as his religious affiliation weakened, his views that he must bear the responsibility for the behavior of others in the family began to weaken, as well. Perhaps others could assume some responsibility for their own choices and behavior. At times, this brought Joshua great relief and actually seemed to move him along his religious trek with more energy. Although the appeal for him was striking—he could lessen his own sense of responsibility by "letting" his wife make her own decisions about life—it also provoked anxiety because making that adjustment would be an overt acknowledgment that he was making some tangible changes in the religious foundation that had governed his life from its beginning.

This is different from how I usually work with gender issues. Typically, if I sense gender role ideology is creating problems in a relationship, then I bring it up and ask about it. But in this case, gender seemed inseparable from religion. As long as he saw religious themes as the central problem, I decided to reinforce questions about gender as he noticed them, rather than introduce them myself.

A second example of how gender entered the discussion was Joshua's concerns about his young boys. "It's my job to teach them values," he said several times. "That's what God wants me to do." This put considerable pressure on him, because he was increasingly uncertain about which views of reality to teach. We talked about whether fathers had to have all the right answers for their children. This widened the discussion from a focus on which doctrines to teach to a consideration of the role of fathers as teachers. Redefining part of this problem as a gender issue allowed him to decide that he could focus on prosocial behavior while they were still young (truth telling, promise keeping, respect for others, etc.) and that he could become more of a resource as they got older and asked doctrinal questions. This began to free him from thinking he had to be the father with all the right answers.

Addressing Father Issues

The fifth theme was the most painful for Joshua. Several weeks into therapy, he decided to address his relationship with his father. In my work with men, more intense emotions seem to be generated around father memories than any other topic. In Joshua's case, the struggle was to distinguish his views of his father from his views of God. Did he want to leave the church or his father? He could not always tell.

He could recall some physical abuse from his father—being hit in the head when he did not think "right," or having his hand whacked when he accidentally dropped some food in the kitchen. The hitting was accompanied by comments about that body part being sinful or bad—as in, "Your hand just made a mess; it must be punished." This issue took him off topic for a while, as he saw it: We were not directly addressing his religious questions and the depression they were creating. But I saw this as important. I have worked with people who learned to dissociate as a result of abuser language that identified certain body parts as separate and bad. Joshua gave no indication of dissociation, but I still invited him to think more about his experiences with his father.

Reluctantly, he came to see that this issue was important in and of itself, regardless of his religious journey. It led to the first intense expression of emotion. It hit him suddenly as he was recalling a particular incident. Tears appeared first, followed by waves of crying that he could not stifle. He kept saying, "This is so embarrassing." My first response was sadness. Empathy comes naturally for me around this issue. I also felt moved by his embarrassment. He did not want to be crying, but he could not stop himself. But I also felt angry that Joshua had been so deeply hurt as a child and had been prevented from expressing his pain at the time. Although it was his task to cry and mine to be supportive, I know that my own emotional responses were conveyed to him in both verbal reflections and in demeanor. This human response seemed to normalize his emotional expressions, and I do not think it moved me out of my role as a therapist in the passenger seat.

Although his emotionality was more intense over this issue than any other, he wanted it to remain secondary, while he tried to figure out what to do with his life. My views were different, however. A week later, I talked with him about the value of emotionality in life. I described emotions as "tools" that can help us identify problems that need to be addressed and that can give us clues about their importance. This notion is often new to men who have associated emotional expressiveness with being feminine. When I can be explicit that I see the ability to express intense emotions as a strength, the result is often a willingness to talk further without fearing my judgment that he has been less of a man.

Outcome

After about 2 years (upward of 75 sessions), Joshua decided to leave his job as a church pastor. This decision was cataclysmic in his life. As he saw it, he was not simply changing jobs. He was changing lives. He was taking on a new identity, a new purpose, and new goals. He decided that he could remain a Christian but that he must find his way in a new group that gave more permission for him to make decisions about his daily life. This was not a sudden decision. In fact, I am not sure that it occurred at a moment in time that he could identify. It was a gradual realization, not a decision. I remember emphasizing the need to find ways of seeing these changes as a continuation of early patterns, not the beginning of an abruptly new life.

Eventually, Joshua decided to go back to school, to get a degree that would allow him to work with troubled children. He had always wanted to be a counselor of kids, but he had been discouraged from doing so early in his life by his parents, who said that mental health services were unnecessary. In part, this decision was fed by his own memories of being a child and feeling threatened. Going back to school was not easy. He continued to feel the masculine pressure to provide for his family, and he had to find a series of jobs to help him get his degree and make his contribution to the family.

Fortunately, his wife seemed both able and eager to begin her own career. She had received training prior to the marriage that she was able to use in finding a job. This apparently gave her something she was needing—a life that included responsibilities in addition to parenting. It also helped put food on the table.

Although highly stressful at times, this new arrangement seemed to improve the chances of survival for the marriage. Joshua reported feeling less pressure to make the right decision all the time, and he said that his wife started to "blossom" in ways that he had not seen before.

It was not surprising that Joshua's depression began to lift as these changes were implemented. At the same time, his anxiety increased as he prepared to leave his occupation, his religion, and many of his friends who would shun him. We often reframed this anxiety as "excitement" or even "exhilaration."

Over the course of therapy, his behavior in my office changed. He stopped wearing his black suit and bringing his briefcase. At one point, he bought several brightly colored polo shirts and was able to laugh about his earlier need to appear "professional." Near the end of our work together, he developed a metaphor rooted in his religious tradition. In therapy, he had started the process of being "re-born again," by which he meant he was being born a third time. His first birth was biological. His second was religious. And his third was personal.

When terminating with someone I have seen for many sessions, it is my practice to make the last couple of sessions a review of our work together. I offer to provide a summary of my memories of the therapy process, and I offer some thoughts about what I see ahead for the person. I invite the other person to do the same and to summarize the experience of therapy as a way of closing the chapter of our work together. This experience is often quite moving for me. Although I do not invite people to bring something tangible to the termination sessions, it is not unusual for someone to do so. For example, one person made a small wall quilt for her home and brought it to the last session; each square summarized a particular theme in therapy. Others have brought poems they have written. A few have composed songs. One made an abstract painting about his therapy that he wanted to hang in his home. Several have brought songs of recorded music that capture various themes in therapy.

Termination is sometimes difficult for me. When I work with someone a very long time, I become connected in ways that seem as much human as professional. This was especially true for Joshua, whose journey had so many similarities to my own. He had written a poem, and brought it to our final session to read. He called it, "From Holy to Whole."

> Birth One
>> was sudden. a noisy exit from life-giving waters of the womb;
>> bright overhead lights revealing every innocent wrinkle;
>> ready to be "straightened out" by nuclear parents.

Birth Two
> was uncertain. a chlorine-drenched emergence from baptismal waters;
> divine searchlights illuminating every unwanted flaw;
> yearning to live the "straight and narrow way" of my sectarian community

Birth Three
> continues. a tearful healing of old after-birth pains;
> dazzling milky way insights expanding my universe;
> therapeutically freed
> to become a full member of my wider human family

AFTERWORD

Why did I choose this case? Joshua's story addresses an issue that is difficult in psychotherapy—the intersection of organized religion and Western psychology. It is rarely an easy interaction. But to me these domains have much in common: an interest in understanding and interpreting the world; a concern with personal well-being and interpersonal relationships; a desire to implement a set of ethical commitments in the larger society; and more. My personal interest in these themes explains my selection of Joshua's case to present to the editors.

Is this case typical of how I work with traditional men? Many parts of Joshua's presentation are quite familiar in my work with traditional men: the reluctance to seek therapy, calling at the suggestion of a concerned family member, the need to be in charge of the therapeutic pace and process, the reluctance to be emotionally expressive, the concern for reputation, the power of the provider role, the hesitancy to consider medication, the fear of failure, and the shame of early abuse.

Several aspects of my approach with Joshua are common in my work around gender issues with traditionally socialized men: avoiding competition or confrontation; finding ways of describing emotions that are masculine congruent; opening up the possibility for deep feelings of shame, pain, or loss; looking for "little experiments" (action plans) that respond to the presenting problem; and finding ways in which he could use his strengths.

How was this case informed by developmental or constructivist notions? It was my view that Joshua could construct his own views about the meaning of his life. He wanted to change some of his views about the universe. With my support, these changes occurred slowly, deliberately, and reflectively over time. He was able to see his present questions from a vantage point that considered his early life experiences. His relationship with me formed a base from which he could explore various ideas about ultimate realities; in effect, he used therapy to "try on" various views of the world. The presenting problems (religious uncertainty and marital problems) were part of a larger pattern of change that involved his identity, attachments, values, and abilities.

QUESTIONS FROM THE EDITORS

1. *What types of gender-based stereotypes were you aware of in counseling this client? How did that impact your therapy with this client?*

I struggled with three stereotypes. The first grew out of my general awareness of television preachers and the stories of personal and financial improprieties that have plagued some of them. Even though I assume that those who have been caught breaking the law represent a small minority of Christian preachers, I was aware of those stories when I first met Joshua. My first response was to tell myself to avoid coloring Joshua in those darker shades. For the first couple of sessions, that was a challenge. His presence filled the room, much as an energetic television preacher fills the screen.

Another stereotype was evoked by Joshua's acceptance of some traditional gender role ideas, especially the need to control life around him. He brought a written agenda to our first meeting and clearly wanted to be in charge. This stereotype hinted at several possible implications: unequal treatment of women, coercive parenting, an inability to acknowledge one's own flaws, and so forth. My approach was not to fight him but to follow along, looking for openings. At the time I am writing these lines, I am reading a biography of Benjamin Franklin. His biographer (Isaacson, 2003) suggests that one reason for Franklin's diplomatic successes was his refusal to confront directly those who believed they knew more than he did. Isaacson (2003) quotes Franklin: "Would you win the hearts of others, you must not seem to vie with them, but to admire them"; and "For these fifty years past, no one has ever heard a dogmatical expression escape me" (pp. 56–57).

A third stereotype is the picture of the "Christian fundamentalist," which in its more extreme forms portrays someone as being judgmental and parochial and acting superior. My challenge was to step back and see Joshua as a fellow human being, struggling to make the best of the hand he had been dealt by his genes and his parenting.

2. *How did your own gender role issues influence your work with this client?*

I am committed to the feminist notion that men and women should be equal politically, economically, and socially. I had to check my own reactions to Joshua's views about the "chain-of-command" approach, which distributes power disproportionately between men and women. It was especially problematic in this case, because these views came directly from the religious perspective that was causing him difficulties. If I challenged his views of gender roles, I would also be challenging his religion.

3. *Looking back on the case, knowing what you know now, would you change the way you worked with this client?*

I think I would do a couple of things differently. I would try to spend much less therapy time listening to him dispute his many religious questions with himself. At the time, I thought it was giving him a safe place to address the central issue as he saw it. But I now wonder if I could have encouraged him to discuss some of those issues with someone else more trained in theological matters while we devoted our time to the more distinctly psychological issues (his mood disorder, personality concerns, and family dynamics).

I also would have emphasized more strongly the need to address the abuse history. I did not at the time because his religious concerns seemed so primary. But I do think he would have benefited from spending more time with this issue. More work needs to be done in this arena. Perhaps he will return to therapy at some point to address it.

4. It seems like therapy was viewed as a last-ditch effort, and then it was perceived as a shameful move. Are these attitudes typical of men that you see, and how do men generally seek help?

Joshua's approach to me was typical of men who adhere to traditional expectations of masculinity. Their initial phone call to me represents an acknowledgment of failure. My first clues along these lines usually come on the phone in the form of the self-protective questions I am asked—about confidentiality, about the content of a "consultation," or about my training and experience. These men come with great reluctance, and they seem to be suffering more when they arrive. They often explain their presence by referring to (or blaming) someone else as the reason they have called.

Not all men approach therapy in this way. Increasing numbers of men seem quite ready to call on their own, to acknowledge their own needs themselves, and to engage early in the process of change. But Joshua was not one of these men.

5. This client presented with a strong religious orientation that appeared to reinforce traditional ideas about masculinity. When you work with religious men, what relationship do you see between masculine ideology (orientation) and religion?

The relationship between gender role expectations and religious teachings is often very close. At times, it is not easy to figure out how to do therapy while respecting religious perspectives that contain strong views about gender. Mike Maples and I have wrestled with this question and have offered a few suggestions elsewhere (Maples & Robertson, 2001).

Some religious men feel reluctant to seek help because they know that others are very critical of their religious views or because their faith prohibits them from coming. It can be a fine line that distinguishes a counselor's respect for the religious journey of a man, on the one hand, and raises questions about the possibility that some of those ideas may be maladaptive, on the other. Minimizing a person's religious views can be quite harmful. To some degree, it is a judgment call as to whether someone is psychologically ready to discard parts of a religious structure. It is also important, it seems to me, to be careful about engaging in behavior that usurps the role of someone's God or religious leader.

REFERENCES

Brooks, G. R. (1998). *A new psychotherapy for traditional men.* San Francisco: Jossey-Bass.

Brooks, G. R., & Good, G. E. (Eds.). (2001a). *The new handbook of psychotherapy and counseling with men: A comprehensive guide to settings, problems, and treatment approaches* (Vol. 1). San Francisco: Jossey-Bass.

Brooks, G. R., & Good, G. E. (Eds.). (2001b). *The new handbook of psychotherapy and counseling with men: A comprehensive guide to settings, problems, and treatment approaches* (Vol. 2). San Francisco: Jossey-Bass.

Cattell, R. B., Eber, H., & Tatsuoka, M. M. (1970). *Handbook for the 16PF.* Champaign, IL: Institute for Personality and Ability Testing.

Dalai Lama, H. H., & Cutler, H. C. (1998). *The art of happiness: A handbook for living.* New York: Riverhead Books.

Ford, D. H. (1987). *Humans as self-constructing living systems: A developmental perspective on behavior and personality.* Hillsdale, NJ: Erlbaum.

Good, G. E., & Mintz, L. B. (2000). Gender and sex in counseling and psychotherapy. *Sex Roles, 43,* 419–421.

Greenberg, L., & Paivio, S. (1997). *Working with emotion in psychotherapy.* New York: Guilford Press.

Isaacson, W. (2003). *Benjamin Franklin: An American life.* New York: Simon & Schuster.

Kilmartin, C. T. (2001, August). *Crimes against nature.* Solo theatrical performance presented at the 109th Annual Convention of the American Psychological Association, San Francisco.

Lyddon, W. J., & Jones, J. V., Jr. (Eds.). (2001). *Empirically supported cognitive therapies: Current and future applications.* New York: Springer Publishing Company.

Mahoney, M. J. (1991). *Human change processes: The scientific foundations of psychotherapy.* New York: Basic Books.

Mahoney, M. J. (1995). *Cognitive and constructive psychotherapies: Theory, research, and practice.* New York and Washington, DC: Springer Publishing Company.

Maples, M. R., & Robertson, J. M. (2001). Counseling men with religious affiliations. In G. R. Brooks & G. E. Good (Eds.), *The new handbook of psychotherapy and counseling with men: A comprehensive guide to settings, problems, and treatment approaches* (Vol. 2, pp. 816–843). San Francisco: Jossey-Bass.

O'Neil, J. M., Helms, B. J., Gable, R. K., David, L., & Wrightsman, L. S. (1986). Gender-Role Conflict Scale: College men's fear of femininity. *Sex Roles, 14,* 335–350.

Rabinowitz, F. E., & Cochran, S. V. (2002). *Deepening psychotherapy with men*. Washington, DC: American Psychological Association.

Richards, P. S., & Bergin, A. E. (Eds.). (2000). *Handbook of psychotherapy and religious diversity*. Washington, DC: American Psychological Association.

8

FACING FEAR WITHOUT LOSING FACE: WORKING WITH ASIAN AMERICAN MEN

SAMUEL PARK

As a psychologist, I have had the pleasure and honor of working with clients across a variety of roles: counselor, coach, and facilitator. As an Asian American (more specifically, Korean American) psychologist, however, I have found that working with culturally diverse populations requires an expansion of the traditional role of counselor; it often includes mentorship, instruction, and a strong personal connection (beyond academic understanding or appreciation) with the world within which clients live and perceive themselves and others. My work at a university counseling center has allowed for the study and, more important, the application of these principles.

As a second-generation Asian American man, I find such efforts to be both rewarding and challenging. By facilitating therapeutic experiences that enhance one's multicultural awareness and identity development, I find much meaning and inspiration in my work. At the same time, however, being an Asian male psychologist can present many challenges. Much of this deals with issues of credibility for the clients—toward me as a helper, as well as the profession of psychology in general (Sue & Zane, 1987). In addition, further challenges can arise when working with men of color, as issues and conflicts between masculinity and nontraditional forms of help-seeking behaviors often become salient (Pollack, 1998; Rowan, 1997; Sue, 2001). It is particularly challenging when working with men from cultures—such as my own Asian culture—that value minimal expression and display of emotion (Sue & Sue, 1990; Uba, 1994). Within traditional Asian cultures, the field of Western psychology, which encourages what may be considered by some cultures as nonmasculine processes (e.g., emotional awareness, request for assistance), is viewed with caution (Atkinson & Gim, 1989; Atkinson, Whitely, & Gim, 1990; Lee & Saul, 1987). In my work with many Asian American men, it is amazing how these sets of values remain in place across generations and ethnicities—from first generation immigrants to fourth generation men.

Such issues of masculinity and credibility serve as forces that continuously remind me of how my role as a Korean American man can assist others in their awareness and definitions of what it means—for each man—to be an Asian American. As a result, I too must be aware of where I stand with my "maleness" and with my culture—what I embrace and appreciate (e.g., strength, hard work, achievement), my insecurities, and also those values with which I struggle to accept as part of my traditional culture (e.g., minimal display of emotions, sexism) and therefore, as parts of myself (Liu, 2002). My integration of these elements, along with a commitment to continuously assess and challenge my position on them, results in a new, dynamic definition of an Asian American man: one that is confident, vulnerable, and at the very least, honorable. It is within this new definition of *honor* that I can find a harmony in my personal challenges with various cultural norms. "Active" (and at times nontraditional) efforts to define the modern Asian American man in essence model the very honorable behavior that is expected of psychologists. It requires passion and commitment (even in the face of resistance), based on establishing and maintaining relationships, in order for the boundaries of culture to be expanded. And given the expansive roles of a multicultural psychologist beyond traditional counselor (Atkinson & Lowe, 1995; Sue, 2001; Sue et al., 1998), I see my work with Asian American men as opportunities to facilitate a process of critical assessment of masculinity, contribute to their development as Asian men, and increase awareness of how their definitions of maleness affect all aspects of their lives.

An essential ingredient to succeed in these efforts is the establishment of the therapeutic relationship. Through a strong interpersonal connection, a relationship can be formed; credibility can be established; and ultimately, masculinity, if necessary, can be redefined (Meth, 1990). The challenge—my challenge—is to be comfortable enough in my multiple roles as an Asian American, a man, and a psychologist to be in a position in which I can facilitate corrective emotional and relational experiences for my clients. There are many sources of my passion with this issue; many are academic, yet the most significant influences are the male and female relationships that have helped shaped my view of masculinity: my father, who took a risk to move his family to the United States, and my mother, who was the breadwinner but adhered faithfully to her ascribed cultural role to comply with the patriarch's decisions.

It is not surprising that themes of leadership, decision making, and importance of the family provided an overall framework in my perception of masculinity. At the same time, values of limiting emotional expression or display, authoritarianism, and sexism also contributed to this foundation. And one value, above all, was given particular attention: Do not disgrace the family; in other words, do not "lose face." This value, "face," has shown to be a consistent and salient variable in Asian American help-seeking preferences and attitudes (Park & Zane, 2005; Zane & Mak, 2003; Zane & Yeh, 2002). *Face* is differentiated from *shame* in that the former is a social and relational construct (Goffman, 1955), whereas the latter is an individually based experience (Ho, 1976). My identity development, influenced by these values and their conflict with my own values, shaped my early years as an adult. I went through a process of appreciating and resenting my culture, which for many years resulted in stagnant identity development. Perhaps this is one way Asian cultures maintain a sense of harmony: Love and dislike balance each other out. But my definition of what it means to be an Asian man did eventually grow through this constant struggle. My movement from culture-bound "harmony" to a path of self-defined harmony was set when I chose the field of psychology and confronted the "shame" that resulted from this decision. Yet in making this difficult choice, I had never felt more like a man, an honorable Asian man, than in those moments of personal struggle—to me, this was harmony. I realized, and continue to realize, that masculinity and "maleness" mean achieving a sense of comfort with the "discomfort" of periodic straying from culture- and gender-bound norms and stereotypes. "Comfort with discomfort"—this is strength, achievement, and sensitivity; I believe this is the contemporary Asian man.

Along with my family, there are a great many influences in my personal and professional journey in the area of working with men. My academic and professional mentors have played major roles in providing a theoretical foundation from which my clinical work, and work with men, are applied. The pioneering work of Stanley Sue and other Asian American researchers provided not only valuable empirical information about personality characteristics, cultural values, and counseling issues with Asian Americans but also revealed that Asian American men were successful in the field of psychology (see Uba, 1994).

My orientation as a therapist is influenced heavily by the humanistic, interpersonal process, dynamic, and experiential schools of psychology. Although trained primarily as a cognitive-behaviorist, the humanistic work of Carl Rogers's (1951) and Edward Teyber's (2000) interpersonal process approach present what I feel is the foundation of counseling: building a healing, corrective relationship guided by respect and genuineness. Pollack's (1998) review on therapy with men provides a framework to help foster such alliances early in treatment that promotes the demystification of the therapeutic process: clarification of the counseling process; establishment of objective goals; and initiation of solution- and task-oriented approaches. Although important in all counseling relationships, these building blocks are particularly essential in work with Asian American men: Respect, genuineness, clarification, and structure (initially) model an understanding to have clients not lose face within a most "shameful" situation (Park & Zane, 2005). In other words, these efforts on the part of the therapist indicate a level of cultural sensitivity and competence with men that, according to "face" theory, maintains the individual's social standing, which increases the chances of establishing a working relationship (Goffman, 1955). Through this process, a change can take place where one experiences masculinity that is not traditionally Asian, but uniquely Asian.

My conceptualization in working with Asian American men is thus integrative. As is strongly recommended by the Asian American literature, I work to establish initial credibility through structured, directive techniques (Sue, 2001; Sue & Zane, 1987); develop trust through respect and integrity (Zane & Sue, 1991); nurture a connection through shared and varied cultural experiences (Sue et al., 1998); and facilitate corrective emotional experiences through modeling and mentorship (Lynch & Hanson, 1992; Teyber, 2000). Through this process, recurring interpersonal themes influenced by issues of masculinity can be safely projected, processed, and worked through. Although not all Asian American men deal with issues of masculinity as their presenting issue, it is not uncommon that this theme underlies or affects the current challenges that bring them to therapy. As stated earlier, such work is both rewarding and challenging. Such was the case with John, as I discuss next.

WORKING WITH ASIAN AMERICAN MEN:
THE CASE OF JOHN

John was a 22-year-old, heterosexual-identified Korean American man in his junior year at a large university. He reported having significant concerns about his recent drop in academic performance, as well as concerns of discomfort in meeting others. Upon arriving at the university, he experienced significant adjustment difficulties. This resulted in an increase in depressive symptoms and anxiety, which affected his academics and willingness to meet others. In describing his background, John reported a history of dysthymia for over a span of 10 years, with distress and sadness regarding relationships with his immediate family members (i.e., father, mother, older brother). He was referred to therapy by his roommate, who had expressed concern (to John) about his mood and anxious behavior. John came to therapy approximately 3 months into the first academic term.

At our first meeting, John reported several physical complaints: stomachaches, fatigue, and headaches. This is not surprising, given Asian American tendencies to present with physical or medical issues as their primary concern (Sue, Zane, & Young, 1994; Uba, 1994). He also had concentration difficulties and a tendency to have memory lapses at a rate beyond his reported "normal" level of functioning, particularly during periods of distress. He reported (with less emphasis) depressive symptoms, moderate anxiety, particularly in social situations, and little to no social support. John also indicated an increase in alcohol use (binge drinking once a month) and smoking, both done alone, since starting at the university. He had no prior experience in therapy (or sought any form of treatment for his physical and emotional complaints), and no current or past suicidal ideation.

At first glance, John appeared to be a "typical" Asian man: medium height, polite, and soft spoken. He was above average in attractiveness and speech and was highly acculturated to mainstream American culture. He stated that although he could tolerate brief interactions with Asians, he felt more comfortable with non-Asians, as he stated he did not feel like a "real" Asian. Although taken somewhat aback by these statements, I was not entirely surprised, given what I felt was a type of conflict often found during periods of transition in one's ethnic identity development (Atkinson, Morten, & Sue, 1993). I felt that making a process comment about me being an Asian (and what it was like to interact with me) at this point in our work may have been too early, as it may have resulted in shame and a loss of face. This may have negatively affected the development of our relationship. Instead, I continued to gather information and stored this piece to use at a later time.

Although he did not appear to be severely depressed, he did possess low mood and presented a minimal range of affect. He appeared cautious of his words and actions—fidgeting in his chair and maintaining minimal eye contact—and would use humor as a way of alleviating anxiety within the session. He would often ask questions that displayed concern regarding his situation and how he was perceived with comments such as "Sounds crazy, doesn't it?" Despite his self-consciousness and concerns about my perceptions, I found him to be interpersonally enjoyable and very pleasant; perhaps his soft-spoken, vulnerable but genuine interpersonal style reminded me in some ways of myself. As I reflected back on my challenges as I transitioned through my own ethnic identity development, I respected his path—although unique, the themes of what it meant to be an Asian American, a man, and seeking personal contentment in this endeavor could be shared and understood. I could truly appreciate and relate with him.

Background

John possessed a challenging personal history. He was born in South Korea and immigrated with his parents and older brother to the United States when he was 6 years old. Upon arriving in the United States, he reported that his parents fought and engaged in frequent verbal abuse; he also reported witnessing periodic domestic abuse. He reported that this and financial instability (due to his father not having stable work) led to his mother leaving the family, remarrying, and eventually moving out of state. John stated he had not had regular contact with her since.

John characterized his father as a selfish and apathetic man, who did not "work hard" in the "Asian way" to support his family or to keep it intact. Throughout his childhood and adolescent years, he communicated little with his father and did not view him as a source of emotional or financial support. When they did communicate, it was primarily unidirectional: his father criticizing him. It is interesting that although possessing the role of being the obedient recipient of criticism and verbal abuse (by both his father and older brother), he would often serve multiple roles that provided for the family's survival: as a worker (he was the breadwinner), homemaker, and interpreter. He had difficulty accepting his role as a compliant and respectful son when he often had to take the role of family "leader" to have the family financially survive.

These issues, combined with a continuous history of relocation (he reported having attended six different high schools) and unsuccessful attempts to connect with his estranged mother, resulted in resentment and anger toward his family and culture. When his father passed away from cancer during his high school years, he experienced a tremendous range of emotions (both positive and negative), which resulted in much guilt. He appeared to have difficulty finding peace with this issue, and this may have contributed to his confusion about his feelings about his own ethnicity and trust toward others, especially Koreans. Despite this challenging history, John excelled in his academics, which served as his chief source for confidence and validation. It was not surprising that his drop in academic performance, a common entry point for Asian Americans, was the primary reason for his decision to come to therapy (Atkinson & Matsushita, 1991).

Conceptualization

The conceptualization for this case draws from multiple perspectives: interpersonal, cultural, and men's issues. On the basis of an interpersonal process viewpoint, John's situation presented a challenging history in which the development and permanence of nurturing object attachments or relations (i.e., father, mother, brother) did not occur (Teyber, 2000). The combination of an abusive and unavailable father, a mother who left the family during childhood, and an unresponsive older brother resulted in inconsistent attachments, poor role models, and a lack of experience trusting others. His current avoidance and wariness of establishing and maintaining relationships appeared to reflect interpersonal attempts to minimize anxiety and suppress fears of rejection and abandonment (Sullivan, 1968).

From a cultural perspective, there appeared to be an ongoing ambivalence toward the Korean culture, a love and hate that appeared to be generalized from his mixed feelings toward his parents. Given these cultural difficulties, he appeared to have difficulty negotiating between Asian and Western values, which are indicative of entry-phase challenges within his ethnic identity development (Atkinson et al., 1993). His reported discomfort being around Asian persons but wishing to be more identified with this group was reflective of this ambivalence. His having been matched with an Asian therapist presented a unique opportunity to address cultural and identity issues, as I served as both a source of anxiety and hope in his wish to be identified as Asian American.

Finally, from a men's issues perspective, there appeared to be conflict and difficulties with John's internalization of masculinity—what it means to be a man (Liu, 2002; Meth, 1990; Pleck, 1995) and more specifically, a Korean man. I suspect that John was struggling with the following questions: Given his model of Korean masculinity from his father, does being a Korean man mean to abide by values that have resulted in disappointment, abuse, or trauma? Does being a man mean not identifying with being Asian? And, finally, is there another way to find a sense of masculinity that embraces the best of both Asian and Western cultures? The interactions between role conflict (Pleck, 1995), father–son themes (Gordon, 1990), and cultural identity (Liu, 2002) were important issues I hoped we would work on together.

My strategy in working with John integrated elements from each perspective and attempted to address interventions that complemented suggestions put forth within the Asian American counseling literature (Leong, 1986). First, given that John appeared somewhat wary and cautious of the counseling process (low ascribed credibility), I worked to establish credibility and an alliance through a series of directive, tangible, goal-oriented discussions and experiences that would demystify therapy, reduce immediate symptoms, and build a sense of self-esteem. This approach is well suited for Asian men (Zane, Hatanaga, Park, & Akutsu, 1994; Zane & Sue, 1991).

With an alliance and credibility established, I hoped to be able to address cultural identity issues and to explore with John through an interpersonal process (using myself as a source for transference of feelings) his thoughts and feelings of being Asian, American, and a man. Through an interpersonal process of exploration of the therapeutic relationship, I hoped that John could not only describe but also experience the range of emotions that he harbored for his family, with the desire being to bring a sense of positive closure with his father and feel hope with his mother and brother. By addressing all these issues—interpersonal, multicultural, ethnic identity, masculinity—and still being sensitive to not allow John to "lose face," I hoped to be able to provide, through modeling and respect, an experience with an Asian man that was not traditionally Asian but presented for John a new way of experiencing and relating to men.

These were indeed lofty expectations. However, I felt that given this integrative approach, it could provide a unique opportunity for growth. In reality, as John and I worked together, the difficulties faced throughout the therapy process were not only his challenges but also my own personal trials in being aware of my own processes—cultural and men's issues—that affected the strategy previously described.

Early Phase: Establishing Credibility

As stated earlier, my initial approach with John was to collaborate with him to establish tangible goals to establish a level of credibility that could facilitate an interpersonal process. At the end of our first formal meeting, John and I discussed specific, objective goals that could be measured in the short term: reduction in physical symptoms; reduction in stress; increases in mood; increases in concentration; and reduction in substance use. The framework for our goals would be to gain a sense of equilibrium from which studying would be less difficult. John appeared appreciative with our setting tangible, specific goals and was active in this discussion.

As we transitioned to setting long-term goals, John was noticeably less enthusiastic. Although I typically do not initiate here-and-now processes too early in therapy (particularly with Asians whose values may not adhere to such interventions), I challenged myself to reflect on this apparent difficulty with him. I suggested that perhaps his difficulty in viewing his life from a long-term perspective was related to his personal experiences of continuously addressing current crises. Working hard to not imply judgment, I attempted to normalize his experience and anxiety and suggested that perhaps this could also be a part of our short-term goals—to analyze the struggle and, eventually, to set long-term goals.

Although taken somewhat aback, he appeared relieved with this approach recommendation. With specific goals established, I sensed an immediate reduction in his anxiety. I suspect I may have provided a "gift" early in therapy of structure and immediate relief that could balance the uncertainty of the long-term relationship. Sue and Zane (1987) stated this type of "gift" is culturally appropriate and is an important part of the early phase of treatment with Asians. I was aware that there were likely several relational dynamics that our match represented: Asian male to Asian male; authority or expert to student; parent to child. Although my orientation suggests that such relational issues and the resulting transference(s) be addressed in therapy, I felt that they would need to be introduced gradually as our process and relationship unfolded. The ambiguity and risk of engaging in such a process would likely have resulted in John feeling discomfort and shame; the literature suggests such interventions are not recommended early in therapy (Park & Zane, 2005).

My interventions set forth at this early point in the relationship were thus structured and concrete. First, I provided a referral to a physician for an examination for his physical complaints and to rule out any physical or substance-use conditions that may be affecting his anxiety, mood, and academics. The results of the examinations indicated no pressing physical conditions, with the physician's recommendations to reduce stress, increase exercise, and reduce substance use. John was compliant with these recommendations. I also referred him for a cognitive appraisal to assess any learning or processing disability for his concentration and memory deficits. As suspected, the results indicated no learning or processing disability but instead indicated an extremely high level of achievement and intellectual functioning. John was relieved and pleased with the results, which led to a reported increase in self-confidence with his academics. Finally, over the next 3 to 4 weeks, I implemented a series of structured, cognitive–behavioral anxiety-reducing interventions to provide strategies for relief of immediate relief during stress (e.g., relaxation techniques, time management skills, exercise) and reduction of substance use.

Within a month, we assessed the progress of therapy. John indicated less immediate anxiety, slight increases in mood, slightly reduced substance use, increases in physical activity, and increased levels of adjustment to the academic demands of the university. He reported noticeable improvement in academic performance, concentration, and slight increases in self-esteem. No memory deficits over the past month were reported. Throughout this entire initial phase of therapy, I was keenly aware of modeling appropriate professional behavior to establish credibility and trust. I was careful to be aware of the cultural component, to dissolve any initial assumptions he may have regarding Asian males (e.g., authoritative, sexist), and to work to be an encouraging coach in assisting him with skill and self-esteem building. In turn, I observed and felt that he was a most "compliant" client—respectful, timely, and with incredible follow-through with "homework" assignments. I could not help but theorize that his compliance was due in part to being a "good" Asian child to the Asian "elder"—perhaps a parallel process that he lived throughout his life. This indicated a most interesting phenomenon— how internalized cultural values affect daily existence—even for those like John who consciously make efforts to not be "Asian." I would need to keep note of this as therapy progressed.

John, however, reported no progress in comfort with initiating social relationships, and continued difficulty feeling comfortable around Asian students. With credibility and a working alliance established, as well as John gaining sets of practical skills to deal with daily academic anxiety, I felt this would be an ideal point to address the long-term goals for therapy. It is interesting that although my approach was "textbook" in terms of establishing credibility and setting and meeting short-term, measurable goals, I realized that from an interpersonal process standpoint, to address issues of ethnic identity and masculinity, my approach would need to deviate somewhat from our initial structured style. I had much information to tell me that relational transferences were occurring. Although the relationship had been established and a discussion of relational issues was indicated, I felt an initial resistance to not engage in an interpersonal process. I realized that I felt particularly sensitive about John's view of therapy; more specifically, with me. Questions such as, How does he like me? Does he view me in the same way as other Asian men? and Do I live up to modeling a different view of masculinity? persisted within me. Teyber (2000) suggested that these types of questions and emotions provide a powerful opportunity for a therapeutic process to occur. Although I had great empathy for John, I constantly self-monitored how I spoke, acted, and related with him, at times providing more (or even less) support than needed—trying very hard to create a "perfect" balance in my approach. My rationalization of these behaviors was that I did not want him to feel uncomfortable during this transition phase of our relationship. In reality though, I suspect it was what made me feel most comfortable in those moments. I realized that my own insecurity in working with him led to me feeling less like "a man," which led to a "safe," but not necessarily personal, approach to therapy. Again, these were issues I needed to note as we entered the next phase of therapy.

Middle Phase: Cultural Identity

Aware of the clinical issues and the interpersonal challenges that this next phase of therapy would elicit, I approached these issues by initiating a discussion about long-term goals. Although not as confused with the question when introduced this time, John continued to reveal difficulties with articulating specific thoughts of what he hoped to see in our long-term work together. I had suspected such difficulties. To gradually introduce an interpersonal process, I asked him to share what he hoped he would be feeling by the end of therapy. John did not appear to struggle as much with this line of questioning; general comments such as "feeling better," "content," and "more comfortable" allowed entry to this process.

Knowing that pursuing questions related to emotions was not something with which many men, especially Asian men, are accustomed, I carefully asked him to describe this goal of feeling "more comfortable." He shared that although his academics had stabilized, he did not feel comfortable around others—a generalized discomfort in social situations, particularly with small groups and individual Asians. He stated that with large groups, he could be anonymous enough to not feel as self-conscious around others. I asked him to be more specific about his "discomfort"—first with surface inquiries (e.g., how long, how often, how much) but then followed with more questions regarding the depth of the fear, which eventually led to my first risk.

I reflected to him that given his discomfort around others, particularly Asians, how challenging his interactions with me might be. This was the first time I had introduced our relationship and myself as specific features of the therapy. He quickly withdrew into a more cognitive stance, stating that we had a professional relationship with layers of legal safety and confidentiality—that given these parameters, working with another Asian was not too difficult. Although I sensed his discomfort (which would typically result in me initiating an interpersonal process), I decided to not pursue our relationship as a topic too quickly. I felt too insecure about the strength of our bond to take such a risk. Although I could frame this decision to withdraw, myself—as "the pace was not ideal just yet" to pursue this process—I realized that I was experiencing anxiety about how I portrayed myself as an Asian man to him. I was so cautious about not damaging him (and protecting myself) that I was actually not allowing him to see me as a true Asian American man. Indeed, a parallel process had developed: He did not want to disappoint me, and I, him. Although I wanted him to like and trust me as a man, I realized that he may need to experience a full range of feelings toward me—not only positive—for a corrective emotional experience to occur (Teyber, 2000).

Knowing that I needed to trust the process, my strategy was to address the issue of culture to guide this next phase of therapy. Through some discussion, we agreed that the next goal of treatment would be to feel increased "comfort" in various anxiety-provoking social situations—namely those with Asian individuals. I began the process of asking him about how he identified himself ethnically and culturally. He responded by stating that he identified himself as Korean ethnically, but more American culturally. This resulted in a cognitive presentation of the definition of *culture*, *identity*, and *race*. However, to initiate an interpersonal process, I wanted to establish, at least at the outset, a balance between cognitions and emotions toward his Korean heritage. I invited him to share his feelings about the Korean culture. This appeared to be an invitation he had never received, as he appeared initially to have difficulty articulating them. By allowing him the time and a safe, nonjudgmental space to practice his expression of feelings, I believe he became more comfortable with this balance. This strategy also allowed for increased comfort on my end as a model of an Asian American man; I could facilitate direction and purpose through sensitivity and empathy. With the increased comfort in my role, I finally began to actually experience the true power and potential of our relationship.

Over time, the ratio of cognitive and emotional disclosures changed. He gradually increased in sharing feelings of anger, disappointment, and confusion regarding his ethnicity. John shared that he disliked the emphasis on the (economic) status in Korean American culture, the practice of unconditionally respecting elders, the strict disciplinary practices, and the lack of positive and supportive emotional communication among Koreans. He said he felt "lost" because he did not feel entirely welcome in either Korean or Western European cultures, which he stated has affected his comfort around others. This confusion and difficulty negotiating between cultures is reflective of early stage dissonance in ethnic identity development (Atkinson et al., 1993) and is not uncommon among Asian American men (Liu, 2002). When confronted with why he would want to identify with Korean culture, given his many reservations about its values, he shared that he believed that it was his "duty" to appreciate Korean culture; more specifically, it was a means to which he could bring some level of honor and respect for a family that he felt was socially shameful and disappointing. The salience of "face" and shame, even for those who are highly acculturated, played a powerful role in this motivation (Zane & Sue, 1991; Zane & Mak, 2003). I wondered whether his feelings toward the Korean culture were more of a reaction to his parents than the culture itself and whether his reluctance to reject his Korean identity was in some way reflective of hope that there might be resolution to his relationship with them.

Finally feeling comfortable to take the risk and modeling such behavior, I took an interpersonal approach. I asked him about his thoughts about working with a Korean therapist. His responses were conservative ("very professional"), polite ("it's fine"), and cautious ("it's helpful"). I asked about his feelings in working with not just any Korean therapist, but me specifically. Although I knew this question would be difficult for him to answer, I wanted to invite a process of discussion that modeled a level of risk taking, leadership, and perhaps, a sense of masculinity within a nonthreatening environment. Not used to such types of questions, John quickly withdrew and stated he did not "feel anything" specific to me. I understood his discomfort—and I shared my appreciation for his honesty in the moment. Perhaps I had introduced the issues of culture too early, or perhaps I had projected my wish to connect with him before he was ready. Although I felt confident that such a risk to reflect on our relationship was timely and appropriate, I suspect that his rejection of my invitation to connect, although painful for me, indicated a defense and pattern of behavior modeled by past disappointing experiences with others with whom he had attempted to connect.

Over the next few weeks, as a means to increase comfort and trust levels, we engaged in a process of "empirical" study through various experiential exercises. Through cognitive–behavioral assignments of monitoring thoughts and emotions around groups of individuals (Asians and non-Asians), we ascertained that his anxiety around Asian men differed qualitatively from his feelings when interacting with Asian women; he stated the former elicited significantly more anxiety and negative self-statements, whereas with Asian women, he reported feeling a wish to be recognized and appreciated. He seemed rather engaged in this process, and although there continued to be a cautious approach to our interactions, he appeared to show increased comfort in interacting with me. It is interesting to note how we both retreated to "safe" interactions after the last attempt to facilitate an interpersonal process. This reminded me of the type of interaction that men (including myself) often engage in as a way to connect with other men—it is as if we were talking about sports or some other traditionally male topic. Interesting and engaging—but safe. This is not what I had in mind in my hope to model the balance of strength and sensitivity of the Asian American man.

The Asian American Man

In time, as discussions about Asian men and women became a salient theme, John did what I believe was a significant step in our work together: At the peak of his confusion and frustration, he asked me about my ethnicity, culture, and how I negotiate between two cultures, as well as my views of Asian men and women. This was the first time he had asked me about my experiences: At last, there was an entry point for an interpersonal process! Mindful of not allowing my insecurities about the relationship to affect the process negatively, I expressed great appreciation for the question, and knowing that self-disclosure can be an important part in working with Asian Americans (Atkinson & Lowe, 1995), especially Asian men (Liu, 2002), I felt and shared my comfort (and nervousness) in engaging in this request. I believed being open and honest with him was critical to model and facilitate a healing process.

I shared with him my process and journey of integrating Asian and Western cultures—their similarities, their differences, and my feelings, both positive and negative. I sensed his attention. I explained some about my history, my family, and how my process of integrating the two was a result of coming to a comfort level with my role as an Asian American man. This meant finding peace with my ascribed Asian role of being a provider, leader, and financial supporter for my family. But this also meant finding acceptance that I did not have to fulfill these roles in a perfect or expected traditional path set by my parents or culture. I indicated that this was not an easy journey. I explained my decision to pursue psychology, my need to be emotionally expressive, and my unyielding respect for women—and how these decisions, although difficult to implement in the short term, resulted eventually with me feeling more close to my culture and more like an Asian man. With this level of integration, I could embrace my culturally expected role as a man rather than feel resentment toward it. In addition, I could thus view and experience both men and women with great respect, compassion, and affection.

I explained to John that this process did not come easy, as it required an honest examination of my own feelings and wishes. I also responded to the second part of his question with a reflection that perhaps his anxiety with men was somewhat related to, rather than different from, his feelings around women—that maybe what we need from both men and women, from humans, is love, appreciation, and validation. Although the core needs are similar across gender, the differences may be reflective of internal dilemmas with past or current male and female figures. This was a significant amount of information and interpretation at one sitting, and I knew I was risking rejection again. This time, however, John engaged himself in the process. He shared his anger and resulting confusion and how he had very much wanted to be Korean or "American" but had never until now felt "good enough" to be either one and felt less like a man for this conflict. For the first time, I sensed hope. I reflected that I appreciated his struggle and respected his process. He thanked me for my disclosures. Unlike my earlier personal hope to receive acceptance, I decided to allow John time to reflect on these issues, as I felt it was a necessary component for his own ethnic and male identity development.

The result of this significant discussion was movement and change: movement from a dissonance stage of identity development to, initially, immersion (to truly assess the pros and cons of his own culture) and then gradual entry into an introspective stage of development. John's growth and interest in finding his own sense of Asian-ness was rapid and intense. He was finding himself interacting more frequently with Asian students (going to Asian student organization meetings and socials), with fluctuating levels of anxiety. Although he was finding empowerment in this process of discovery and integration, with the consistent anxiety around others, I questioned whether the "pace" of this discovery was forging ahead of issues that I felt continued to affect his view of himself: his relationship with his father and mother.

As our relationship grew in terms of comfort and respect, I posed this "projective" question to John: If you could take a snapshot of (a good) "quality of life," what would the picture look like? After some hesitation (I had never used such an intervention in our work together), he stated that the picture would be one in which he would be at home with his wife and children making dinner. We talked about the picture, his feelings about it, and his hopes, which were to be loved by a woman and to provide love to his children. The talk eventually led to a discussion about what type of father and husband he would like to be. He stated he wanted to be loving, giving, and strong—things he stated he did not receive from his father.

I realized we were at a critical point in our relationship. His answers reflected the hurt, anger, and disappointment with his relationship with his parents, especially his father. The theme of guilt surfaced repeatedly; he stated that even though he harbored resentment toward his father, he still longed for his love—which was now reflected in his longing for acceptance among Koreans and, perhaps, from me. Now that his father had passed away, John would not be able to share his feelings, anger, and love with him. John felt that he had been a disrespectful son and was not worthy of closure with his father. Reflecting on the cultural appropriateness of his feelings and thoughts, I asked him what he would say to his father if he were alive. There was tremendous resistance to this suggestion (which was expected).

Instead of retreating for fear of my own rejection, I inquired about the resistance and stated that throughout our entire work together, when themes of emotions about relationships with his father or me were introduced, there was a noticeable change in his mood and behavior. I asked him what he feared. After a moment of silence, he said that he feared being alone, and, given his pattern of isolating from others, he was scared "all the time." I asked whether this fear of being alone was related to the lack of validation he received throughout his life. He shared that it was easier to be alone than to work hard to meet someone who would ultimately disappoint him. He stated that relationships are "not worth it." I asked, "Is your relationship with your father worth it?" No response. "Is your relationship with your mother worth it?" No response.

Finally, I asked him if our relationship was "worth it." He murmured "no"; another rejection—but I felt quite optimistic with this process, as he finally began to assert and take ownership of his feelings. He stated that at some point in our work together, he began to "like" me and that despite his progress in therapy, he believed that he would somehow not meet my expectations for him—that he would be a disappointment and that I would realize he was "not worth it." He shared that his pattern of behavior in such situations would be to simply not care as a way to emotionally protect him from an anticipated rejection. He stated he was torn—that he wanted very much to withdraw from our work together but at the same time felt committed to stay because he did not want to place more shame on himself, his family, and me.

As interpersonal process theory would predict, John had transferred the fears he had with his parents to me, another Asian male figure. He experienced the conflict, anxiety, and sadness he had repeatedly felt throughout his life. Instead of working to have him experience immediate relief, which would normally be done in the early stages of working with Asian Americans, I worked to keep the fear salient in order for us to work through it together. Indeed, to be in such an unpredictable situation, to try so hard, and to not know the outcome of a process certainly presented a most uncomfortable scenario. I stated that interactions are indeed scary and that there is a natural tendency for all humans to accept predictable and familiar paths when fear arises. His path was to retreat from others when fear increased. I asked him how he, in this moment, could confront the fear and not run away.

With what felt like several minutes of silence, he asked me the following question in a most gentle and vulnerable manner: "Do you . . . like me?" I realized this was a monumental action on his part—risking rejection by asking me of my feelings. I stated that I truly appreciated his courage and inquired about his feelings in the moment. He shared that he felt anxious, but paradoxically stable—"strong." This is what I had hoped for John: to gain a comfort with the "discomfort" of uncertainty. By confronting his fear of rejection by taking a risk with me, an Asian man, he was establishing his own sense of power, leadership, and vulnerability—a sense of his own masculinity. I felt a range of emotions, from happiness (realizing he was moving toward his goals) to sadness (knowing that our work would likely be ending soon).

I answered his question honestly. First, I thanked him for asking me the question. I then disclosed that I truly liked and appreciated him—not only for his commitment to our relationship but mostly for his courage to confront all the parts of himself, strong and vulnerable, to establish a sense of identity for himself, and that it was through this acceptance that peace with his culture, father, and mother could possibly result. I thanked him for the opportunity to learn so much from him and about him. I shared that I accepted and respected him for all he represented, that he did not shame himself or his family, and that I felt closest to him in that very moment when he was most at risk. He was not shaming himself, his family, or me—through his courage, he was bringing honor to them. He wept quietly. In that moment, I felt a strong sense of connection and closeness with John—not as a counselor, friend, or colleague—but as a man. I cherish that moment.

He appeared overwhelmed, not necessarily because of my words, but because he had confronted his many fears by asking me, without knowing the outcome, what I felt for him. I believe that this experience facilitated, on some level, a corrective emotional experience for John, as well as providing a redefining moment for him in his quest to find comfort with being an Asian American man. Perhaps this is what it meant, for him, to be an Asian American man: strength, courage, expressing emotions, and fear. I asked him about his feelings; he responded quietly by saying "different." I believe that John at that point recognized that he could carve his own path, traditional or nontraditional, toward being an Asian man. Although still affected by his past, he was no longer reliving, through isolation and distance, the trauma of rejection. Although he could not change history, he could now change the course of the future through his masculinity: courage, sensitivity, and respect—all components of what many perceive is the true Asian American male (Liu, 2002; Sue, 2001).

Termination

This emotional experience facilitated a most gentle final phase of therapy. John's overall levels of anxiety decreased slightly in social situations, as he reported increased comfort in interacting with Asian, especially Korean, students. He also reported gradual increases in mood and overall outlook. He seemed to be experiencing a growing pride as a Korean American, although there continued to be internal struggles to synthesize his identity. I believed this was productive, as it indicated movement beyond his immersion stage of development (Atkinson et al., 1993).

John used our time together to work through the varied emotions toward his father, even engaging in an empty-chair exercise to share his feelings. And he began considering working on reestablishing a relationship with his mother (he actually started composing a letter to his mother). His wariness of men and women did not decrease immediately but was gradual; his projection of feelings from his father and mother continued to be influential—but his awareness of these emotions and patterns was present. Again, this awareness and periodic risk-taking reflected movement; as with cultural identity development, when there is movement, there is a higher likelihood for change (Atkinson et al., 1993).

Finally, I suspect that our relationship became more relaxed and collegial as we ended our work together. I attempted, through drawing on an integration of the Asian American literature and interpersonal process theory, to model for him a type of masculinity and mentoring that he had not experienced prior to therapy. We shared our appreciation for each other more frequently, and there appeared to be genuine affection and respect for each other. At times John would even joke with process comments such as "I'm feeling [internal] pressure to be an obedient Asian son"—to which we would laugh and then process. At times, we would attempt to speak Korean in therapy, which allowed John to display his strength in language and allowed me to reveal my vulnerable side (because I am not proficient in speaking Korean); we would process this interaction. Again and again, there was movement.

John and I ended our therapy 6 months after we began. In that time, I felt truly happy for John's commitment, courage, and growth. I shared that I would miss him very much; he shared similar feelings. I felt more secure about my work and portrayal of an Asian man—with strengths and vulnerabilities—and this, in a way, allowed me the experience of gaining insight into my own masculinity. I referred him to an interpersonal process group as the next phase. He cautiously accepted this offer and risk and stated that he saw it as a way to feel more comfort around men and perhaps to receive feedback and advice on how to speak more confidently to women. John had what I believe was his first opportunity to experience the start and end of a healthy relationship with a man. He was coming into his own as an Asian man, and I was happy for his movement.

FINAL THOUGHTS

John is, without question, one of my most memorable clients. For me, John represented an integration of principles of multicultural counseling competence, psychodynamic theory, and interpersonal process therapy with men.

As I periodically reflect on this case, I am amazed at how ingrained cultural values can be, even across generations. Themes of Asian masculinity, cultural conflict, and parental figures represent many issues that Asian American men currently face (Liu, 2002; Sue, 2001). And in accordance with multicultural counseling competencies, therapists must not only attend to the salient cultural issues but may need to go outside the traditional role of "therapist" and into more nontraditional roles of mentor, healer, advocate, and self-discloser—roles that suit a particular culture and individual (Lynch & Hanson, 1992).

Research on Asian Americans indicates that establishing credibility, gift giving, trust, and an initial directive counseling style with clients often results in continued use of services (see Uba, 1994). For me, this meant often delaying my need to "process" until John was able to confront his fears—at his pace. This resulted, at times, in "rejection." But even with John's initial rejections, I felt that his statements of not being ready to move with me were an indication of him building a sense of strength and asserting his own masculinity. I appreciated that process because it allowed me to keep in check my issues about wanting to be a perfect Asian man for other Asians; I was reminded repeatedly that his sense of masculinity did not, and should not, necessarily have to match mine. I left John with the following statement that I must remind myself of: "Trust the process."

QUESTIONS FROM THE EDITORS

1. *What types of gender-based stereotypes were you aware of when counseling this client? How did that impact your therapy with this client?*

Although John presented as a sensitive and thoughtful individual as therapy progressed, his initial presentation was typical of many Asian American men: cognitive, intellectual, and removed from emotion (Liu, 2002). As described in the chapter, early attempts on my end to examine emotions were confusing to (or avoided by) him, which is not surprising. Also, in his interactions with me, the issue of cultural norms surrounding respect to elders and experts became salient. His interactions with me throughout the course of therapy were quite respectful, and I certainly felt at times he wanted me to serve in the expert, leadership role. He was deferent, nonconfrontational, and quite respectful, even if he did not completely understand the nature of some of my comments or interventions. In addition, he was quick and efficient in following through with any homework or assignment I suggested—a sign of respect to maintain harmony in relationships. Such actions in Asian male–male relationships exist, particularly if face-issues are salient in the relationship. The goal of my work with John was to (a) not devalue or disrespect the importance of such traditionally culturally appropriate interactions but also to (b) work with him to gain insight and skills into critically assessing the values, roles, and expectations within the Korean culture.

2. How did your own gender role issues influence your work with this client?

This is an excellent question for this case. My work with John allowed me the challenging opportunity to honestly examine my own gender role issues. I found myself wanting to be the perfect therapist for John. I placed so much pressure on myself to perform and be the best helper for John—which tied into my own stereotypic male drive to win—that it affected my course to facilitate the therapeutic process. When I might have normally made a process comment, I would hesitate initially with John. When he did not understand an intervention on my part, I sometimes felt disappointed in myself. I also noticed that at the early stages of therapy, I sometimes was thinking more than feeling, or the ratio would be unbalanced. When I allowed myself to confront my fears of not being perfect, I felt I could ultimately be a good therapist for John. In the end, I believe that is the true masculine approach. I find that the issues of perfection, winning, and an outcome-based definition of *success* are things that I must continually monitor and reflect on. When I can do this, I know I am growing, even when the growth is at times uncomfortable.

3. Looking back on the case, knowing what you know now, would you change the way you worked with this client?

As I reflect on this case, the first thing that comes to mind is that I wish I had been able to do more with the countertransference I felt in working with John. In my wish to be a positive role model of the Asian American man, I became at times too concerned with his reactions to me. I felt much compassion for John—I truly liked him as a person. I also wanted to be liked, but this prevented me from doing some things I know could have had quite a positive impact. Knowing that I had established a sound foundation of trust and respect, I wish I had addressed the powerful components of our connection earlier in therapy. That would have modeled a type of courage and strength that, in my view, is representative of the healthy Asian American man. Fortunately, I was able to use these feelings later in the therapeutic relationship—with positive results. However, I know that had I been courageous, I could have had a wonderful opportunity to process our relationship in a time frame that would have been just as appropriate.

4. It seems that when working with Asian American clients, you are very aware of your cultural background. How does that appear with non-Asian clients?

I am constantly aware of the issue of culture and my cultural background in my work with clients—both Asian American and non-Asian. My efforts to be a multiculturally competent counselor demand this type of awareness, knowledge, and appreciation for differences. I believe that all interactions are cross-cultural and that every meeting with a client presents an opportunity to address culture. My work with Asian American clients often allows for an immediate, ascribed type of credibility and understanding, in which cultural similarities and unique differences are not only articulated but are also felt and experienced (many times without words). In my work with non-Asian clients, I attempt a similar approach: to use my cultural background as a way to address cultural similarities and differences as a means to connect with clients. However, with Asian clients, discussions regarding cultural etiquette, customs, and interaction styles are less frequent in comparison to non-Asians. As is to be expected, there is often more education with non-Asian clients on the Asian culture. Although my experiences with Asian clients are often very different from non-Asian clients, the ingredients are the same to build the relationship: respect and trust. I see the concept of "culture," cultural differences, and my cultural background as strengths in my therapy with clients, not necessarily an "issue."

5. *How do you see the concepts of "honor," "shame," and "saving face" when working with Asian American men?*

The concepts of "honor," "shame," and "saving face" play out often in my work with Asian American men. The issue of "saving face" has been found to be a most salient and impacting variable for Asian Americans— often impacting disclosures, behaviors, and relationships. I believe the core elements of Asian culture, such as balance, community, and harmony, have persisted because of the concepts of "shame" and "maintaining face." With Asian American men, the issues of family honor, being the leader of the family, and male interpersonal etiquette continuously are indeed present— and this seems to cut across generation and acculturation levels. Asian American men work to not lose face, not be the cause of another person losing face, and show respect for male elders and experts. Therapy presents a situation that is highly threatening to face and (stereotypic) masculinity. It is thus not surprising that interactions with Asian American men are often the most difficult for me at the outset of therapy. Establishing trust and respect often must be done within the ground rules or boundaries of face-saving interactions: "gift giving" (immediate symptom reduction), which allows for the start of an exchange type of relationship; directive efforts on the part of the therapist to reduce the ambiguity of the exchange; and not having the client engage in face loss early in therapy. If these elements are established early in the relationship, there is tremendous potential for the therapy to be effective.

SUGGESTED RESOURCES

Asian American Psychological Association: http://www.aapa.org/

Chin, F. (1991). *Donald Duk*. Minneapolis, MN: Coffee House Press.

Lee, A. (Director). (1994). *The wedding banquet* [Motion picture]. United States: 20th Century Fox.

Lin, J. (Director). (2003). *Better luck tomorrow* [Motion picture]. United States: Paramount Pictures.

Men's Health Network: http://www.menshealthnetwork.org/

MenWeb: http://www.menweb.org/throop/index.html

Okada, J. (1976). *No-no boy*. Seattle, WA: University of Washington Press.

REFERENCES

Atkinson, D. R., & Gim, R. H. (1989). Asian American cultural identity and attitudes toward mental health services. *Journal of Counseling Psychology, 36*, 209–212.

Atkinson, D. R., & Lowe, S. M. (1995). The role of ethnicity, cultural knowledge, and conventional techniques in counseling and psychotherapy. In J. G. Ponterotto, J. M. Casas, L. A. Suzuki, & C. M. Alexander (Eds.), *Handbook of multicultural counseling* (pp. 387–414). Thousand Oaks, CA: Sage.

Atkinson, D. R., & Matsushita, Y. J. (1991). Japanese American acculturation, counseling style, counselor ethnicity, and perceived counselor credibility. *Journal of Counseling Psychology, 38*, 473–478.

Atkinson, D. R., Morten, G., & Sue, D. W. (1993). Within-group differences among racial/ethnic minorities. In D. R. Atkinson, G. Morten, & D. W. Sue (Eds.), *Counseling American minorities: A cross-cultural perspective* (4th ed., pp. 19–39). Madison, WI: Brown & Benchmark.

Atkinson, D. R., Whitely, S., & Gim, R. H. (1990). Asian American acculturation and preference for help providers. *Journal of College Student Development, 31*, 155–161.

Chua, P., & Fujino, D. C. (1999). Negotiating new Asian American masculinities: Attitudes and gender expectations. *The Journal of Men's Studies, 7*, 391.

Goffman, E. (1955). On face-work: An analysis of ritual elements in social interaction. *Psychiatry: Journal for the Study of Interpersonal Processes, 18*, 213–231.

Gordon, B. (1990). Men and their fathers. In R. L. Meth & R. S. Pasick (Eds.), *Men in therapy: The challenge of change* (pp. 234–246). New York: Guilford Press.

Ho, D. Y. (1976). On the concept of face. *American Journal of Sociology, 81*, 867–884.

Lee, D. B., & Saul, T. T. (1987). Counseling Asian men. In M. Scher, M. Stevens, G. E. Good, & G. A. Eichenfield (Eds.), *Handbook of counseling and psychotherapy with men* (pp. 180–191). Thousand Oaks, CA: Sage.

Leong, F. T. L. (1986). Counseling and psychotherapy with Asian-Americans: Review of the literature. *Journal of Counseling Psychology, 33*, 196–206.

Liu, W. M. (2002). Exploring the lives of Asian American men: Racial identity, male role norms, gender role conflict, and prejudicial attitudes. *Psychology of Men and Masculinity, 3*, 107–118.

Lynch, E. W., & Hanson, M. J. (1992). Developing *cross-cultural competence: A guide for working with young children and their families*. Baltimore: Brooks/Cole.

Meth, R. L. (1990). The road to masculinity. In R. L. Meth & R. S. Pasick (Eds.), *Men in therapy: The challenge of change* (pp. 3–34). New York: Guilford Press.

Park, S., & Zane, N. W. S. (2005). *A test of two explanatory models of Asian American and White students' preferences for a directive counseling style*. Manuscript in preparation.

Pleck, J. H. (1995). The gender role strain paradigm: An update. In R. F. Levant & W. S. Pollack (Eds.), *A new psychology of men* (pp. 11–32). New York: Basic Books.

Pollack, W. S. (1998). Mourning, melancholia, and masculinity: Recognizing and treating depression in men. In W. S. Pollack & R. F. Levant (Eds.), *New psychotherapy for men* (pp. 147–166). New York: Wiley.

Rogers, C. R. (1951). *Client centered therapy*. Boston: Houghton-Mifflin.

Rowan, J. (1997). *Healing the male psyche: Therapy as initiation*. London: Routledge.

Sue, D. (2001). Asian American masculinity and therapy: The concept of masculinity in Asian American males. In G. R. Brooks & G. E. Good (Eds.), *The new handbook of psychotherapy and counseling with men: A comprehensive guide to settings, problems, and treatment approaches* (Vol. 2, pp. 780–795). San Francisco: Jossey-Bass.

Sue, D. W., Carter, R. T., Casas, J. M., Fouad, N. A., Ivey, A. E., Jensen, M., et al. (1998). *Multicultural counseling competencies: Individual and organizational development*. Thousand Oaks, CA: Sage.

Sue, D. W., & Sue, D. (1990). *Counseling the culturally different: Theory and practice* (2nd ed.). New York: Wiley.

Sue, S., & Zane, N. W. S. (1987). The role of culture and cultural techniques in psychotherapy: A critique and reformulation. *American Psychologist, 42*, 37–45.

Sue, S., Zane, N. W. S., & Young, K. (1994). Research on psychotherapy with culturally diverse populations. In A. E. Bergin & S. L. Garfield (Eds.), *Handbook of psychotherapy and behavior change* (4th ed., pp. 783–817). New York: Wiley.

Sullivan, H. S. (1968). *The interpersonal theory of psychiatry*. New York: Norton.

Teyber, E. (2000). *Interpersonal process in psychotherapy: A guide for clinical training* (4th ed.). Pacific Grove, CA: Brooks/Cole.

Uba, L. (1994). *Asian Americans: Personality patterns, identity, and mental health*. New York: Guilford Press.

Zane, N. W. S., Hatanaga, H., Park, S., & Akutsu, P. (1994). Ethnic-specific mental health services: Evaluation of the parallel approach for Asian American clients. *Journal of Community Psychology, 22*, 68–81.

Zane, N. W. S., & Mak, W. (2003). Major approaches to the measurement of acculturation among ethnic minority populations: A content analysis and an alternative empirical strategy. In K. M. Chun & P. B. Organista (Eds.), *Acculturation: Advances in theory, measurement, and applied research* (pp. 39–60). Washington, DC: American Psychological Association.

Zane, N. W. S., & Sue, S. (1991). Culturally respective mental health services for Asian Americans: Treatment and training issues. In H. Myers, P. Wohlford, P. Guzman, & R. Echemendia (Eds.), *Ethnic minority perspectives on clinical training and services in psychology* (pp. 49–58). Washington, DC: American Psychological Association.

Zane, N. W. S., & Yeh, M. (2002). The use of culturally based variables in assessment: Studies on loss of face. In K. S. Kurasaki & S. Okazaki (Eds.), *Asian American mental health: Assessment theories and methods* (pp. 123–138). New York: Kluwer Academic/Plenum Publishers.

III

EXPLORING CONNECTION: BUILDING THE THERAPEUTIC ALLIANCE WITH MEN

9

THE CASE OF THE
ANGRY BLACK MAN

JAY C. WADE

This case exemplifies how race, gender, masculinity, and power can enter into the room when working with men. Individual counseling and psychotherapy may take place within a room, but that room exists within a larger social, cultural, and political context. In this particular instance, the room existed in an acute inpatient psychiatric ward, within the mental health system, where I was the only African American man on the staff. Working within the mental health system, I found that many issues particular to men were not given the attention they deserved. From a medical, pathology-based model of treatment, the focus was on management of psychopathology, with little attention paid to nonpathological kinds of issues that can affect men's lives. Male clients would be concerned about such things as employment, divorce, marital and relationship satisfaction, child custody, male friendship, money, parenting, and so on. Each of these issues was couched in feelings and beliefs about oneself as a man and became more complex when racism, oppression, and discrimination were added to the mix. Through my individual and group work with men, I was able to address these issues, but all too frequently, I found that my colleagues did not. My desire to provide effective treatment with men motivated me to request men as clients or patients at the places where I worked and to write about how to work with men in counseling and psychotherapy.

One of my first scholarly endeavors was to write about the issues and concerns of African American men and how to best address these issues in counseling and psychotherapy (see Wade, 1994a, 1994b). In particular, I found clinicians often would ignore the environmental and societal influences that contributed to the clinical picture of Black men who were receiving psychiatric treatment. For example, a patient would state that he is abusing alcohol and cocaine because he cannot find a job. The common response from clinicians would be to ignore the fact that a Black man with limited skills and supports, who must face racial discrimination in hiring practices, may abuse substances when unable to find employment. Rather, clinicians would focus on the abuse, and they would essentially tell the patient, "You can forget about employment until you are abstinent."

Another neglected area of concern to Black men that I felt was not being addressed and was misrepresented in the literature was the father–son relationship. This literature has historically pathologized Black men because of father absence, that is, the belief that Black men are absent and uninvolved fathers and that this leads to problems in masculine identity development in Black men. Many men with whom I came into contact were single fathers disconnected from their children because of their inability to financially provide for their children. These fathers were often denied access to their children and longed for a father–child relationship. However, there were other fathers who were very involved with their children and viewed parenthood as a source of pride and accomplishment. I thought it important to stop blaming the victim and to consider the social and historical contextual factors that have influenced the plight of Black men and their role as fathers.

DEVELOPING IDEAS ABOUT WORKING WITH MEN

Eventually, these experiences as a clinician motivated me toward developing a model for working with men in counseling. In examining the literature, I found O'Neil's (1981, 2002) concept of "gender role conflict." This model stimulated some of my early thoughts on developing a model. I found aspects of this model to be applicable to many of the men I worked with, yet I questioned why some men did not experience psychological conflict related to traditional gender roles. I wondered why some men adhere to traditional masculinity standards whereas others do not. I also wondered to what extent gender role conflict was an issue for African American men who may have a different masculinity, and how gender role conflict might differ for African American men. Similarly with Eisler's (Eisler & Blalock, 1991; Eisler & Skidmore, 1987) concept of "masculine gender role stress," I wondered what factors might mediate the experience of gender role stress, that is, what would make one man view a particular situation as stress producing whereas another man would not?

The Model of Male Reference Group Identity

Based on my own experiences as a man and on encounters with other men I had known, as well as a review of the literature on men and masculinity, I developed the theory of male reference group identity dependence (Wade, 1998). The theory concerned male identity and stated that men will differ in their feelings of psychological relatedness to other men. Such differences have significance for the extent to which and how men use a male reference group for their gender role self-concept (i.e., one's gender-related attitudes, attributes, and behaviors). The theory argued that

1. A man's gender role self-concept develops in relation to other males through feelings of psychological relatedness.
2. Males will vary in the extent to which they feel psychological relatedness to other males.
3. Psychological relatedness to other males, along with differences in male reference groups, underlies differences in masculinities.

There are three hypothesized male reference group identity statuses that are characterized by differences in feelings of psychological relatedness to other men. The *no reference group* status is characterized by a lack of psychological relatedness to other males; the *reference group dependent* status is characterized by feelings of psychological relatedness to some males and not others; and the *reference group nondependent* status is characterized by feelings of psychological relatedness to all males. The qualitative differences in feelings of psychological relatedness have implications for the gender role self-concept and the quality of one's gender role experiences.

For the no reference group status, there is confusion about oneself as male—not in terms of core gender identity but rather in terms of the socio-cultural and personality aspects of being male, because there is no image of maleness or group of males that the individual feels similar to or with whom one identifies. There is confusion, alienation, insecurity, and anxiety associated with gender role experiences. For the reference group dependent status, there is identification with an image or group of males perceived as similar to oneself while not so with males perceived as dissimilar to oneself. For example, there is rigid adherence to gender roles (i.e., of the reference group, whatever they may be), stereotyped attitudes, and limited or restricted gender role experiences and behaviors. For the reference group nondependent status, there is identification with all males. Although there may be an image of maleness or group of males the individual feels he is like or most similar to, there is no prepotent male reference group and there is an appreciation of differences among males. The individual is able to be relatively flexible, autonomous, pluralistic, and unlimited in his gender role attitudes, attributes, and behaviors.

Male reference group identity assumes that one's gender role attitudes, standards, and attributes develop within a cultural context and that the cultural context may differ among individuals. Originally, the male reference group is the cultural purveyor, and through psychological relatedness, one internalizes and makes one's own the gender role attitudes of the male reference group. Both psychological relatedness and reference group selection may have different psychological consequences for males of different races, ethnicities, sexual orientation, religious affiliations, ages, and so on.

Working with men, I found that men who are more likely to experience conflict associated with the male role are also more likely to have internalized a rather rigid masculinity that has been characterized in the literature as "traditional." This masculinity is predominant, and many men do not see how their attitudes, behaviors, and beliefs are associated with how they were socialized to be a man. Such men would be characterized as reference group dependent according to my theory and would be men who are more likely to experience gender role conflict. However, it should be noted that because there are many masculinities, male reference group identity theory focuses more on the adherence to reference group norms of masculinity rather than on the norms themselves. When working with men who may be characterized as reference group dependent, the therapist would have the goal of developing a male identity that is personally defined and relevant.

How I Work With Clients

Because traditional masculinity norms limit men's experiencing and expressing emotions other than anger, I have found and the literature suggests (e.g., Allen & Gordon, 1990; Brooks, 1998; Clark, 2000; Lee & Owens, 2002) that men tend to be more cognitive and behavioral than affective and emotional in their approach to things. Men tend to want to solve problems on their own rather than to seek help, and their approach to problem solving tends not to be through expressing tender emotions. Perhaps because of masculinity norms, as well as my own personality, I tend to be cognitive and behavioral in my own approach to counseling and psychotherapy. However, a limitation of this approach is that it can neglect addressing one's affective experience, and oftentimes men need an approach that focuses on feelings. Typically, but depending on the client's style, I initially use a more cognitive–behavioral approach when working with men and focus less on feelings and interpretation. I listen for cultural messages and try to tease out what may be culturally related versus personality versus psychopathology. I try to evaluate the client's thinking and behavior in terms of whether it is maladaptive. Eventually, however, I engage clients in more affective work by using a psychodynamic approach. I use Rogerian counseling attitudes: empathy, unconditional positive regard, acceptance, genuineness, and a nonjudgmental stance. I let the client know that I recognize the difficulty of the situation for him, in terms of being in a situation in which he has either sought help or has been coerced or forced to seek help (e.g., being hospitalized involuntarily, receiving court mandated treatment, or being pressured from a wife or mate to seek treatment).

THE SETTING AND CIRCUMSTANCES IN THE CASE OF GEORGE

I was working as the activity therapy supervisor on the acute inpatient unit of a private hospital when George was hospitalized for depression, aggressive behavior, and substance abuse. He told his wife, while intoxicated, that he was going to kill himself. It seemed to me that this was a cry for help. His wife called the police and told them George had made a suicidal attempt, which according to George was actually not the case. The police brought him to the emergency room, where he was evaluated by a psychiatrist, diagnosed as depressed and suicidal, and hospitalized.

In the presentation of his case history to the staff, the following details were disclosed. George was a 42-year-old married African American man who had a master's degree and worked in social services. He was the father of three children. After his mother had died, approximately 1 year prior to admission, he moved from recreational alcohol use to alcohol and cocaine abuse. In this process, he lost his job in a federal social service program. While under the influence of substances, he would be argumentative, with frequent altercations with his wife and sometimes with the police. He would wander off for days on drug and alcohol binges.

The inpatient unit was a locked ward with 22 beds. The staff consisted of the chief psychiatrist, three psychiatric residents, a clinical psychologist and two interns, an art therapist, a social worker, four daytime nurses, two psychiatric technicians, and myself. The orientation was psychodynamic. The staff was predominantly White, with three African Americans: two female nurses and myself. The average length of patient stay was around 28 days, and there was administrative pressure to have patients discharged within those 28 days. The patients were predominantly White and had private insurance, and they ranged in age from adolescence to the elderly. Two or three beds were reserved for patients on Medicaid or Medicare. Treatment consisted primarily of medication, activity therapy groups, community meetings, and individual therapy.

After several days of being in the hospital, several observations were made by the staff with respect to George and his behavior on the unit. George was intelligent and articulate, and he tended to use his intelligence and verbal skill in an aggressive manner toward the staff. Initially he was angry, hostile, demanding, arrogant, and devaluing of the hospital and staff. On the ward, he was argumentative, and the staff had difficulty controlling his verbally aggressive behavior. Most of the predominantly White staff were either fearful of him or disliked him. My view of George's behavior was consistent with the other staff members' views. However, I did not feel intimidated by George, nor did I feel defensive, angry with him, or devalued by him. I did not like or dislike him, rather I viewed his behavior as ego defensive and mostly felt the desire to help and protect him. When he spoke with me, the only African American man who was a professional on the staff, I noticed he behaved in a manner opposite to what was observed on the unit.

Several of the staff members were frightened of George, and many were angry with him. The Black female nurses on staff also had difficulty managing him. He was assessed to be manipulative, attention seeking, potentially violent, and able to divide the staff. I did not agree with this assessment, except that he did seem to make the staff work harder than usual to come up with a unified way of managing him. The initial intervention involved using medication and setting consistent limits with George. Although in this inpatient unit only the psychiatric residents were assigned as primary therapists, I asked the team if I could be assigned as George's primary therapist. I explained that a rapport was developing between George and me and that I could work individually with George to help him through his inpatient stay. I purposely phrased it this way to indicate that his behavior was an expression of his difficulty being a patient rather than his behavior being primarily difficult for staff. Nonetheless, the staff wanted him controlled, and if I could do it, they were behind it, especially the attending psychiatrist, who approved, stating that it was an excellent idea. I would be the primary therapist in collaboration with the psychiatric resident assigned to the case. It should also be acknowledged that this was a staff that recognized that the patient might work best with another Black man, or someone who was sensitive to issues of race and gender.

To understand George, I found it important to recognize race- and gender-related factors in conceptualizing the case and determining how to intervene. I viewed the situation from the perspective of George fitting the stereotype of the angry Black man, and therefore he was feared by some of the staff, in particular some of the White clinicians and most of the female staff. The stereotype is a media-driven image that emerged in the 1960s and portrays Black men as hostile, dangerous, threatening, criminal, and violent (Steinhorn, 1999). As a result, African American men's public expression of assertiveness is mistranslated into aggressive behavior (Franklin, 1998). Some staff were able to express their fear of George in clinical staff meetings. Although George had not actually threatened any staff or patients on the unit, his behavior was described as "threatening," and female nursing staff stated they were afraid he might act out violently. Others expressed their anger and exasperation. This was understandable because George often made racial remarks about the White staff and their incompetence. Nevertheless, it was somewhat difficult for me in these meetings because I thought the staff was not handling George the best way possible and felt uncomfortable with their characterization of him. I did not see him as threatening or frustrating, rather I saw the staff as mostly having a hard time dealing with a patient who challenged our authority and refused to be the nice, docile patient. Clinical staff that led the community meeting used a psychodynamic approach, using interpretations to respond to George's complaints and criticisms about the unit and staff. This seemed to only fuel George's anger, who would intelligently but hostilely tell the leaders they were ignoring the issues, using "psychobabble," and trying to manipulate and control the patients. The staff wanted him controlled and compliant, which is understandable, given the nature of psychiatric inpatient treatment. Although medication was one way to intervene and seemed to have some effect on his behavior, limit setting was not working too well.

The psychodynamic method of running a community meeting overall did not sit well with me. Interpretation of patients' complaints tended to go over the patients' heads, and I believed the patients deserved a concrete response from staff that let them know they were being heard and understood, and that their concerns were being addressed. In part, I suppose that made me empathize with George and internally side with his point of view. To some extent, I saw this conflict as a racial/cultural issue that was being acted out, as well as a control and power issue. George would not be able to "win" in this situation, nor would he benefit from his inpatient stay if he continued to engage in these struggles with the staff. Consequently, I viewed the primary goal in working with George as him changing the way he interacted with staff to be more productive.

Initial Sessions With George: Conceptualization and Catharsis

I met with George three times a week, which were the only days I worked on the unit. George had been on the unit approximately 1 week before I started working with him individually, and he was eager to work with me. He felt he could trust and talk with me, because I could identify with his particular situation as an African American man. Rapport developed very quickly, in part because I was another Black man and therefore he assumed that I would understand him. I understood why he had criticisms of the staff, from my own experiences as a Black professional working within the mental health system. Based on my experiences, one of my first publications was an analysis of institutional racism in the mental health system (Wade, 1993). However, with George, I did not understand the intensity of the anger directed at the staff.

I used specific techniques that allowed for and encouraged the rapport. First and foremost, I told him that I was on his side and recognized how difficult it must be for him to be hospitalized. I was supportive and initially did not challenge him. I used reflections of content, common language rather than psychological terms, and recognized race and gender as important factors in why he was having difficulty on the unit and why staff were having difficulty with him. For example, I would respond to George's various criticisms of the staff with reflections like the following: "You feel angry with the staff because they are not listening to you or respecting you as an intelligent Black man"; "The staff don't know how to best deal with a Black man of your stature"; "You have some legitimate complaints, but you feel that because of race you aren't being heard." The first couple of meetings were basically spent getting to know George and allowing him to complain to me about the staff. In addition to reflecting, I would respond by letting him know that I understood why he was angry and that he had a right to be so. I told him, "Yes, the staff are more concerned with your presentation than the truth of what you say"; "I can understand how some of the staff can get you upset when they ignore your point and focus on your behavior"; "At times it does seem like they are treating you in a way that could provoke anger."

Initially, one of the goals of the counseling was for him to express his anger so that there would be a catharsis and so he would therefore have less anger to direct at staff. So when he criticized staff, I did not defend the staff's actions, yet I was careful not to collude with him against the staff. For example, when he would say a staff person was a racist, I would say, "I can see why you think so, but I can't say for sure"; "Sometimes people don't see what they say or do as having a racist undertone to it"; "Well, you know Whites often don't perceive racism existing when Blacks perceive it does." Additionally, I knew that I would have to help him to be able to deal with his anger at the staff in a way that was more productive and to eventually get at what was at the root of his anger, which seemed more like a rage that was far too intense for the situation.

In my professional life, I have had the experience of working in both a predominantly Black mental health program and a predominantly White mental health program. Communication styles, among other things, were very different between the two places, which I later came to understand as culturally based differences in styles of communicating. Although this is somewhat of an oversimplification in the description of the two environments, I would characterize the communication style of Blacks as being more emotional, with truth being based on what one feels to be true. Conversely, I would characterize the communication style of Whites as being more rational, with truth being based on science and logic. While at the predominantly White work site, there were a few instances in which I expressed my opinion about something usually having to do with what we as a team were doing clinically with a patient or with respect to the treatment program. Granted, I expressed my opinion with passion and emotion, a manner that would go without comment when working with the predominantly Black staff. However, with the White staff the response would be to ignore my point and address my delivery by generally saying, "You seem to be upset. Is there something bothering you that we can help you with?" Although I did not feel upset, by my colleagues making that suggestion I began to wonder whether I was upset and did not know it, making me question myself. The other relatively common occurrence was when I would make a suggestion for an intervention of some sort, and it would go ignored. Then, some other staff member would make basically the same suggestion for an intervention, support the suggestion with some scientific literature or research, and it would be accepted. Given these experiences, I could identify and empathize with George and the difficulty he was having on the unit. However, in gauging my own emotional response to these kinds of incidents, I did not have the kind of anger bordering on rage displayed by George.

My experience working in the mental health system suggested that systemic intervention was needed with staff on behalf of George. For George to benefit from treatment, he would need more than medication and limits setting. In my opinion, many of George's complaints were valid—partially out of a countertransference reaction, yet primarily because in my professional opinion, what George identified were actually things that could be improved on. George's concerns were mainly about things an inpatient staff gives little thought to: right to privacy, cleanliness of the facilities, quality of the food, manners, the regimen, and so on. Nonetheless, the way George expressed himself did not allow for any other response from the staff but to pathologize his behavior and control it.

My experiences working in the mental health system also informed my conceptualization of George's problems on the unit. Inpatient hospitalization is typically about reducing psychiatric symptoms through the right dosage of medication, and quickly so as to make beds available for more patients. Thus, the primary goal of psychotherapy when conducted by a psychiatrist (or resident, in this case) tends to be in line with the goals of inpatient treatment: reduction of symptoms through finding the right dosage of medication. Other areas of a patient's functioning tend to be secondary. This can be at odds with the way Black men view their problems and the way they need to be addressed. George did not think that he needed medication, although he agreed to take it. I believed George needed to be listened to, respected, validated, and responded to concretely and that what needed to be explored was what was underlying his rage at the system.

Using Black racial identity theory (Cross, 1991, 1995; Helms, 1990, 1995; Vandiver, Cross, Morrell, & Fhagen-Smith, 2002) to understand George, I saw him as having characteristics associated with the immersion stage of racial identity. This identity status is characterized by the idealization of Black people and culture and the rejection and denigration of White people and culture. Anger is associated with this status, and much of George's anger was directed toward White people. Although his anger at Whites would make it difficult for him to work with a White clinician, it does not mean that he could not benefit from working with someone who was White. If he were able to develop trust and rapport through the skills of the clinician, this could have the potential of quelling his rage, potentially allowing the clinician access to the root of his anger. Further, White racial identity theory (Helms, 1990, 1995) suggests that the clinician's racial identity status would be a factor. Additionally, some Black clinicians would have had difficulty working with George and the racial content of his issues because of their own racial identity.

In terms of gender role conflict and stress, George was experiencing conflict and stress associated with living up to the standards of traditional masculinity. George was representative of what was found in my research on African American men's gender role conflict (Wade, 1996), in which I found that the immersion status of racial identity was related to gender role conflict with regard to success, power, and competition issues and restrictive emotionality. In particular, George was having difficulty dealing with emotions related to death and loss and, more specifically, the death of his mother and later the loss of his job. His anger at the losses was being acted out, and feelings of depression and anger were in part acted out through alcohol and drug abuse—a rather typical way that men deal with such feelings (Pollack, 1998). As a Black man, I figured the loss of his mother had particular significance, given the importance of the mother–son relationship in African American culture.

After the first couple of sessions in which I got to know George and let him vent his anger, I began to focus on helping George differentiate his angry feelings by using reality testing. He would describe an incident that had occurred on the ward or some incident in which he had confronted staff and then vent his anger about the situation. The goal of my interventions now was to help him gauge how much anger was appropriate for the situation and how to best express or control the anger so as not to cause more difficulty for himself. The following is an example of how I responded to George in such instances:

George: The staff here doesn't care about the patients. You know that woman who is always interrupting in the community meeting with her crazy talk? They just let her wander around and don't watch after her. She goes into people's rooms without being invited. When I mentioned it to the head nurse, she just ignored me and basically told me to mind my own business. She really pissed me off! I told her, You nurses are all incompetent!

Me: What did the nurse actually say to you, her exact words?

George: Well, she said that they were aware of what she was doing and that they were handling it. But they weren't handling it and she just dismissed me!

Me: What is it you would have the nursing staff do?

George: Stop the woman from going into other people's rooms!

Me: How do you think they should do this?

George: I don't know, but they should.

Me: So you are primarily angry with this nurse because she doesn't know how to control the patient's behavior but also because she didn't do what you asked?

George: Yeah, I guess so.

Me: And perhaps this lack of your control, in this situation, is what infuriates you?

George: Well, yeah, sort of. But I also am mad at the nurse. She doesn't know how to treat people.

Me: I would guess in your work, at your job, you have run across people like that—people who don't treat people with respect and courtesy. How do you normally handle it?

George: Well, you have to deal with them. I tend to ignore it, unless it's directed at me personally, in which case I let the person know I didn't like what they did.

Me: Do you get angry, raise your voice, or criticize the person?

George: Well, not really. I just let them know.

Me: But here, in the hospital, you really get mad with the staff when that happens, and the result is that you end up getting into trouble with the staff. They respond by making it harder for you here because you make their job harder. They don't want to have to deal with your anger and criticisms.

Oftentimes, George would talk about how difficult it is to be a Black man, how he had to deal with White people (e.g., on the job, in the hospital) all the time who disrespected him, and how difficult a struggle it was to maintain a home and family while having to deal with racism. George knew I understood him. It was evident in what he said and the way he related to me. He would say things like, "As a brother, you know what I mean" or "You have to deal with the same thing, being a Black man in a White man's world." I would respond to these types of statements affirmatively, because they were true. Given the rapport that had been built, I felt confident in moving on to interventions that focused more on making some therapeutic changes. I explained to George that although he had a lot to deal with as a Black man, husband, and father, what he needed to work on was getting better and getting out of the hospital. I pointed out that if he continued to have these run-ins with the staff, it would only make his stay more unpleasant and longer:

He had been dealing with racism all his life, he could not change the staff, and he needed to change how he was handling the situation. I enjoyed working with George, and the feeling was mutual. He was receptive to my point of view and guidance, and I felt pleased with him and the progress of therapy. Building on our relationship, we moved on to other deeper issues.

Intervening With Men: Deconstructing Traditional Masculinity

It was around the fourth session that George made the statement that the staff in the hospital killed his mother. When I asked him to explain what he meant, he said that when his mother was sick, he brought her here to the hospital, and she died. He felt that her death was due to the hospital's incompetent staff. I specifically did not challenge this perception; rather, I expressed that perhaps he blamed himself for bringing her to this hospital and that perhaps he felt guilty for not taking better care of her. George began to discuss how bad he felt about her dying, that he had let her down, and that perhaps he had not done what was best for her to keep her alive. When he mentioned that the hospital had killed his mother, one could see the anger in his body language and feel its intensity. After mentioning his possible feelings of guilt, his affect changed to sadness as he described how he felt he had let his mother down. He went on to explain the entire circumstances surrounding his mother's death.

With this new information about George and what might be behind his rage at the staff, I felt it necessary to let the staff know this information in the next clinical rounds so that they might respond a bit more sympathetically to him. In general, with my explanation the staff was able to obtain a different perspective and more empathic understanding of George, feel more comfortable in interacting with him, and be more objective in planning treatment interventions for him. I felt I had to advocate for George so that he could best benefit from treatment within a mental health system that often has little regard for the person.

Because of George's revealing his feelings about his mother's death, subsequent sessions focused less on anger at the staff and White people and more on his thoughts and feelings about himself as a Black man. I felt we had hit a crossroads in that he had begun to talk more about himself and less about the staff, and central to George was his identity as a Black man. In particular, I focused sessions on the various roles and obligations he had in his life, and trying to get an understanding of how his life went out of control to the point where he ended up in a psychiatric hospital. Because of his history of substance use and abuse, I wanted to be relatively sure that the abuse was a symptom versus a cause of his problems. To some extent they were both: As a symptom, substances were used to medicate himself, so to speak; as a cause, substance abuse was also the behavior that led him to be hospitalized. Through an examination of his usage history, I felt confident that the abuse was primarily a symptom, that is, a way to deal with his feelings of anger, loss, and depression. Further, George concurred and felt that he was not able to control his usage (primarily drinking) after the loss of his mother and especially after the loss of his job. When he lost his job, he said, he gave up. I told him perhaps he gave up because he had felt he had failed as a son and as a man, that he could no longer do those things that defined his manhood: caring for his mother, working, and being a husband to his wife and a provider for his family. However, there are other aspects of being a man, and with some effort he could return to work and to being a husband and provider. This led to a discussion about what it means to be a man.

It was sad to hear George's story about how after his mother died, he lost all confidence in himself, his sense of manhood, and his passion for life. The loss of his mother was the primary issue and trigger, but this deterioration was, from my point of view, intimately tied into his masculine ideology. I wanted to let George define for himself what it meant to be a man. Here, I was coming from the perspective of male reference group identity dependence. I viewed George as being primarily reference group dependent, in which male identity is conformist and there is strict adherence to masculinity norms. To develop a nondependent male identity, it would be necessary to challenge his notions of what it is to be a man and have him develop a more personally defined male identity. Using a cognitive approach, I challenged George on some of his definitions of manhood. For example, I asked George, "How would you define what it means to be a man?"

George: A man takes care of his responsibilities and doesn't take any crap from anyone. He is strong both mentally and physically.

Me: So when a man is unable to take care of his responsibilities, for legitimate and valid reasons, he is not being a man?

George: Well, yes, I guess, in a way.

Me: Suppose a man loses his job and is now unable to pay his mortgage and fully provide for his family. Is he now less of a man?

George: He is still being a man if he does whatever he can to remedy the situation.

More important, however, I wanted to address his thoughts and feelings surrounding the loss of his mother. The idea I had was that his cognitions about what had happened, and why, were connected to his beliefs about his role as a man. More specifically, he believed he had failed to take care of his mother, which is what he believed a man is supposed to do. So, through the process of his describing what it means to be a man and the extent to which he had failed to live up to those standards, I was able to move the counseling into talking about his mother.

Me: You believe it was your responsibility, as a man and son, to take care of your mother. Is that right?

George:	Yes, of course.
Me:	Did you?
George:	Well, yes I did. The hospital didn't take care of her though. I never should have brought her here. If I had taken her to a better hospital, she could still be alive today.
Me:	So like you said, being a man is taking care of one's responsibilities. You said that you did this with regard to your mother, but you feel that you failed to be responsible for her by taking her to this hospital where they let her die. However, you believe that as long as a man is doing whatever he can to remedy the situation, he is still a man. Do you believe you did everything you could to remedy the situation with your mother?
George:	No. I failed her.
Me:	What more could you have done?
George:	I could have taken her to a different, better hospital.
Me:	So, you are angry with yourself for not taking her to a different hospital, as well as angry at this hospital. Both you and the hospital failed her. As a man, in particular as a Black man, you are supposed to take care of your mother and protect her. You feel you didn't live up to your role as the good son.
George:	I couldn't save her.
Me:	You were the only one who could do this, take care of your mother, because you were the only family member and you were the man. [George's only sibling was deceased, and he had no contact with his father.] But what more could you have done? You took care of her, and whether or not the hospital is at fault, it seems to me that you were a very loving and caring son. Would she agree with me, if I were able to ask her?

Through these particularly intense sessions that focused on his sense of failure, as a man and as a son, I was able to reduce George's feelings of guilt around the loss of his mother and soothe his damaged ego. I wanted to communicate my care and concern for him, which comes in part from my own personality and masculinity but also from the positive aspects of masculine culture in the Black community. As Black men, we are all "brothers."

George was still angry at the hospital, but through the counseling he began to accept that he had done the best that he could do to care for his mother. I told him he was also a good husband and father and that he needed to focus on them now: do the best he could for them. This meant getting better and getting out of the hospital, returning to his wife and children, and to work. At one point in clinical rounds subsequent to these few sessions when George's case was discussed, there was a notable difference in the staff's discussion of his behavior on the unit. I had noticed a difference in the community meetings, where he was less disruptive and argumentative. This was very rewarding for me to see, because I felt the counseling was working and George was feeling and doing better. Although he continued to be the voice of the community, the angry tone and presentation had gone away. Staff had remarked on his being less angry and more cooperative, which they believed was due to his responding to the medication. However, I knew that he had come to certain realizations. Through the counseling, George was able to differentiate between the reasons for his anger: anger that stemmed from his mother dying in the same hospital where he was now being hospitalized, anger at himself for letting his mother down, and anger due to being frustrated at efforts to achieve and relate in "the White man's world."

His descent into drug and alcohol abuse was tied to his inability to grieve for his deceased mother and his anger at himself for not being able to fulfill his role as a man and son and keep his mother alive and well. He developed insight into how the socialization of masculine gender roles may have played a part in his feeling responsible for keeping his mother alive, expressing painful feelings through anger, and using substances to both suppress and express feelings.

George was hospitalized on the inpatient unit for approximately 4 weeks. The individual sessions with George began in the second week of his stay and continued three times per week until he was discharged 3 weeks later. I knew when George's discharge was approaching, on the basis of reports on George's treatment plan during clinical rounds. Because of my being part-time staff, I did not know exactly when he would be discharged and was not working the day he left the unit. As such, there was no clear ending with George. Given the nature of inpatient services, discharge generally occurs when the patient has recompensated, is stable on medication if medication is warranted, and has a place to stay. With regard to George, this meant no longer having suicidal ideation and aggressive behavior, being compliant with staff and treatment, and being able to return home to his family. As these goals were reached, our final few sessions were less intense, and we primarily discussed his improvements and plans after discharge. They focused less on therapeutic goals and were more focused on providing support and encouragement.

SUMMARY

My experience working within the mental health system has shown me that at times it is at odds with the way Black men view their problems and the way they need to be addressed. This is also true for men of other races; however, I wanted to present this case to demonstrate the particular situation of African American men who are receiving treatment. Racial factors, perhaps not understood because of racial and cultural differences between patient and staff, sometimes need to be understood and addressed in concert with masculinity issues.

Anger in men often conceals hurt, disappointment, and depression. It is important to acknowledge legitimate sources of anger and yet differentiate angry feelings when working with men. In the case of George, his anger was displaced onto all White people and the White clinical staff in particular. The counseling needed to acknowledge the legitimate sources of his anger at the staff as well as uncover, identify, and label those feelings that the anger signified. Until George's legitimate sources of anger were validated, he was not able to recognize and accept that there were other subconscious sources for his anger. Psychiatry tends to treat excessive or "inappropriate" affect with medication, whereas psychology tends to do so with counseling and psychotherapy. I view both as valid treatment paradigms, but both paradigms are culturally infused. Thus, cultural considerations are oftentimes important in designing a plan for treatment. I believe this was accomplished because of my sensitivity to racial, cultural, and masculinity issues; my advocacy on behalf of George; and a staff that was receptive to viewing race and gender as important factors to consider in this case.

QUESTIONS FROM THE EDITORS

1. *What types of race- and gender-based stereotypes were you aware of in counseling this client? How did that impact your therapy with this client?*

The gender stereotypes that I was aware of were related to the expression of emotion, being responsible and in control of everything, being strong both mentally and physically, and being aggressive and competitive. These stereotypes operated as masculinity prescriptions or scripts that I believed were operating within the patient. The extent to which George felt he was able to enact these prescriptions was related to his feelings about himself as a man. Perhaps he had been able to successfully enact these prescriptions prior to his psychological deterioration leading to hospitalization. However, being hospitalized was a very real manifestation of his belief that he had failed as a man. Being hospitalized, he was not mentally strong nor was he in control of his life. Perhaps to compensate for this failure, he exaggerated those aspects of masculinity that he in some way could manage to hold on to. So, George was overly aggressive and competitive with the staff and tried to be in control of what he could on the unit (e.g., the community meetings), and he expressed hurt, disappointment, and embarrassment through anger and intimidation. Given this conceptualization of George, the therapy had to address his definitions of masculinity, deconstruct those definitions, and construct new ones.

2. *How did your own gender role issues influence your work with this client?*

It is hard for me to figure that I had any gender role "issues," per se. I like to think that I then as well as now am a nontraditional man as compared with the "traditional man." So, I can best answer this question by saying how being nontraditional in my masculinity or gender roles influenced my work with George. First and foremost, I respected George and saw him as having a very hard time on the unit. I felt a bond with him as another African American man, and he had no problem viewing me in the same manner. I was not threatened by his behavior or his expression of masculinity; rather, I felt he needed support and protection—protection from the potentially harmful effects of the psychiatric system. I sensed a caring and sensitive man underneath the bravado and aggressiveness he was displaying. In working with George I felt I could bring that out in him, support it, and reinforce it and that I could be a caring and sensitive man with him. Granted, George was a man who was intelligent and mature, and not all men or African American men would have necessarily accepted my way of being a man. I was once told by a 23-year-old African American male client I worked with that I was a "sell-out" and just like a White boy. This was not said in anger, but to let me know how different I was from him. This statement did not insult me, and nonetheless the young man did benefit from being in counseling with me. I give this example to illustrate how George did not have a problem with me or my masculinity, whereas it could very possibly have been different.

3. *Looking back on the case, knowing what you know now, would you change the way you worked with this client?*

I could have possibly done some other work with George had I been a full-time staff member. With more time, I would have helped him to reconnect with his wife and children and to reassume his position as the head of the household. I may have explored more about his relationship with his father. It might have changed the entire dynamic with staff if I were full time, in that staff might have viewed me more as fully one of them. Being part time and relatively new to this staff, I had to be somewhat reticent in speaking my opinion about the staff's case conceptualization and treatment of George. It was a delicate balance, given that George (the difficult patient) and I (the staff person) were both African American men and there were not any other African American men on the unit that I can recall. I had to be one of the staff, like them, and at the same time inside feeling I was one of the Georges, a Black man, who was causing the staff problems.

4. *Scholars write about the existence of multiple "masculinities" based on cultural factors. Are there specific aspects of masculinity related to being an African American man?*

There are specific aspects of masculinity related to being African American, primarily because of having a racial minority status and common history of slavery and racism. African American men have had to define their masculinity in opposition to the dominant masculinity, and without the freedom to enact the dominant masculinity. Let it first be said that African American men are diverse in their masculinity, given social class and age differences. African American men have many masculinities. However, there are some aspects of African American masculinity that seem to be more widespread and understood across all economic strata and ages of African Americans. One is a respect and care for one's mother, an aspect that was evident in the case of George. Another is brotherhood. Other African American men are viewed as one's brothers. However, some African American men limit this type of brotherly affection and care to only those who are a part of their circle. African American men have generally been free to be emotionally expressive and to express affection to other African American men with whom they are close. I believe this male-to-male expression of closeness is a relatively new acceptance of a gender role norm that came about in the 1960s. There is also the expectation that one is to act like a Black man, without specifically knowing what that is other than to not act like a White man. This expectation comes mostly from other African American men, but African American women and European Americans also subtly and sometimes not so subtly express it. In general, as an African American man you must be psychologically and emotionally strong and tough to survive in an environment that is potentially hostile to you for being something you have no ability to do anything about, that is, being Black and male.

5. *You wrote about feeling that the staff was stereotyping the client as an "angry Black man." Part of your treatment was intervening with the staff to address this stereotype and presenting an alternative description of the client. Is that typical of your work?*

What has been typical of my work, in particular within the mental health system, is intervening with staff on behalf of any client. When I worked in psychiatric treatment settings, it was not always the angry Black man type but it often was on behalf of Black men receiving psychiatric treatment. Although I do not discriminate among patients with respect to the quality of care I provide them, I take particular interest in the welfare of "my people," so to speak. Because of my being an African American man and because I have seen the lack of understanding and quality of care African American men often receive, I have made it my business to advocate for them within the mental health system. Often the interventions with staff took the form of depathologizing the conceptualization of the patient's behavior. Other times it was just ensuring that the patient received the quality care he deserves, such as addressing premature discharge plans or termination of treatment, or questioning the efficacy of medicating the patient's behavior.

REFERENCES

Allen, J. O., & Gordon, S. (1990). Creating a framework for change. In R. L. Meth & R. S. Pasick (Eds.), *Men in therapy: The challenge of change* (pp. 131–151). New York: Guilford Press.

Brooks, G. R. (1998). *A new psychotherapy for traditional men.* San Francisco: Jossey-Bass.

Clark, C. F. (2000). *Why men hate therapy.* Retrieved January 10, 2004, from http://www.psychod.com/MIWhyMenHateTherapy.pdf

Cross, W. E., Jr. (1991). *Shades of Black: Diversity in African American identity.* Philadelphia: Temple University Press.

Cross, W. E., Jr. (1995). The psychology of nigrescence: Revising the Cross model. In J. G. Ponterotto & J. M. Casas (Eds.), *Handbook of multicultural counseling* (pp. 93–122). Thousand Oaks, CA: Sage.

Eisler, R. M., & Blalock, J. A. (1991). Masculine gender role stress: Implications for the assessment of men. *Clinical Psychology Review, 11,* 45–60.

Eisler, R. M., & Skidmore, J. R. (1987). Masculine gender role stress: Scale development and component factors in the appraisal of stressful situations. *Behavior Modification, 11,* 123–136.

Franklin, A. J. (1998). Treating anger in African American men. In W. S. Pollack & R. F. Levant (Eds.), *New psychotherapy for men* (pp. 239–258). New York: Wiley.

Helms, J. E. (1990). *Black and White racial identity: Theory, research, and practice.* Westport, CT: Greenwood Press.

Helms, J. E. (1995). An update of Helms's White and people of color racial identity models. In J. G. Ponterotto & J. M. Casas (Eds.), *Handbook of multicultural counseling* (pp. 181–198). Thousand Oaks, CA: Sage.

Lee, C. C., & Owens, R. G. (2002). *The psychology of men's health.* Philadelphia: Open University Press.

O'Neil, J. M. (1981). Male sex role conflicts, sexism, and masculinity: Psychological implications for men, women, and the counseling psychologist. *The Counseling Psychologist, 9,* 61–80.

O'Neil, J. M. (2002). *Twenty years of gender role conflict research.* Paper presented at the 110th Annual Convention of the American Psychological Association, Chicago.

Pollack, W. S. (1998). Mourning, melancholia, and masculinity: Recognizing and treating depression in men. In W. S. Pollack & R. F. Levant (Eds.), *New psychotherapy for men* (pp. 147–166). New York: Wiley.

Steinhorn, L. (1999). *The noble Negro stereotype: The black image in the white mind.* Retrieved January 10, 2004, from http://www.tompaine.com/feature2.cfm/ID/2503

Vandiver, B. J., Cross, W. E., Jr., Morrell, F. C., & Fhagen-Smith, P. E. (2002). Validating the Cross Racial Identity Scale. *Journal of Counseling Psychology, 49,* 71–85.

Wade, J. C. (1993). Institutional racism: An analysis of the mental health system. *American Journal of Orthopsychiatry, 63,* 536–544.

Wade, J. C. (1994a). African American fathers and sons: Social, historical, and psychological considerations. *Families in Society, 75,* 561–570.

Wade, J. C. (1994b). Substance abuse: Implications for counseling African American men. *Journal of Mental Health Counseling, 16,* 415–433.

Wade, J. C. (1996). African American men's gender role conflict: The significance of racial identity. *Sex Roles, 34,* 17–34.

Wade, J. C. (1998). Male reference group identity dependence: A theory of male identity. *The Counseling Psychologist, 26,* 349–383.

10

A NEW UNDERSTANDING OF THE MACHO MALE IMAGE: EXPLORATION OF THE MEXICAN AMERICAN MAN

JOSEPH M. CERVANTES

Latino men, regardless of ethnic background, have historically been viewed as hypersexualized, aggressive individuals who are prone to fits of anger, alcohol abuse, and involvement in multiple sexual affairs (Baca-Zinn, 1982; Cromwell & Ruiz, 1979; Fragoso & Kashubeck, 2000). A defining characteristic among Latino men based on some combination of myth, stereotype, or anthropological observation, has been the label of *macho*, or *machismo*. This description makes reference to a culturally expected and stylized set of actions from Latino men with respect to hypersexual and aggressive behaviors and a propensity to defy relational rules in a permanent partnership. A more detailed overview of the concept of "machismo" will be presented toward the end of this chapter.

Mexican and Mexican American men, in particular, have been described as being especially prone to machismo in their behavior, almost as if this internalized innate construct defines their actions and emotional repertoire (Casas, Turner, & Ruiz de Esparza, 2001; Falicov, 1998; Gowan & Trevino, 1998; Quintero & Estrada, 1998; Rodriguez, 1996). In this chapter, I explore the concept of "machismo" with a case description and analysis of a Mexican

American adult man and interweave this writing with my historical and biographical observations. As a Mexican American man with strong cultural and indigenous awareness, I have had the opportunity to observe the unique challenges of growing up in the 1950s postwar era in which overt prejudice and discrimination was still a defining characteristic for the United States. This was a time that predated the now-colloquial macho attitude but nevertheless was an assumed characteristic toward Latino men, thus the Mexican American or Chicano man was suspect. Although the term *Chicano* can be a label that has differing sociopolitical connotations in various parts of the Southwest, it is interchanged with the identification of Mexican American. (See Velasquez, Arrellano, & McNeill [2004] as a reference for added inquiry.)

This writing will proceed with an overview of the experience of being Mexican American, highlighting personal, family, and professional conflicts. The case of a 40-year-old Mexican American man who I treated for identity issues is next, followed by analysis of the counseling process. Last, a literature review of Mexican American maleness is presented to initiate a dialogue that may have relevance for psychological treatment and possible future research. Summary and conclusions provide relevant observations about this understanding.

THE EXPERIENCE OF BEING A MEXICAN AMERICAN AND INDIGENOUS MAN

I was born in Southern California in 1950, a place and time where the confines of a small community allowed for strong interfamilial ties while overt prejudicial practices were evident both in school and in the broader environment. These overt racist practices impacted the attitudes that were evident from the majority toward Spanish-speaking people and behaviors that dictated when Mexicans could swim in the local city pool, where they could sit in the one city theatre, and what side of town they lived on. Spanish was not an esteemed language but was rather a language of the disempowered and unacceptable class of people. These were the views seen through the eyes of a 5- or 6-year-old as I grew into a consciousness of those attitudes and feelings.

My life was framed within the scope of a strong Mexican/Indigenous upbringing with a large extended family and two parents who were dedicated to the rearing of their children and to their community. My mother, a product of an indigenous background and born in New Mexico, was well-educated for her time, having graduated from a Catholic high school in the mid-1940s with intentions of being a nurse, a career that never became at least formally fulfilled. My father, from a small ranch community in Jalisco, Mexico, turned businessman upon his arrival in the United States at the age of 14 and eventually owned and managed the first grocery store in the community and then a restaurant for several years. He was prone to providing food to those who could not afford it and treats to children during holiday periods.

My life was also framed by a maternal grandmother who was from indigenous cultural origins in Mexico and was a *curandera*, an indigenous folk healer. As the first male grandson, I was given the privilege of being cared for by her on several occasions. During these times, she often taught me about the interconnectedness of all living things. I learned as a child that flowers communicated to each other and to human beings, if they would listen; that animals shared a special place in the world with humans; and that the world was a place of magic and wonder that was embraced in the arms of Mother Earth, the protectress of all living things. In this context, the icon, Our Lady of Guadalupe, became a prominent fixture in my psyche as well as on the shelf in our respective homes. I was fortunate enough to observe several healing sessions that my grandmother conducted with various neighbors and referred clients into her home. These experiences encouraged me to be socially responsive to people, an observation that had also been reinforced by my own parents.

Experiences of being Mexican American, awareness of the sacredness in everyday life, and the observations of overt racism and oppression were an interesting blend of cultural socialization and personal awareness. I was exposed to a Roman Catholic primary and secondary education, where nuns demonstrated their own form of ethnic and racial discrimination. The nuns would forbid the Spanish language either in the classroom or in the playground, and by doing so intimated the lower quality of citizen that they felt characterized those who were Mexican. Although we could not verbalize the discrepancy at such early ages, this was an interesting contrast from teachers who were supposed to model Christian ideals and virtues to us as schoolchildren. The stigma of being Mexican American, speaking Spanish, and holding family values that were not mainstream was disregarded and rejected. Consequently, there were alternating, disjointed images of being a Mexican American male that characterized my upbringing.

The first of the additional influences that impacted my development as a Mexican American male was my entry into a Roman Catholic seminary after the eighth grade, which extended from the ages 13 through 21. This time frame reflected a significant generational era of political, racial, and cultural strife. My adolescent development was captured by the impact the Vietnam War had in the United States; the 1960s protest movements of African American, Chicano, and Native American peoples; and the belief that we, as disempowered people, were a holistic community that should support humanitarian efforts over the needs of government and big business.

The second influence occurred following my decision to leave formal seminary training and enter graduate school in psychology at the University of Nebraska—Lincoln in the early 1970s. It was during this time that I confronted my own personal, autobiographical history as I became involved with the Wounded Knee incident in South Dakota, a highly politicized and emotionally charged conflict between members of the American Indian movement and the United States government. It was with the impetus of this incident that I started to realize my own indigenous history and ancestral calling. It was also during this tentative formation that I became increasingly aware of the fact that my Mexican-ness was also Indian-ness and that my grandmother had played a critical role in that early shaping. Following her death in the 1980s, I took on a more direct role in the evolution of my ancestral calling, given that her death spurred several dream experiences in which my grandmother would continue the initiation of my indigenous heritage and commitment to be a healer. This awareness set the tone for personal and professional development, and subsequent theory building that was to follow (Cervantes, 2004a, 2004b; Cervantes & Ramirez, 1992; Tello, 1998; Valdez, Baron, & Ponce, 1987).

The construct of a macho male, although evident in my socialization and later development as a young adolescent boy, proved to be a meaningful awakening in my identity. This awakening emphasized descriptors of "protector of the family," "being responsible," and "leader in the community," which were held as expectations to be modeled and a salient part of development as a Latino male. Although the negative characteristics often associated with Mexican men and Mexican American men were evident and portrayed Latinos as domineering, aggressive, fearless, authoritarian, promiscuous, and virile (Niemann, Pollak, Rogers, & O'Connor, 1998; Quintero & Estrada, 1998), I did not integrate these into my own sense of personal identity as a man. Rather, the more affirming aspects of being a Latino male were prominent in my autobiographical education, which included expectations like keeping your word and having honor and respect for your family and less fortunate members of society (Baca-Zinn, 1982; Casas, Wagenheim, Banchero, & Mendoza-Romero, 1994; Ramirez, 1999; Torres, 1998).

CONCEPTUAL LENS AND PROFESSIONAL INFLUENCES

My professional practice has been influenced both by the ethnic and cultural traditions and experiences I have had and by nearly 3 decades of working with Spanish-speaking populations, primarily Mexican, Mexican American, and Chicano families. These observations of working with Chicano/Mexican American families are outlined in another source (Cervantes & Sweatt, 2004). Emphasized in that writing is the need to understand contextual background, immigration history, language issues, and social and oppressive, discriminatory experiences. The major part of my influence as a Mexican American man and how that affects my treatment as a professional has been shaped by those male members of my immediate and extended family who affirmed a strong sense of responsibility, loyalty, and respect for one's family. The elders in my early, developmental community of boyhood and young manhood experiences have mirrored many of the writings that are found among American Indians who described accounts of maleness consistent with honor and protection of the community. For example, one of my inspirations was the experiences of the medicine man Black Elk as communicated through his biographer Neihardt (1961), who wrote poetically about this man's life, mission, and his mystical visions to alert and protect his people. I have also been influenced by the writings of Lame Deer (Lame Deer & Erdoes, 1972), a holy man of the Lakota Sioux Tribe who told the story of manhood as it is experienced through oppression, discrimination, and protection of his ancestral land. A similar theme is noted by Montoya (1992), who described in his writing of poetry, drawings, and short stories a picture of the Chicano/Mexican American male who has had to struggle with the impact of cultural oppression and racism while attempting to integrate a sense of manhood. He observed that the indigenous history has gone underground as a result of generations of oppression and nonrecognition of the ancestral background of Mexican and Mexican Americans. Nevertheless, the relevance of staking claim to a manhood interwoven with respect and protection of one's community is also echoed by Montoya (1992).

The results of continuous exposure to my grandmother, the recognition of the distinct cultural backdrop of my heritage, and the writings from American Indian elders have influenced the foundation of specific philosophical tenets about life. These tenets have impacted my professional work and continue to evolve as I advance my clinical experience. A summary of these tenets appears with more detail in other writing that I have done (Cervantes, 2004a) and includes the following:

> All life is interconnected and sacred.
>
> A strong belief in energies and cosmic forces.
>
> Oppression, discrimination, and racism can form a salient background to the personality development of individuals and their later access to charting the course of individual lives.
>
> Life is a journey that is interwoven with both the sacred and the secular, and the successful navigation of these dimensions allows growth to proceed along a designated and more authentic path.
>
> It is important to recognize one's religious and spiritual beliefs, traditions, and rituals.
>
> Service to others is the natural order of things, following a realization of one's life journey.

More traditional influences in the psychological literature have come from Ramirez (1983, 1998), who described the Mestizo perspective that establishes an interconnectedness among the beliefs and values of indigenous peoples throughout the Americas. This concept of "Mestizo" has been broadened by Cervantes and Ramirez (1992) on counseling practices with Chicano families. A salient foundation to my work with Chicano and Latino families came from the influence I received through Minuchin (1974) in his initial treatise on families and family therapy. Minuchin spoke about the family system as it was experienced within my familial and cultural household. The constructs of parental systems, boundaries, alliances, and hierarchy were to both ground my personal experience and understand it with the many families that I would see in the future. A family systems perspective is closely interlinked with a transpersonal psychology framework for me that provides the theoretical language and rationale for how I typically work and view the healing process.

CASE DESCRIPTION AND ANALYSIS OF JUAN DIEGO ALEGRIA

Practice as a psychologist for almost 3 decades has afforded me the opportunity to examine many variations of Latino families especially with Mexican/Mexican American and Chicano populations (Cervantes, 2004b). Within that context, I have seen many Latino men in this designated ethnic group who have presented a wide variety of personal and relational problems, including marital difficulties, sexual orientation concerns, internalized distress resulting from experiences of oppression and discrimination, addiction problems, acculturation difficulties, professional development, and identity issues. The case of Juan Diego Alegria (a pseudonym to protect personal identity) is a case that I followed for 3 years, which has provided me the opportunity to look in depth at personal, familial, and relational history as it has impacted his development of manhood. The case of this client, hereinafter referred to as "Juan," begins with a description of relevant background history as related to the presenting problems that initiated treatment. Juan was seen in an outpatient private practice setting, in which the presenting problem was existential anxiety, framed within a lack of meaningful connectedness with others, difficulty with alcoholism, and a general feeling that personal problems were now beginning to affect professional work.

Juan was a 40-year-old man of Mexican American background who was born in a small mining town in northern Arizona. His parents were Mexican immigrants from a village community in Michoacan, Mexico, and were illiterate, young farmers who, because of the expectations of their era, married as adolescents. Marriage at a young age was typical in these communities because of the need to support population growth that provided economic stability, although at a low subsistence level. Juan was the third oldest of five children, with two older sisters who were born in Mexico prior to the parents' arrival in the United States. The parents immigrated when Juan's mother was pregnant with him and they arrived through the assistance of a "coyote" that transported the family across the border in a rented, windowless van. A "coyote" is a smuggler of people across Mexico and United States borders. From Juan's recollections of conversations with his mother, this van was crammed with other immigrants from Mexico and Central America. Juan reported that when his parents arrived in Arizona, his father worked for the mines and his mother rotated her duties between being a full-time homemaker and cleaning homes for other families. Juan's parents were only able to complete the second grade and thus had limited vocational and work opportunities.

Juan's family lived in poorly constructed housing situated along the railroad tracks where most Mexican and other Spanish-speaking people resided. In this community, like many others, there was an obvious divide between Latinos and Anglos, between English and Spanish, and between those families struggling with significant economic deprivation and those that had better financial means. Also described were cultural and religious systems of Mexican beliefs that tended to view this population as more Catholic, ritualistic in their manner, and inclined toward large families. These differences have historically been some of the basic ingredients for development of prejudicial and ethnic bias in communities across the country. Religion has been a defining factor in the development of attitudes toward Mexicans and Mexican Americans (Matovina & Riebe-Estrella, 2002).

Juan reported that growing up in his family was economically difficult, given that his father would work 14-hour days in the mines, rising 6 days a week to report to work at 4:30 a.m. and remain until 6:30 p.m. He would work largely in the dark and silent shafts of the mines, not arriving home until early evening, exhausted, frustrated, and frequently angry with his superiors for the unsanitary and unsafe conditions around which he and his coworkers were employed. His mother was found to carry similar resentments for the long hours that she would spend taking care of her children and ensuring that she was still able to clean several houses during the week to make ends meet. Juan reported that their two-bedroom, unheated home was frequently an uncomfortable environment for his family, with his parents frequently tired, angry at their life circumstances, and insensitive to the changing emotional and developmental needs of himself, his sisters, and younger brother. These issues were made more complicated by father's increased frustration brought on by the discriminatory and prejudicial experiences in his work environment as well as in their community. Juan recalled an episode in a second grade school conference when his father became incensed with the teacher deriding Juan for his continued use of the Spanish language in the playground, which she felt detracted from Juan's development of appropriate English speaking skills. His father became enraged, referring to the teacher's educational philosophy as prejudicial, which apparently caused the teacher to feel threatened. The local police authority was called, and his father was taken into custody and jailed on the charge of disorderly conduct. He was placed in protective custody for 48 hours, released on bail, and subsequently forced to pay a fine. These experiences served to harden his father's feelings toward "the gringo," which added significant strain to an already unsteady household. The family environment became more complicated with his father's development of leukemia. The family blamed the noxious air in the mines and the high stressors evident with living in this community with the development of this severe medical condition. His father subsequently died at the age of 35, when Juan was only 9 years of age.

Juan stated that his life after the death of his father proved to be difficult, with his mother assuming the single parent role in the raising of five children. Juan stated that besides feeling the vulnerability and loss of his father, he and his older sisters were frequently teased by their White classmates about their ethnicity and their Spanish language communication with each other. The teasing became more aggressive after Juan's oldest sister was raped by two of her White male classmates, causing a significant uproar in the community, with suggestions she had brought on the attack. This incident resulted in his sister being branded a "loose woman," a designation that became a pervasive sentiment in her community. These impactful negative reactions were followed by her quitting school, becoming pregnant, and eventually dying during childbirth when she was 20 years of age. Other relevant issues in Juan's background were his reports of teachers who minimized his intellectual abilities and assumed that he should be taking the non-college track toward a vocational trade. Further, Juan recalled growing up with an attitude that "he and his race" were just a bunch of "macho Mexicans" whose only interest was in alcohol abuse, philandering, and avoiding responsibility. This attitude was implicitly supported by some adults in his community, who would engage in those stereotypic behaviors because of the discriminatory and oppressive factors that were operating and the lack of opportunity for any level of advancement in the Mexican family's economic situation. As a result, Juan stated that he became determined as a young adolescent not to identify with being "Spanish" or Latino heritage and to minimize his speaking of the Spanish language. Juan reported that he wanted to "become like the rest of the White boys" who could seek upper mobility, do well in school, and not feel the sting of prejudice. With this attitude, Juan was quickly able to gain some favor among the majority community, performed well in high school, and graduated on time with many of his White classmates.

Juan stated that his mother died by the time he was a senior in high school of a combination of a broken heart, the sadness of racial and ethnic inequality in their lives, the loss of her daughter, and what appeared to be the increased emotional instability of her other children. Although Juan successfully completed high school, Juan's two other sisters became pregnant during early adolescence, thus terminating any potential opportunities to advance themselves in life. Juan's younger brother became involved in drug abuse and subsequently had to also quit school in ninth grade and began working to support himself in the mines. Juan's mother died from cancer following the initiation of stomach difficulties, causing her an inability to eat. By Juan's high school graduation, he and his siblings were orphaned. Juan spent the next 3 years trying to maintain a household working in construction while providing a home and physical stability for his brother and sisters.

By age 21, Juan felt compelled to leave the small mining town and escape to Southern California to begin a new life. He reported that he drifted in and out of various odd jobs until through the aid of a girlfriend, he felt more secure to enter college. Juan stated that the good study habits he gained in high school allowed him to finish a 4-year university degree in 3 years, majoring in biological sciences, and subsequently gain entry to a prestigious medical school, where he graduated with honors. Following a residency in internal medicine, Juan was employed at a local medical center and established a private practice in internal medicine.

In spite of his academic and professional successes, Juan stated that he struggled with bouts of depression, alcohol abuse, and an unstable relationship history with women. Juan indicated that since his denial of his Latino ethnicity, he had never used this ethnic grouping for entry into any university or medical school and advanced solely on the merits of his academic scholarship and university transcripts. However, these accomplishments did not come without some shame and insecurity about who he was. Juan reported that on several occasions when the Spanish-speaking housekeeping staff in the various hospitals and clinics would speak to him in Spanish, he would become nervous. He would ignore them if other colleagues or professionals were within hearing distance. Juan stated that his Spanish language had gone underground and he did not wish to reinforce his Spanish speaking ability among those who might begin to view him with prejudiced eyes. As a result, Juan refused to treat any Spanish-speaking patients other than through the use of a translator even though he could speak Spanish fluently. By the age of 30, Juan was able to hide the fact that he spoke Spanish from his classmates, colleagues, and related medical professionals.

Juan's first marriage to a "gringo nurse" lasted only 4 years as a result of "value conflicts" and communication difficulties. His use of the word "gringo" appeared to have a salient emotional reactivity that implied anger and relational distance on the basis of cultural differences and past life experience. A second marriage a year later to a White female physician lasted only 3 years also because of more value conflicts and difficulty understanding each other. Juan stated that he wandered for the next few years without any significant relationships in his life, which also caused his medical practice to suffer. Juan seemed unable to rebound from his history of two failed marriages. At the time that Juan presented himself for outpatient psychotherapy, he reported that he was depressed, alone, and confused about who he was. His increased alcohol drinking pattern was now feeling out of control and was impacting his relationships with fellow colleagues.

Initial Phase of Treatment

At the time of request for services, Juan presented as a haggard, depressed, sullen 40-year-old Latino man who reported himself to be addicted to alcohol and whose profession he described as "trying to keep up with patients' medical needs." This quote turned out to be prophetic, with a presenting complaint of always feeling behind in his medical care and of being unable to fulfill the emotional needs of his patients. In addition, Juan complained of "feeling overwhelmed by life's demands"; a recent history of sleep difficulties with recurrent insomnia; decreased energy level; increased abuse of alcohol, which was now starting to interfere with work; and confusion over how he perceived his role as a medical practitioner. Juan impressed me as an individual who seemed appropriately concerned about his life circumstances, however, was very superficial in his own self-analysis and deeply troubled over the course of his personal and relationship history. The worry lines noted in his face and the unhappiness that seemed to both frame his features and be communicated through his slightly slumped body posture denoted a man who felt emotionally empty and distressed. He also appeared to carry a huge weight on his shoulders that seemed to confirm the personal and professional pressures and insecurities that characterized his person.

During the initial phase of treatment with Latino men, I frequently find myself needing to establish a common ethnic or cultural bond to secure a more meaningful therapeutic exchange. In addition to establishing therapeutic trust and confidence in the initial phase of treatment, I have found that working with Latino males requires a building of commonality to decrease the level of defensiveness or related concerns that the client may have with the assumption of being identified as having a more serious mental health problem. Latino men have an image of manhood to uphold that is different from the socially constructed nature of masculinity (Lara-Cantú & Navarro-Arias, 1986; Thompson & Pleck, 1995). "Manhood" tends to imply a cultural expectation that Latinos must be more in control and authoritative than females. This cultural role is embedded in the expectation that Latino males tend to view themselves as needing to be protectors of their respective families and significantly less prepared to view themselves with weakness (Falicov, 1998).

Although there can be wide variation of this theme, it tends to be a common observation I have made in treatment with both Mexican and Mexican American men that they are prone toward feeling more powerful at the expense of females to establish a relational hierarchy that promotes the male as head of the family system (Baca-Zinn, 1982). Consequently, these initial visits with Juan were intended to establish some common bonds that would allow him to view my role as both professional and personal without developing confusion or developing inappropriate dynamics in the therapeutic relationship.

I noticed that this delicate balance between being professional yet personally relating was accomplished with the interweaving of Juan's background of family history and stories that would provide a context to comment on a sense of familiarity and commonality. By doing this, I found Juan to be more self-aware of the observations he made relative to his personal history and to recognize the relevant commonality that was being mutually shared. This dialogue allowed for an intimacy of shared cultural beliefs that furthered a therapist–client bond between Juan and myself. It was during this time of initial culture sharing that I purposely interweaved some Spanish language into our therapeutic dialogue. My goal was not only to evaluate the level of resistance Juan may have to communicate bilingually but also to give permission for him to express himself in Spanish if he chose.

The initial phase of treatment with Juan focused predominantly on the stabilization of his mood and addressing the problem that had now become chronic alcohol abuse. The first handful of visits with Juan found him to be resistant and prone to minimize the weaknesses that he had been demonstrating for the past few years in his personal and professional life. In the years of my practice, I have noticed that when resistance is evident with regard to demonstrating any personal weaknesses, this is a sign that some related role modeling from myself may be helpful. I learned in the relationship with my grandmother that the use of storytelling was often an effective way to both transmit ancestral history and provide a commonality between the listener and the storyteller that would invoke feelings of mutuality and connectedness.

Given Juan's personal history with his father working in the mines, I elected to disclose some of my own father's personal history as an adolescent who, upon arrival in the United States, picked oranges in the groves for several years. This story was interwoven with examples of the struggles that my father endured with long hours doing hard labor beginning with work that frequently started at 4:30 a.m. under harsh weather conditions. The personal struggles that were detailed regarding my father's history appeared to have a similarity in Juan's recollection of his own father's working conditions and the human energy needed to rise in the morning and work until dark. This disclosure proved to be a vital exchange between Juan and myself, as he was able to see some congruence between my assumed life circumstances and his. Working with Spanish-speaking populations for many years, I have found that varying levels of disclosure can be helpful to bridge and deepen a therapeutic relationship. This was observed to be true also with Juan, who subsequently viewed our emerging professional relationship as one that he could come to trust and perceive as syntonic with his own personal life experiences. Thus, this storytelling has been a frequent therapeutic tool that I have used with clients, particularly with Latino families as a way to bridge a mutual understanding and awareness of cultural beliefs that have allowed for a deepening of the exchange between the client and myself.

The opening of this relational portal found Juan to be increasingly more compliant and invested in addressing those personal issues and limitations that had begun to accumulate over the past several years. Juan's depression was in part addressed through the use of a psychopharmacology consultation with a Latino psychiatrist colleague. I found the depression to be embedded in the history of his father's alcoholism and subsequent emotional distancing, his mother's own depression, and the untimely loss of both his father to leukemia and his sister to acute sadness and life's overwhelming obstacles. In addition, the loss of his mother at the time of his senior year in high school proved to be particularly difficult in that he felt he could not admit vulnerability because of the expectation that he must now be strong for his brother and sisters. Consequently, the accumulation of the immediate family losses, the abrupt termination of his childhood with the death of his father, and the required psychological fortification to meet the new demands of his family were all salient elements in the psychological profile that was emerging with Juan. These major themes were interwoven throughout treatment with Juan as he struggled to resolve past losses, grieve, and reorder his emotional priorities toward more mature functioning.

The issue of alcoholism proved to be a very difficult theme, yet one that appeared to reach some resolution after he was able to heal some of the dynamics of his immediate family. Alcoholism for Juan was tied to memory of his father's own abuse history as well as the now evident feelings of loss that he had successfully put aside during his young adult years. The ungrieved losses were now becoming a conscious force that was demanding recognition. However, he was unwilling to enter a drug and alcohol program because he perceived that his reputation would be sullied and he would be unable to be excused from his medical duties and responsibilities. Consequently, Juan agreed to try Alcoholics Anonymous (AA) for four to five times a week and to secure a sponsor. Within a month of a combination of AA group meetings, psychotherapy twice a month, and consultation with a psychiatrist who provided antidepressive medications, Juan was able to curb his alcohol intake substantially and to manage his medical duties more responsibly. The help of a sponsor, also a Latino, assisted Juan immensely in the management of his alcohol abuse, bringing it to a standstill within 3 months of his initiation of Alcoholics Anonymous. The more difficult agenda lay in dealing with the loss of his father, mother, and sister.

It was also during this period after a year of treatment that Juan became more comfortable speaking in Spanish with me. A bilingual language therapy soon became a salient hallmark of our interaction.

Middle Phase of Treatment

The first 4 to 6 months of Juan's care were spent exclusively on stabilizing his emotional functioning, curbing his alcohol abuse, and ensuring that he would be able to manage his daily professional duties in a responsible and competent manner. The coordination of services with both the psychiatrist and his sponsor proved to be helpful in developing a group support system that allowed Juan to feel cared for. Some of the initial psychological issues addressed during this first phase of treatment included his feelings of hopelessness, emotional loss of family, and the importance of his being strong at all costs. This last theme proved to be more detailed and interwoven in his attitude and overall functioning. This attitude was also tied to what Juan came to label the "macho man syndrome," which he described as the need to feel protective and strong for his remaining family members and to demonstrate an attitude that he could "handle it all." Consequently, the most devastating aspect for Juan at the initiation of treatment was his inability to do it all, as he reported, and to not admit defeat in the face of his family members, patients, and medical colleagues. The "macho man syndrome," as Juan self-diagnosed, proved to be a significant aspect of the second phase of treatment, and subsequently, this theme was a major discussion of the ensuing dialogue for the remainder of his psychotherapy treatment.

The ability to stabilize Juan's drug and alcohol abuse was an important goal of the treatment plan to address the more difficult psychological issues that have been part of his developmental and familial experience. As I stated previously, my orientation in psychotherapy tends to be a blend of family systems, humanistic, and transpersonal work. I place emphasis on the importance of family roles and hierarchy, and integrate an understanding of religious and spiritual aspects of the individual. This combination of theoretical bases has been prompted by my cultural worldview and the experiences I have gathered through relationship with my maternal grandmother and my several years in the seminary. Although Juan was baptized Roman Catholic and participated in Sunday services with his mother, he did not consider himself a practitioner but nevertheless incorporated the essentials of that particular belief system. Those basics included a belief in God, a reverence for Our Lady of Guadalupe, and a cosmological understanding of his own indigenous roots which he perceived as coming from Aztec traditions and beliefs (Carrasco, 1990; Matovina & Riebe-Estrella, 2002). This indigenous orientation is common among many Mexicans and Mexican Americans who practice Catholicism (Matovina & Riebe-Estrella, 2002). Thus, although Juan had historically rejected his Latino roots, he had not rejected the religion and spirituality that had historically been a foundation in his life and that was interlaced throughout his beliefs and values.

These traditions were ones that Juan learned from his own mother, which included a belief that the world is interconnected, that there are various unseen entities that provide an influence in human experience, and that prayer is a powerful method of having communication with God. His beliefs were important to ascertain to evaluate the potential resources and innate traditions that could be used in the psychotherapy process. With many

Chicano/Latino males, it has been my experience that one's worldview of religion and spirituality continues to play a salient role in one's existential belief system. The psychotherapist's awareness about one's religious beliefs and practices can provide an opportunity to ask more specific questions relevant to early religious background and later spiritual development. I believe the comfort level to inquire about this arena has evolved for me because of my own seminary training, which fostered an appreciation for religion and spirituality as a significant dimension to human experience.

Following a description of the therapeutic methods and rationale, Juan was initiated into a counseling process that involved the cleansing of mind and spirit before proceeding with any further therapeutic dialogue. I have learned that with the initiation of any deepening work in therapy, particularly if there has been trauma associated with the experience, some preparation or cleansing is important. As part of my own background, the use of ritual and ceremony is an important aspect in preparing one's consciousness for entry into more difficult emotional agendas. It has been my experience that ritual helps to prepare the mind for any difficult emotional or physical undertaking, whether it be participation in a sweat lodge or in the difficult therapeutic dialogue that occurs when therapist and client are moving into the examination and experience of psychological trauma (Imber-Black, Roberts, & Whiting, 2003).

In my tradition and learned beliefs, the burning of sage is a way to cleanse the physical space and signal the start of an important ritual toward preparing one's consciousness to discuss traumatic life events. Sage has historically been used by indigenous people in the Americas to initiate ceremony and to begin a process that could involve anything from the confession of one's misgivings to the start of ceremonies (Falicov, 1999; Gafner & Duckett, 1992). Burnt sage often evokes a very subtle but powerful effect on the consciousness of the individual. Many individuals in healing ceremonies and counseling sessions experience the scent and smoke that arises from sage as enabling one to cross from one level of consciousness to another. I have observed this crossing over with clients as they appear more relaxed, open, and free to discuss intimate thoughts and reactions. Although I do not understand how the scent of sage affects an individual biochemically, I know from the use of it over several years that the scent of its sweetness often initiates a state of relaxation for the client, who will frequently report feelings of peace and tranquility and a readiness to advance the therapeutic work. In Juan's case, the use of sage assisted in helping him to become more self-reflective and forgiving in his life review of developmental losses.

I would like to acknowledge that the use of sage in psychotherapy is not a recognized process in traditional counseling practice. However, as Falicov (1999) and Matovina and Riebe-Estrella (2002) have noted, counseling with Mexican and Mexican American clients may require the use of indigenous methods that infuse an old-world healing process with more modern therapeutic strategies. Although they described nontraditional frameworks in a more generic way, Krippner and Achterberg (2000) comment on the salient role that these frameworks and healing paradigms can have on the understanding and resolution of psychological problems.

Orienting Juan to the use of a cleansing ceremony to assist in more emotionally intimate, therapeutic work was not alien to his own memory of religious ceremonies. Reminding him of the use of incense in the Roman Catholic Church, particularly during seasons of high mass, helped Juan to connect the scent of the incense and the feelings of holiness that were part of his experience with the Catholic Church when he was a young boy. Juan was able to recall a shift that occurred for him whenever he experienced the scent of incense in a church ceremony, and how it made him feel elevated and spiritual. This same understanding was applied to the use of sage with regard to helping him move from a secular to a sacred mindset as a way to cleanse the physical space, and metaphorically to cleanse one's thoughts and feelings in preparation for a particular therapeutic exploration. I have also observed that once the use of sage or sweetgrass becomes introduced, the scent from either of these plants allows the client to feel more relaxed toward facilitation of the therapeutic work related to emotional or psychological traumas. The use of this procedure with Latino and Chicano individuals has not been a difficult process to explain, given the consistent familiarity between the use of incense in the Catholic Church and the similar effect it tends to create in one's mental and emotional consciousness.

Exploration of these losses resulted in Juan immediately becoming tearful over the missing of his long deceased family members and becoming regretful over the unspoken feelings he individually harbored for each of them. This intimate exploration was sharpened through the use of a flathead drum to prompt a trance state that allowed Juan to enter the emotional memories of his past. The drumbeat, simulating the rhythm of the heart, has been a powerful tool that I have used with many Latino clients who have wanted to do inner work that involves deeper emotional or historical examination. I characteristically initiate the introduction of the drum by having the client move into a state of relaxation with deep breathing while allowing the drumbeat to move at the same rate of breath observed with the client. The coordination of the drumbeat with the breath rate allows the monotone rhythm to direct the breath, thus producing a deeper state of relaxation.

This examination with Latino clients has frequently involved early developmental losses, instances of migration trauma, and other related traumatic experiences (i.e., rape, incest survival, work-related accidents). The use of the drum as the initial focal point has assisted in the facilitation of deeper self-realization, identification of relevant aspects of the traumatic events, and the emoting of long-held uncomfortable and self-destructive feelings. It is within this context that Juan would interweave his recollections of the familial, cultural, and societal labeling of the "macho man syndrome." A deeper state of relaxation allowed Juan to have more immediate access to relevant historical memories that would produce images and feelings about how he viewed himself in relation to other boys. Some of these recollections included peers who would brag about their sexual conquests or be challenged by the emotional experiences of oppression, which would cause the excessive abuse of alcohol. Sometimes the experience of guilt for having left his boyhood community would cause Juan to become tearful. It seemed that he compared his departure with the leaving of his buddies on a war-ravaged battlefield.

Relevant to the "macho man syndrome," Juan's interpretation of this labeling and the expectations accompanying the meaning involved being protective, in charge of the family, and proud of his manhood. These learned aspects of being "macho" were tagged alongside some of the more conflictual images that he also integrated into the label of "macho," including abuse of alcohol and aggressiveness. Juan observed that among some of his adolescent friends many years ago, being "macho" sometimes involved more negative aspects than the examples of manhood he had been exposed to by his family of origin. These examples have been cited particularly as related to hyper-sexual engagement, alcohol abuse, and anger management problems (Anaya, 1996; Casas et al., 1994).

The middle phase of treatment focused on the cleansing of the old energies that had peaked with long-held self-destructive emotions. These themes involved guilt and anger over the loss of his parents and sister, the resentment in his being in charge of his family, and the struggles against racism and discrimination that he had experienced as a youth and through much of his formal education. Toward the end of this phase, Juan was moving toward increased resolution of his long held self-destructive feelings and felt more settled in saying goodbye to the losses of his family members.

My involvement with Juan during the middle phase of treatment appeared to have a profound effect not only in his relationship with me but also in producing memories and images from my own past that prompted personal reflection on long-forgotten old history. I recalled images of two older half-brothers, who were prominent gang members in my community, and who themselves had become "leaders" in their own right by proving themselves to be "men." This proving of manhood was exhibited through aggressive physical engagement with gangs from other parts of the neighborhood and city. In the 1950s, the use of drugs and firearms was not prominent; rather, the method of handling disputes and protecting one's turf was through physical altercations with each other to prove who was "tougher." It is these images as well as those of my father, who would oftentimes work 18-hour days in his grocery store to provide for the family, that also reminded me of what I had been exposed to as a young boy and what may be expected of me as I became older.

These images, which became increasingly more apparent to me, had an interesting effect on my relationship with Juan. I felt that he and I shared a very similar bond with each other and almost seemed as if we could communicate nonverbally about these specific background experiences that reinforced our conscious, but unspoken, mutuality. I feel that this level of therapeutic dialogue, both verbal and nonverbal, was a prominent outcome of the work that we engaged in as therapist and client and that it led to a positive rapport that facilitated the final phase of treatment.

Final Phase of Treatment

Following a year and a half of work with Juan, he was observed to be more capable, functional, and responsible at work; had received a year chip from his AA support group for being clean and sober; and had started dating again. Nevertheless, there was still some occasional depression that would incapacitate him, causing missed work and feelings of self-worthlessness. However, these reactions had decreased in frequency, and he felt more capable managing these uncomfortable moments.

A therapeutic practice that I typically give to Latino clients as a homework assignment, depending on their level of motivation and emotional and mental preparedness, is to locate and travel to a place that they find healing for themselves. Examples of these healing environments typically include the mountains, the forest, the ocean, or one's backyard. I encourage the clients to fast for the day and to allow the spiritual energies of that environment to speak to them so that the guidance of a prayer, song, or affirmation may be presented. It is a version of asking for a vision that is a commonly practiced ritual among some indigenous communities in the Americas. The difference in this therapeutic strategy is to have a prayer that is "gifted" to the client and occurs within a designated period of personal reflection (typically within 24–36 hours) alongside the use of fasting. The goal of a subsequent visit with the individual following that personal ceremony is to talk about the experience, listen for the prayer or song that may have been realized, and allow this "transpersonal gift" to be a significant affirmation of one's personhood, well-being, and spiritual connection to the Creator. In this regard, it is salient to note the content of the prayer that has been realized by the client, as it can often detail many of the anxieties and the past history of crisis that have impacted the individual historically.

The use of a day fast helped Juan to be mentally prepared. He was agreeable to using the process of fasting to further his own emotional understanding, given that he had experienced me and our work together as meaningful and helpful. The use of sage, the beat of the drum, and the deep relaxation process were in many ways very unique to Juan's prior understanding of the therapeutic process, as he felt that these methods and my therapeutic relationship with him were affirming and healing. Juan's experience with the fasting ritual left him mildly anxious throughout much of the day, fearing that he would not receive any message from this period of reflection and personally guided prayer. His place of sacredness was designated as a hillside in the country that he had frequented over the past few years to feel relaxed from the burden of his medical practice. This is where he would go for brief periods of time to find some respite and clarity of mind; he spent the majority of his day there in reflection and meditation. This self-imposed day of fasting proved to be helpful to Juan, who spent the next several sessions talking about memories of his past family background and forming a perspective of himself that aided in the development of a more defined role as a Latino man.

The receiving of a prayer during this fast helped Juan to feel that a gift was provided that would allow for a more trusted experience of his inner wisdom. The prayer content from his fast reflected a resolution of the past guilt and anger at his losses. It was recommended to Juan that he use this prayer as a morning ritual that would help set his intentions for the day and provide him the necessary fortitude to handle the various stressors and expectations that were routine for him as a physician. This prayer seemed to aid him in the emotional handling of his professional duties, allowing a more mature guidance and intelligence to complement an increasing confidence in his abilities. In addition, Juan quickly came to understand that although some of his family members had physically died, his memory of their love and support always remained with him.

Juan was instructed to incorporate prayer into his everyday reflection and affirmation. This is a typical recommendation that I make with a client as a way to reinforce the internalization of the personally developed positive affirmations. However, the use of prayer in particular is introduced only if it is consistent with the client's belief system.

Following approximately 3 years of work, Juan was terminated from my practice with a more full sense of his abilities, increased competency in his feelings as a man, and a reaffirming presence in the lives of his own patients. Juan's new perceptions of being male appeared to reorder his priorities about what he felt to be important. He described his sense of a newfound maleness as a way to appreciate a greater beauty in the patients he served and an increased awareness for the role he played in his community. Further, his view of maleness appeared to transcend any concerns about his own past history that previously made him feel that he was not measuring up to prior images of being a man.

Juan reported being increasingly sensitive and aware of his patients' needs while developing a deeper understanding for the mental and emotional suffering that often framed their physical complaints. He did express frustration with a health care system that required less than optimal support of patient care. Nevertheless, Juan described having more confidence that he was able to handle those constraints while giving added respect for the patients that he cared for and the manner in which he was able to handle the emotional agendas that they brought to his office.

MEXICAN AMERICAN MALENESS: A BRIEF OVERVIEW

Juan's case was beneficial for me at several different levels. Initially, the therapeutic relationship helped to affirm my sense of competency with other health professionals within the context of an evolving indigenous healing practice. Second, I came to painfully recall the psychological wounds and their impact on Mexican American/Latino men as a result of discrimination and racial prejudice that I also had experienced. Last, the labeling and stigmatization of the "macho man syndrome" further made me remember some early developmental memories and expectations about how Mexican American manhood had been communicated in my youth. Many studies over the past 25 years have clarified the labeling and understanding of "machismo" in Mexican American males. The following brief discussion is intended to provide an overview for some of the salient themes relevant to the understanding of this concept.

Being macho or machismo for Latino males, particularly those who have identified as Chicano, Mexican American, or Mexican, has been a significantly misunderstood label (Casas & Pytluk, 1995; Casas et al., 1994). Prior descriptors of this term have been the result of stereotypic images (Cromwell & Ruiz, 1979), racist inaccuracies (Mirandé, 1988, 1997), inappropriate extrapolations from traditionally oriented rural communities (Madsen, 1964), or misunderstood differences of manhood as defined by these Latino groups (Abreu, Goodyear, Campos, & Newcomb, 2000; Mirandé, 1997). In addition, other writers (i.e., Gilmore, 1990) have observed that developmental expectations of machismo are not unique to Latinos but are evident in many world cultures.

A more useful and culturally syntonic view of "machismo" is to view this set of behaviors and attitudes as tied directly to the socioeconomic and historical elements of a given society (De la Cancela, 1986; Mirandé, 1988; Rodriguez, 1996). This perspective is a distinct change from a view that pathologizes the individual or group and is a fresh contrast from thinking long-proposed by Diaz-Guerrero (1967) and Diaz-Guerrero, Lichtszain, and Reyes (1979). Consequently, it is inaccurate to continue portraying the Latino man as authoritarian, womanizing, alcohol-prone, and self-destructive. A sociohistorical context, as noted by Freire (1972), creates an appreciation for how colonization promotes the development of internalized oppression leading to potential self-destructive acts and varied expressions of manhood.

The cultures of Mexican and Mexican American men, as commented on by several authors over the past 50 years (Casas et al., 2001; Diaz-Guerrero, 1967; Peñalosa, 1968; Torres, Solberg, & Carlstrom, 2002), have identified a wide range of manhood expressions that incorporate elements of machismo. This understanding has frequently been described in relation to the salient religious and spiritual undercurrents involved in protection of the community. Anaya (1996) observed that macho themes and images of manhood are pervasive throughout the Southwest landscape. Examples of the variety of these observations noted by Anaya (1996) include indigenous patterns of caring for one's community; the ability to withstand physical and emotional pain (i.e., the concept of *aguantar*) to be strong for one's family; Pachuco males with crosses affixed to their exterior clothing, worn as badges of protection and manhood; and highly customized, low-rider vehicles with painted images of beautiful women alongside images of the Virgen de Guadalupe, protectress of the Américas. It is significant to note that even in these highly exaggerated images of manhood, they are specific to a particular sociocultural context and socioeconomic status. A conclusion reached by Torres et al. (2002) is that Latinos are diverse in their interpretation and demonstration of manhood and thus generalizations about machismo behaviors are not valid.

This brief review suggests that the concepts of machismo are interwoven with religious and spiritual connotations and expectations that have direct application to a male's participation in his respective family and community (Tello, 1998). Thus, exaggerated aspects of Latino manhood behaviors appear to be the result of an impaired or oppressed ability to perform the necessary and related aspects of one's psychological and social role as a man. It can be argued that the display of dysfunctional machismo can be displaced anger over an inability to handle aspects related to one's social and cultural responsibilities and a difficulty in taking responsibility for the assumed role assignment that a male is expected to integrate into one's personal, social, familial, and work behavior. It has been my experience that levels of acculturation and experiences of oppression and discrimination will play a significant role in how the role definitions of *machismo* are handled by Chicano/Latino men.

SUMMARY AND CONCLUSIONS

The case of Juan presented in this chapter provides a version of his internalized image of machismo, formed through various familial, community, and sociopolitical forces that included role modeling from his father, direct and indirect messages from his mother, and the experiences of racism and oppression during his youth. Similarly, it was his development of a "macho man syndrome" that propelled him out of the small Arizona mining town and toward the road of academic excellence. The will to succeed in spite of the odds resulted in the conviction that he would advance himself. In reference to definitions of *machismo* and the case of Juan, several lessons are salient that can generalize to counseling and psychotherapy with Mexican American men. Initially, this case helps to illustrate that sociocultural and historical context are significant informants in the assessment and relationship building process. It was necessary to review Juan's relevant background and contextual history to understand the broader picture of his particular life circumstances. Failure to evaluate this relevant background would have left a major gap in the assessment and treatment process.

Second, I found self-disclosure with this Latino man, and with many Latino men in past psychotherapy experiences, to be a significant dimension in the formation of meaningful therapeutic contact. The opportunity to self-disclose can assist in joining a relationship that emphasizes similarities of human experience and underscores the positive attachment and subsequent contact that can ensue from this process. As has been recognized by many writers in the past (Wachtel, 1998), self-disclosure should not proceed without a conscious recognition that such related information from the therapist is primarily to assist on behalf of the client's best interests.

Third, it is important to understand that the concept of "machismo" refers to a universal set of behaviors and that they are not just specific to Mexicans and Mexican Americans (Casas et al., 2001; Gilmore, 1990; Torres et al., 2002). Thus, it is important to recognize that *machismo* refers to a culturally specific set of behaviors that denote challenging dimensions to manhood; behaviors that are formed from specific familial, communal, social, and political experiences; and attempts to advance oneself in life. To catalog them solely as behaviors that are intent on manipulating women and exaggerating one's sense of manhood in a pathological way is to provide an inaccurate assessment of the individual and, at least with Mexican American males, to propagate a continued perception that is prejudicial and racist in nature.

Fourth, it is important to recognize the presence of religious and spiritual themes in counseling with Latinos and how they provide clues to unspoken psychological concerns (Cervantes & Parham, 2005). In addition, these themes may open up opportunities for meaningful rituals in the healing process, as noted from the treatment of this case. Ritual provides a useful mechanism for the movement of consciousness that can serve to initiate readiness for psychological inquiry, more in-depth psychological exploration, and problem resolution. These processes were demonstrated with the treatment of Juan.

Fifth, practitioners should be prepared to confront their own professional bias toward Mexican American males. Stereotypes continue to abound regarding men, and in particular with the Mexican American population. Mexican American men have been portrayed unfairly and inaccurately with regard to their level of motivation for treatment, participation in the therapeutic process, and stereotypic descriptions of who they are as men. As a result, these stereotypes have served to prejudice treatment and have led service providers to view Mexican American males as family members who may not be included in the counseling process as a result of this inherit bias (Falicov, 1998; Torres et al., 2002).

Sixth, this case reinforced the need to understand the interrelated dynamics of migration history, acculturation stress, and the merging of a Mexican American/Chicano, mainstream identity. These dimensions are complex and have significant emotional agendas tied to them, which create important therapeutic avenues of assessment and inquiry. There are likely several familial and personal background stories that need to be discussed, as they may form a backdrop to some of the presenting complaints and relational history that have brought male clients to counseling (Brooks, 2003).

Last, Atkinson, Brown, Casas, and Zane (1996) identified several therapeutic roles that are useful in conceptualizing one's professional involvement. This issue is underscored by Casas et al. (2001) in their application of these various role assignments to working with Latino males. These roles are described as including a counseling process that defines the therapist as advisor, advocate, facilitator of indigenous support systems, facilitator of indigenous healing systems, consultant, change agent, counselor, and psychotherapist. These roles may provide salient avenues of meaningful and therapeutic relationship building for those wishing to work with Mexican American males.

This chapter has focused primarily on a description of a psychotherapeutic case with a Mexican American man whose life outlined several contextual factors that have included sociocultural, language, sociopolitical, and professional issues. The review of the literature and the recommendations made might be helpful to the practitioner who is working with this significant population and might lead to an appreciation of the various factors that are relevant in meaningful therapeutic contact and treatment.

QUESTIONS FROM THE EDITORS

1. *What types of gender-based stereotypes were you aware of in counseling this client? How did that impact your therapy with this client?*

Juan's profession as a physician immediately brought up two stereotypes about his professional background. Initially, I perceived Juan's specialty in internal medicine as being more insensitive to the psychological and emotional understanding of patients. Further, I have found that I view physicians as having limited bedside manner, which takes away from the humanistic elements of practice. A second stereotype also related to Juan's physician status as rejecting of mental health professionals. This stereotype was formed on the basis of my prior experiences in hospitals in which the power hierarchy seemed to cross over into ethnicity beyond just medical or professional specialty. Hence, Latino physicians tended to abide more in the trust and confidence of their Anglo counterparts as opposed to cultural groups who shared similar cultural background and related identity.

Initially, these stereotypes gave me reduced confidence about the way in which I would work with Juan. I felt that Juan's own professional boundaries would prevent him from addressing any of the specific emotional and psychological concerns that were affecting him. As a result, I maintained more of an emotional distance and was less inclined to address the cultural backdrop as it may have impacted his personal difficulties. However, as I explored his personal and familial history, I became aware of significant emotional abuse and community oppression that allowed me to identify with Juan. This awareness provided me the confidence to take more emotional risks and begin addressing personal and cultural issues that may have also affected Juan's functioning. Much of this internal dialogue for me was the result of my own prejudices toward male physicians and was emphasized by his being Latino. This is an interesting commentary for me to make, given that I had assumed that I was able to bridge many personal insecurities of working with other Latino professionals. Indeed, this case demonstrated to me that there are still personal issues related to gender and culture that I must continue to address.

2. *How did your own gender role issues influence your work with this client?*

I was raised with a strong male role provided by my own father, uncles on both sides of my family, and other extended family members who generally demonstrated behaviors and expectations that were consistent with how I perceived being a Mexican American male (Gonzalez, 1996). These learned gender roles included being head of household, taking responsibility for one's action, and demarcating the jobs for both men and women. Many of these experiences shifted for me as I became older and was exposed to a broader world with more sophisticated and diverse value systems. It is with this specific gender role bias that I contextualized the issues provided by Juan. His description of life circumstances appeared to be consistent with my own childhood. It is interesting that I was able to relate to the suffering and abuse in a very intimate way, particularly as Juan highlighted the oppression and racism that he experienced.

3. *Looking back on the case, knowing what you know now, would you change the way you worked with this client?*

The stereotype of working with Latino male physicians was prominent in my relearning with Juan. I was able to view his humanness more directly than I anticipated, which gave me permission to work more intimately with his emotional concerns and suffering. In addition, I had become more acutely aware of the feelings of oppression and racism that I myself had experienced. Although this was not a novel feeling for me, the depth of emotion and experiences expressed by Juan allowed me to delve more deeply into my own emotional scarring, which reopened strong feelings of sadness and anger over discrimination I had experienced with Roman Catholic nuns, priests, and the general community where I had lived as a boy. This was significant learning for me, but I believe it prevented me from being more authentic and attuned to the wide range of emotions that were likely experienced by Juan in his personal experiences of oppression and racism (Long & Martinez, 1997).

Hence, what I would change is the initial responsiveness with which I began my relationship with Juan. I feel I would now increase security to my therapeutic position and blend a personal resolution of my own experiences as I listened to how his life had evolved.

4. You outline a way of working with men that is grounded in traditional Latino spirituality. Your client, however, had essentially disavowed his cultural roots and worked to hide his identity. How were you able to create a working therapeutic relationship with this distance between the two of you?

I recognized that there was an existing stereotype on my part with regard to this client's professional standing that initially made me skeptical about the level of emotional conviction and willingness that he may have toward counseling. It is interesting to note that I had a similar reaction, which made me question whether my stereotypes would get in the way of working effectively with Juan. I believe that what assisted me in moving beyond the stereotype and understanding his specific human condition was being able to evaluate and listen for the child abuse and discrimination that were part of his personal history. It is these two arenas that provided me the opening to develop a more intimate tie with this individual.

Second, learning that Juan was a man who had a religious background, I asked him (as I routinely do with clients) how he had been socialized to his Catholic beliefs and spirituality, and I asked him about the specific disruptions that had challenged the interplay between his interpretation of religion and related psychological concerns. I believe, however, that there is a more detailed awareness that I received in working with Juan that was part of my own healing process. That awareness had to do with the personal background and his struggles to move through a society that labeled him negatively on the basis of the color of his skin, his language, and his ethnicity. This theme was a salient personal factor in my connection with this man, and I believe this created a strong therapeutic alliance. The sting of discrimination and oppression formed both a spoken and unspoken bond that supported a collaborative relationship and fostered a mutual respect.

5. How did machismo appear in the session between the two of you?

If *machismo* is defined as trying to do a one-upmanship on the other, that dynamic never played out in my therapeutic relationship with this individual. What was more evident from the start was a relational dance in which we navigated how to further our mutual understanding of each other. There was some apparent defensiveness on each of our parts, which seemed related to our specific stereotypes and prejudices associated with our professional status as Latinos and the specific professional disciplines that each of us held. As already reported in the chapter, the emotional distance initially gave way to a greater appreciation for Juan's personal and familial history and the impact it had on me as the provider. This awareness was a particularly strong therapeutic agent in the bridging of our mutual understanding and in the multidimensional aspects of our healing work.

REFERENCES

Abreu, J. M., Goodyear, R. K., Campos, A., & Newcomb, M. D. (2000). Ethnic belonging and traditional masculinity ideology among African Americans, European Americans, and Latinos. *Psychology of Men and Masculinity, 1,* 75–86.

Anaya, R. (1996). I'm the king: The macho image. In L. Rodriguez (Ed.), *Muy macho: Latino men confront their manhood* (pp. 57–73). New York: Anchor Books.

Atkinson, D. R., Brown, M. T., Casas, J. M., & Zane, N. W. S. (1996). Achieving ethnic parity in counseling psychology. *Counseling Psychologist, 24,* 230–258.

Baca-Zinn, M. (1982). Chicano men and masculinity. *Journal of Ethnic Studies, 10,* 29–44.

Brooks, G. R. (2003). Masculinity and men's mental health. *Revision, 25,* 24–37.

Carrasco, D. (1990). *Religions of Meso America.* San Francisco: Harper & Row.

Casas, J. M., & Pytluk, S. D. (1995). Hispanic identity development: Implications for research and practice. In J. G. Ponterotto, J. M. Casas, L. A. Suzuki, & C. M. Alexander (Eds.), *Handbook of multicultural counseling* (pp. 155–180). Thousand Oaks, CA: Sage.

Casas, J. M., Turner, J. A., & Ruiz de Esparza, C. A. (2001). Machismo revisited in a time of crisis: Implications for understanding and counseling Hispanic men. In G. R. Brooks & G. E. Good (Eds.), *The new handbook of psychotherapy and counseling with men: A comprehensive guide to settings, problems, and treatment approaches* (Vol. 2, pp. 254–279). San Francisco: Jossey-Bass.

Casas, J. M., Wagenheim, B. R., Banchero, R., & Mendoza-Romero, J. (1994). Hispanic masculinity: Myth or psychological schema meriting clinical consideration? *Hispanic Journal of Behavioral Sciences, 16,* 315–331.

Cervantes, J. M. (2004a). *Mestizo spirituality: A counseling model for Chicano and Native/Indigenous peoples.* Unpublished manuscript.

Cervantes, J. M. (2004b). Mexican-Americans: A prospective analysis and counseling paradigm. In C. Negy (Ed.), *Cross-cultural psychotherapy: Toward a critical understanding of diverse client populations* (pp. 85–113). Reno, NV: Bent Tree Press.

Cervantes, J. M., & Parham, T. (2005). Toward a meaningful spirituality for people of color: Lessons for the counseling practitioner. *Cultural Diversity and Ethnic Minority Psychology, 11,* 69–81.

Cervantes, J. M., & Ramirez, O. (1992). Spirituality and family dynamics in psychotherapy with Latino children. In L. Vargas & J. Kross-Chionio (Eds.), *Working* with culture: Psychotherapeutic interventions with ethnic minority children and adolescents. New York: Jossey-Bass.

Cervantes, J. M., & Sweatt, L. I. (2004). Family therapy with Chicana/o families. In R. Velasquez, L. Arrellano, & B. McNeill (Eds.), *Handbook of Chicana and Chicano psychology and mental health* (pp. 285–322). New York: Erlbaum.

Cromwell, R. E., & Ruiz, R. A. (1979). The myth of macho dominance in decision making within Mexican and Chicano families. *Hispanic Journal of Behavioral Sciences, 1*, 355–373.

De la Cancela, V. (1986). A critical analysis of Puerto Rican machismo: Implications for clinical practice. *Psychotherapy: Theory, Research and Practice, 23*, 291–296.

Diaz-Guerrero, R. (1967). *Psychology of the Mexican: Culture and personality*. Austin: University of Texas Press.

Diaz-Guerrero, R., Lichtszain, J. L., & Reyes, L. I. (1979). Alienacion de la madre, psicopatologia y la practica clinica en Mexico [Alienation of the mother, psychopathology, and clinical practice in Mexico]. *Hispanic Journal of Behavioral Sciences, 1*, 117–133.

Falicov, C. J. (1998). *Latino families in therapy: A guide to multicultural practice*. New York: Guilford Press.

Falicov, C. J. (1999). Religion and spiritual folk traditions in immigrant families: Therapeutic resources with Latinos. In F. Walsh (Ed.), *Spiritual resources in family therapy* (pp. 104–120). New York: Guilford Press.

Fragoso, J. M., & Kashubeck, S. (2000). Machismo, gender role conflict, and mental health. *Psychology of Men and Masculinity, 1*, 87–97.

Freire, R. (1972). *Pedagogy of the oppressed*. New York: Herder & Herder.

Gafner, G., & Duckett, S. (1992). Treating the sequelae of a curse in elderly Mexican Americans. *Clinical Gerontologist, 11*, 145–153.

Gilmore, D. (1990). *Manhood in the making: Cultural concepts of masculinity*. New Haven, CT: Yale University Press.

Gonzales, R. (Ed.). (1996). *Muy macho: Latino men confront their manhood*. New York: Anchor Books.

Gowan, M., & Trevino, M. (1998). An examination of gender differences in Mexican-American attitudes toward family and career roles. *Sex Roles: A Journal of Research, 38*, 1079–1093.

Imber-Black, E., Roberts, J., & Whiting, R. A. (Eds.). (2003). *Rituals in families and family therapy*. New York: Norton.

Krippner, S., & Achterberg, J. (2000). Anomalous healing experiences. In E. Cardeña, S. J. Lynn, & S. Krippner (Eds.), *Varieties of anomalous experiences* (pp. 353–395). Washington, DC: American Psychological Association.

Lame Deer, J., & Erdoes, R. (1972). *Lame Deer, seeker of visions*. New York: Washington Square Press Publications.

Lara-Cantú, M. A., & Navarro-Arias, R. (1986). Positive and negative factors in the measurement of sex roles: Findings from a Mexican sample. *Hispanic Journal of Behavioral Sciences, 8*, 143–155.

Long, V. O., & Martinez, E. A. (1997). Masculinity, femininity, and Hispanic professional men's self-esteem and self-acceptance. *The Journal of Psychology, 131,* 481–488.

Madsen, W. (1964). *The Mexican-American of South Texas.* New York: Holt, Rinehart & Winston.

Matovina, T., & Riebe-Estrella, G. (Eds.). (2002). *Horizons of the sacred: Mexican traditions in U.S. Catholicism.* Ithaca, New York: Cornell University Press.

Minuchin, S. (1974). *Families and family therapy.* Cambridge, MA: Harvard University Press.

Mirandé, A. (1988). Que gacho es ser macho: It's a drag to be a macho man. *Azlan: A Journal of Chicano Studies, 17,* 63–89.

Mirandé, A. (1997). *Hombres y machos: Masculinity and Latino culture.* Boulder, CO: Westview Press.

Montoya, J. (1992). *Information—20 years of Joda.* San Francisco: Chusma Press Publications.

Neihardt, J. (Ed.). (1961). *Black Elk speaks: Being the life story of a holy man of the Oglala Sioux.* Lincoln: University of Nebraska Press.

Niemann, Y. F., Pollak, K. I., Rogers, S., & O'Connor, E. (1998). Effects of physical context on stereotyping of Mexican-American males. *Hispanic Journal of Behavioral Sciences, 20,* 349–362.

Peñalosa, F. (1968). Mexican family roles. *Journal of Marriage and the Family, 30,* 680–689.

Quintero, G. A., & Estrada, A. L. (1998). Cultural models of masculinity and drug use: "Machismo," heroin, and street survival on the U.S.–Mexican border. *Hispanic Journal of Behavioral Sciences, 16,* 315–331.

Ramirez, M., III. (1983). *Psychology of the Americas: Mestizo perspectives on personality and mental health.* New York: Pergamon Press.

Ramirez, M., III. (1998). *Multicultural/multiracial psychology: Mestizos perspectives in personality and mental health.* Northvale, NJ: Jason Aronson.

Ramirez, M., III. (1999). *Multicultural psychotherapy: An approach to individual and cultural differences* (2nd ed.). Needham Heights, MA: Allyn & Bacon.

Rodriguez, L. (1996). *Muy macho: Latino men confront their manhood.* New York: Anchor Books.

Tello, J. (1998). El hombre noble buscando balance: The noble man searching for balance. In R. Carrillo & J. Tello (Eds.), *Family violence and men of color: Healing the wounded male spirit* (pp. 31–52). New York: Springer Publishing Company.

Thompson, E. H., & Pleck, J. H. (1995). Masculinity ideologies: A review of research instrumentation on men and masculinities. In R. F. Levant & W. S. Pollack (Eds.), *A new psychology of men* (pp. 129–163). New York: Basic Books.

Torres, J. B. (1998). Masculinity and gender roles among Puerto Rican men: A dilemma for Puerto Rican men's personal identity. *American Journal of Orthopsychiatry, 68,* 16–26.

Torres, J. B., Solberg, V. S. H., & Carlstrom, A. H. (2002). The myth of sameness among Latino men and their machismo. *American Journal of Orthopsychiatry, 72,* 163–181.

Valdez, L. F., Baron, A., & Ponce, F. Q. (1987). *Counseling Hispanic men.* In M. Scher, M. Stevens, G. E. Good, & G. A. Eichenfield (Eds.), *Handbook of counseling and psychotherapy with men* (pp. 203–217). Thousand Oaks, CA: Sage.

Velasquez, R., Arrellano, L., & McNeill, B. (2004). *Handbook of Chicana and Chicano psychology and mental health.* New York: Erlbaum.

Wachtel, P. L. (1998). *Therapeutic communication: Knowing what to say when.* New York: Guilford Press.

11

HELPING A BOY BECOME A PARENT: MALE-SENSITIVE PSYCHOTHERAPY WITH A TEENAGE FATHER

MARK S. KISELICA

For the past 26 years, I have worked with troubled adolescents and their families in a variety of settings, including a private psychiatric hospital, a public junior–senior high school, an outpatient mental health setting, two correctional facilities, an inpatient brief therapy unit, and several private practices. Over the course of this time period, the United States has had one of the highest rates of teenage pregnancy in the world and a skyrocketing rate of teenagers who give birth to babies out of wedlock. Consequently, it is not surprising that I have encountered through my work as a psychologist hundreds of unmarried boys and girls who are, or were about to become, parents during their teenage years.

As I counseled teenage parents during the late 1970s and throughout the 1980s, time and time again I was confronted by a disturbing practice: Mental health and social service agencies were appropriately very attentive to the needs of adolescent mothers but they tended to ignore and dismiss the needs of young fathers. In response to this neglect, I considered it my professional responsibility to try to understand the concerns of teenage fathers and to be their advocate and counselor. Later, when I became an academician during the 1990s, I developed a systematic line of research on the subject of adolescent fathers, which included a careful examination of the existing literature on the subject; the launching of numerous studies to investigate attitudes about, and services for (or the lack thereof), teen fathers; and the development of male-friendly approaches to counseling boys who become fathers when they are still teenagers.

My efforts to change the way society views and treats teenage fathers has put me in touch with an ever-widening circle of professionals who share my passion to help boys and men and who have supported and informed my work as a practitioner. For example, when I first dove into the literature on teenage fathers, I was greatly influenced by the work of two particular scholars, Bryan Robinson of the University of North Carolina at Charlotte, and Leo Hendricks of Howard University. Robinson's work affirmed what I had witnessed repeatedly in clinical settings: Teen fathers are the victims of harmful stereotypes depicting them as a callous lot who abandon their partners and their children. In his groundbreaking book, *Teenage Fathers*, Robinson (1988) demonstrated through his thoughtful critique of the literature that contrary to popular myths about adolescent fathers, most young men involved in an out-of-wedlock pregnancy have caring, supportive relationships with their partners and their children. Robinson also described the many heart-wrenching hardships of teen fathers, which was supported by the pioneering empirical findings of Hendricks (1988) and his colleagues, whose cross-cultural research on the subject documented that young fathers do, indeed, experience a wide range of difficulties and that they require practical help and guidance with the transition to fatherhood.

I had the opportunity to talk with both men about their work when I was a professor at Ball State University from 1990 through 1994. I once called Robinson to tell him how much his work had influenced me and to ask whether he was still doing research on the subject. He reported that he had moved onto other topics, but he thanked me for my call and encouraged me to continue with my attempts to make the public more aware of adolescent fathers, for he still believed that society had not changed its views about this population. To my great fortune, I successfully recruited Leo Hendricks to give a keynote address on teen fathers for the Annual Conference of the Indiana Council on Adolescent Pregnancy (Hendricks, 1992). During the wonderful time we shared at the conference, Leo urged me to pursue my scholarly interests on the subject, noting that adolescent pregnancy and parenthood was one of the most urgent social issues of our time.

I will always be grateful to these two eminent men for their support, yet I am sad to say that not much has changed in society's treatment of young fathers. In a series of studies conducted during the 1990s, I repeatedly found that service programs are much more likely to provide services for teen mothers than for teen fathers (Kiselica, 1996, 1998b; Kiselica & Sturmer, 1993, 1995). Furthermore, I constantly meet people who say to me, "Oh, you work with teen fathers—I bet you meet some real losers with that bunch." And I am often contacted by reporters who, after discovering my many publications on the subject, want to learn more from me about teen fathers because—as they confess to me—"We always hear about young mothers, but we rarely hear anything about young fathers." It has become my life's work to change these sorts of reactions.

If we really hope to help teen fathers to become caring, competent, and committed parents, then we must begin by thinking complexly about these young men. I admit that I have struggled over the years to attain such an understanding. When I was a teenager myself, I knew nothing about teenage fathers and their difficulties. As I began to work with this population, I quickly discovered that becoming a father as a teenager is a very stressful crisis. I also learned that many boys facing this crisis are condemned, rather than helped in any substantive way, during their transition to parenthood. I became so upset by society's treatment of teenage fathers that I went through a phase of overidentifying with them, focusing my attention only on pregnancy and parenthood from their perspective. I have finally reached a more complicated understanding about these young men by learning to seek out and trust the empirical data on the subject, which have demonstrated that there are many different types of teen fathers. Some—which, I must emphasize, represent the minority of teen fathers—are antisocial in their attitudes and behavior, using their partners as sexual objects and never intending to take responsibility for their role in an out-of-wedlock pregnancy. Most, however, have genuine feelings for their partners and their children, but a large number of these young men gradually reduce their contact with their partner and child because of a host of interpersonal, educational, and economic difficulties, including conflicts with their partner and their partner's families, confusion about the role of a father, a tendency to drop out of school, and financial problems (see Kiselica, 1995). All teenage fathers need help to understand what their conceptions of masculinity and fatherhood are, who shaped those conceptions, and how they want to define themselves as men and fathers. Much of my work has been focused on assisting them with those vital challenges.

Another thrust of my work has been directed at helping mental health professionals to understand how to adjust the process of psychotherapy so that it better fits with the relational style of boys. In a series of publications dedicated to this issue (Kiselica, 1999b, 2001, 2003a, 2003b), I have observed that there tends to be a mismatch between conventional approaches to counseling and the relational style of boys. For example, although many boys naturally open up to their friends during informal activities, such as playing sports, hanging out, or working on cars, counselors continue to insist that boys work with them in formal office settings where they are expected to disclose intimate thoughts and feelings in face-to-face encounters. Although this approach is successful with some boys, especially those who are very verbally and emotionally expressive, it creates an understandable reaction of discomfort in other boys, who are often erroneously viewed by the practitioner as being resistant or oppositional to therapy or constitutionally incapable of establishing deep relationships with others. However, the problem does not reside in the boy—it rests with a well-intentioned but misguided approach to working with the boy. In these situations, there is a tragic mismatch between the boy's relational style and the therapist's conception about how therapy should proceed, all too often resulting in an unsuccessful intervention that is blamed on the boy for his alleged flaws.

To correct for this mismatch, I have suggested that helping professionals transform their traditional ways of doing therapy by adopting what I have referred to as a "male-friendly psychotherapeutic process" (Kiselica, 2003b, p. 1226). By "male-friendly," I mean practicing a male-sensitive approach to counseling that includes the use of informal settings, flexible time schedules, instrumental activities, humor, self-disclosure, and psychoeducational groups. Specifically, this involves talking to boys in their language and doing with them the types of things that boys naturally do as a means of establishing friendships with others. So, for example, when counseling a teenage father, rather than expect the boy to sit in my office, spilling his guts about the pregnancy, I talk with him while we walk outside, shoot baskets, or eat a meal, gradually learning about his interests and concerns as he grows more comfortable with me (Kiselica, 1995, 1999b).

I try to help teen fathers to become supportive partners and loving fathers by infusing this male-friendly psychotherapeutic process into a multicultural family therapy framework, which recognizes that there are universal issues associated with adolescent paternity—that is, issues that cut across cultures, such as resolving the crisis pregnancy, preparing for fatherhood, negotiating changes with the immediate and extended family, and sorting out educational and career plans. These universal challenges are played out in a unique family system and within cultural contexts with culture-specific perspectives about the world. For example, there is still a strong social stigma among White, non-Hispanic Americans toward adolescent, premarital childbearing, which helps to explain why White families have tended to resolve unexpected pregnancies by forcing the young couple to marry. African American families commonly have a historical mistrust of the social service and mental health systems due to the effects of institutional racism, which deters many Black teen fathers from seeking the assistance of a professional counselor, social worker, or psychologist. Hispanic teen fathers raised in a household adhering to traditional gender roles are likely to experience vexing values conflicts if their partners have been socialized to embrace the androgynous gender roles that have become more commonplace in mainstream society (Kiselica, 1995). So, as I consider the universal challenges a teen father must master, I form culture-specific hypotheses about the contextual factors that will influence his route and response to paternity.

I illustrate the male-friendly counseling process and the multicultural family therapy approach here through my discussion of a case study featuring Carlos, an adolescent boy who became an expectant father at the age of 16. His name and key details regarding his case have been altered to protect his anonymity.

COUNSELING CARLOS, A TEEN FATHER

I learned about Carlos C., a 16-year-old Mexican American boy, from a priest who had read about my work with teen fathers in a local newspaper. The priest called me to ask whether I would be willing to work with Carlos and his family, whose lives had been seriously disrupted when he broke the news of the pregnancy to his parents. The priest reported that he learned about the pregnancy from Mrs. C., who had sought the priest's spiritual guidance at the onset of the crisis. He added that Carlos came from a very traditional, Mexican family and that he had not yet had any contact with Carlos's father regarding the pregnancy.

Because Mrs. C. had taken the initiative to get help for her son, I realized that she was the person through whom I could establish contact with the family. I asked the priest to tell Mrs. C. that I would give her a call, and I followed up by contacting Mrs. C. over the phone. During this first conversation, I encouraged Mrs. C. to ventilate about the pregnancy and its shocking impact on her family. I empathized with her fears about her son's readiness to be a father and assured her that I would be happy to help her family to resolve this crisis, no matter how long it would take.

Recognizing that in traditional Hispanic culture, fathers typically represent the family to the outside world, I asked Mrs. C. if she had let her husband know that she planned to be in touch with me. She replied that she had and that her husband had responded by giving his consent for her to talk with me because of my relationship with their parish priest. Despite this consent, I realized that I had better establish a relationship with the father soon as a sign of my respect for his authority. I asked Mrs. C. to notify Mr. C. that I would pay him a visit to solicit his opinion as the head of the family on the pregnancy.

Several days later, I called Mr. C. and asked if I could visit him that night to talk about Carlos and his situation. Mr. C. agreed, so I stopped by his house, where he greeted me with a firm handshake as I entered his modest row home, which he shared with his wife, Carlos, and two daughters: Maria, who was 13, and Wilma, who was 12. I joined him at the dining room table, where he had invited me to sit and share some soda and coffee cake while we talked.

During this first conversation, I told Mr. C. I was honored to meet his family, and I showed him some photos of my own parents, my wife, and my three children. I told him I understood how important family is and that this must be a very difficult time for him. He responded by telling me how angry he was at Carlos for getting his girlfriend, Carmen, pregnant and for shaming the family. Furthermore, he was conflicted about how the family should handle the situation, on the one hand, wanting Carlos to marry Carmen—which was the honorable thing to do—and on the other hand, wishing Carlos would finish school first. Both Mr. and Mrs. C. had dropped out of school and had worked in low-paying jobs ever since—he as a laborer for a landscaping company, she as a child-care worker. He wanted his son to have a future spared of the hardships he and his wife had faced, and he feared that the pregnancy would jeopardize his son's chances of having a better life. I told Mr. C. how much I admired him for his selfless dreams for his children, and I shared with him how my parents had sacrificed and struggled to give my siblings and me an education. I promised him that I would do everything I could to help him and his family, and I asked his permission to meet with Carlos to discuss the pregnancy.

Due to the success of this visit with Mr. C., I earned access to Carlos and now faced the challenge of winning his trust. Even though his father had required Carlos to meet with me—which was a critical step in the therapeutic process—that did not guarantee that Carlos would cooperate with me. To gain his confidence, I had to recall what my mentor, Leo Hendricks, had taught me through his writings and lectures: A young man facing an unplanned pregnancy approaches counseling with a central question in his mind, "What's in this for me?" In other words, teen fathers have their own agenda when they enter counseling. For some, the top agenda item is getting help to find a job; for others, their first priority is calming down the family. Some others just want comfort and assurance that everything will be okay. I had to figure out what Carlos's key need was.

When Carlos entered my office, he looked like an angry, defeated young man who felt coerced into seeing me. As I looked at him, I tried my best to understand what it must be like for him to be forced to come see a stranger against his will. I realized I would get nowhere with him unless I affirmed these feelings and helped him to see that I was willing to become a part of his world, rather than expecting him to fit into mine. Also, because so many of the boys I have worked with have feared that psychologists would mess with their minds, I recognized that I had to let him know how I practice counseling. So, I immediately told him I understood that he might want nothing to do with me but that he should know that I cared for him, his family, and Carmen. I explained to him that I had helped a lot of guys who were in his situation and that I was not the kind of shrink who would play games with his head. I promised him that I would tell him what I was thinking at all times so that he would not have to worry about me playing any mind games with him. I assured him that all I wanted to do was to get to know him, and if he then felt I was okay, we could take it from there.

Carlos relaxed his defensive posture a bit after I shared these thoughts with him, and I immediately capitalized on this slight change in his mood by asking him if he would like to take a walk with me to get a bite to eat at a convenience store around the corner from my office. He replied, "That's cool," and I led him out the door and to the sidewalk as we headed to the store. Along the way, I told him a little bit about my family, and I asked him about his interests. He told me that he and his friends liked to work on cars, and I shared with him my experiences doing minor repairs in cars when I worked as an attendant in gas stations during my teenage years. I confessed to him that I did not know much about automobile mechanics, although I had done quite a few oil changes and tune-ups on cars during the early 1970s. This led to a nice conversation about how complicated engines have become, with Carlos gradually doing more and more of the talking, telling me about the types of things he and his buddies liked to do with cars, such as entering them in races at a nearby race strip.

We continued to talk about cars as I purchased, and then we consumed, two sodas and two candy bars during our return trip to my office. Once we settled back into my office, I sensed that Carlos was now comfortable with me, and I asked him if he hoped his baby would be a boy, and if so, would he like him to be a mechanic.

This probe sparked the first of countless conversations between Carlos and me about the pregnancy, Carlos's relationship with Carmen and his parents, and fatherhood. He told me about how shocked he was when he learned about the conception. He was too young to be a father, and he had been scared to tell Carmen's mother and then his parents about the pregnancy because of the shame it would bring to both families. Doing so had been devastating, because Carmen's mother had cried and his father had blown up at him in response to the news. Their reactions had left him depressed, and he was confused about how he would manage his life now that he was about to become a father. More than anything, he wanted to decide on a course of action, but he was unsure about what he should do next. So, I offered to help him to negotiate a plan for managing this crisis with his and Carmen's family—an offer of assistance that Carlos eagerly accepted.

PRENATAL COUNSELING

So, over the next 2 weeks, I had several talks with Carlos, his parents, and Carmen and her mother about how they hoped to resolve the pregnancy, which is an important task associated with the prenatal phase of counseling with teen parents. Mr. and Mrs. C. met with Carmen's mom, Ms. V., who was a single mother; all three adults and both of the expectant teen parents agreed that they were opposed to an abortion. They also agreed that the children were too young to marry, even though they recognized that it was fairly common for teenagers to marry in their culture. The parents wanted their children to complete high school, and they accepted my offer to help them to map out a plan that would allow them to provide for the needs of the baby while making it possible for the young parents to continue with their studies.

It was fortuitous that the families cooperated. Often, the families of the teenagers involved in an adolescent pregnancy take on adversarial roles and blame each other for the crisis. Instead, Mr. and Mrs. C. and Mrs. V. empathized with each other's point of view and became a source of mutual support, which was a great asset to me in my counseling with Carlos. I felt relieved and fortunate to be able to work with these caring, constructive parents. Another indication of the constructive tone established in this case occurred when Mr. C. gave me his signed consent to discuss matters with Mrs. V., an arrangement that Carlos supported as well. This cooperation enabled me to be of service to both families as they attempted to work together in the best interests of the young parents and the baby.

During the remainder of the prenatal phase, I contacted a school counselor, who put Mrs. V. and Carmen in touch with the coordinator of a school-based program for teen mothers. The program was designed to help expectant and parenting teenage girls to remain in school. Once enrolled in the program, Carmen took classes in child development and parenting skills and enrolled in several academic courses she would have to finish to complete her diploma.

I also supported Mrs. V. and Carmen emotionally as they coped with their fears of Carmen having a child at the tender age of 14. A big development in allaying their fears was steering them toward a university hospital that had excellent obstetrical and gynecological (OB/GYN) services. Throughout her pregnancy, Carmen received state-of-the-art medical care, which helped her and her mom to feel less scared about her delivering the baby while Carmen was so young.

Although it was fairly easy to find prenatal services for Carmen, there were no programs to which I could refer Carlos for support as he approached parenthood, which is often the case when it comes to adolescent fathers. In the absence of a structured fatherhood program, I proceeded to work extensively with Carlos and his family. Two of my goals with Carlos during the prenatal phase were to engage the support of Carlos's parents to prepare him for fatherhood, and to fill in the gap when his parents could not help him. For example, during our individual counseling sessions, I encouraged Carlos to think about the kind of father he would like to be and to discuss this topic with his parents. Based on this suggestion, Carlos enjoyed many frank talks with his parents, especially his father, about the responsibilities of parenthood, which forged a new closeness between Carlos and Mr. C. Although many years earlier Carlos had internalized his father's fine qualities—such as Mr. C.'s dedication to family and to hard work—he had not been aware of how keenly his father had embraced these values until the two began to have conversations about Carlos's transition to fatherhood. Mr. C. used this period of transition to teach his son about his views on being a provider, about giving to the next generation, and about protecting the family, and Carlos happily soaked up the lessons his father was sharing with him, enjoying a newfound closeness with his father in the process. Nevertheless, Carlos was still uninformed about child development, so I lent him some of my videos on parenting babies, which he observed and we discussed during our individual counseling sessions. During these discussions, we talked about his reactions to the videos, including his understanding about appropriate expectations for children and the developmental changes children experience over time. As important, I told Carlos about the joys I have experienced holding my children, teaching and playing with them, and watching them grow and how parenthood has enhanced the bond I have with my wife. Sharing these disclosures with Carlos solidified my relationship with him and helped him to look forward to fatherhood with optimism.

Carlos found it difficult to concentrate in school during this period, because he took a part-time job—as you might have guessed, working in an auto-repair shop doing maintenance on cars—as a means to financially support Carmen. He was tired from the additional hours at work and missed hanging out with his buddies. To help him remain inspired with his work in the shop and at school, I asked a former client of mine, John, who had been a teen father many years earlier, to serve as an informal mentor for Carlos. John kindly agreed to visit Carlos, and the two developed a nice friendship. According to Carlos, talking with John about their respective experiences might have been the best help of all during his efforts to be a caring partner and father.

Sometimes, supportive parents, a teen father mentor, and counseling are not enough to keep an expectant adolescent father in school. So, I called another friend of mine, Bill, who was a teacher at the technical high school where Carlos was learning to be a mechanic, and asked him to check in on Carlos from time to time. Bill was glad to help, and he pushed Carlos to complete his studies.

Another crucial goal with Carlos prior to the birth of the child was to foster his support of Carmen, who continued to live with her mother, while Carlos lived with his parents. Throughout the pregnancy, Carlos and Carmen experienced an up-and-down relationship. At times, they were very affectionate and concerned for each other, but at other times they experienced conflicts and distance. Therefore, a major issue in our therapy was teaching Carlos that he had to find a way to support Carmen through these swings in their relationship. For example, Carlos participated with Carmen in Lamaze classes and went with her to some of her OB/GYN visits during the pregnancy. He did this despite the fact that he and Carmen talked about "breaking up" several times throughout the pregnancy. Because he managed to stay focused on helping Carmen, however, he was present with her on the day she gave birth to their 6-pound baby girl.

POSTNATAL COUNSELING

The birth of the child was a temporary source of joy for both families. Carlos was a proud father, even though he looked inept whenever he held his tiny daughter. Although a part of him still was in a state of disbelief that he was a father at this point in his life, another part of him felt that he had become more of a man by having a child. Now that he had taken this important step of becoming a father—albeit an unexpected one—he was determined to show the adults in his life that he would rise up to the expectations that they, especially his father, had for him: to be a provider; to help with the care of his daughter, Juanita; and to protect her and her mother, Carmen. Many people from both the paternal and maternal families welcomed Juanita into their lives, and they expressed their pride in Carlos as they witnessed his efforts to be a good father. But this happy atmosphere was soon tempered by the many adjustments that are required when teenagers have children.

The magical feelings soon evaporated as Carmen experienced sleepless nights caring for a colicky infant. Carmen became irritable, prompting frequent spats between her and Carlos. Carlos was testy too, overwhelmed by his new responsibilities, and he was often short with Carmen and insensitive regarding her frustrations with the baby. Both teenagers began to dump the baby on their parents, expecting the grandparents to watch Juanita while the teens went out with their friends. The grandparents became critical of their children's child-rearing practices, and Carlos and Carmen sometimes responded by telling their parents to butt out.

To quell these conflicts, I met separately with each family to better define the roles and boundaries in the families. We clarified the schedule for who would watch Juanita and who had the ultimate say with decisions regarding the child. This was a tricky process because I had to help the grandparents to walk a fine line between being helpful to their children, while not completely taking over. In the end, signed contracts detailing responsibilities and schedules led to fewer disagreements among all of the parties involved.

Throughout the postnatal period, I continued to use the assistance of school personnel to help Carmen with her education and parenting skills. She took Juanita to a child-care center at her school, and she decided she would acquire training to be a medical assistant. Meanwhile, Carlos kept plugging away in the technical school and at the garage, bolstered by the continued encouragement of John and Bill and inspired by the impressive work ethic of his parents.

In spite of these varied forms of support, Carlos and Carmen continued to have their difficulties. As time passed, each of them developed romantic interests in other people and strongly ambivalent feelings about each other. Although they both gradually recognized that they were too incompatible to marry, they still felt deeply tied together, bonded by their surviving the crisis of an unplanned pregnancy and sharing a beautiful daughter. Eventually, they both married other people, but they each remained committed to their daughter.

I terminated counseling with Carlos shortly after he graduated from high school, approximately 2 years after I had first met him. At that point, it was clear to me that he had developed a mutually supportive, although at times conflicted, relationship with Carmen, and that he had become a good father who cared for his child emotionally and financially on an ongoing, reliable basis. As he became more settled into his role as a parent, we agreed that we would see each other on an as-needed basis. We had a special celebration in his home after he graduated from high school. I accepted his parents' invitation to visit their home and gave Carlos a card in which I expressed my admiration for all that he had accomplished. I observed that he had been involved in a pregnancy when he least expected to, and rather than ignoring his responsibilities, he had confronted his fears about parenthood, learned all that he could about raising a child and supporting his daughter's mother, finished school, got a job, and became a loving father to Juanita and an amicable friend to Carmen. I also gave Mr. and Mrs. C. a card expressing my respect for the way they had supported Carlos and Carmen and their baby. In return, they thanked me for my dedication to their family and said they would always remember me and my family in their prayers—sentiments that touched me deeply.

Carlos is now the father of a second child and is employed full-time as a mechanic. He stops in to see me about once or twice a year and sends me an e-mail from time to time to let me know how he is doing. He is a fine young man and a fine father.

DISCUSSION

This case study illustrates that effective counseling and psychotherapy with boys involves adjusting the therapeutic process to fit the personality and culture of the client. In this particular case, my client, Carlos, was forced into counseling against his will while he was in the middle of a crisis pregnancy. A key challenge for me was to recognize that his anger and defensiveness about counseling were neither a sign that he did not want help nor symptoms of "resistance" but rather the justifiable reactions of a boy who was thrust into unfamiliar and frightening territory at a tender age. The key to earning his trust was to acknowledge the legitimacy of these feelings while adapting the counseling process to match his needs and culture. Because Carlos faced the crisis of an unplanned adolescent pregnancy, his needs included learning about child development and child rearing, defining for himself what it means to be a father, supporting his partner during and after the pregnancy, being linked to adults in his life who could support him, completing school and finding a job, and most important, becoming a caring parent. All of these challenges were played out in a cultural context in which Carlos's parents were Mexican Americans with traditional views on gender roles. Therefore, I had to earn the trust and endorsement of the parents to gain access to Carlos, and I had to be careful not to impose my own biases about gender roles on him or his family. Although I personally am a nontraditional man, I made sure to respect that Carlos and his father favored more traditional gender roles for men in their culture. Embracing these values and the skills that other professionals and I taught Carlos gave him the confidence to take on the demands of fatherhood during his teenage years.

I recently ran into Carlos in the gym one evening when we both had decided to work out. On that night, I noticed how much he had physically matured as he rhythmically lifted an easy-curl bar, pumping up his well-defined biceps in the process. Between doing sets of bicep curls, he approached me to say that he and his daughter were doing well and that he was thinking of starting his own business. In one of those fulfilling professional moments that will stay with me forever, he added that he often remembers the times we had spent in counseling and what they had meant to him. I told him that I was glad that he and Juanita were well, wished him well with his new business venture, and thanked him for his kind comments about our work in counseling, adding that I, too, often remembered him with fondness.

As I drove home that night, I reflected on the fact that I had helped a confused teenage boy to sort through the crisis of an unplanned pregnancy to become a caring, committed father and a successful young man. When I arrived home, my three children were asleep, so I quietly stepped into each of their bedrooms to watch them as they lay sleeping peacefully in their beds, thinking to myself that Carlos understood this same experience of what it means to love your child. With that thought, I ended my day grateful for the life I have and the lives of the young men I have touched and who have touched me.

QUESTIONS FROM THE EDITORS

1. *What types of gender-based stereotypes were you aware of in counseling this client? How did that impact your therapy with this client?*

Throughout my work with Carlos, I was keenly aware of one particular stereotype about boys that permeates the helping professions: Boys who have difficulty expressing themselves emotionally in therapy are developmentally impaired. (For a full critique of this stereotype, see Kiselica, 2001, 2003a, 2003b, and Kiselica & O'Brien, 2001.) Although it is true that some men experience a clinical condition referred to as *alexithymia*, which is defined as extreme deficits in the ability to access, recognize, and express emotions, the extant empirical findings on the subject indicate that there are no consistent gender differences in alexithymia. Furthermore, these findings show that the vast majority of people, including males, are in the normal range of the ability to express emotions (Kiselica, 2003b; Kiselica & O'Brien, 2001; Wester, Vogel, Pressly, & Heesacker, 2002). Moreover, biases about men being hypoemotional have been associated with an alarming tendency by mental health professionals to blame men for the problems they bring to therapy (Heesacker et al., 1999). Therefore, the assumption that there is something constitutionally awry in all boys who have difficulty expressing themselves during traditional psychotherapy is an unfair stereotype that can impede efforts to help boys. In my work with Carlos, I hypothesized that his initial hostility toward me was a legitimate reaction to his forced participation in therapy and his fear that I would not adapt to his way of relating to the world, rather than a sign that he was a victim of flawed male development. By challenging this stereotype and using a male-friendly approach, I was able to establish a strong therapeutic bond with Carlos, rather than set him against me.

2. How did your own gender role issues influence your work with this client?

Throughout my work with Carlos, I was conscious of my own biases about gender roles and I was very careful not to attempt to impose my own values regarding gender roles on Carlos and his family, which might have alienated them from me. Although my father, my brothers, and I are androgynous men, Carlos and his family practiced traditional gender roles. So, I respected these differences and helped Carlos to clarify the gender role that best suited him and his family.

3. Looking back on the case, knowing what you know, would you change the way you worked with this client?

On the whole, I feel very good about my work with Carlos and his family. The counseling process and interventions I used were successful, so there is little I would change. However, I do now wonder whether part of Carlos's initial hesitation about seeing me in counseling might have been associated, in part, with the traditional male tendency to avoid seeking help from professionals during times of trouble. Related to this idea, if I were to do anything differently with Carlos, I might have reached out to him more often after we had terminated counseling to see how things were going with him. Although I did not initiate these extra contacts because Carlos did stop in to see me from time to time after the termination phase and we seemed to have a strong degree of trust between us, I now wonder whether he could have used my help in the years following the end of my counseling work with him.

4. *How did your race and social class position impact the work you did with this client?*

I recognize that I am an Irish–Slovak, Catholic, fair-skinned White man with blond hair and blue eyes. Although I was born into poverty, I now am a member of the upper middle class. As I have stated elsewhere (Kiselica, 1998a, 1999a, 1999c), I realize that my physical appearance as a very light person and my current status as a member of the upper middle class have afforded me unfair advantages and privileges that often have been denied to darker skinned people, particularly those from lower socioeconomic levels, because of our nation's history of racism. Therefore, it is understandable that people from some historically oppressed groups, such as African Americans and Hispanics, might resent me for what I represent as a White person in a racist society. So, when I work with clients who are Hispanic, as Carlos and his family were, I keep these historical experiences in mind and use both culture-specific and universal tactics to bridge any cultural barriers that might exist between us (see Kiselica, 1995). For example, with Carlos's family, I used a culture-specific strategy of respecting the Hispanic tradition dictating that the father represents the family to the outside world, which is why I contacted Mr. C. first when I initiated my first visit with Carlos's family. I also hypothesized that I was more likely to be accepted by the family by demonstrating *personalismo*, the practice of being warm, personal, and emphasizing people over ideas, which is how I presented myself to each member of the family. Furthermore, my use of a family counseling approach was consistent with the traditional Hispanic emphasis on the family, rather than the individual. I complemented these culture-specific considerations by joining the family through discussions of universally shared experiences, such as the struggles of our respective ancestors to overcome hardships and the dreams we have for our children. Through these measures, I was able to transcend and honor the cultural, historic, and socioeconomic differences between me and Carlos and his family.

5. *As a father, what is it like to mentor expectant fathers? What experiences from your personal life contribute to your passion for working with young expectant fathers?*

I am a most fortunate person because I was raised by two loving parents, including a father who is my hero. My dad overcame numerous hardships, including the death of his dear mother when he was just 8 years old, his father's alcoholism and exploitation, poverty, a learning disability, dropping out of school after the eighth grade, and a severely injured leg and hip, to become the most wonderful father a son could ever ask for. He always worked hard, provided for his family, helped my mom with domestic chores, assisted my siblings and me with our homework, and most important, was a sweet and kind man. It is not surprising that my transference to men is positive, thanks to my relationship with my dad, and the warm feelings I have for men makes it easy for me to regard young fathers with fondness. Teenage fathers working with me sense my warm regard for them, so this transference energy makes it easier for young, expectant fathers to trust me. Helping adolescent fathers with their adjustment to parenthood is also a satisfying and generative experience for me, because I feel that I am sharing a wonderful legacy with them—the legacy of my precious father.

REFERENCES

Heesacker, M., Wester, S. R., Vogel, D. L., Wentzel, J. T., Mejia-Millan, C. M., & Goodholm, C. R. (1999). Gender-based emotional stereotyping. *Journal of Counseling Psychology, 46,* 483–495.

Hendricks, L. E. (1988). Outreach with teenage fathers: A preliminary report on three ethnic groups. *Adolescence, 23,* 711–720.

Hendricks, L. E. (1992, April). *Expanding the initiative with teenage fathers.* Keynote address conducted at the Annual Conference of the Indiana Council on Adolescent Pregnancy, Indianapolis, IN.

Kiselica, M. S. (1995). *Multicultural counseling with teenage fathers: A practical guide.* Newbury Park, CA: Sage.

Kiselica, M. S. (1996, June). *The service needs of teenage parents: Results of a national ASCA survey.* Paper presented at the Annual Convention of the American School Counselor Association, Indianapolis, IN.

Kiselica, M. S. (1998a). Preparing Anglos for the challenges and joys of multiculturalism. *The Counseling Psychologist, 26,* 5–21.

Kiselica, M. S. (1998b, March). *School-based services for teenage parents: Results of a state survey.* Paper presented at the World Conference of the American Counseling Association, Indianapolis, IN.

Kiselica, M. S. (1999a). Confronting my own ethnocentrism and racism: A process of pain and growth. *Journal of Counseling and Development, 77,* 14–17.

Kiselica, M. S. (1999b). Counseling teenage fathers. In A. M. Horne & M. S. Kiselica (Eds.), *Handbook of counseling boys and adolescent males: A practitioner's guide* (pp. 179–198). Thousand Oaks, CA: Sage.

Kiselica, M. S. (1999c). Reducing prejudice: The role of the empathic–confrontive instructor. In M. S. Kiselica (Ed.), *Confronting prejudice and racism during multicultural training* (pp. 137–154). Alexandria, VA: American Counseling Association.

Kiselica, M. S. (2001). A male-friendly therapeutic process with school-age boys. In G. R. Brooks & G. Good (Eds.), *The handbook of counseling and psychotherapy with men: A comprehensive guide to settings, problems, and treatment approaches* (Vol. 1, pp. 43–58). San Francisco: Jossey-Bass.

Kiselica, M. S. (2003a). Male-sensitive counselling with boys. *Counselling in Education,* 16–19.

Kiselica, M. S. (2003b). Transforming psychotherapy in order to succeed with boys: Male-friendly practices. *Journal of Clinical Psychology: In Session, 59,* 1225–1236.

Kiselica, M. S., & O'Brien, S. (2001, August). Are attachment disorders and alexithymia characteristic of males? In M. S. Kiselica (Chair), *Are males really emotional mummies: What do the data indicate?* Symposium conducted at the 109th Annual Convention of the American Psychological Association, San Francisco.

Kiselica, M. S., & Sturmer, P. (1993). Is society giving teenage fathers a mixed message? *Youth and Society, 24,* 487–501.

Kiselica, M. S., & Sturmer, P. (1995, August). *Outreach services for teenage parents: Has gender equity been realized?* Paper presented at the 103rd Annual Convention of the American Psychological Association, New York.

Robinson, B. E. (1988). *Teenage fathers.* Lexington, MA: Lexington Books.

Wester, S. R., Vogel, D. L., Pressly, P. K., & Heesacker, M. (2002). Sex differences in emotion: A critical review of the literature and implications for counseling psychology. *The Counseling Psychologist, 30,* 629–651.

12

COUNSELING MEN: PERSPECTIVES AND EXPERIENCES OF A WOMAN OF COLOR

MELBA J. T. VASQUEZ

This chapter describes the theoretical orientation of a woman of color who works with a variety of clients, including White men, in psychotherapy. A case is presented, and descriptions of the beginning, middle, and end of psychotherapy are described. The unique challenges of this combination of gender and ethnic background (Latina psychotherapist and White male client) are described.

INFLUENCES

What is my theoretical orientation in conducting psychotherapy, and how is it influenced by my role as a woman-of-color therapist providing psychotherapy to a White, middle-aged male executive? I describe my theoretical orientation as reflecting a multicultural, feminist perspective. That is, in addition to considering intrapsychic, interpersonal cognitive, and behavioral familial issues and dynamics as contributing to one's development, I consider societal messages and factors that have influenced each individual with whom

I work. The broader social context is critical in understanding human behavior. The feminist and multicultural perspective includes the belief that when psychological theory ignores the sociopolitical realities of the culture in which it arises, it can render only a fragmented interpretation of human experience (Miller, 1984). This means that as a psychotherapist I always assess and listen for experiences and influences in each person's narrative.

More specifically, my style of psychotherapy is influenced by a feminist relational–cultural perspective. A basic premise of relational–cultural theory (RCT) is that people grow through action in relationships with others. This perspective is based on the belief that development is a result of the interplay of affecting and being affected and of mutual responsiveness and care (Jordan, 2003). Relationships are thus viewed as being the primary source of healing and growth. RCT is built on an understanding of people that emphasizes a primary movement toward, and yearning for, connection with others throughout the life span. This perspective is contrary to traditional approaches to psychotherapy that view development as a trajectory from dependence to independence and from an existence governed by feeling to one guided by logical, abstract thought (Jordan, 2003). In RCT, disconnection is viewed as the primary source of human suffering. Psychological health is viewed as increasing levels of complexity, fluidity, choice, and articulation within human relationship as a marker of developmental maturity. Psychological development takes place in and through increasingly complex relationships; psychological health is a function of participation in relationships in which mutually empowering connections occur (Jordan, 2003). The model also assumes that connection inevitably entails conflict and that this conflict can also be a source of growth and is in fact, necessary. Given that this model was particularly developed to understand and work with women, one may ask how the RCT translates to working with White men, for whom autonomy and independence are often highly valued. I hope to demonstrate this in the discussion of my work with my client in the remainder of this chapter.

My clinical practice is very much influenced by the principles espoused in the *Guidelines on Multicultural Education, Training, Research, Practice, and Organizational Change for Psychologists* (American Psychological Association, 2003). The first guideline encourages psychologists to commit to cultural awareness and knowledge of self and others. With every client, I assume that we both enter the relationship with cultural histories that give rise to particular relational images. Walker (2004) suggested that when these cultural histories are not addressed, these images may flourish underground, perpetuating the distortions that impede the flow of relational movement.

My history as a Latina who grew up in a socially segregated, somewhat discriminatory community, means that at times, I have issues of trust and discomfort with White, majority culture individuals. It is critical as a psychotherapist that I am aware of what "triggers" the feelings of distrust and discomfort, as well as of the negative relational images that clients may have of me. Walker (2004) suggested that in a racially stratified culture, people are divided into dominant and subordinate, superior and inferior roles. Relational images are then based on premises of "better than" and "less than." Thus, it is possible for me to have a variety of negative emotional reactions to a client whom I may perceive to be better than or who may communicate in various ways that I am less than. It is my job as a psychotherapist to manage and process my reactions for the good of the relationship with the client.

Several multicultural experts have written about the therapeutic experience with a racial–ethnic minority group member paired with a White group member in the counseling dyad. Helms (1984, 1990) described an interaction model of counseling based on the identity development of racial–ethnic minority groups and of White identity development. She described four possible types of relationships, including parallel, crossed, progressive, and regressive. In the case presented here, the relevant relationship is a "crossed" relationship; that is, the counselor and client are at diametrically opposite stages of racial consciousness, with different attitudes about racial–ethnic minorities and Whites. Because of this difference, my ability to be empathic with the experiences of the client was especially important to avoid risk of disconnection. Disconnections are viewed in the RCT model as destructive to the growth process and occur in psychotherapy as a result of empathic failures and misattunements. Power dynamics influence the relationship in personal, societal, and psychotherapy experiences. Less powerful members of society are often relegated to positions of shame, which creates immobilization, self-blame, and a profound sense of isolation. However, conflict can be a source of mutual growth and understanding and can deepen the relationship. The RCT model is designed to help clients who have been rendered powerless in personal and societal situations to fortify against shame and disempowerment. Again, the question may arise, How does this model apply to a middle-aged, White male executive? My belief is that shame and disempowerment are relevant experiences for everyone, including powerful White men. The manifestations and behaviors may vary, and it is this information about which I have to be aware. Whereas women and people of color may behave in ways that are recognizable as feeling shameful and may reflect behaviors typical of feeling downcast and oppressed, White men may behave in more aggressive ways when they feel similar shameful feelings. Clearly, I run the risk of stereotyping with these observations, but these are tendencies that I have observed and that are supported in the literature (Addis & Mahalik, 2003; Brooks & Good, 2001). Of course, not all White men act in this way, but many do.

When a White client enters my office, I am aware that in general, I enter a relationship with someone who has been culturally indoctrinated to believe himself or herself to be superior to me, just as I have been culturally socialized to believe that I am inferior. Although these dynamics are not always in play and may be subtle when they are, they are nonetheless powerful (Walker, 2004). As a psychotherapist, I have the responsibility to manage these dynamics and images when they surface in myself, as well as to try to watch for them in my clients. The client whom I describe in this chapter did evoke vigilance along these issues on my part. He did so by virtue of being a White, corporate executive, over 6 feet tall. He initially displayed overt confidence, and appeared quite privileged. These are all factors that have historically evoked intimidating images for me.

McIntosh's (1989) essay *White Privilege: Unpacking the Invisible Knapsack* has been informative to me in my understanding of a racially stratified culture. "White privilege" is the unearned advantages and benefits that accrue to White individuals by virtue of a system normed on the experiences, values, and perceptions of their group. White privilege automatically subordinates groups of color and confers dominance to one group. Relational images of this dynamic occasionally surfaced in our psychotherapy for me, including at our first session. My client, Mike, spoke in loud, confident tones, and began by saying that it was someone else's (his wife's) idea to be there. He thought he was fine. Yet, I reminded myself that given the consistent findings that men tend not to seek professional help (Addis & Mahalik, 2003; Brooks & Good, 2001; Levant, 1995), it was meaningful that this man was attempting to seek help, even if the pressure to do so came from elsewhere. I assumed that he must be in significant pain; furthermore, he was willing to seek help from a Latina psychologist. I wondered what views and stereotypes he had of me, and what he had had to do to be willing to see a Latina therapist. Although I did not know the answers to these questions at this point, these perceptions of mine overrode the initial feelings of intimidation.

DESCRIPTION OF THE CLIENT AND THERAPY PROCESS

Mike entered therapy on the insistence of his spouse. His presenting concern was difficulty in his marital relationship, which he reported to be in crisis. In fact, the 20-year relationship had been difficult for the past 2 years. The "crisis" aspect was the result of his admission to having an "emotional affair" with a coworker. That is, he had begun to share thoughts and feelings in an intimate context with his coworker; although the relationship had not become physically intimate, Mike was feeling very attracted to her and knew that he was at risk of an affair. He had begun to behave in a distant and cold manner toward his wife, and his wife confronted him about the significant amount of time that he and his coworker seemed to be spending together by phone as well as at work.

I explored Mike's perspective of how he and his wife had been interacting in the past year. Mike's view revealed that there was significant criticism, contempt, defensiveness, and passive–aggressive behavior on both their parts. These are all indicators of a marriage in trouble (Gottman, 1994). I suggested that he and his partner seek couples therapy, in addition to agreeing to work with him in individual therapy. Over the next few sessions, Mike reported significant stress at work, noting that he had been reassigned to a position that reflected demotion, in his perspective. Mike felt a great deal of anger and shame for the demotion, and at first glance, did not take responsibility for contributing to any difficulties in the workplace (I often find that women overattribute responsibility for failure to themselves and men attribute responsibility to others.) When we tried to explore his shame, initially, he simply shut down and blamed those around him. Although this was momentarily distancing to me, I reminded myself that most men are socialized to be confident, self-reliant, physically tough, and remain in emotional control (Addis & Mahalik, 2003). Thus, acknowledging vulnerability or mistakes, especially initially in our relationship, would not have been allowable for him to maintain his sense of self. This awareness allowed me to remain in connection with Mike.

Assessment and Beginning of Psychotherapy

As part of the assessment process, I value hearing the client's story, or narrative. It became clear that Mike had internalized many traditional socialized male ideologies. Those ideologies include, for example, the position that men should be tough, competitive, and emotionally inexpressive (Addis & Mahalik, 2003). He decided, for example, at age 8, to never cry again, as a result of being made fun of by other boys for crying when hit. When I expressed sadness about these experiences, he responded in a bravado manner, adding that he had become even stronger by being successful in school and elsewhere. He initially could not accept my empathy for his historic pain. Yet, my continuing to convey understanding and empathy was important. He "softened" in his stance with me gradually.

Although Mike's parents were "somewhat comforting," there was significant stress, trauma, and loss in the family, and apparently, little time for him. He had a difficult family history with parental divorce and various forms of rejection. These experiences of loss and rejection very likely led to Mike's way of coping, including the idea that he must be successful, powerful, and competitive, to be a worthwhile person.

Mike had never been in psychotherapy before and, despite a lifelong struggle with mood instability, had never been on antidepressants. He sought a sense of worth through advanced education and high-status jobs. Levant (1995) described how the more men endorse traditional masculinity ideologies, the more they experience a host of potential presenting issues, including poor self-esteem, problems with interpersonal intimacy, greater depression and anxiety, abuse of substances, problems with interpersonal violence, greater biomedical concerns, as well as greater overall psychological distress. At the same time, the strengths associated with traditional masculine ideologies include abilities in problem solving, logical thinking, appropriate risk taking, and assertive behavior. Mike struggled with, on the one hand, a need to be confident (which he later admitted was often perceived as arrogance), successful, and in control; on the other hand, he struggled with poor self-worth, lack of intimacy, and depression, and he was abusing alcohol when he entered psychotherapy. Although he was not outwardly aggressive, he displayed sarcasm and various passive–aggressive behaviors, such as neglecting to finish projects that his wife wished completed, forgetting to run errands that he had agreed to, and continuing to talk to the coworker after committing to his wife that he would not.

We began to work on several cognitive–behavioral strategies to alleviate the symptoms of depression. I strongly recommended exercise, among other proactive behavioral strategies. Research has clearly supported the use of exercise in increasing one's health and mental health (Hays, 1999; Vasquez, 2002). Hays (1999) reviewed a wide range of studies that illustrated the psychological benefits of exercise with such disorders as depression, anxiety, stress, self-esteem issues, obesity, substance abuse, posttraumatic stress disorder, and recovery from medical illness. Furthermore, exercise as a strategy in psychotherapy can help increase a client's feelings of effectiveness in one's life. In addition, I encouraged him to be proactive in taking steps to accomplish other tasks that he had been avoiding.

After several weeks of showing an inability to begin exercise or to make any other significant behavioral changes to help alleviate his depression, Mike agreed to begin taking antidepressants. It was a struggle for him to take medication, as he saw it as determining that something was wrong with him. He sought information and decided what medication he wished to try before meeting with his physician. This was in keeping with his need for independence, self-determination, and control. The antidepressants did help Mike feel less depressed, and he slept better; however, the stresses and strains of life (finances, relationship, children, etc.) were still often overwhelming.

Although addressing the depression seemed difficult for Mike to control without the use of medication, he showed other abilities and strengths. To his credit, Mike was able to use his logical thinking to stay away from alcohol. Because he had set as a goal to develop integrity and improve his marriage, he worked hard to not engage in destructive arguments with his wife. Mike also experimented with being more assertive at work at the appropriate times. For Mike, work was difficult. He was under considerable stress, with a major reorganization after employee cutbacks in his corporation. He was in a "middle-man" role and felt the responsibility of the company to perform well, yet he felt that he had little authority. So we used therapy to help him with his work-related challenges. We role played methods of delegating and directing employees; Mike had received feedback that he was perceived as disdainful and contemptuous in his directives. He thought he was being humorous in a sarcastic way, yet it seemed that he had a tendency to ridicule others, to emphasize their weaknesses in front of others in a jocular manner, and to underestimate the negative impact of this approach. In as compassionate a manner as possible, but also in a direct way, I continued to provide feedback to him about the possible unintended consequences of his interpersonal style.

Middle of the Therapeutic Process

About 4 months after entering psychotherapy, Mike was laid off from his high-tech job. Although he had known that this was a possibility, given the state of the economy and the fact that his organization was "top heavy," he was devastated, hurt, and humiliated. Furthermore, a challenge to our relationship came when he declared being "victimized" by the fact that some ethnic minority personnel, whom he perceived to be less important or capable, were kept on, probably because of "affirmative action."

I felt immediately upset by what I perceived to be Mike's biased opinion and his attempt to scapegoat others rather than take responsibility. I remember feeling the immediate flush of anger and negative countertransference. However, it was important to me to be the "good therapist"; that included managing my own issues and being empathic with his pain and fear as a result of the loss of his job and source of income. I also knew that although he had improved during the course of therapy in his capacity to take more responsibility, the trauma of the job loss likely resulted in his "relapse" to old defenses of blaming others.

Perhaps one of the biggest challenges for me as a psychotherapist is being able to be attuned to clients well enough to know when to support and when to challenge, especially when the client is expressing what I perceive to be destructive or self-destructive sentiments, thoughts, and opinions. This is especially true when my own reactions (countertransference) and issues are triggered. In this case, I decided to put aside my feelings in the moment, given that he was in pain and seemed oblivious to the impact of his statements on me (which was information in and of itself). In my perspective, he was abusing his White privilege (McIntosh, 1989) in assuming that he was the one who should have maintained the job and in assuming that he was more competent. However, I also conceptualized that Mike was fragile in his ability to incorporate "fault" in his responsibility to what he may have contributed toward the decision to let him go and his need to "scapegoat" others. Although I did not perceive this to be "healthy coping," it was what he needed to do in that moment. I gently explored his feelings, and over the next few weeks, he was able to identify feelings of disgrace, shame, and despair, and he began to acknowledge that perhaps his performance was compromised in the past year. After my initial negative reaction to his method of coping, I think that I was able to be truly empathic and concerned for Mike's well-being. I did this by understanding that my responsibility was to care for him in the moment and that opportunities to challenge his blaming and perception of ethnic minority colleagues' unfair advantages could come later.

I realize, in retrospect, that I missed an opportunity to share, in a more immediate way, my personal reactions to Mike. Jordan (2003) and Walker (2004) have spoken of how when the therapist can be empathic with his or her own experience of racial degradation, he or she can be more attuned to the whole fabric of the client's social and emotional world. Empathy across levels of stratified power begins with self-empathy. By developing empathy for our own racial–ethnic privileges and deprivations, our strengths and weaknesses, we transform disconnection into a source of connection. Thus, I missed an opportunity to move toward a deeper connection to Mike by avoiding the processing of my reaction to Mike's biased attributions as to why he lost his job. I withheld the opportunity for both of us to engage in a growth-enhancing discourse about my feelings and reactions.

During the therapeutic period after his job loss, Mike was able to explore patterns in his previous jobs that were distancing and problematic. We explored his history and patterns of what he described as "arrogance." Mike was able to acknowledge that he did a good technical job but that a lot of people, both above and below him, "loathed him." He was able to admit that his arrogant style was actually compensation for his insecurities. When Mike took the time to truly analyze and consider his behavior, he was shocked and perplexed by how he treated others. He wept as he acknowledged that he likely came off as a "know-it-all," pontificated, and evoked dislike in people. Mike asked me whether I saw him in that negative light. I gently told him that although he had initially come across in that manner, and I gave him examples, I knew that underneath, he was a gentle, tender, vulnerable person, trying to be worthwhile. I also communicated that I knew that most people would not know that about him unless he demonstrated it. That seemed to be a helpful perspective to him. I missed another opportunity to challenge the discriminatory comments he had made. However, it may have been inappropriate during this period. I did not trust myself enough to feel at this point that those were not "my issues," so that I could manage the discussion in a way that would be constructive; I may have also assessed that he was not ready to hear this from me.

We balanced the powerful insights about Mike's destructive and self-destructive behaviors with the perspective that the state of the economy was indeed a challenge to corporations and that in other times, his difficulties may have been tolerated. It was important that Mike not feel entirely at fault but that he could use this painful period as an opportunity to develop insights about himself and to modify his behaviors for improvement.

We talked about the importance of pushing through his depression and avoidance in changing patterns and habits, as well as in pursuing work in the future. He went through questioning about whether he had the capability to deal with people. In addition to holding up "a mirror" for him to see his destructive behaviors (challenge), I also worked to help him identify his skills and strengths (support) on an ongoing basis.

One of the themes in the relationship between us had to do with an ongoing feeling of "shame" about my helping him with anything. Mike was able to describe his reactions as his "ego bristling"; he felt embarrassed and resisted being in the role of being helped. We explored both the societal messages about masculinity that he had received as well as his role in the family: He was not expected to need anything. The expectation in his family, given that his mother remarried and he had two different stepfathers, was that he not be a bother. He was, in fact, expected to be an asset to the family, and one who made his mother and stepfathers proud. However, he rarely got credit for his achievements. We processed his anger about that, including how those dynamics existed in his current relationships, both at home and at work. We also processed whether he felt that I gave him credit for his achievements in psychotherapy. It became a gentle joke between us for me to underscore his therapeutic achievements from then on.

Mike especially had difficulty being in a position of not knowing something. We explored, several times, his difficulty in accepting information, help, or support, especially from a woman of color. He was able to acknowledge that sometimes that was easier (to receive support from a woman of color) and at times it was difficult (to be in a position of knowing less about something than I).

At one point, several months after his loss of employment and after he had obtained another job, I was able to gently give feedback about how I was distanced by his anger about losing his job because of affirmative action. The issue came up because he was surprised that he had gotten a job, given that he was competing with a variety of women and persons of color. Mike recognized that his comments were examples of how he did not always consider the consequences of his statements. We further processed his feelings about being a White man in a world that was changing in regard to the increase of women and people of color in the workplace. Although it was productive to our relationship that we process this, given the distance from the actual event, the discussion was not as conflictual or immediately raw as it might have been months prior. Whether addressing my feelings about his statements was more or less productive is a continuing question for me. Authentic responsiveness is not always or necessarily full disclosure (Walker, 2004); timing is important. The ability to judge a client's readiness for a particular challenge or intervention is critical. These therapeutic decisions are more complex when the therapists' own feelings are stirred up and when they are experiencing countertransference. This interaction has served as a learning experience for me.

In general, kindness and compassion were "not pervasive" in the culture in which he grew up. One of our goals throughout therapy was for Mike to move from a pessimistic, cynical attitude to one of hope, optimism, and joy. He acknowledged that our relationship had evolved into one that reflected genuineness, authenticity, connection, and integrity. However, he was reluctant to assume that he could trust the capacity of most people to engage with him in those ways. He acknowledged that he was "attached" to his pessimistic thinking, and he saw optimistic people as naive and unrealistic. Yet, he stated that he would like to feel differently.

Despite several breakthroughs and progress in therapy, there were also several difficult sessions. In one session, for example, Mike talked about how he realized that his childhood was significantly shame based. Despite the fact that his parents were well educated and that both had master's degrees, they also were emotionally volatile, fought frequently, and were emotionally abusive to him and his siblings. He perceived his father to be weak and dominated by his mother. After this session of exploring the significant pain he felt as a teenager over his parents' emotional abuse, fights, and subsequent divorce, he returned the following session and determined that he could not "have another session like that." He was too devastated afterward. What I heard was that the pain was overwhelming; he had trained himself to not experience pain and emotion, and now that he was feeling it, he did not have the skills to process it. I gently suggested that experiencing emotions took "getting in shape," like physical work. I worked to demystify pain and suggested that although it is uncomfortable, pain is simply something to get through. I also acknowledged that given his depression, pain may indeed be very difficult to experience. I suggested that I check with him as to whether he wanted to explore family sources of current difficulties, as they arose; the choice would be in his control. Mike agreed to that; he acknowledged later that that level of respect was powerful for him and allowed him to feel that he was somewhat in control of his emotions. The choice for Mike to even explore his emotions seemed relatively remarkable and courageous to me. Mike had decided during adolescence that all emotions (including the expression of anger) were wrong and that he had only himself to rely on. Over time, Mike cultivated skills of debate and facility with language as a manner to fend off emotions. Mike was now aware that he had developed a superior, verbally bullying style; his anger and hurt had both been misdirected in that way. I normalized his experience as similar to that of many, if not most, men whom I have worked with in therapy.

In the end, it turned out that exploring Mike's familial history was very important for him. Mike was able to realize that in his initial relationship with his wife, he had become dominant, probably in an attempt to not be dominated like his father. Mike realized he had "become his mother," yet in the worst possible way. Mike also acknowledged how important it was for him to tune in to his children and parent them according to their needs, rather than according to his own needs. Mike wanted a lot for them, and he wanted to provide guidance but not "browbeat" them as Mike had been by his parents. Mike did not want his children to become "armored beasts" like himself.

Termination

I worked with Mike off and on for a total of 4 years. During the termination phase, Mike acknowledged that he had changed his image from that of a "know-it-all" who postured to one who was quietly and warmly supportive of others and that he could share knowledge as appropriate. From my perspective, he had indeed become much more approachable and humane, and I gathered that this had been internalized from the reports and feedback he brought in about his interactions with others. Mike was embarrassed as he reminisced about his past pretentiousness. He felt more able to reach out to others and their "good parts." Mike wanted to continue to work to not isolate himself and to find other ways to feel joy and reward, other than achievement. Despite this openness and hope for a new way of being in the world and in relation to others, Mike continued to have an "existential struggle" in becoming more optimistic and sincere. Mike acknowledged that my "system" was "as good as any," but his confidence had been shaken, and part of him felt he could not let people know of his deep vulnerabilities and fears. Thus he still teetered between being open and closed. I acknowledged that there are times and places to be truly open and other times and places not to be. Psychotherapy had provided him with a place that he had craved all his life. He had wanted someone to show interest in what he was going through, but he could not ask for it (his brief "emotional affair" was due to this need, he had come to understand). Mike had concluded during his adolescence that people are self-interested, so he decided that he could not rely on others to care about him and hence remained "needless" of others. Through his psychotherapy experience, Mike realized that at least part of that belief was erroneous. And now Mike was working to shed those beliefs; being "armored" did not serve a healthy purpose any longer. Toward the end, Mike also acknowledged that when I pointed out that he was an angry person who felt victimized, he felt "pissed off." But it rang true to him, and he felt he was still working on acknowledging when he was angry, struggling with ways to deal with it more directly, or learning how to let it go. Otherwise, Mike had learned that his thoughts and feelings of victimization fed into cynicism and reactivity, which got in the way of his goals and with his attempts to get along with other people.

Mike felt he was trying to nurture the part of him that wanted to connect with people. He felt he had greater clarity of vision about what happened to him during the period he lost his job and fell into an affair. He was still working on setting aside resentments, because as he did so, he could "almost enjoy his life." Although his marriage was still lacking, it was improved, and he felt more hopeful now than when he entered therapy. More important, he was beginning to nurture friendships among some male colleagues.

Mike also felt more able to manage mood swings and that allowing himself to slip into a depressive state was "destructive indulgence" that he could fight back with my "optimistic reframes." As we ended our time together, Mike chose to "stop out" and perhaps return on an as-needed basis. Mike's perspective about his psychotherapy was that he had brought in numerous crises, trials, and tribulations. He had learned a more positive approach to dealing with life's challenges and had begun to feel more worthwhile. Mike was more accepting of himself and others, including weaknesses and mistakes and saw those as simply a part of being human. He felt that he understood many of the sources of his maladaptive behavior patterns and had begun to replace those with new skills

This therapeutic experience was a rich one for me. As therapists, we are constantly learning and simultaneously participating in amazing healing and transformation in the lives of individuals with whom we work. It is an honor, and yet the task is humbling and can fill both the client and the therapist with anxiety and uncertainty. This experience was highly productive for both Mike and me. I learned, once again, that the stereotypic White, male corporate executive, who may be off-putting to me, is just as vulnerable as anyone else. We all struggle with the pain of life. Although I do not lose sight of the fact that there are significant unearned opportunities and advantages for most White men, it does not obliviate the reality that life is painful and challenging for everyone and that White men can benefit significantly from psychotherapy. I was consistently very touched by Mike's struggles; in particular, his loneliness was especially poignant and moving. I marveled as Mike became able to be open and to connect and work with me. I believe that in this relationship, we were able to transform the politics of stratification in our gender and racial–ethnic roles into a healthy and mutually powerful relationship with each other. We were both able to take some risks in the shared journey of this relational endeavor. We both became more authentic in the therapeutic relationship. I believe that I have carried some aspects of this authenticity with this White man into my relationships outside of the therapy experience; I hope that Mike is able to take his experience with a Latina outside of the therapy experience as well. Each similar encounter is a comparable growth experience for me. In sum, I believe a mutually empowering connection occurred between Mike and me. The social construction of gender is such that men are generally not allowed to consciously need connection, yet relationships are important for good mental health for all human beings. Over time, in the context of psychotherapy and in our relationship, Mike developed increased levels of complexity, fluidity, choice, and articulation in his relationships, all markers of developmental maturity and increased mental health, according to the RCT (Jordan, 2003). So did I.

The following text was published in a "Life Is Short" segment of the *Washington Post* and reflects my value of the importance of relationships as part of health and healing, as well as the poignant socialized norms against men's connection with men:

Seeing two old men walking down the street, comfortable in their familiarity, I begin to feel my mortality. I've seen them in Ghana, Brazil, Europe and Washington; friends for life. A man without a friend is truly
alone. Even family cannot replace that loss. I asked other men if they feel
this void, this isolation, and each was surprised that he is not the only
one. We have all lost and we grieve. Sometimes driving alone, or in a
quiet mood, we cry for our lost buddies. No one sees us, no one hears us.
No one knows. (Brooking, 2003, p. D1)

QUESTIONS FROM THE EDITORS

1. *What types of gender- or race-based stereotypes were you aware of in*
counseling this client? How did that impact your therapy with this client?

Mike initially presented in a confident, aloof, arrogant, tough, competitive, and emotionally inexpressive manner, which was stereotypic of male
ideology, as described by Addis and Mahalik (2003), Brooks and Good (2001),
and Levant (1995). I was initially intimidated and distanced, given my "relational images" based on my cultural indoctrination to believe that White
men are superior to me. I feared that because he had likely been similarly
indoctrinated to feel superior to me, he would not be able to be my client and
to assume the role of allowing me to help. I think I may have also feared that
if he did allow me to help, it would be in the role of my providing a service for
him, rather than in the role of a mutual relationship.

2. *How did your own gender role issues influence your work with this client?*

I am aware of initially having to work to feel worthy of working with a
middle-aged, White male corporate client. This meant that I had to struggle
through my internalized, oppressive negative relational images of inferiority
and subordination and feeling "less than" Mike. These negative images were
initially triggered in part simply by virtue of his existence, more so by his
initial style. I am also aware of my socialization as a woman and Latina that is
trained to give, nurture, and care for others. Those values can be destructive
if carried to an extreme, if one cares for another at the expense of oneself.
However, in this case, I believe that the values facilitated my ability to see
beyond Mike's negative coping behaviors to be able to help him with his
pain, and the sources of his difficulties. I believe I was able to reach past my
and his negative relational images to enlarge the relational capacity for both
of us. That is, we were able to participate in the therapeutic relationship in
more and more complex levels, which allowed for growth.

3. *Looking back on the case, knowing what you know now, would you*
change the way you worked with this client?

I do wish that I had not been intimidated at times by Mike. Although I
think that I was usually able to move past those feelings fairly quickly each

time they came up, I know that the negative relational images, which evoked negative feelings, also evoked distrust in my responding or interacting in an authentic manner. I wonder, for example, if I had taken more of a risk to respond more immediately to my hurt feelings when Mike made reference to affirmative action as the cause of his loss of job, would the ensuing potential conflict have allowed for a deeper working relationship more quickly? Would it have disrupted the relationship? When we did later process the event, I suspect that we did not delve as deeply as we might have. This seemed to be a lost opportunity.

4. *How did you respond personally to his cynical manner? How did you stay engaged with him when you may have wanted to pull away?*

Initially, I was quiet in response to Mike's cynicism; I did not like it, it was distancing. Soon after the beginning of therapy, however, I was able to "hold up a mirror," identify the cynicism, and talk about the impact on me ("it pushes me away and makes me not want to engage with you"; "it feels unsafe to interact with you"). We also processed the likely similar impact on others. After that, I pointed out his cynicism each time I experienced and perceived it. Soon, he was able to identify it as well.

I stayed engaged with Mike when I felt like pulling away by understanding his behavior and by feeling the responsibility of my role as a psychotherapist. I told myself that he was simply feeling threatened, fearful, or hurt and was engaging in old, maladaptive behaviors to manage that pain. I also told myself that it was my responsibility to help him learn over and over to identify the pain or discomfort that evoked those behaviors and how destructive those patterns were, and to support his practice in replacing those behaviors and attitudes with other, more productive ones.

5. *This therapy is an example of multicultural counseling across multiple dimensions (e.g., race, sex). In reference to multicultural counseling, what were you aware of culturally in session, and is there a cultural dimension that was not addressed?*

Helms's (1990) description of counseling types of relationship, based on the identity development or racial–ethnic minority groups and of Whites, suggests that my and Mike's relationship was a "crossed" relationship. That is, I was aware of the impact of my socialization experiences as a woman and as a Latina in this culture. Mike was initially not aware of how his White identity, his height, his education, and his socioeconomic status granted him privileges and the subsequent feelings of entitlement accorded him in society. Although my awareness of this "crossed" aspect of our relationship influenced me to carefully avoid the risks of disconnection, I also wonder whether I might have addressed these more openly and directly once a working relationship had been established. I believe that we could have done so. Perhaps I used the protection of my responsibilities to not "lay" my countertransference on Mike to avoid my own pain. Walker (2004) talked about how in the relational–cultural model, the therapist accepts responsibility for engaging the complexity of empathy, the vulnerability of authenticity, and the nuances of mutuality. Although I think I accomplished this for the most part with Mike, there are clearly ways in which I might have been more effective.

REFERENCES

Addis, M. E., & Mahalik, J. R. (2003). Men, masculinity, and the contexts of help seeking. *American Psychologist, 58,* 5–14.

American Psychological Association. (2003). Guidelines on multicultural education, training, research, practice, and organizational change for psychologists. *American Psychologist, 58,* 377–402.

Brooking, D. T. (2003, November 23). Life is short. *The Washington Post,* p. D1.

Brooks, G. R., & Good, G. E. (Eds.). (2001). *The new handbook of psychotherapy and counseling with men: A comprehensive guide to settings, problems, and treatment approaches* (Vol. 1). San Francisco: Jossey-Bass.

Gottman, J. (1994). *Why marriages succeed or fail . . . and how you can make yours last.* New York: Fireside Books.

Hays, K. L. (1999). *Working it out: Using exercise in psychotherapy.* Washington, DC: American Psychological Association.

Helms, J. E. (1984). Toward a theoretical explanation of the effects of race on counseling: A Black and White model. *The Counseling Psychologist, 12,* 153–165.

Helms, J. E. (1990). *Black and White racial identity: Theory, research, and practice.* Westport, CT: Greenwood Press.

Jordan, J. V. (2003). Relational–cultural therapy. In M. Kopala & M. A. Keitel (Eds.), *Handbook of counseling women* (pp. 22–30). Thousand Oaks, CA: Sage.

Levant, R. F. (1995). Toward the reconstruction of masculinity. In R. F. Levant & W. S. Pollack (Eds.), *A new psychology of men* (pp. 229–251). New York: Basic Books.

McIntosh, P. (1989, July/August). White privilege: Unpacking the invisible knapsack. *Peace and Freedom,* 8–10.

Miller, J. B. (1984). The development of women's sense of self. *Work in progress* (No. 12). Wellesley, MA: Stone Center Working Paper Series.

Vasquez, M. J. T. (2002). Latina women, exercise, and empowerment from a feminist psychodynamic perspective. *Women and Therapy, 25,* 23–38.

Walker, M. (2004). Walking a piece of the way: Race, power, and therapeutic movement. In M. Walker & W. B. Rosen (Eds.), *How connections heal: Stories from relational–cultural therapy* (pp. 35–52). New York: Guilford Press.

IV

EXPLORING MASCULINITY: EXAMINING GENDER ROLE CONFLICTS WITH MEN

13

HELPING JACK HEAL HIS EMOTIONAL WOUNDS: THE GENDER ROLE CONFLICT DIAGNOSTIC SCHEMA

JAMES M. O'NEIL

At the age of 44, Jack Smith entered therapy to make a career transition and change his self-defeating behavior. He felt alone, angry, and confused by his continuous life problems. My therapeutic approach to Jack was guided by my own assumptions about doing therapy with men and a diagnostic schema to assess men's gender role conflict (O'Neil, 1990; O'Neil, Good, & Holmes, 1995). In this case study, I use this diagnostic schema to explain my therapeutic process with Jack in the context of his gender role socialization and his family-of-origin issues. During the therapy, he wrote out his thoughts and feelings and shared these writings with me during the course of our sessions. Throughout the case study, I include Jack's written statements to elucidate what he experienced during our therapy. Furthermore, I also share how I felt during my therapy with Jack.

THERAPEUTIC ASSUMPTIONS THAT GUIDE MY THERAPY WITH MEN

My therapeutic approach is based on feminist principles and the recognition that many of men's psychological problems emanate from patriarchal sexism and restrictive gender role socialization experiences. I was strongly influenced by feminists in the 1970s and the 1980s who argued that sexism and restrictive gender roles were significant mental health issues for women. The emergence of the new psychology of men over the past 2 decades has reinforced these feminist perspectives as they relate to men's mental health. Furthermore, my training as a counseling psychologist fostered an eclectic approach to using different theories and techniques in psychotherapy. I am fundamentally an existentialist and humanist who is clinically anchored in psychodynamic, cognitive–behavioral, and family systems theories. I strive to be an authentic and compassionate person in my therapeutic roles, believing that people can heal their emotional wounds when therapists are trusted, have well-developed skills, and show authentic compassion for their clients.

I have six assumptions that guide my therapy with men:

1. Many men seeking therapy have been socialized to restrictive and sexist stereotypes of masculinity and femininity and therefore they will need to "journey with their gender roles" (O'Neil & Egan, 1992a; O'Neil, Egan, Owen, & Murry, 1993).
2. Many men seek help because of unconscious gender role conflicts that negatively affect their lives.
3. Many male clients in therapy need to experience gender role transitions (O'Neil & Egan, 1992b), in which they redefine certain gender role themes that allow for greater cognitive, affective, and behavioral flexibility.
4. Many male clients' reactions to therapy will activate gender role conflicts (O'Neil et al., 1995). These conflicts can be assessed by therapists and worked through during therapy.
5. Much of my therapeutic process with men involves assessing defenses (O'Neil & Nadeau, 1999), working through resistance, and creating nonthreatening structures that use men's strengths. Furthermore, I assume that men usually need to understand how their family of origin, their gender role socialization, and any gender role traumas have affected their growth and problem solving.
6. I approach therapy with men by assessing past and present gender role conflicts through the use of an operationally defined diagnostic schema (O'Neil, 1990). This schema is described in a later part of the chapter.

In the following sections of this case study, I summarize Jack's family dynamics, describe how I used the gender role conflict diagnostic schema to assess his emotional and psychological problems, and describe the therapeutic process and quote directly from Jack's weekly writings as he redefined his masculinity and healed his wounds. Throughout the case, I report my experience being Jack's therapist.

Jack Smith's History and Family Dynamics

Jack was socialized into a fragmented, Irish-Catholic family of lower-middle-class socioeconomic status. He was the youngest child and was socialized in the shadow of his two older sisters. The Smith family was tense, cold, and emotionally vacant. Jack's father, an alcoholic, was an ineffectual spouse, father, and provider. Mrs. Smith had matriarchal control over the family and Jack described her as "domineering, controlling, and a critical mother who disliked men at a very basic level." She controlled the emotional climate of the family by espousing the values of hard work, discipline, frugality, God, church, and the defeat of communism.

"Being a man" was an issue in the Smith family because Mrs. Smith observed her husband as weak, ineffective, alcoholic, and powerless. She had intense disappointment, anger, and rage at her husband. Young Jack observed his mother as a powerful feminine force that frequently emasculated his father. She also vented her anger and rage at young Jack. He became her personal project: "a man in the making." As Jack put it, "If her husband was a loser, her son was going to be a winner and redeem the family name."

Jack's childhood and teenage experiences in his family and school were dysfunctional, tense, and conflictual. He described himself as a troubled child. Jack developed authority, control, and power conflicts by reacting to his overpowering mother and older sisters. Jack felt his sisters always had the edge, adding, "My sisters were always seen as better than me. They would play word games with me and I always lost." How to win control and have power over women became a critical issue for Jack. He wanted his mother's affirmation but was angry at her coldness, disapproval, and high expectations. Young Jack never knew the warmth of a loving mother and father because he received no supportive parenting. As he put it: "I was numbed by my childhood anger." Jack's relationship with his parents is best described in his own words:

> I am thinking about how I must have learned to try to get around Mother and Dad, creep up on issues, and try to manipulate situations to my advantage. Oblique ways of dealing with Mom and Dad. Couldn't deal with anything directly. With my mother, I must have felt like a victim, impotent to have an impact on events and communications and outcomes. With Mother, one couldn't have a dialogue. She was single minded and zealous in communicating her viewpoint and her will. One gentle little boy, who had lots of thoughts of his own and wanted to emerge and have some impact on the situations of life, was left to succumb . . . and to duck the direct interaction . . . and to resent the oppression. And I learned to be more subtle and manipulate situations indirectly, through sex and a kind of personal pressure that took the form of charisma and charm and personality. I developed guile and ways of getting approval and attention that were built on a superficial strategy of manipulation. I soon didn't have time to discover what I really wanted in situations or how to just be

direct in communication. I lost sight of who I was and what I needed (really needed) and how to be direct in the pursuit of my needs.

Restrictive emotionality, as a family norm, kept much of Jack's conflicts covert. He vacillated between being a compliant, good little boy and becoming aggressive, angry, and rebellious. He acted out his anger through antisocial pranks that infuriated and worried his mother. Progressively, she exerted more control and sanctions to ensure Jack's "success in the world." In high school, many of Jack's gender role conflicts were evident, yet he was unaware of their source and meaning. He had difficulty demonstrating back-to-back success in the classroom and in athletics. Jack's fear of failure and difficulties taking responsibility were barriers to his personal and academic maturity. He would vacillate between being the teacher's pet and exhibiting obnoxious, disruptive, and rebellious behavior. Jack challenged authority outside the home because his mother could never be challenged at home.

Jack left the family to attend a large and well-respected university, but it was difficult because of his dependence, limited self-confidence, and the intense pressure from his mother to succeed. He was unable to concentrate and meet the academic demands and finally flunked out of college. Jack re-enrolled in a local university and successfully graduated from college. His pattern was to fail and then to pull himself together and succeed. After graduation, he married, moved to another state, and entered a psychology graduate program. His marriage was unfulfilling and again, he could not study. By the end of the second year of graduate school, he flunked out. After his son was born, he felt intense pressure to be the breadwinner but his energy went to numerous extramarital affairs. The stress of familial responsibilities produced avoidance and distance from his wife and son. Three years later, he divorced his wife and left his 3-year-old son. He was an angry man on the run, unaware of the significance of his emotions and actions, and unable to be a nurturing spouse or father.

After his divorce, he began a series of intense relationships with women. For 4 years, he experienced an emotionally abusive relationship that mirrored the adolescent version of his unfeeling, angry bond with his mother. Jack had a strong need to dominate and control women both personally and sexually. It seemed like he was unconsciously replaying the destructive power and control dynamics with his mother and sisters. He objectified women, viewed them as sexually attractive objects to be manipulated. He could not emotionally bond with women; was fascinated by their bodies; and experienced fear, anger, and power struggles with women. As with his mother and sisters, he would usually lose, thereby stimulating rage at women and feelings of personal powerlessness and self-hatred.

Jack's career development revealed a man running away from himself. Over a 7-year period, he had six different jobs in seven different settings. Jack did complete a master's degree in special education at age 32 but many

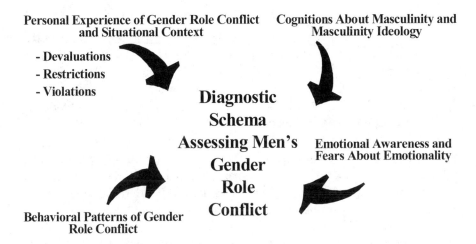

Personal Experience of Gender Role Conflict and Situational Context

- Devaluations
- Restrictions
- Violations

Cognitions About Masculinity and Masculinity Ideology

Diagnostic Schema Assessing Men's Gender Role Conflict

Emotional Awareness and Fears About Emotionality

Behavioral Patterns of Gender Role Conflict

Figure 13.1. Gender role conflict diagnostic schema.

of his gender role conflicts were evident in his work. After 4 years of teaching, he became dissatisfied with the special education work, felt "burned out," and unappreciated as a professional. At age 40, Jack entered therapy with much despair, depression, and career dissatisfaction. He had just ended another abusive relationship with a woman that mirrored the dependent and angry dynamics that he had before with his mother.

Diagnostic Schema to Assess Men's Gender Role Conflict in Therapy

The therapy with Jack used my diagnostic schema (O'Neil, 1990) to assess men's gender role conflict. The simplified version of the schema is shown in Figure 13.1 and includes four gender role conflict assessment domains: cognitions about masculinity and masculinity ideology, emotional awareness and fears about emotionality, behavioral patterns of gender role conflict, and personal experiences of gender role conflict in situational contexts. The gender role conflict assessment domains are described as follows.

Cognitions about masculinity are how men think about gender roles in the context of relational, work, and family roles. The current theoretical concepts to describe men's cognitions about masculinity are *masculinity ideology* (Pleck, 1995), *masculine norms* (Levant et al.,1992; Thompson, Grisanti, & Pleck, 1985), and *masculine conformity* (Mahalik et al., 2003).

Emotional awareness is defined as the ability to label, experience, and express human emotions and the ability to receive others' emotional expressions. Fears about emotionality result when emotions are not considered to be human experiences but are seen as feminine and weak and therefore antithetical to the expected masculine norms and ideology.

The behavioral patterns of gender role conflict include restrictive emotionality, health care problems, obsession with achievement and success, restrictive and affectionate behavior between men, control, power, competition issues, and homophobia (O'Neil, 1981a, 1981b; O'Neil et al., 1995). Empirical research over a 25-year period shows these patterns are significantly related to higher levels of depression, anxiety, stress, aggression toward women, and other mental health problems (O'Neil, 2002, 2005).

The personal experiences of gender role conflict occur when men experience gender role devaluations, restrictions, or violations while they either adhere to or deviate from the stereotypes of masculinity and femininity. The situational contexts of gender role conflict include gender role devaluations, restrictions, and violations within the man himself, from others, or expressed toward others.

These four assessment domains were used during my clinical assessment of Jack and throughout his therapy. To orient the reader to the therapy process, I have included the following brief summary of how the assessment was made.

CLINICAL ASSESSMENT USING THE GENDER ROLE CONFLICT DIAGNOSTIC SCHEMA

In the sections that follow, how the four assessment domains were used with Jack are discussed. These domains are presented as separate areas, but they interrelate with each other in dynamic ways.

Assessing Jack's Cognitions About Masculinity and Masculinity Ideology

I assessed Jack's thoughts about masculinity to determine how his masculinity ideology might contribute to his emotional, interpersonal, and career problems. Overall, Jack internalized restrictive masculine norms of manhood that existed in the 1940s and 1950s. Jack learned from his mother the masculine norms of power, control, strength, hard work, moral integrity, career success, and community involvement. She pressured Jack into these masculine norms and highly sex-typed masculinity. She gave little nurturing support and was highly critical when he failed to meet the traditional norms of masculinity. Jack endorsed his mother's masculine norms, but he was also anxious, rebellious, and feared failure in meeting these high standards of manhood. He had no awareness of his masculinity ideology and how it affected his psychological functioning.

Assessing Jack's Emotional Awareness and Fears of Emotions

I assessed Jack's emotional capacity and concluded that he had learned restrictive emotionality from his mother and father. He could describe some feelings intellectually, but he could not experience them emotionally. The only feeling he could express was anger, and these emotions were discharged through abusive sarcasm and manipulative "mind games." Jack was afraid of his emotions, particularly the ones repressed in his childhood. During one of our sessions, he disclosed, "It is the fear of coming face to face with my own pain that keeps me in an avoidance posture with others, keeps me from assuming responsibility, keeps me from reaching out with intimacy and vulnerability."

From my clinical assessment, I concluded that Jack had internalized angry feelings about femininity, his mother, and women at a very early age. The assessment process analyzed how Jack's fears about emotionality affected his current interpersonal functioning. Jack's continuous attempts to control women were based on his deep fears of being controlled by their emotions. He feared the feminine (O'Neil, 1981a, 1981b, 1982; O'Neil, Helms, Gable, David, & Wrightsman, 1986), but was also dependent on it for his self-understanding. Many times, Jack's fear of femininity turned to anger and manipulative power plays with his mother and subsequently with other women in his life. At some very basic level, he wanted to control, dominate, and sometimes destroy the feminine. These dynamics made his unconscious emotions primary areas of assessment during the therapy.

Assessing Jack's Behavioral Patterns of Gender Role Conflict

Jack's gender role conflicts were unconscious to him. Therefore, I made assessments of his behavioral patterns of gender role conflict using the Gender Role Conflict Checklist (O'Neil, 1988). He reported conflict with restrictive emotionality with control, power, and competition issues; restrictive sexual and affectionate behavior; and problems with success and achievement. Jack's restrictive emotionality was maintained by his intellectualization of emotions and inability to experience vulnerability. Furthermore, his inability to give up control and his need for power kept feelings internalized, causing him to feel insecure and at times unstable. Jack's restrictive emotionality narrowed his range of communication to "a war of words," particularly with women.

Control, power, and competition issues were also assessed. Problems with power were observed through Jack's written statements about his relationship with his mother. He indicated that he regretted how much power he had given to his mother and how damaging it was. As control was discussed in the therapy, he was able to make his own assessments into his interpersonal process. He wrote, "I am struck tonight with how much I seem to need to control the feelings of women. I am letting go of control, letting go in so many areas of my life, I am letting go and falling back on myself."

Jack's restrictive sexual and affectionate behavior was also assessed. He craved and needed affection, but he had been deprived of it most of his life, and therefore it was an ambiguous area of his life. He erroneously equated affection and intimacy with impersonal sexuality. Because sex was defined as an act to dominate and control women (the feminine) he experienced ongoing restricted sexual and affectionate behavior in his intimate encounters. From the sessions, it was apparent that sex was a conquest and that power and control mediated all sexual involvement.

Jack also experienced conflicts around his achievement and success as a man. He sought therapy initially because he was disappointed with his low level of achievement and success. He felt little professional success and was afraid to try new things because of past failures. Much of his depression resulted from his failure to achieve prestige, wealth, and influence. These achievement values were central to his masculinity ideology learned from his mother. He had failed to meet his mother's success standards of status, upward mobility, and recognition in the community. Jack feared failure and was not confident or assertive in promoting himself or meeting his achievement needs.

Assessing Jack's Personal Experience and the Situational Contexts of Gender Role Conflict

Jack's gender role devaluations, restrictions, and violations were apparent from his personal statements but also unconscious to him. I assessed how gender role conflict was personally experienced, how others contributed to his conflict, and how he expressed the conflict toward others. Self-devaluations were common with Jack. He devalued himself for his failure, lack of success, manipulation of others, lost potential, immaturity, and for needing psychotherapy. He feared personal devaluation from others because he worked with grade school children, not in corporate America. He also received much devaluation from others for his lifestyle and his personality problems. For example, his parents, sisters, and girlfriends all negatively devalued him for his failures and unstable life. He would react to these personal devaluations by playing angry, interpersonal games and devaluing their femininity. Pointing out "women's darker sides" allowed Jack to vent accumulated rage at his mother and other women.

Jack's gender role restrictions were assessed by observing his restrictive emotionality and needs to be in total control during interpersonal exchanges including our therapy sessions. Restrictive emotionality and control inhibited his capacity for authentic contact and intimacy. He did not trust his feelings, except for anger, because he had never explored them. He lacked the interpersonal skills to initiate and maintain honest relationships with women and men. His restrictions were apparent from his written statements to me, such as,

> Time is passing me by. I feel it! Will I ever find another woman whom I find attractive and lovable? Who are all these women walking around,

sitting across from me on park benches? I feel inept, a fumbler who doesn't know where to begin. I don't feel in possession of those social skills that I have relied on. I'm not sure I even know what to say to a woman.

Jack's mother had restricted his freedom to grow socially and emotionally and therefore a cohesive self did not develop. His father did not provide any model of positive masculinity and was not involved in Jack's life. Jack's emotional and behavioral restrictions negatively affected his own marriage and limited his intimacy and communication with women, his wife, and his son.

Jack also violated himself regularly with his anger, fear, alcohol abuse, self-hatred, and depression. Jack was not just a passive victim of violation; it was apparent that he violated others by his dishonesty, interpersonal behavior, and emotional abuse. He violated women by objectifying them sexually, by manipulating their feelings and bodies, and by not respecting their dignity and human rights. He violated his own masculine values regularly and felt guilty and depressed afterward. Many times violations from others would stimulate his punishment and self-loathing. He clearly felt violated by his mother, sisters, and multiple relationships. Jack wrote his feelings of being devalued and violated by his mother and shared them with me:

> My own life is numbed by childhood anger at you for not having loved me, for actually minimizing me, putting me down. My path toward offering you unconditional love would be easier if the lack of the expression of love was your only failing toward me. But you did more. You also punished me. Can you believe it, Mother? You punished me for years and years, with your glances, your expressions, and your attitudes. And did you know why? No you didn't. Mother, you punished me simply because I was male. What a jolt that would be for you now, to hear me say this. And it is painful for me to say it, but it is brutally true.

Assessing Mother Blame

Jack blamed both of his parents for his childhood and adult problems. He specifically blamed his mother for her authoritarian control and unsupportive pressure to be a successful man. This theme of mother blaming was a dominant theme throughout the therapy. As the previous quote suggests, Jack blamed his mother for her sexism ("You punished me simply because I was male"). To me, this was a good example of how mothers and family dynamics can be sexist toward young boys and men. But was it an accurate portrayal of what really happened? During the therapy, I wondered whether this mother blaming and claims of sexism were justified. Was there any hard evidence of sexist abuse and maternal harshness, or was it Jack's own sexist misogyny? I had him seek additional evidence that his mother was sexist and harsh by asking his sisters to describe how his mother treated Jack. They confirmed his view that Mrs. Smith was indeed abusive. He also invited me to read all his college letters from his mother that documented much that he reported. From these two sources, I determined that there was credible evidence that Jack was treated in an abusive way that resulted in his excessive mother blaming. The question of how to help Jack with blaming his mother, others, and himself became critical issues in the therapy.

Using the Diagnostic Schema During the Therapy Process

I saw Jack in therapy consistently for 3.5 years. The therapy process described in this section illustrates how the assessment schema was translated into therapeutic interventions. During an early session, Jack gave a composite history of his life and expressed his despair and fear about growing older.

My initial impressions of Jack were that he was a polished educator, articulate, powerful, and controlling. The early sessions with Jack were typically "electrically charged." He would rapidly fire ideas and penetrating questions at me. There were times when I struggled to keep up with the speed and intensity of his statements. I remember feeling the need to be more prepared than usual because Jack had a well-defined agenda with me. He was interpersonally competitive, and I felt pressure from him to have complete answers to complicated life issues. His "in-your-face" confrontations were abrasive at times, but they were usually mediated by a boyish charm, humor, and charisma.

I was drawn to his charm and charisma, but I could also feel the angry core of his personality. He was adamant about wanting his therapy to exclusively focus on his career conflicts and burnout. He indicated in an angry tone, "I have already experienced psychotherapy and want my career to be our exclusive focus." The exact focus of the therapy was the first power issue that we faced and Jack's first form of resistance and defensiveness in therapy. I remember reflecting to myself that power is almost always an issue with men in therapy, but with Jack it was his primary way of relating to me. His anger caught me off guard and it was unclear at first how to use the power issues and resistance to move the therapy along. I agreed to respect his decision to focus only on career issues. I also communicated that sometimes career issues and emotional problems were intricately linked; consequently, deeper issues may need to be explored.

I liked Jack personally, but at times his strong presence and powerful and controlling demeanor intimidated me. I can remember processing my intimidation immediately after sessions and between sessions. I am not one to be easily intimidated by clients, so I wondered why Jack affected me so strongly. Maybe it was that he was highly articulate, but it probably was that he knew how to use power. Moreover, I wondered about the meaning of his bold and strident posture. I concluded that his intimidating behavior toward me (trying to make me afraid) was reflective of his own fear of being in therapy. I got to feel his masked fear through his intimidating demeanor.

After doing a complete assessment of his career situation, I shared that his career conflicts were probably related to deeper emotional issues. This feedback set up an intense power and control dynamic between us. He quizzed me on how much experience that I had doing therapy with middle-aged men. He disclosed that he had doubts about how I could help him, given that I was 10 years younger. I recognized that these doubts and distancers would need to be mediated if the therapy was going to work. Like many times during the therapeutic process, there was no apparent intervention to resolve the power and control dynamics. He felt out of control during these early sessions, and this frightened him. I walked the tightrope of letting him have the control (staying with the career issues) and periodically asserting my own diagnostic insights that deeper emotions were causing the burnout and career dissatisfaction.

There was also another provocative and critical exchange. It occurred when I showed full caring and compassion as Jack expressed his dark depression about his "meaningless" job as a special education teacher. It was easy to show care because his vulnerability and pain touched me deeply. Jack angrily challenged my caring calling it "a trained role that was fake and lucrative" for me. This kind of put-down was at first annoying, and I felt unfairly judged. As I moved past my feelings of insult, I decided that this was a significant test from Jack. His personal and professional devaluation of me was more than just challenging my caring and personal integrity. What he was testing was whether I could handle his anger and rage. Was I tough enough, skillful enough, and "man enough" to get him past his lifelong anger?

I reframed his invalidation of my caring by asking him whether he received care from his parents and family. He indicated that he had never felt anyone really cared for him, especially his parents. Jack doubted that anyone could care for him and his needs. Whether I cared was the overt issue, but the real issue was whether I could be fully trusted. Would this room be a place where he could share his deep hurt?

It seemed like I passed these early tests and he began to open up. He expressed feeling weak because he needed therapy and was worried that therapy was an unmasculine activity. Jack feared that I devalued him as a man because he needed help. During one session, he said, "Aren't strong men able to solve their own problems?" My response was, "Most everyone has a problem in life that they cannot solve on their own and need someone's special help." I explained that seeking help could be a sign of strength and personal wisdom. I was overly cautious at this point, recognizing that Jack had not really committed himself to the therapy process. Being in the room with Jack at this point was like "tiptoeing through the tulips," meaning that I had to watch exactly where I was going. When I am cautious with clients, it usually means there is something critical to understand or something dramatic that I need to do.

I made an intentional and clinical intervention at this point. Jack appeared to be a good candidate to terminate therapy because of his fears about losing control and addressing deeper emotional issues. I sensed from his posture, facial expressions, and late arrivals that he was uncommitted to confronting his pain and problems. I confronted him on my perception of his vacillation about continuing therapy. He disclosed being "on the fence," unsure of what to do. I proposed a therapeutic structure where he could be in control, but he would share some of the control with me. I decided that Jack's positive resources as a man, his literary and intellectual strengths, could be affirmed and used therapeutically. I asked him whether he would be willing to write out some of his feelings every week and do some reading on men's issues, specifically on the patterns of men's gender role conflict (O'Neil, 1981b).

This therapeutic structure appealed to him, because he liked to write and read. This structure was validating for him because he could show his abilities, self-worth, and strength to me through his written prose and ideas. The structure was a way of mediating his fears about therapy being unmanly. What was therapeutically important is that he could feel some control in the process, while vacillating about whether to release the intense emotions that simmered below. The therapy structure gave Jack hope that he could understand his complicated personality dynamics and still retain some of his control. As he wrote out his feelings and began to discuss his masculinity issues, I gave him encouragement and affirmation.

Slowly, I asked questions about whether his early family dynamics might be relevant to understanding his career and interpersonal problems. I asked whether he had ever defined himself as a man, because he reported his mother had complete control over his life. I probed his reaction when he received harsh criticism from his mother or when he was discrepant with the masculine stereotypes that she so strongly enforced. I asked how he felt when observing his mother emasculating his father. He listened to these probing questions but had little to say. The room filled with darkness, gloom, and nervous tension when these family-of-origin questions were raised. Because these questions were an opening to his pain, he was unwilling to relinquish control during these sessions. I waited impatiently as he decided whether to take the emotional journey with me. I was impatient, but I knew from my own personal breakthroughs and from my previous clients, that resistance and impasses have to be worked through slowly.

I kept intermittently pushing the family-of-origin issues with Jack. I encouraged him to express his feelings of anger, fear, and despair experienced as a child. This was difficult for him to do because of his learned restrictive emotionality, inability to give up control, and fears about vulnerability. He could rationally describe the feelings and fears but not express or experience them emotionally. Restrictive emotionality had been a family norm and many of Jack's fears and emotions were deeply repressed. Many of the sessions focused on assessing whether Jack could express and experience feelings at all. I decided to teach him an expanded emotional vocabulary that he could use to access his inner experience. He learned the vocabulary quickly, but how to help Jack experience and release the emotions became the therapeutic challenge.

During one session he began to disclose,

> I feel so emotionally crippled, Jim. It must stand out to others who notice that I never remarried. You can't comfortably go through life locked up inside and protecting every feeling, every potential wound. I don't trust one damned feeling I have. I am in such turmoil with new feelings and new ways of dealing with things that I can't know the truth of anything. I have no ballast. I hate this discomfort. And yet, I have known worse pain. I have to bear that in mind.

Jack not only feared facing his emotions but also the pain associated with his childhood. The critical breakthrough with Jack's restrictive emotionality came when he was able to recognize that emotions are neither masculine nor feminine but represent core human dimensions of every person. Furthermore, I introduced another therapeutic paradigm for Jack to consider. The paradigm suggested that negative emotions and pain could be transformed into positive energy. I provided him with my pain paradigm that elaborated on the following: (a) embracing and labeling pain, letting pain be pain; (b) journeying with pain; (c) letting go of pain, using it; and (d) deriving the benefits of pain—new energy (O'Neil & Egan, 1992a). I explained that the process of working with pain could help him turn the past pain into a more positive life experience. He was skeptical about any benefits from working with pain, because his experience was just the opposite. Yet, he was intrigued by a new way to look at pain and more important, the hope that his life could be improved. Hope became one of the central themes in Jack's therapeutic process. Again, this therapeutic structure was acceptable to him, and we could proceed to the deep pain that he had repressed for many years.

Jack began to reexperience his childhood pain only when I began asking questions about it. Much of this process involved rediscovering his childhood emotions that affected his current ability to work and love. He would write out the feelings during the week, and we would process them during our session. As the pain came up, so did his resistance and defenses. Being vulnerable in this way was new territory and a major gender role conflict for the therapy process.

As the pain came, so did the direct anger and blame at his mother and father for their inept parenting and neglect. Yet after the anger came the unexpressed childhood tears and some relief.

I had done therapy for over 15 years, but this man's pain touched me deeply. I remember that as Jack journeyed with his pain about his father, it activated some of my own pain and unfinished business with my own father, who had died 5 years earlier. In this case, the countertransference was useful because I could validate and empathize with Jack's pain and loss. I worked with my own pain and Jack's emotions simultaneously, as we rolled through the loss and childhood memories together. As Jack faced his father, he had to accept his distance from his own son, with whom he had lost contact. Pain from not having a father was quickly transformed into pain and guilt about being an ineffective father himself. Furthermore, he was now able to sense the pain of the neglected children that he worked with daily. Through these children, he was able to recapture more of his own pain, emotional deprivation, and childhood depressions. Multiple layers of pain were now operating in our therapy.

We went from guarded emotional control to floods of feelings over a 3-week period. This emotional upheaval was at times frightening and scary for Jack and therefore an issue for me. With so much emotion flowing, I kept asking myself whether we had the "right dose" of emotion (not too much, not too little) to have Jack heal his wounds. I told him that managing the pain could increase his confidence and that he could "stay afloat and swim with the pain." This encouragement became the stimulus for further change and greater emotionality in the therapy sessions.

The next intervention was to help Jack discover the "little boy inside the adult man" (Scher, 1979). These two parts of himself, the little boy and the adult man, were in constant intrapsychic and psychological warfare (O'Neil & Egan, 1992b). He called this vulnerable boy "Little Jackie" and accepted that this child coexisted with the adult self. I encouraged him to have internal dialogues between these two parts of himself. Many therapy sessions were spent exploring how Little Jackie was socialized to manipulate, control, act out, and achieve through deception. Additionally, working parallel processes, we explored how these boyhood dynamics affected his current interpersonal relationships with women, men, and children. He became acutely aware of how the little boy in the adult man was part of his own gender role devaluations, restrictions, and violations. Furthermore, he realized that this hurt child devalued, restricted, and violated others. He began to use his insights, and we moved on to gender role transitions related to power and control.

As we journeyed with his pain, I directed the therapy to Jack's gender role conflicts related to power and control. From my assessment, it was clear that he had serious difficulty with power and control in all relationships. I reminded him of how we had worked through the power and control issues in our earlier sessions by sharing power and control. I indicated that the same process could work with his relationships. Power and control had been defined in the combative relationship with his sisters and mother as "power and control over others." He had learned that power, control, and position were essential for him to feel like a real man and secure in his relationships. His primary power conflicts were directly related to his mother. He wrote,

And it's all clearly tied to my relationship with my mother. What a sick, fucking relationship I had with her. I detest the power I have given her over my life. I am so pissed at myself sometimes about all this. The damage was extensive to my psyche, and this struggle is a bitch. And far too late in my life.

Power and control were gender role themes (O'Neil & Fishman, 1992) that needed to be redefined for Jack to find his true power. Jack had learned that power was something external to himself that was to be taken from others. He needed to see that real power and control, in their most profound ways, are the internal experience of positive self-worth, self-control, and developing strength. Real power and control could be redefined as the ability to influence and empower self and others. I asked Jack whether he could redefine power and control in a different way and begin to experiment with new ways of interacting with people. He explained that he was not sure that he could change, but he wanted to test it with his career failures and impotency at work.

Jack's gender role self-devaluations about his career underachievement and failures were fully explored. He disclosed his intense pain and emasculation when his mother and other women devalued him for his lost potential. I remember internally processing the following as Jack described his lost potential and inability to use his personal power: "One of the greatest human and existential tragedies is to know you have personal potential and not demonstrate it to yourself and use it to help others." I felt this tragedy with Jack's expressed fears and tears. As I listened, moments of my father's lost potential flashed through my mind.

Jack needed to have a cognitive sense of what contributed to his lack of success. We attached labels to his lack of confidence and assertiveness, low self-esteem, and fears about taking responsibility. We analyzed his learned fears of failure that resulted from not having effective parents and having few back-to-back successes in his life. I listened to him devalue himself as a man in terms of being lazy, unmotivated, and apathetic. I reflected back to him that these self-devaluations were learned in childhood from his family and were not really fixed and unchangeable personality attributes. He disclosed his envy and devaluation of men he knew who were successful. He also devalued men who were failures, with special attention to his own father and a series of public figures who had disgraced themselves. He began to ask questions about my career and success in academia and men's studies. Clearly, he was comparing himself to me, but the abrasive competitiveness expressed in our earlier session was gone. He was now yearning for concrete ways to create his own success. He also discussed difficult work experiences, particularly conflicts with authority figures that abused their power. These authority figures were triggers for Jack's unconscious rage at his abusive mother who he resented for not supporting his personal and career development. He became conscious of this relationship between the past and present abuses of power, and he began to use his insights in his work setting.

Jack began to use his personal power and verbal skills constructively in his school setting. His ability to do self-processing between the hurt child (Little Jackie) and the adult man were much more observable. Jack had to deal regularly with a particularly abusive work supervisor. I encouraged him to effectively use his internal power by identifying personal feelings and becoming more assertive and direct. For example, he described his struggle with his abusive work supervisor,

> Fighting depression! My boss called this AM and has moved me from my favorite school to a lesser one. He lied and did it for political reasons. I'm not a "team player" in that I don't play administration games so far as manipulating the PPT process. I'm angry and feel impotent. I was not consulted. Feel pushed around by an irrational authority. But Little Jackie is not to be found here. Jack, the adult, is holding sway. I am staying busy and doing chores and little, one-step-at-a-time organization tasks. I feel depressed but do not want to succumb. I feel strong! It's a wonderful feeling. In control. Positive power!!!

Jack used his positive power in a number of leadership roles and in his career and interpersonal roles. He gained confidence, demonstrated success, and received praise from others. These successes helped him believe that he could effectively assert his power and change his life. He had moved past his father's passivity and learned new skills that were the opposite of the manipulative power and control dynamics that he had learned from his mother. I cheered him on and told him that he had this ability to recreate himself and turn the past pain into positive power.

Having made some gains with his career, the therapy moved to Jack's interpersonal functioning with women. Every relationship—from his mother, to his ex-wife, to multiple sex partners—was analyzed. Jack began to see how his mother and childhood experiences affected his relationships with women. Numerous sessions focused on Jack's desire to control and dominate women. We explored how he thought and felt about his mother and the women in his life. Deep feelings of pain, loneliness, and anger were evident in his emotional disclosures that were occurring more frequently.

Jack began to monitor his interpersonal and sexual encounters with women. In one relationship, he was able to actually develop some authentic personal caring, separate from any sexual involvement. What followed this deep caring were personal deception, rebellion, and manipulation. The pattern of making positive change and then regressing to old patterns was fully explored. We began to explore his illicit affairs with married women or sexual encounters in which domination and control were the primary outcomes of sexual intercourse. His sexual practices, thoughts, and fantasies during masturbation were fully examined. He was drawn to depersonalized sexual experiences but felt disgust, guilt, and anger after these encounters. He disclosed previous impulse control problems where he had felt both aggressive and sexual feelings toward anonymous women. We discussed these painful dynamics and began to generate hypotheses about their meaning.

Jack was able to understand that his anger at women was expressed through dominating them sexually. Jack's struggles with his anger and sexuality with women were documented in his writings about "the rush of forbidden sex":

> I can really feel the internal struggle between my needs for a "sexual rush" and my needs to be more patterned, more steady, and responsible. I mean it is literally a feeling of pressure inside. I feel quite horny and in need of sexual release, but it is not Jan [a woman Jack felt true intimacy with] to which I feel the need to turn. It is the illicit, clandestine, "unacceptable" encounter that I want. My mind is searching through mental files, and I am thinking of ways to arrange a meeting with someone who could fit this definition. But so far I am hanging on. I am doing nothing but living with myself and my feelings. I want to maintain control, but it is hard. What grabbed me yesterday was how what I have always thought were deep feelings of love for these eroticized women, is really depression and self hate for what I am doing . . . something that I do not value for my life or anyone else's.

To sexually dominate women was particularly important to Jack's manhood. Because he had been emasculated at home during his formative years, he needed to develop power that he had never possessed. He was attracted to depersonalized sexuality that was unemotional and distant. Personal intimacy and human sexuality had not been integrated. He had to strike out at the feminine, control it, and penetrate it sexually. He acted as though penetrating women sexually was the only way to control a woman and the feminine. I questioned him whether on some unconscious level, these sexual dynamics had anything to do with his mother. He agreed that his mother was "present" during sexual intercourse. After much emotional discharge, Jack asked this question, "What might personal closeness and intimacy without the anger and control really mean?" In other words, he asked the question, Will I ever be able to love someone in an intimate, sexually satisfying way? The gender role transition to intimacy had begun.

My next intervention was to help Jack bring closure to his rage at his mother. I felt this closure would open up more emotional space for him to love himself and others more fully. The goal was to have him forgive his mother by more deeply understanding her pain. Forgiveness many times requires more knowledge of the victimizer and new contextual information about how and why the violation occurred (Enright & Fitzgibbons, 2000; O'Neil, Davison, Mutchler, & Trachtenberg, in press). To accomplish this, we both read again Jack's letters from his mother while he was in college. These letters brought out the forgotten parent–child dynamics and a deeper understanding of his mother's pain. Jack had numerous discussions with his mother using Perl's Gestalt (Corey, 2005; Levitsky & Perls, 1970) empty chair technique. He summarized some of these exchanges in writing:

> I am crippled by dictators of the past, by my battle with my mother. This siren who would dash my life against the rocks, sang to me, while not sweetly, a powerful tune that tried to mold me into a strong man, but offered no love and affection along the way. Oh, Jim, she was so awesome, so strong, that I wilted under her messianic power. God how I loved her, still do! Mother why didn't you love me more easily? I was a good kid, as capable as any child a mother could have. Were you so lonely in your own life that I got lost? Were your own pain so great, your own loneliness so encompassing, and your sense of survival so strong that your feelings, your love, got lost along the way? You never really felt love in your life, did you? Dad was such a disappointment, offering so little support in the raising of children, so little emotional warmth in his heart, so alone unto himself. You had to survive the best you knew how, and that included controlling feelings and tender emotions that were a big part of who you were. All the dreams of your youth were compromised, weren't they? You aspired to so much more than you became, as you said to me, "I just did what I had to do." I want to forgive you, Mother, for your lack of understanding of what I needed and how to give it to me. I want to forgive you and offer my love to you, give to you what you never had. I am trying, please understand, but I can't open up yet. My own hurt is so deep, you'll have to wait.

Jack did have some actual encounters with his mother, in which he appropriately asserted his power and began the forgiveness process. He videotaped a 2-hour session with his mother where he probed the family dynamics and history. Mrs. Smith, who was now age 83, avoided some of the questions and remembered only fragments of the past. Jack was able to control and process his feelings toward his mother; something that he was never able to do as a child. He was proving he could be assertive, compassionate, and use his power effectively. What he could not communicate to her directly he wrote to himself:

> You might understand the anger I feel for you and the way you treated me. And it is this anger that I can't shake, Mom. But I want you to know, that when I work it all through, when I get the anger out and develop more constructive ways of dealing with it, I will give you the love you never had from your father or your husband. It will be a little late, Mom, for you perhaps. But not for me . . . . By forgiving you, and loving you, I will be able to love another woman someday. It's getting late, it seems, but I do hope it will be possible for me to know the kind of love that you never did. I just wish it weren't so hard.

I was very moved by Jack's forgiveness process as he cried out his loss and confronted his mother for her neglect and harshness. Jack was developing compassion and empathy for his mother. This compassion mediated some of the rage and opened up some possibilities of letting go of the pain experienced with his mother. Jack actually took care of his mother as she was dying and this became a very healing part of his therapy. To take care of his mother, who had not taken care of him, was truly a sign that a significant transformation was occurring in Jack's life. It was one of those moments in therapy where you observe human healing triumph over past trauma and hurt. He faced her with compassion and a new sense of power. He did not back off when challenged, reprimanded, or punished. He had faced his mother as a powerful feminine force and felt strong and positive about himself. He was putting the past behind him and the therapy sessions began to focus on his current interpersonal relationships.

Jack began to see how his mother and childhood experiences affected his relationships and sexual affairs. Numerous sessions covered Jack's multiple relationships and his desire to control and dominate women. His feelings and thoughts about his mother and women became the focus of the therapy. Deep feelings of pain, loneliness, and anger were evident in his emotional disclosures that occurred more frequently. For example, he wrote me these feelings:

> I am awake this morning with a terrible loneliness, the kind I have always run from as soon as I can. This morning I am trying to "embrace the pain." I am realizing how lonely and alone I really am in my life. The superficial social nature and friendly personality hides underneath a very lonely man. I have been out walking, thinking of all my relationships with former girlfriends, and I am aware of the inability that we all have had to give emotionally to each other.

During all of this, Jack had developed an emotional vocabulary that allowed him to monitor how emotional states caused interpersonal conflicts and stresses. He had been able to work with both the masculine and feminine parts of himself. Consequently, he was more comfortable confronting the feminine in women and the masculine in other men. Most important, he was beginning to know who he was and not retreat from the truth of who he had been. He began to assert his rights without manipulating others and defined his own gender role values in both work and interpersonal relationships. He began to use his positive power and vulnerability as an asset for self-understanding and personal healing. Rather than pushing pain and anger away, he began to face it. He wrote this to me:

> Thanks to our sessions, I was able to embrace the pain and to recognize my old patterns of adding punishment to myself. Little Jackie tried to take hold of me this afternoon, but he was unsuccessful. I feel stronger tonight also, even as I am sad and unhappy about my loss. But even more, this morning, I am aware of what vulnerability I am going to have to develop, learn about, demonstrate. I am desperately lonely for love

and meaningful commitment, and yet I ask for it first with weak promise that I might give it in return. I realize this morning (for the first time in my heart) that I am going to have to give love if I am to receive it. And isn't this the philosophy expressed just about everywhere by great thinkers? The Bible is a very lengthy expression of this one "lesson." Schweitzer, Martin Luther King, Jr., have shown the very love that I want to express. But they were made extremely vulnerable by doing so. I realize that I can deeply care for a woman as I do and not feel inadequate or like a loser because in deeply caring I have to let my mother die. I am free to just care, no power struggles, etcetera. I expressed this to her today. It was a wonderful and yet strange feeling during lunch.

Jack began to approach relationships more honestly and directly. He learned to set boundaries in relationships and express his honest feelings without manipulation and hidden agendas. When he was congruent with his new masculine values, he sensed an emerging confidence in his work and personal relationships. He began to like himself more, devalue himself less, and seek less confirmation from others.

After 3.5 years of therapy, Jack decided to end therapy, with the option of returning at a later time. Jack wanted to continue his growth without the weekly therapy sessions. The termination process lasted 8 weeks and involved reviewing the therapy process and the issues still unresolved. Jack had resolved a number of problems and expressed satisfaction with his growth and positive change. There were doubts about his ability to find intimacy and how to maintain the self-sustaining changes made over the therapy period.

Four months after termination, I contacted Jack to obtain a release on the case material used in this chapter and to inquire on how he was doing. Jack reported that he was doing quite well without therapy and that he was successful in maintaining the changes made in therapy. He reported that he had lost 20 lbs. and was beginning to initiate relationships with women. He also reported some personal rejections from women but that the old destructive dynamics of the past had not occurred.

SUMMARY OF THE CASE:
AN EXAMPLE OF HEALING GENDER ROLE TRAUMA

My overall assessment was that Jack was a victim of sexism because of his sexist gender role socialization and family life. Furthermore, in my diagnostic opinion, Jack experienced what Pleck (1995) described as "male gender role trauma." Masculine gender role trauma is not very well developed in the men's literature but has been used to explain boys' negative experiences in sports, coming out as gay, separation from mothers, and having fathers absent. I think gender role trauma was fully evident in Jack's life during both his childhood and adulthood. According to Pleck, trauma strain occurs when a man attempts to meet, or actually meets, the gender role expectancies during gender role socialization and this process has long-term negative effects. Furthermore, male gender role trauma implies sexist experiences that negatively shape a boy's personality and psychosocial functioning. Jack's dysfunctional family dynamics, including his neglectful fathering and oppressive mothering, resulted in numerous personality problems and dysfunctional behaviors that limited his growth and development as a young boy and adult man. You would have had to be "in the room" for those 3 years to grasp the full degree of the trauma that Jack experienced and lived out. Established theories of victimization and trauma (McCann, Sakheim, & Abrahamson, 1988) help explain Jack's traumatizing experiences in his family. Many times victims experience distorted cognitive and affective schemas during and after their trauma. Clearly, Jack learned distorted gender role schemas (O'Neil & Nadeau, 1999) from his family of origin related to power, control, intimacy, safety, assertion, self-esteem, and trust. These distorted gender role schemas had significant negative effect on his developmental growth, restricted him in accomplishing major developmental tasks, and prohibited him from developing a positive masculine identity. He developed what Blazina and Watkins (2000) describe as a "fragile masculine self."

Long-term therapy with Jack challenged me, and it also allowed me to conceptualize his healing process using the gender role conflict diagnostic schema. The case also demonstrates how family-of-origin issues can be intricately related to men's gender role conflicts. Jack's therapy was really a gender role journey (O'Neil & Egan, 1992a, 1992b; O'Neil et al., 1993) because he discovered how his sexist gender role socialization contributed to his emotional problems. Furthermore, in the therapy he went through a number of gender role transitions (O'Neil & Egan, 1992b). These gender role transitions included mediating heterosexual antagonism, developing a capacity for intimacy, redefining power and control, processing emotional pain, and healing the wounded child. He also redefined numerous gender role themes that allowed him to experience his pain and heal some deep wounds. The gender role themes included control, power, emotionality, vulnerability, trust, intimacy, and sexuality.

I encouraged Jack to recreate himself and told him that he did not have to be defined by the past. Therapeutic structures were created for Jack that emphasized his strengths as a man and helped him mediate his fears related to emotions, trust, intimacy, power, and giving up control. The therapeutic structures that Jack used in his personal transformation included knowing his gender role conflicts, examining his family of origin, learning how to process and use pain, learning how to redefine his masculinity, taking back the power he had given up, healing the hurt child, developing an emotional vocabulary, experimenting with new roles and definitions of power, and forgiving his mother and himself. Jack was able to profit from the therapy because he was bright, educated, articulate, and motivated to change. He personalized the information about men's gender role conflicts and wrote out his feelings, which helped him experience the anger and release it. He was willing to experiment with a new sense of power in his career and his relationship with women. These experiments were successful and gave him confidence and hope that he could change his life.

This case study was originally written 10 years ago. During this time, I sought Jack's consent to publish his therapy. He read the entire case and wrote back a three-page reaction with factual corrections and suggestions that improved the accuracy of his therapeutic process. Therefore, I believe that the case study does have additional validity, given Jack's evaluation of it. Recently, I contacted Jack to have him reread this revised version of the case and to obtain his additional feedback. I found out that he is deceased. This knowledge brought up emotion for me and many questions. When did he die and how was his life after therapy? Did the positive changes that he reported 4 months after therapy endure over the years? Was there regression and relapses into his anger and pain? Did he find the intimacy that he sought? I wanted to contact his family to obtain some information about his life in the 1990s, but there are significant ethical and confidentiality issues that prohibit me from making this contact.

Knowledge of Jack's death increased my commitment to fully document his therapy. He indicated on numerous occasions that he wanted his therapy process to be known to other men and women. He was not concerned about being anonymous and told me, "I hope that publishing my therapy process will help therapists help other men recovering from their boyhood pain and adult masculinity problems." In this regard, Jack wanted his therapy to be a stimulus for increased understanding of men in therapy. For him, to know that his therapeutic process and pain would not be lost but would be used by others was another aspect of his healing. I hope that Jack's case study does add to other therapists' knowledge about doing therapy with men. Jack would have been pleased if this happens. I would be pleased with receiving feedback on this case study and hearing other therapists' experiences with men "in the room."

QUESTIONS FROM THE EDITORS

1. *What types of gender-based stereotypes were you aware of in counseling this client? How did that impact your therapy with this client?*

I do believe that my stereotypes about men did operate during my therapy with Jack. The primary stereotypes operating were that men are unemotional, controlling, power oriented, invulnerable, and many times masked (Lynch & Kilmartin, 1999). These stereotypes about men were quite congruent with how Jack presented himself. I held these stereotypes about men, and Jack validated them. The stereotypes also served as criteria for how Jack could redefine and change his masculine identity. In other words, I held these masculine stereotypes but also knew that these same stereotypic qualities were shallow and illusory attributes to establish a human identity. Jack and I broke down, evaluated, and worked through the stereotypes of masculinity as part of the therapeutic process. In my own gender role journey, I had evaluated the shallowness and destructiveness of the masculine stereotypes and how they emanated from patriarchal sexism. On the basis of my own evaluation of the stereotypes, I could help Jack make his own evaluations. For Jack, redefining masculine stereotypes was a formidable and challenging task, but one that he ultimately embraced.

2. *How did your own gender role issues influence your work with this client?*

My unresolved power and control issues with men were activated when Jack was unwilling to relinquish any control in the therapy during the initial sessions. Jack's evaluative statements about me being an uncaring therapist, and focused on making money, activated past anger at men who have judged me or questioned my integrity. Jack's description of his father's wounds activated some unresolved feelings about my own father. Furthermore, my perspective that men can be traumatized and victimized by sexism operated during the therapy. I had to sort out and relive my own experiences as a child, as Jack revealed his traumatic socialization experiences. All of these issues made me feel vulnerable and activated some countertransference issues that I had to deal with during and after each session. They also allowed me to more personally understand Jack's pain in a much deeper way than if I was unaware of my own gender role journey.

3. *You incorporated readings about masculinity and extensive writing interventions. How did you use these interventions in the therapy?*

Both the readings and writing activities made therapy acceptable to Jack. The readings served as a way for Jack to think about himself in term of gender role conflict. I actually had him rate himself on the six patterns of gender role conflict, using one of my therapy checklists. Jack's weekly diary writings were his way of learning self-processing and preparing for the weekly therapy session. He could write out his deep feelings before the session and then use the therapy sessions to express the emotions to me. This gave him control over his feelings and the option of sharing them with me. We varied how he processed his weekly writings. Sometimes, he sent them to me in advance to study. Sometimes he read them to me. Other times, he had me do the reading out loud. In all cases, he was finally facing and processing his emotions and putting the anger in constructive action and use.

4. *The gender role conflict model notes that homophobia is one of the hallmarks of gender role conflict. How did homophobia appear in the room? Did it*

influence your ability to let the client know how much you appreciated and liked him?

Homophobia was operating in the room but not in any overt way. We never discussed homophobia, but it was a subterranean dynamic in our process. I consider homophobia to be one of the most important issues in liberating men from their sexism and gender role conflict. Consequently, I have spent much energy in trying to understand my own homophobia. I did not experience any homophobia when working with Jack. Our therapeutic closeness did not make me anxious or limit me in expressing my affection and caring for him. However, I do think that Jack experienced some aspects of homophobia, given that he had never opened up to any other man with such vulnerability. Furthermore, when two men break down the stereotypes of masculinity, become emotionally vulnerable, share feelings and tears, homophobic and irrational fears are more possible. These are stereotypic feminine qualities that "real men" are not supposed to show and many times inappropriately attributed to gay men. Our therapy operationalized these "feminine qualities," and therefore homophobia may have been operating in a covert way but it is unclear exactly how.

REFERENCES

Blazina, C., & Watkins, C. E. (2000). Separation/individuation, parental attachment, and male gender conflict: Attitudes toward the feminine and the fragile masculine self. *Psychology of Men and Masculinity, 1*, 126–132.

Corey, G. (2005). *Theory and practice of counseling and psychotherapy* (7th ed.). Belmont, CA: Brooks/Cole.

Enright, R. D., & Fitzgibbons, R. P. (2000). *Helping clients forgive: An empirical guide for resolving anger and restoring hope.* Washington, DC: American Psychological Association.

Levant, R. F., Hirsch, L., Celentano, E., Cozza, T., Hill, S., & MacEachern, M. (1992). The male role: An investigation of contemporary norms. *Journal of Mental Health Counseling, 14*, 325–337.

Levitsky, A., & Perls, F. S. (1970). The rules and games of gestalt therapy. In J. Fagan & I. L. Shepard (Eds.), *Gestalt therapy now: Theory, techniques, applications* (pp. 140–149). New York: Harper.

Lynch, J., & Kilmartin, C. T. (1999). *The pain behind the mask: Overcoming masculine depression.* Binghamton, NY: Haworth Press.

Mahalik, J. R., Locke, B. D., Ludlow, L. H., Diemer, M. A., Scott, R. P., Gottfried, M., & Freitas, G. (2003). Development of the Conformity to Norms Inventory. *Psychology of Men and Masculinity, 4*, 3–25.

McCann, I. L., Sakheim, D. K., & Abrahamson, D. J. (1988). A model of psychological adaptation. *The Counseling Psychologist, 16*, 531–594.

O'Neil, J. M. (1981a). Male sex-role conflicts, sexism, and masculinity: Implications for men, women, and the counseling psychologist. *The Counseling Psychologist*, 9, 61–80.

O'Neil, J. M. (1981b). Patterns of gender role conflict and strain: Sexism and fear of femininity in men's lives. *The Personnel and Guidance Journal*, 60, 203–210.

O'Neil, J. M. (1982). Gender role conflict and strain in men's lives: Implications for psychiatrists, psychologists, and other human service providers. In K. Solomon & N. Levy (Eds.), *Men in transition: Theory and therapy* (pp. 5–44). New York: Plenum.

O'Neil, J. M. (1988). *The Gender Role Conflict Checklist*. Storrs: School of Family Studies, University of Connecticut.

O'Neil, J. M. (1990). Assessing men's gender role conflict. In D. Moore & F. Leafgren (Eds.), *Men in conflict: Problem solving strategies and interventions* (pp. 23–38). Alexandria, VA: American Association for Counseling and Development Press.

O'Neil, J. M. (August, 2002). Twenty years of gender role conflict research: Summary of 130 studies. In J. M. O'Neil & G. E. Good (Cochairs), *Gender role conflict research: Empirical studies and 20-year summary*. Symposium presented at the 110th Annual Convention of the American Psychological Association, Chicago.

O'Neil, J. M. (2005). *Twenty-five years of research on men's gender role conflict using the Gender Role Conflict Scale: New research directions and clinical implications*. Manuscript submitted for publication.

O'Neil, J. M., Davison, D., Mutchler, M. S., & Trachtenberg, J. (in press). Process evaluation of teaching forgiveness in a workshop and classroom setting. *Marriage and Family Review*.

O'Neil, J. M., & Egan, J. (1992a). Men and women's gender role journeys: A metaphor for healing, transition, and transformation. In B. Wainrib (Ed.), *Gender issues across the life cycle* (pp. 107–123). New York: Springer Publishing Company.

O'Neil, J. M., & Egan, J. (1992b). Men's gender role transitions over the life span: Transformations and fears of femininity. *Journal of Mental Health Counseling*, 14, 306–324.

O'Neil, J. M., Egan, J., Owen, S. V., & Murry, V. (1993). The gender role journey measure (GRJM): Scale development and psychometric evaluations. *Sex Roles*, 28, 167–185.

O'Neil, J. M., & Fishman, D. M. (1992). Adult men's career transitions and gender-role themes. In H. D. Lea & Z. B. Leibowitz (Eds.), *Adult career development: Concepts, issues, and practices* (2nd ed., pp. 161–191). Alexandria, VA: American Counseling Association Press.

O'Neil, J. M., Good, G. E., & Holmes, S. E. (1995). Fifteen years of theory and research on men's gender role conflict: New paradigms for empirical research. In R. F. Levant & W. S. Pollack (Eds.), *A new psychology of men* (pp. 164–206). New York: Basic Books.

O'Neil, J. M., Helms, B. J., Gable, R. K., David, L., & Wrightsman, L. S. (1986). Gender role conflict scale (GRCS): College men's fear of femininity. *Sex Roles*, *14*, 335–350.

O'Neil, J. M., & Nadeau, R. A. (1999). Men's gender role conflict, defense mechanism, and self-protective defensive strategies: Explaining men's violence against women from a gender role socialization perspective. In M. Harway & J. M. O'Neil (Eds.), *What causes men's violence against women?* (pp. 89–116). Thousand Oaks, CA: Sage.

Pleck, J. H. (1995). The gender role strain paradigm: An update. In R. F. Levant & W. S. Pollack (Eds.), *A new psychology of men* (pp. 11–32). New York: Basic Books.

Scher, M. (1979). The little boy in the adult male client. *Personnel and Guidance Journal*, *57*, 537–539.

Thompson, E. H., Grisanti, C., & Pleck, J. H. (1985). Attitudes toward the male role and their correlates. *Sex Roles*, *13*, 413–427.

14

ADAM AND THE PAIN OF DIVORCE

ROBERTA L. NUTT

How could I be interested in and teach women's issues without developing an interest in men's issues? I asked myself that question many times as early as the 1970s as I was developing a graduate course in the psychology of women. In this course I found myself frequently discussing some issues in the course that were important to women, yet companion issues related to men would emerge. It did not seem possible to adequately cover one side of an issue without the other. Yet it also seemed that many of these issues were not in opposition to women but were unique to the experience of men. Hence, my interest in men's issues grew naturally from my interest and investment in women's issues. For me, it seemed that much of what was taught in gender role socialization restricted the full development of both men and women. On a personal level, I saw it in the consequences I paid in high school for not listening to the cultural message to "play dumb," and I saw it in the adulation of football players to the detriment of all the bright and talented boys who were not athletic. I was also impressed by men I met in the early years of the women's movement who supported equal rights and the Equal Rights Amendment. These men talked about being tired of the stress of carrying the sole burden of provider as their primary role, which resonated with my desires to avoid the traditional women's roles of homemaker, secretary, second-class helper, and so on.

It seemed only natural that as I developed the psychology of women course, I wanted to add companion literature on the new psychology of men—as opposed to the literature developed on traditional men. In the 1970s, there was already a wealth of writings concerning women's issues, because the women's liberation movement had begun in the 1960s, but it was more difficult to find literature concerning the socialization of men and its accompanying critique. I did eventually find the work of such writers as Joseph Pleck, Herb Goldberg, Warren Farrell, Sam Osherson, and many others, and later the work of Jim O'Neil, Ron Levant, Gary Brooks, Glenn Good, Murray Scher, Andy Horne, Mark Kiselica, Frank Pittman, and Bill Pollack.

As a psychologist, I remember when the Society for the Psychological Study of Men and Masculinity became a division of the American Psychological Association (APA). At the time, I felt that it was important for feminist women to support this process. These were the men who understood both men's and women's issues and were working toward the mental health of both sexes. I helped gather petition signatures and recruit members. I explained to feminist women how our agendas matched. As the new Division 51 formed, I worked on the bylaws, served as the first fellows chair, and was elected on two separate occasions to the women's seat as member-at-large on the Division 51 executive board. I have particularly enjoyed writing for the newsletter, serving on the editorial board of the journal *Psychology of Men and Masculinity*, and chairing the search for the new editor of that journal.

Sometime around 1989, Gary Brooks asked me to join him, Don-David Lusterman, and Carol Philpot in presenting a symposium on men's and women's issues in relationships. We presented similar symposia a number of times at APA and American Association of Marital and Family Therapists meetings. We enjoyed the interchange and eventually we decided to put our thoughts and strategies into a book. After several false starts, we completed our book *Bridging Separate Gender Worlds: How Men and Women Clash and How Therapists CAN Bring Them Together* (Philpot, Brooks, Lusterman, & Nutt, 1997). We were determined as two women and two men to write this book in one voice—a voice that believed men and women were socialized differently but that they could learn to understand and accept each other. Our premise fit everything I believed. It was a wonderful, growth enhancing process as four persons of two sexes deepened their understanding of each other.

During this growth period, I developed other projects related to men's issues. One particularly important one was writing an article, later also published as a book chapter, on training issues for male students (Nutt, 1991b) in a gender-sensitive doctoral program. This writing forced me to consider how I integrated men's gender role socialization as well as women's gender role socialization into everything I teach and how I directed and administered a doctoral program. Some favorite examples include a conversation I had years ago with a doctoral student who was changing careers from business to psychology. We processed the difficulty he was having transitioning from business hierarchy and structure to the more open atmosphere of the doctoral program in which all voices were valued. Then there was the first student who insisted on staying local for his clinical predoctoral internship—because his wife was completing her medical residency in the area—this student knew he had me with a great role reversal. Other male students have expressed appreciation for the program's support of their fathering roles and times when their children were a higher priority than a particular class or meeting.

My therapeutic work with men has been personally rewarding in that they have provided numerous examples of gender role conflicts and stress to illustrate what I had earlier learned from my academic studies and involvement with Division 51. My clients have made that material come alive. Men have shared with me in their therapy more fully than they would ever share with a woman in their personal lives, particularly their fears and struggles to live up to the masculine ideal. They have talked about their feelings of incompetence around their earning power, sexual prowess, and dealing with their deepest feelings and insecurities. I feel privileged to have their trust. They have enabled me to see much more clearly the similarities between men and women at the most basic levels that are often masked by gender role socialization. These experiences have made me more sensitive to my male friends, colleagues, and relatives. I understand when a male colleague expresses, with humor and embarrassment, the conflict between his desire to be with his family over holidays when he is busily working in his office to get ahead in his career. I can strongly support the male colleague who cut back on his professional service to be home more during his children's early years and understand his pain at being criticized and misunderstood by other men. My experiences with male clients have given me a much healthier attitude toward, and relationship with, men than I would have ever had on the basis of my personal life experience alone, and I am grateful.

MY THERAPEUTIC APPROACH

In my approach to working with male clients, I consider first how difficult it often is for male clients to enter therapy and counseling (Brooks, 1998; Carlson, 1987; Goldberg, 1976; Good, Dell, & Mintz, 1989; Heppner & Gonzales, 1987; Ipsaro, 1986; Robertson & Fitzgerald, 1992). It often, although not always, takes a fairly major crisis in a man's life to overcome his socialized resistance to therapy. I am sensitive to the probable overload of pain that brought this man to my office. Therefore, I initially spend time being sensitive to the help-seeking process.

Second, I recognize that men are generally less likely to have been socialized to begin therapy by sharing and exploring deep feelings. Some men may not even be aware of deep feelings (termed *alexithymia* by Levant, 1992;

see also Balswick, 1988; Farrell, 1987), and some men are likely looking for a quick fix through actions. As with any client, it is crucial to join with the male client where he is. Listening, accepting where he is, and talking in language that matches his will create an initial feeling of safety and forms the foundation of a working relationship. I believe that many men will consider entering new territory, such as exploring emotional issues, only by first being accepted for who they are as a man. I have noticed that male clients may make less eye contact than many female clients and that many male clients are more comfortable fiddling with a pen or some other object when they are talking. I generally do not push for deep feelings in the first session or two, and I do not interpret the fiddling activities. It seems to me that all of these reactions and behaviors speak to a male way of "being" in the therapy room.

Yet I am deeply convinced that men are born with the same kind of basic needs and feelings as women and that socialization accounts for the majority of differences measured and observed in adulthood (Bergman, 1995; Betcher & Pollack, 1993; J. H. Pleck, 1995; Pollack, 1998). Therefore, it is possible for men to explore history and feelings and come to deep understanding of themselves (Keen, 1991). It is also possible for them to analyze gender role socialization around relationships, career, success, identity, sexuality, and so on (Bernard, 1981; Bograd, 1991; Brooks, 1995; David & Brannon, 1976; Doyle, 1995; Farrell, 1974, 1993; Goldberg, 1979, 1987; Horne & Kiselica, 1999; Kelly & Hall, 1992; Levant & Brooks, 1997; Mahalik, 1999; Morris, 1997; Nutt, 1991a; O'Neil & Roberts-Carroll, 1988; Robertson & Fitzgerald, 1990; Scher, Stevens, Good, & Eichenfield, 1987; Zilbergeld, 1978, 1992) and to make new decisions for what it is for them to be men (Philpot et al., 1997; Pittman, 1985). This process may be slow and may necessitate different stages to achieve, such as participating in all-male groups as an initial step to help men safely explore the expression of feelings with other men (Andronico, 1996; Brooks, 1998; Good, Gilbert, & Scher, 1990).

After rapport is established, I usually find it helpful to explore the male client's family-of-origin messages about manhood (Osherson, 1986); his experiences as a boy; and his messages from peers (the male chorus—Pittman, 1990), schools, media, and religion (Good, Gilbert, & Scher, 1990; Keen, 1991; Lee, 1987; Moore & Gillette, 1990); and his personal gender role journey (O'Neil, 1981, 1982; O'Neil & Egan, 1992). Men are often unaware of the power of these messages in their current lives and find it helpful to make the connection—It makes current problems more understandable (Cook, 1990; Gilbert, 1999; Gilbert & Scher, 1999; Mahalik, Cournoyer, DeFranc, Cherry, & Napolitano, 1998; Meth & Pasick, 1990). In particular, I have found that respect for the client's struggles with competition versus intimacy with other men (Messner, 1992; Nardi, 1992) and an understanding that male anger often masks fear, hurt, and insecurity are critical. My background in studying men's gender role socialization is especially useful when I can use it to suggest hypotheses that convey an understanding of male gender role expectations (Brooks, 1998; Faludi, 1999; Fischer, Tokar, Good, & Snell, 1998; Levant & Pollack, 1995; Pittman, 1990, 1993; E. H. Pleck & Pleck, 1980; J. H. Pleck, 1981, 1995; J. H. Pleck & Sawyer, 1980; Pollack, 1995, 1998; Scher, 1981), which can significantly put a male client at ease because he feels understood. Plus, with my female gender role socialization, I may be better at early stages of therapy at putting the issues and feelings into words. It may be necessary to be more active with male clients in labeling feelings or suggesting meanings to give them hope for progress. As words to describe feelings may not come easily to male clients, my attention to body language, posture, facial expressions, and tone increases in importance to help me understand and follow the client.

THE CASE OF ADAM

Course of Counseling

Adam entered counseling with me to address the pain of a difficult divorce process. Mary Ann, his wife of 16 years, had left him for her golf instructor and moved to California. Adam was hurt, angry, and frustrated with himself for not recovering more quickly. During the first session, Adam said he chose a female psychologist because he thought it might help him understand how women think. I saw him for approximately 30 sessions over the course of a year.

When Adam entered counseling, he was 37 years old and a successful executive vice president in a major corporation. He was tall, handsome, and well-dressed. Physically taking care of himself was important to him, and he exercised frequently. With his looks and success, he was used to getting his own way. My initial reaction to Adam was mild surprise at his entering therapy. In my experience, men who have developed such a successful public persona are often not willing to admit emotional defeat or to seek help through therapy. Often their appearance and success indicate an investment in traditional gender roles, and these men feel that therapy puts them in a one-down position that violates the expectations of the male gender role. Traditionally, successful men are supposed to be able to solve their own problems. My immediate thought upon seeing and meeting Adam was that he had obviously reached his pain threshold and was suffering beyond his expectations.

It became clear in the next few sessions that not only was Adam hurt at being betrayed by his wife, he was ashamed and embarrassed to admit that he was in so much pain and confusion. This embarrassment seemed understandable in lieu of the traditional male role that continually says, "suck it up." Adam reported having a number of male friends, but when questioned, I discovered that although they shared many activities (e.g., sports, happy hour), discussing personal issues seemed off-limits. Adam's friends knew Mary Ann had left and were concerned for him, but his friends responded to Adam by telling him to start dating and forget about her. In the face of this feedback and "support" from his friends, Adam did not want to admit how lonely, anxious, and confused he felt. This reluctance to reveal his sadness and hurt to his male friends reminded me of Pittman's (1990) concept of the "invisible male chorus" that men sense is always watching their actions. Adam did not want his friends to see his real feelings and criticize or ridicule him. He felt vulnerable and had lost some self-confidence, plus he felt guilty for any part he may have played in causing her to leave. Adam further revealed that he was having difficulty sleeping and was smoking and drinking "too much." It became clear by his continuing discussion of his pain with me that Adam felt safer admitting these "weaknesses" to a woman whom he assumed would be less critical than his male friends. I felt how important it was for me to accept and validate Adam's feelings in him to make it easier for him to accept them himself.

Early in therapy, Adam was still responsive to communication from Mary Ann and desperately wanted reconciliation. Whenever she came to town and called Adam to meet, he eagerly went, only to have his hopes dashed when Mary Ann left again and never called. Adam described his feelings of being "like a yo-yo on a string stuck in a pattern" he could not or would not break. Adam seemed well aware of the power Mary Ann held over him and he resented her for it. Adam could see the manipulation when she told him she cared about him and then disappeared, but he felt helpless. I was again struck by how difficult it was for Adam to admit Mary Ann's power over him and how much safer it felt to him to admit it to me rather than his male friends. I thought it was therefore important for me to accept and validate his feelings of being stuck and normalize his embarrassment. I hoped that my comfort with his feelings would lead him to feeling more comfortable with his feelings as a whole.

We tried to work through his idealized version of his marriage versus the reality of it. In truth, it appeared that Adam had always been more committed to the marriage than Mary Ann was. She enjoyed having a good time and when his job cut back travel time and party budgets, she seemed to resent the change in lifestyle. Adam also commented that Mary Ann was a spendthrift who did not respect his viewpoints on money. Through our discussions in therapy, he eventually began to see the reality of his marriage more clearly. Adam began to view Mary Ann as superficial in her values, but seeing her in person still wrenched his emotions. She continued to call when she was in town and invite him over, and Adam felt unable to resist. Adam commented that Mary Ann would flirt with him, hint that she was reconsidering their marriage, and then disappear. Adam continued to fall for her "game" a number of times because his attachments ran deep and commitment was a serious event in his life. Watching Adam go through this relational pattern with Mary Ann was difficult for me to watch. I could truly feel his hope each time he would talk about seeing her again; conversely, I would also feel his pain at seeing her go away and not call him back.

In time I came to realize that part of Adam's strong marital attachment resulted from the strong marital relationship modeled by his parents. Adam was closest to his mother who nurtured him, and his parents were close to each other. From his mother, Adam learned to make strong connections. He also probably learned to express emotions and to respect women from her. During our time in therapy, Adam commented that his mother eventually admitted that she had never liked Mary Ann and that she had found Mary Ann cold and uncaring. Whereas Adam could talk about his mother, he was more conscious of the critical side of his conservative, rigid father. Even as an adult, Adam felt he was always striving to live up to his father's expectations. Adam revealed that at his core he was not sure if he could. He was the oldest of four boys, and so he particularly felt his father's judgment and strove to achieve. Conceptually, I tied his birth order to my awareness of achievement pressures often felt by firstborn children. Adam surely seemed driven and he clearly gained a significant part of his self-esteem from his accomplishments.

Following the advice of his friends, Adam tried the "dating scene" but hated it. Women flocked to him and expressed interest, but he was suspicious of their intentions. Adam feared that women saw him as a meal ticket—a "success object." To defend against his fears, Adam would protect himself by being intimidating rather than by revealing his anxiety and fear. Adam realized and clearly expressed to me that he was a man who preferred the married life to the single life, but he felt frightened that he would never find the right partner. I was reminded once again that society's stereotypes of women desperate for marriage and men preferring multiple, fleeting partners are just not true. One of the best parts of being a therapist for me has been learning, contrary to society's stereotypes, how many men do prefer to be in a loving relationship and how important emotional connections are to many men.

After Adam had started to date and expressed his fears about being alone, I suggested he read Tannen's (1990) book *You Just Don't Understand* to examine differences in men's and women's socialized conversation patterns. I have found her linguistic analysis to be incredibly helpful with heterosexual couples. After reading this book, Adam saw how he had frustrated Mary Ann by trying to solve her problems for her rather than just listening. Adam also realized that he had inquired too frequently about her whereabouts and saw how that may have felt controlling to her. Finally, Adam recognized how he had tried to calm his fears and anxiety with dominance and control. The book was helpful to him for understanding and normalizing his feelings and behavior. He was able to identify feeling guilty about this past behavior and resolved not to repeat it in the future. I felt hopeful about

Adam's ability to be aware of his past communication patterns, and he seemed committed to working toward changing these patterns.

Over a few months, he went through numerous rounds of realizing Mary Ann was not the woman for him, making plans for a new life without her, and then reverting back to feeling hurt and confused from missing her. I felt that my role at this time was to not judge him or try to force him to move emotionally away from these feelings. That seemed to be what his friends were doing. Instead, it was important for me to accept him where he was and not push him in any direction. He needed the time and space to actually feel his emotions from start to finish, without feeling the pull to hide them or perform for the male chorus. In this way, his emotions were honored and validated, and he could progress at his own pace.

Eventually Adam met someone new whom he liked, Cathy, but she was 6 years older than him and had a more advanced degree. He found that challenging. Although Cathy was attractive and accomplished, Adam worried about the age and educational differences. Would she eventually look older than he did? Would his male friends be critical of his attachment to an "older woman"? Would she eventually find him boring because he had only a bachelor's degree? Although reporting these feelings in session made him feel shallow, they were nevertheless true expressions of how he felt. In retrospect, I think Adam needed the space to actually voice these fears with a supportive audience. Although Adam wavered between Mary Ann and Cathy for several months—always being honest with Cathy about his ambivalence (we spent much time discussing the importance of honesty in a close and lasting relationship)—he did eventually divorce Mary Ann and focused his attention on his relationship with Cathy. Cathy was concerned about becoming the transitional object after his divorce, but Adam reassured her that he had dated enough in his life to be satisfied that he did not want to return to that lifestyle.

Individual therapy terminated when Adam obtained the divorce from Mary Ann and felt that he had emotionally disconnected from her. He continued his relationship with Cathy, and even now they schedule appointments with me occasionally as a couple to smooth out relationship stresses or misunderstandings. One of the plusses of maintaining a long-term practice in the same geographic area is the ability to follow a number of clients through many life growth stages. I have enjoyed watching Adam negotiate his new relationship and actively use lessons he learned in therapy with me. For example, he is much less controlling with Cathy and more willing to share his feelings in an honest, straightforward manner. He is sensitive to discriminating when Cathy wants a listening ear and when she wants ideas for solutions when she describes a frustrating problem at work. It seems like Adam was able to use his therapy experience to be more fully capable of negotiating the rigid expectation of traditional masculinity so that he can also tap into the emotional world of relationships.

Conceptualization

So, how did I conceptualize working with Adam from a gender role socialization perspective? I found him to be an interesting mixture of traditional man and new age man. His emphasis on career and the identity he derived from his occupation and income displayed the traditional side. He had been well socialized by his father to be a "good provider." He took pride in his accomplishments and his philanthropic activities. He dressed carefully, whether he was in a business suit or casual clothing and was well-groomed as a way of expressing his success. The opinion others held of his achievements was important to him, and he used his status to establish rapport with me early in the counseling process. Knowing that I was a university professor as well as a practicing psychologist, he emphasized his degrees and his donations to the universities he had attended. I have noticed numerous times that status-conscious clients like to feel that somehow they have chosen a therapist that they can also view as having status—it seems to reinforce their personal self-view and value. My background appeared to serve this function for Adam, and I was comfortable allowing that to function in this way.

That Adam chose a woman for counseling was no surprise to me. Many male clients have expressed their preference for a female therapist, especially when they are working on an emotionally laden issue like divorce. Men assume they will be less criticized by a woman for expressing or displaying emotions. I have also been told informally by male psychologists that there is an element of competition in the male-client–male-therapist pairing that I, of course, have never experienced (Brooks, 1998; Heppner & Gonzales, 1987; Ipsaro, 1986). Adam also expressed the hope that by seeing me, he could get some new ideas regarding a woman's perspective. There were times when he actively requested my perspective as a woman, which I gave cautiously with disclaimers for the parameters of his situation. I am not particularly comfortable when a client asks me for a "woman's perspective," because I do not want to be perceived as speaking for all women. I am very aware that my perspective may not match the perspective of specific women in the client's life, usually women I do not know. I do not want to add to his assumptions but prefer to provide new ideas to consider.

On the less traditional side, Adam was more willing and able than average to express feelings in sessions. He could express sadness with tearfulness and describe feelings of depression and the temptation to drink too much. He was in touch with his anger and hurt and was able to grasp that he was in a grieving process, and he was able to express his loneliness and the difficulty he had being alone. Although Adam was not proud of this dependence on a female partner, he owned it, at least in therapy (probably not with friends). As therapy progressed, he was also able to acknowledge the darker side of his feelings—his wanting revenge. Adam found it helpful to talk about these feelings and things he would like to do to Mary Ann, but he never expressed any intent to follow through, nor did he ever take action. I am sometimes uncomfortable with revenge issues if I think the client might take action, but I have found "revenge fantasies" to help many clients relieve angry feelings. His willingness to acknowledge and express emotion made it easier for me to work with him because I could use a full array of emotional, cognitive, and behavioral interventions.

Looking back, I expect his close relationship with his mother, both as a child and an adult, was a significant factor in the development of his nontraditional side. Adam often discussed his relationship with his mother and felt supported by her. Their relationship probably played a large part in the ease with which he entered the therapeutic relationship with me. He was used to being understood and validated by a woman. I believe that made it easier for him to trust me with sharing his vulnerable feelings.

Adam did often display the traditional male desire to fix things and get past all his pain and problems, but through the ups and downs of his emotional state, deep down he knew there was no quick fix. It was critically important to his progress that I accepted both the times he was making progress and getting on with his life and the times he had backslid and let Mary Ann manipulate his life and his emotions. Using a boxing metaphor, I framed these events as rounds and I let Adam decide when he had had enough rounds. In that sense, I was probably his boxing coach and someone who could teach him ways to survive these "rounds." One reason Adam seemed willing to reveal his deepest fears and feelings was that I was patient with his timing when none of his friends were. This acceptance helped deflect the self-criticism and frustration Adam sometimes felt when he had fallen for another of Mary Ann's seductive bait-and-switch approaches. My acceptance also allowed him to accept his backsliding as normal. This kind of patience reminded me of the same kind of patience a therapist must have when working with a battered woman who struggles numerous times to leave her abuser. The specifics are, of course, very different in that he was not being physically battered and abused, but some of the struggle to work through emotional ties and the respect for an individual's timing and readiness are similar. Often mental health care providers struggle with being patient with the amount of time it takes a client who has been abused to leave the abusive relationship. Realizing that people have to break emotional connections and leave on their own timing can be difficult. Solutions seem easier to see from an objective distance, but therapists must remember that the client's perspective has both strong emotional and cognitive components.

His sensitivity to being a "success object" was revealing. Given his success and attractiveness, he could have led an active dating life to fit many adolescent fantasies, but Adam did not want that life. He liked marriage and the security it provided. I think that many men actually feel this way but are not willing to admit it. Adam even recognized that part of his desire to be in a marital relationship was a result of insecurity he felt from lack of approval from his father.

Adam was deeply embarrassed by his concerns regarding the age difference between him and Cathy. He recognized that he had been socialized to view his female partner as partly an attractive object for his friends to admire (Brooks, 1995). Being with an attractive woman gives a man status in the eyes of other men. Adam was concerned that his friends could tell that Cathy was older and then be critical (the male chorus, again). Although he knew there were more important variables to consider in an intimate relationship, like emotional support, shared interests and values, and mutual respect, Adam really struggled with this issue. Although I appreciated his honesty and the genuineness of his struggle, I must admit I often had to bite my feminist tongue to remain accepting on this issue. As I am considerably older than both Adam and Mary Ann and have seen a number of successful couples in which the woman was older, I did not see age as particularly relevant. Yet I am sure I was reacting to the traditional cultural stereotype that the male partner is supposed to be older, taller, better educated, and make more money. Eventually, the quality of their relationship did overcome his concerns.

I chose to present this case because it is fairly typical of how I work with men, and Adam's presenting concern is a common issue that men bring to therapy. My sensitivity to men's struggles with male role socialization, which often inhibits early and comfortable recognition and expressions of feelings, and my assumption that overwhelming pain often brings men to therapy are my usual beginning hypotheses. I use my understanding of male gender role socialization to put men at ease, to help them feel understood, to validate their feelings and struggles, and sometimes to help them find words to describe the feelings. My acceptance of the belief in basic human needs that are relevant to both men and women often helps male clients accept their needs and feelings that may violate their socialization expectations. It is also typical for me to explore messages from family of origin, peers, and media to understand a man's own socialization so he can make informed choices about himself and his future.

QUESTIONS FROM THE EDITORS

1. *What types of gender-based stereotypes were you aware of in counseling this client? How did that impact your therapy with this client?*

According to cultural stereotypes, handsome and successful men who get their way are more likely to be rewarded for being socialized as traditional men and unlikely to come to therapy. Therefore, I felt some surprise when Adam first entered therapy, but it quickly became clear to me that he was very sincere about his pain and feeling stuck in the relationship. I also have a stereotype that men who are used to being in control or in charge are more likely to push for power in the therapeutic relationship and quick problem solving, but I never had that experience with Adam. I just had to sit with my stereotypes and watch Adam defy them.

2. *How did your own gender role issues influence your work with this client?*

I always wonder in working with male clients if I am not being sufficiently confrontational regarding the depth of their feelings. Between the stereotype of women being nurturing and protecting male feelings and the stereotype of men being unable to recognize and express feelings, I am always concerned that I could be colluding with the stereotypes. I did monitor these issues in working with Adam, and I have no evidence that I did not confront emotional issues sufficiently, but this is an issue that I constantly question.

3. *Looking back on the case, knowing what you know now, would you change the way you worked with this client?*

Looking back on this case, the one issue to which I wish I had given greater attention was Adam's fear of being alone. When therapy terminated, I was concerned that he had committed too quickly to a new relationship. I did express some of this concern, but he was resolute. I think there would have been important growth to be gained by his examining his anxiety about being alone and his learning to enjoy his own company. By extending our examination of being alone, I think that Adam would have become better equipped to make judgments about the desirability of future relationships and to also feel better about time spent by himself.

4. *As a feminist, what type of attitude do you need to have to work with male clients who talk about women in a demeaning or degrading manner?*

I think it is important to begin by understanding that the client's attitude is learned. Therefore I gently question the origins of these attitudes rather than confront the content immediately. An attitude of initial acceptance on the part of the therapist is critical. It is important to explore the client's history, messages from family and peers, influences of culture, and past experiences in relationships with women to understand the purpose of the hostility in the man's life. This exploration should provide the avenue to confront the attitude and its costs to the client. Often, the client begins the confrontation and can see how these attitudes are incongruent with the man he wants to be. Further, the therapeutic relationship can also serve to overcome such an attitude if the therapist is viewed as both helpful and powerful. Yet I also believe that a male client who deeply feels demeaning or degrading toward women and is not willing to examine it is also not likely to seek assistance from a female therapist.

REFERENCES

Andronico, M. (Ed.). (1996). *Men in groups: Insights, interventions, and psychoeducational work*. Washington, DC: American Psychological Association.

Balswick, J. O. (1988). *The inexpressive male*. San Francisco: New Lexington Press.

Bergman, S. J. (1995). Men's psychological development: A relational perspective. In R. F. Levant & W. S. Pollack (Eds.), *A new psychology of men* (pp. 68–90). New York: Basic Books.

Bernard, J. (1981). The good provider role: Its rise and fall. *American Psychologist, 36*, 1–12.

Betcher, R. W., & Pollack, W. S. (1993). *In a time of fallen heroes: The re-creation of masculinity*. New York: Atheneum.

Bograd, M. (Ed.). (1991). *Feminist approaches for men in family therapy*. Binghamton, NY: Haworth Press.

Brooks, G. R. (1995). *The centerfold syndrome: How men can overcome objectification and achieve intimacy with women*. San Francisco: Jossey-Bass.

Brooks, G. R. (1998). *A new psychotherapy for traditional men*. San Francisco: Jossey-Bass.

Carlson, N. (1987). Woman therapist: Male client. In M. Scher, M. Stevens, G. E. Good, & G. A. Eichenfield (Eds.), *Handbook of counseling and psychotherapy with men* (pp. 39–50). Thousand Oaks, CA: Sage.

Cook, E. P. (1990). Gender and psychological distress. *Journal of Counseling and Development, 68*, 371–375.

David, D. S., & Brannon, R. (1976). *The forty-nine percent majority: The male sex role*. Reading, MA: Addison-Wesley.

Doyle, J. A. (1995). *The male experience* (3rd ed.). Dubuque, IA: W. C. Brown.

Faludi, S. (1999). *Stiffed: The betrayal of the American man*. New York: Morrow.

Farrell, W. T. (1974). *The liberated man*. New York: Bantam Books.

Farrell, W. T. (1987). *Why men are the way they are*. New York: McGraw-Hill.

Farrell, W. T. (1993). *The myth of male power*. New York: Simon & Schuster.

Fischer, A. R., Tokar, D. M., Good, G. M., & Snell, A. F. (1998). More in the structure of male role norms: Exploratory and multiple sample conformity analysis. *Psychology of Women Quarterly, 22*, 135–155.

Gilbert, L. A. (1999). Reproducing gender in counseling and psychotherapy: Understanding the problem and changing the practice. *Applied and Preventive Psychology, 8*, 119–127.

Gilbert, L. A., & Scher, M. (1999). *Gender and sex in counseling and therapy*. Boston: Allyn & Bacon.

Goldberg, H. (1976). *The hazards of being male: Surviving the myths of masculine privilege*. New York: New American Library.

Goldberg, H. (1979). *The new male: From self-destruction to self-care*. New York: New American Library.

Goldberg, H. (1987). *The inner male: Overcoming roadblocks to intimacy*. New York: New American Library.

Good, G., Dell, D. M., & Mintz, L. B. (1989). Male role and gender role conflict: Relations to helping seeking in men. *Journal of Counseling Psychology, 36,* 295–300.

Good, G. E. , Gilbert, L. A., & Scher, M. (1990). Gender aware therapy: A synthesis of feminist therapy and knowledge about gender. *Journal of Counseling and Development, 68,* 376–380.

Heppner, P. P., & Gonzales, D. S. (1987). Men counseling men. In M. Scher, M. Stevens, G. Good, & G. A. Eichenfield (Eds.), *Handbook of counseling and psychotherapy with men* (pp. 30–38). Thousand Oaks, CA: Sage.

Horne, A. M., & Kiselica, M. S. (1999). *Handbook of counseling boys and adolescent males: A practitioner's guide.* Thousand Oaks, CA: Sage.

Ipsaro, A. J. (1986). Male client–male therapist: Issues in a therapeutic alliance. *Psychotherapy: Theory, Research, Practice, Training, 23,* 257–266.

Keen, S. (1991). *Fire in the belly: On being a man.* New York: Bantam Books.

Kelly, K. R., & Hall, A. S. (Eds.). (1992). Mental health counseling for men [Special issue]. *Journal of Mental Health Counseling, 14*(3).

Lee, J. (1987). *The flying boy: Healing the wounded man.* Austin, TX: New Men's Press.

Levant, R. F. (1992). Toward the reconstruction of masculinity. *Journal of Family Psychology, 5,* 379–402.

Levant, R. F., & Brooks, G. R. (Eds.). (1997). *Men and sex: New psychological perspectives.* New York: Wiley.

Levant, R. F., & Pollack, W. S. (Eds.). (1995). *A new psychology of men.* New York: Basic Books.

Mahalik, J. R. (1999). Interpersonal psychotherapy with men who experience gender role conflict. *Professional Psychology: Research and Practice, 30,* 5–13.

Mahalik, J. R., Cournoyer, R. J., DeFranc, W., Cherry, M., & Napolitano, J. M. (1998). Men's gender role conflict and use of psychological defenses. *Journal of Counseling Psychology, 45,* 247–255.

Messner, M. A. (1992). *Power at play: Sports and the problem of masculinity.* Boston: Beacon Press.

Meth, R. L., & Pasick, R. S. (Eds.). (1990). *Men in therapy: The challenge of change.* New York: Guilford Press.

Moore, R., & Gillette, D. (1990). *King, warrior, magician, lover: Rediscovering the archetypes of the mature masculine.* New York: HarperCollins.

Morris, L. A. (1997). *The male heterosexual.* Thousand Oaks, CA: Sage.

Nardi, P. M. (Ed.). (1992). *Men's friendships.* Thousand Oaks, CA: Sage.

Nutt, R. L. (1991a). Ethical principles for gender-fair family therapy. *Family Psychologist, 7,* 32–33.

Nutt, R. L. (1991b). Family therapy training issues of male students in a gender-sensitive doctoral program. *Journal of Feminist Family Therapy, 2,* 261–279.

O'Neil, J. M. (1981). Male sex-role conflict, sexism, and masculinity: Implications for men, women, and the counseling psychologist. *The Counseling Psychologist*, 9, 61–80.

O'Neil, J. M. (1982). Gender-role conflict and strain in men's lives: Implications for psychiatrists, psychologists, and other human service providers. In K. Solomon & N. B. Levy (Eds.), *Men in transition: Changing male roles, theory, and therapy* (pp. 5–44). New York: Plenum.

O'Neil, J. M., & Egan, J. (1992). Men's and women's gender role journeys: A metaphor for healing, transition, and transformation. In B. R. Wainrib (Ed.), *Gender issues across the life cycle* (pp. 107–123). New York: Springer Publishing Company.

O'Neil, J. M., & Roberts-Carroll, M. (1988). A gender role journey. *Journal of Counseling and Development*, 67, 193–197.

Osherson, S. (1986). *Finding our fathers: How a man's life is shaped by his relationship with his father*. New York: Fawcett Columbine.

Philpot, C. L., Brooks, G. R., Lusterman, D.-D., & Nutt, R. L. (1997). *Bridging separate gender worlds: Why men and women clash and how therapists can bring them together*. Washington, DC: American Psychological Association.

Pittman, F. (1985). Gender myths: When does gender become pathology? *Family Therapy Networker*, 9, 25–33.

Pittman, F. (1990). The masculine mystique. *Family Therapy Networker*, 14(3), 40–52.

Pittman, F. (1993). *Man enough: Fathers, sons, and the search for masculinity*. New York: Perigree Books.

Pleck, E. H., & Pleck, J. H. (Eds.). (1980). *The American man*. Englewood Cliffs, NJ: Prentice-Hall.

Pleck, J. H. (1981). *The myth of masculinity*. Cambridge, MA: MIT Press.

Pleck, J. H. (1995). The gender role strain paradigm: An update. In R. F. Levant & W. S. Pollack (Eds.), *A new psychology of men* (pp. 11–32). New York: Basic Books.

Pleck, J. H., & Sawyer, J. (1980). *Men and masculinity*. Englewood Cliffs, NJ: Prentice-Hall.

Pollack, W. S. (1995). No man is an island: Toward a new psychoanalytic psychology of men. In R. F. Levant & W. S. Pollack (Eds.), *A new psychology of men* (pp. 33–67). New York: Basic Books.

Pollack, W. S. (1998). *Real boys: Rescuing our sons from the myths of boyhood*. New York: Random House.

Robertson, J., & Fitzgerald, L. F. (1990). The (mis)treatment of men: Effects of client gender role and lifestyle on diagnosis and attribution of pathology. *Journal of Counseling Psychology*, 37, 3–9.

Robertson, J. M., & Fitzgerald, L. F. (1992). Overcoming the masculine mystique: Preferences for alternative forms of assistance among men who avoid counseling. *Journal of Counseling Psychology*, 39, 240–246.

Scher, M. (1981). Men in hiding: A challenge for the counselor. *Personnel and Guidance Journal*, 60, 199–202.

Scher, M., Stevens, M., Good, G. E., & Eichenfield, G. A. (Eds.). (1987). *Handbook of counseling and psychotherapy with men*. Thousand Oaks, CA: Sage.

Tannen, D. (1990). *You just don't understand: Women and men in conversation*. New York: Morrow.

Zilbergeld, B. (1978). *Male sexuality*. New York: Bantam Books.

Zilbergeld, B. (1992). *The new male sexuality: The truth about men, sex, and pleasure*. New York: Bantam Books.

15

QUEER EYE ON THE STRAIGHT GUY: A CASE OF GAY MALE HETEROPHOBIA

DOUGLAS C. HALDEMAN

Lesbian, gay, and bisexual (LGB) clients seek psychotherapy in relatively greater numbers than do heterosexuals (American Psychological Association [APA], 2000). The reasons for this are unclear, but one familiar hypothesis has to do with the added stress and trauma accrued from growing up and living as an LGB man or woman in American culture. Like many gay psychologists, I suppose the earliest influences on my theoretical approach to the practice of psychotherapy were derived from my own experiences as a client. In 1978, as a young high school teacher in California, I had been terrified by the prospect of a ballot initiative to ban gay men and lesbians from teaching in the public schools. As odd as this may seem today, at that point in time, the threat to my livelihood—as well as a significant element of my identity—was real. Therapy helped me frame my anxiety as a normative response to a serious social stressor. Parenthetically, it also led to the recognition that what I liked most about my job as a teacher was the opportunity to interact with my students in a personal way. My decision to become a psychologist was born of my desire to help my community deal with the psychological effects of a hostile social environment, along with my fascination with interpersonal process.

To this day, I see that period in my life as illustrative of how crisis often leads to opportunities for growth. For although I also work with men who identify as heterosexual and bisexual, it is the gay community to which I feel the greatest allegiance—and responsibility. Recent reports suggest that gay men and lesbians may indeed experience more mental health dysfunction than their heterosexual counterparts (Cochran, 2001). It is likely that the effects of social stigma play a significant role in this finding. Difficult as it was to leave the teaching job that I loved, the stress associated with being a gay teacher in the 1970s led me to develop a career that combines clinical, research, and policy work aimed at improving the mental health of lesbian, gay, bisexual, and transgender (LGBT) individuals.

My initial influences as a psychotherapist were a veritable smorgasbord of theoretical approaches. When I was in training, the legendary film *Three Approaches to Psychotherapy* was still in use. I envisioned myself an amalgam of Rogers's compassion, Perls's confrontational skill, and Ellis's rational sensibility as evidenced in the film, providing endless opportunities for growth to a parade of chain-smoking, Gloria-like patients. The theoretical focus of my training program was eclectic–humanistic, which suited me well. I felt free to tailor treatment by combining elements of several different approaches, depending on the needs of the patient.

As I started an internship at an LGBT mental health agency, however, my mentors changed. I never abandoned my interest in clinical theories, but the more work I did with my own community, the more prominent the work of social psychologists came into my therapeutic repertoire. The symptoms common to gay men that had historically been taken as evidence of homosexuality as a mental illness were explained as normative responses to a hostile society. The work of Herek (2000) was particularly pivotal in my understanding of the prevalence of antigay attitudes and behavior, and the effect of such behavior—in the form of harassment, discrimination, and violence—on the lives of gay men and lesbians. Another important theorist was Malyon (1982), who coined the term "homophobia." Although not a "phobia" per se, this phenomenon refers to a set of beliefs and attitudes that cause devaluation and stigmatization of same-sex sexual orientation. Malyon examined the ways in which homophobia leads to a number of antigay behaviors. Of particular clinical use, however, was his concept of how homophobia on the part of gay men can be turned inward on the self, or internalized. *Internalized homophobia* was seen as a central element in depression, anxiety, and low self-esteem on the part of many gay men. Homophobia has since been implicated as a factor that inhibits the ability of heterosexual men to form and sustain close friendships with other men and handicaps them in developing emotionally intimate relationships with women (Brooks, 2002).

In contrast, the parallel concept of *heterophobia* has gone unnoticed in the literature. This is somewhat surprising, because the abuse that many gay men suffer at the hands of heterosexual boys and men, in early life and beyond, is well documented. However, the common fear that many gay and bisexual men harbor of heterosexual men as a result of traumatic experiences has not been studied as such. Heterophobia may manifest as an avoidance of situations in which heterosexual men are present, as stress responses when obliged to interact with heterosexual men, especially in groups, and as self-devaluation and shame (Haldeman, 2002). Additionally, heterophobia may be expressed as a gay man's wholesale devaluation of heterosexual men and heterosexuality in general. Is the heterophobic gay or bisexual man who holds such fear at risk for avoidant relationships with heterosexual men or even for impairment in relationships with other gay men? Given the paucity of research in this area, it is not yet possible to answer these questions. The case described in this chapter, however, begins the clinical discussion of a gay male phenomenon that is more common than one might think.

My own practice with gay men has evolved significantly over the years. In the 22 years that I have been in practice, I have seen significant social change reflected in the lives of my patients. There was a time when coming out was the primary issue that gay men wanted to address in therapy. This included questions of how to integrate an evolving understanding of one's sexual orientation into existing family relationships, how to navigate the social world of gay men, and attempting to understand the implications of coming out in relation to career issues. Although coming-out issues still are commonly presented, current clients—particularly younger men—have typically come out at an earlier age and have already developed a base of support in the gay community as well as in the dominant culture. This is not to suggest that antigay harassment no longer exists or that people are no longer traumatized by antigay attitudes and behaviors. Antigay bias is alive and well in many of society's institutions, including the military and many religious organizations. Furthermore, many jurisdictions offer no civil rights protection to LGBT individuals. Nevertheless, it is my observation that the kinds of issues gay men bring to therapy have evolved such that adjusting to and integrating sexual orientation per se is often no longer the primary concern. What do gay men focus on? Relationship concerns, vocational and career issues, existential issues, health-related concerns, and family problems—not unlike many heterosexual clients, but within a vastly different contextual backdrop.

Society's increased acceptance with respect to LGBT issues is due in part, I think, to the evolution on the part of organized mental health and its research. For over 30 years, psychology and psychiatry have opposed the view of homosexuality as a treatable mental disorder. And although attempts to change homosexual orientation still persist, these ideas are primarily advocated by conservative religious groups and fringe practitioners who cling to long-dismissed concepts of same-sex sexual orientation as the result of arrested psychosexual development. Additionally, it used to be that few clinical training programs in psychology paid any attention to LGBT issues. That, too, has changed; most recent graduates will report having at least some instruction in LGBT issues, as part of a larger diversity curriculum, or even on its own. To supplement training, the APA-adopted *Guidelines for Psychotherapy With Lesbian, Gay, and Bisexual Clients* (APA, 2000) serve as a research-based summary of common themes in psychotherapy with LGB clients. They are not exhaustive, nor are they mandatory; rather, they provide a framework for clinical work that is grounded in the recent literature.

PSYCHOTHERAPY WITH GAY MEN: THE RULES OF THE GAME

In therapeutic style, I consider myself a true eclectic/humanist. I believe in tailoring an individual approach according to the client's unique needs, history, and style. And although there is no one-size-fits-all format for my approach to psychotherapy, there are certain basic rules that I try to follow with all of the gay men in my practice. They are related to the foundational concepts of clinical practice, as well as common sense; I outline them in the following sections.

Safety First

Working with gay men who have been harmed in prior therapy experiences has taught me that safety and respect cannot be overemphasized in psychotherapy. The therapy setting must be a safe place for gay men to speak openly about their life experiences and to expect—at the very least—understanding and empathy in return. Obviously, if the client is met with negative judgment or aversion in response to his issues, there can be no proceeding with an enterprise as risky or intimate as therapy. If a therapist's personal prejudices or religious beliefs are such that it is impossible to validate the normative life experiences of gay and bisexual men, it is the therapist's ethical duty to refer gay clients elsewhere. Too often have the wounds of a hostile society been exacerbated by an incompetent therapist promoting "conversion therapy" to a vulnerable gay client.

Safety, however, extends beyond overt prejudice or homophobia. Some passing familiarity is required with the normative life experiences of gay men to be able to work effectively with them. The aforementioned APA (2000) *Guidelines* serve as a valuable clinical resource, but it is important that the therapist also have some understanding of what it is like to live—and work, and love—as a gay man in this culture. The client should never have to educate the therapist about differences (or similarities) between gay and heterosexual people in social and sexual interaction patterns.

Respect

Respect for the client's life experience is demonstrated by a number of therapist behaviors. Of primary importance is the therapist's ability to understand significant relationships in the client's life. Those individuals identified by the client as "family" may include individuals who are not legally or biologically related. Primary relationships are not to be diminished because they cannot be legally sanctioned. Various concerns specific to gay couples—how to reconcile different degrees of "outness" of the partners, resolving conflicts about how to spend the holidays, how to integrate children into the family structure—cannot be properly understood by even the most well-intentioned therapist who lacks a frame of reference for the normal lives of gay people. It was once thought that gayness foreclosed the possibility of children. For many gay men, however, children are an integral part of the concept of family, hence the rise in gay adoption, surrogacy, and foster parenting.

A corollary process by which heterosexual therapists unintentionally disrespect their gay clients has to do with responding in ways that minimize the client's experience under the guise of normalizing it. I recently saw a new client who had gone to see another therapist in town but had stopped after three sessions. When I asked him why he had stopped, he reported that he had been discussing early life experiences of harassment and abuse by other boys at his school who suspected that he was gay. The therapist was quick to point out that "adolescence is a difficult time" and that "everyone gets abused at some point." Although the therapist had assured the client in the first session that she was perfectly comfortable with his sexual orientation, he concluded: "She didn't 'get' me. It felt as though she was trying too hard to be 'accepting,' which made me feel as though she wasn't accepting at all." A therapist who is quick to draw parallels between gay and heterosexual relationships in an effort to "join" with the gay client may actually distance him by discounting the very real and unique differences that exist.

One overt form of disrespect is the therapist's attribution of a client's problems to his or her sexual orientation. Research has suggested that therapists attempting to steer a distressed, vulnerable client into some form of conversion therapy will frequently draw the link between the client's problems and his sexual orientation (Shidlo & Schroeder, 2002). This study also found that many such therapists also deliberately mislead the client about what being gay is like (i.e., that gay people are all chronically miserable or that they are incapable of forming healthy relationships). Although the current gay marriage movement clearly demonstrates otherwise, these therapist behaviors violate those sections of the APA Ethics Code that pertain to treatment of LGB individuals (APA, 1998).

Investigate

Until American culture is free from sexual prejudice, the therapist should assume that nearly all LGBT clients have experienced some kind of trauma related to harassment, abuse, discrimination, or violence in their lives. Because this is one of the factors that may affect the way in which the client sees the world around him or her, it is particularly important to carefully assess this area. Nothing intrinsic about same-sex sexual orientation predisposes one to mental or emotional dysfunction, but the effects of antigay trauma can have a significant and long-term impact on psychological functioning. If a gay client has experienced chronic depression or anxiety or has become intimacy avoidant in relationships, it is possible that there is unresolved trauma in the client's background.

There are additional factors that both enrich and complicate the lives of many gay men: race/ethnicity, age, and ability status. Sexual orientation is, after all, a continuum that cuts across all aspects of the diversity spectrum. Therefore, the challenges faced by gay men of color are different than those faced by gay White men. Many models of sexual identity development address the importance of connection to the gay community as an individual's gay identity evolves. But for many gay men of color, the gay community can be a difficult place in which to create a home—sometimes while the community of color from which the individual comes has shut him out (Greene, 1994).

Gay men on both ends of the chronological age spectrum face their own particular challenges. For gay youth, the hostility of some school environments can lead to academic problems, drug use, or dropping out of school altogether. Many young gay people, and those who are presumed to be gay, still face harassment on a daily basis. For this reason, a special high school for LGBT youth was opened in New York in 2004. Still, this is not without controversy, given that a sheltered educational environment such as this gives gay youngsters no experience in coping with the mainstream world, nor does it facilitate mainstream educators taking responsibility to ensure that their schools are safe learning environments for all students.

Older LGBT individuals—and in the minds of some, this group includes anyone over the age of 30—struggle against ageism in the gay community. Frequently, elder gay men will report that they feel "invisible" if they go to a gay bar or walk the streets of the gay district in their city. This is the time of life in which all of the normative concerns related to aging—health care, loss of partner and loved ones, financial stability—can be exacerbated by the mainstream culture's general neglect of LGBT people and by the gay community's marginalization of elder persons.

Finally, the construction of a "queer community" locates the resources, businesses and social outlets of importance to LGBT individuals under an efficient umbrella descriptor. The community itself is exceptionally diverse. Given the multiple meanings that identifying terms can have, and the variety these terms are assigned within and between generations, it is always safer to ask clients how they identify themselves rather than to assume. Some younger people may adopt a more generic term, such as "queer," or they may avoid any descriptor at all. Some middle-aged or older people may find the term "queer" offensive. There are common social and political goals among the groups, but striking differences as well. As anyone who has ever worked to organize a Pride Celebration (the annual LGBT event held during the summer in most cities to commemorate the advent of the gay liberation movement) will tell you, the potential for disagreement between these groups is considerable. Bisexual and transgender individuals may feel some degree of overlap with the lesbian and gay communities, but they may also feel that they do not quite fit in. Fortunately, the LGBT communities in most large urban areas are now diverse enough to accommodate most that wish to belong.

Question Your Assumptions

As already noted, the diversity of life experience—social, political, economic, romantic, cultural—among gay men is extraordinary. Anyone who does enough clinical work with gay men will eventually find all preexisting stereotypes shattered. If you believe that LGBT people are all highly social, hypersexual beings, you will encounter what some call the "Home Depot" gays—men whose ultimate ambitions are domestic and sedate. If you believe that LGBT people are politically all Democrats, you will meet a "Log Cabin Republican." And if you think that LGBT people all want to have full marriage rights, you will discover those of us who disavow marriage as heteromimetic.

Some of us have interests more similar to stereotypical heterosexual men than stereotypical gay men. Some of us are indeed style conscious and spend our weekends perpetually redecorating, although at least an equal number spend their weekends watching sports and working on their cars. It is worth remembering that straight or gay, men are all socialized as men in this culture; as a result, normative male alexithymia (Levant, 2001) is a condition common to gay men as well as straight—often driving our partners up a wall. Finally, if you think that the current wave of gay media exposure is something that all LGBT people embrace, you will likely meet someone who fears that the trend toward "mainstreaming gays" threatens our uniqueness, jeopardizes the individuality that we so cherish, and invites dangerous backlash.

A stereotypic view of gay men and gender roles would probably consider the concepts of homosexuality and masculinity to be oxymoronic. In reality, nothing could be further from the truth. Gay men define themselves, in part, by an attraction to other men; thus, some traditional concepts of "masculinity" are revered among gay men. The "clone" movement of the 1970s—in which gay men sought to "hypermasculinize" themselves through developing muscular builds and dressing in blue-collar male attire—is still the dominant style of the gay male community. Our first awareness of homoeroticism is most often directed toward a heterosexual man, and they remain, for better or worse, the "gold standard" in the minds of many gay men.

"Straight acting" or "straight appearing" is still a typical attribute sought in gay personal advertisements. Team sports are among the most popular of social and interest groups in any gay community. Our sense of masculinity is absolutely central in our gay identities (Harris, 1997). When explaining his aversion to effeminate gay men, one client remarked: "I'm gay because I dig *real* men. If I wanted a woman, I'd get a real one." Of course, it has also been observed that a gay man's tolerance of his effeminate gay brothers is actually a barometer of his own security.

THE CASE OF DAN: THERAPY WITH A HETEROPHOBIC GAY MAN

Dan was referred for therapy by his primary care physician, who had been treating him with medication for depression. Dan reported that his principal depressive symptoms were in the realm of social withdrawal and interpersonal anxiety. The medication was helping somewhat, but Dan felt that there were some issues he would like to talk over. When we set up the initial session on the phone, Dan told me that he wanted to confirm that I was indeed gay. There was a time when the majority of gay male clients would first want to determine that I was gay before seeing me for the first time. Up until 20 years ago, given organized mental health's historical pathologizing of homosexuality and support for conversion therapies, mental health practitioners were often seen as doing more harm than good by many gay men. This is no longer necessarily the case, and I was reminded that it had been some time since I had spoken with a prospective client who seemed to require that level of up-front reassurance that I was gay.

I felt an initial sense that this might be someone who had been wounded in the world of men, and I started paying attention to further cues that under the somewhat tough exterior, there lay a foundation of hurt. At the first session, I was struck by the contrast between Dan's outward appearance and his interpersonal demeanor. Like all of the men in my family, including myself, Dan was a tall, blond Scandinavian American. I always find myself feeling a familiar kinship with such men, but at the same time become vigilant so that I do not overidentify with them. And like other men in my family, his interpersonal style was definitely reserved and stoic. During that first session, I noticed my own behavior as well, watching for my tendency to do backflips to draw out the strong, taciturn Nordic guy.

The suspicion that Dan revealed during his intake gave way during the first session to self-doubt and discomfort. His lack of eye contact and quiet, hesitant speech further validated my impression that Dan had been abused, at least socially, and that his mistrust of men in general had possibly contaminated his ability to connect with other gay men as well. I could feel my heart softening. As is my custom, I invited him to ask any questions he had of me. He had a number of them. What was my philosophy of psychotherapy? Did I work mostly with other gay men? What was the nature of the research I had done? What was the focus of my work with the American Psychological Association? Although it is rare in my experience to be interviewed this extensively by a prospective client, I must confess that such conversations have, in the past, elicited some minor impatience on my part. Whatever impatience I might have felt with Dan was mitigated by a genuine feeling of protectiveness that I developed very quickly for him. I resolved that I would address his questions in whatever time and detail he wanted, bearing in mind that above all else, I would not replicate whatever harm he had experienced elsewhere by minimizing or expressing impatience with his concerns. In terms of my background, he seemed most interested in my work as a critic of so-called "reparative" or "conversion" therapies for homosexuality, as well as my practice with survivors of such treatments.

"Have you been involved with conversion therapy yourself?" I asked.

"No. I was just interested in hearing about your work with gay men."

"What about that is important for you?" I asked him.

"Let me put it this way: I don't trust straight people," Dan replied, looking directly at me for the first time. Dan reported that this was why he felt awkward in his current work setting, in which he worked as an executive manager. He also acknowledged that he had a difficult time sustaining intimate relationships with other gay men. And so the facade began to give way to the bedrock of pain underneath. My initial sense of being distanced by Dan's closed demeanor quickly was replaced by wanting to reach out to him. I felt I could genuinely validate his fears about heterosexual men because I had experienced them, too. I had spent a good amount of time in personal therapy working through my fear and distrust of heterosexual men—not just in the overt sense, as bullies, but also in the covert sense—as emotionally distant and unavailable. For a gay man, this is an even greater problem than for a heterosexual man, because it is with other men that we gay men create the nuclei of our romantic and familial lives.

Dan's Early Life

My validation and attempts to connect with Dan seemed to pay off, because in the early sessions he opened up about the emotionally traumatic and distancing experiences he had had with heterosexual men—starting with his own father and brothers. Dan was the middle of three boys, and he recounted a not-unfamiliar scenario for gay men: a distant, rejecting father and an older and a younger brother who were both athletically inclined. Dan, of a more academic and artistic bent, simply did not match what was expected of boys in this family. During an early session, Dan recounted a particularly memorable humiliation in adolescence, bitterly remembering how his father had failed to support him. He mentioned that he could almost recall the day some years earlier, when Dan was 8 years old, that his father withdrew his love and affection. "It was like a switch turned off," he explained.

"Did you love your father?" I asked.

Dan stopped. "Did I what?" Clearly, this caught him off guard.

"Love him. Did you love him?"

Dan's eyes filled with tears as he struggled for words. Mine did too, as I knew what was coming.

"I adored him," Dan finally whispered. "That's what made it hurt so much."

Although I grew up without a father, I spent a great deal of time as a child fantasizing about what it would be like to have one. I could imagine that a perfect dad's sudden emotional withdrawal would be devastating. Dan shared his early memories of a loving, engaged father who would roughhouse, hold him on his lap, and read stories. As he described that coming to a grinding halt, the grief exploded in the room. There was nothing to do but relive it. I rarely touch clients, let alone hold them, but this was a time I made an exception. It felt right in the moment, and in consultation afterward, I became clear that there are times when breaking one's "no physical contact" policy actually reinforces healthy boundaries, because it promotes healing.

Therapy proceeded with Dan's growing insight that he had misinterpreted his father's distance as a withdrawal of love, when in reality it was his father's strategy for toughening his sons. Furthermore, Dan came to recognize that, as children do, he blamed himself for his father's inexplicable distance. Still, this was a case in which insight alone was insufficient. The losses of childhood are not compensable, and Dan would never be able to recreate an emotionally fulfilled early-life connection with his Dad. Nevertheless, in the context of our therapeutic relationship, I felt that a significant element of Dan's healing was coming from my emotional connection with him. I made clear to Dan—through my own emotional response to him—that I was moved by his grief and that I could certainly understand some of his fears about straight men. As I got to know him better, I came to recognize that resolving his fears about heterosexual men and addressing intimacy concerns with other gay men was accomplished in part by my connection with him. Dan could use the trust and self-confidence he was developing in our relationship and apply it elsewhere.

In retrospect, I think that sharing my own feelings with Dan in response to his experiences was more valuable than any insights I had to offer. He started relating to me more openly and acknowledged that his core fears of straight men were deep and tied up with a sense of shame. Dan's stories of abuse at the hands of heterosexual men and boys were numerous and still painful. He was able to neutralize some of the shame he felt in recounting these events, which he had not previously shared with anyone. There was value for Dan in telling the truth on two counts: First, it helped him to resolve the residual grief and anger that he had been carrying, and second, he came to understand that what had happened to him was not his fault.

Connecting the Past and the Present

With Dan, as with many gay clients recovering from emotional neglect, I frequently reinforced the notion that the past must be understood so that it does not continue to influence the present. Decisions made about men out of self-protection in early life would inhibit adult friendships or romantic relationships with other men. I observed one day that our work seemed to have focused almost exclusively on his past, so I asked Dan if he was ready to connect his history to his present-day life.

"Well, I've actually been talking more to my father. And he always thought that I was the one who rejected him!" Dan explained, as he reported that the two of them were starting to enjoy a deeper relationship after years of superficiality.

I felt genuinely happy about that, and told him so. Wanting to encourage a focus on Dan's intimacy issues, I asked: "Do you think this is having an effect on your relationships with your friends? Or with romantic partners?"

From the length of the pause, I realized that I had struck a nerve. "Well, that's probably something I need to talk about," he finally admitted, with all the enthusiasm of someone contemplating a root canal.

"So let's talk," I said gently. "What's going on in that department?"

"Not much," he said. Another pause. This was going to be tough. I noticed that what I wanted to do was leap in and say, "Why wouldn't you be dating? I'd think that guys would be lined up waiting to go out with you." Instead, I reassured him that whatever he was doing—or not doing—was okay with me.

Dan exhaled. "See, I don't want you to think I'm not very good at 'being gay.' And I do date—just not for very long." I was correct in attributing some of Dan's reticence to a transferential concern that he would disappoint me. Although I did not want to linger on this point, given that there was more crucial intimacy-oriented work to be done, I recognized that we needed to address this before we could go further. "Look," I said, "you have made it with me 100%. Who you are—as a man, as a gay man, is exactly who you need to be." I could literally feel the fondness and respect I had for him as I said these words. "What we need to focus on is changing your behavior and your outlook—on men and on yourself—so that your life is in line with your goals."

From his subsequent description, it appeared that there were many other men who thought Dan was wonderful, too. He had no trouble getting dates. Dan's ability to sustain romantic relationships, however, was limited. Typically, after several weeks, Dan would begin to find flaws in his boyfriends.

And although they were sometimes magnifications of inconsequential is-sues, they were often the result of Dan's having selected someone with whom he had little in common other than sexual attraction. As we began work on Dan's intimacy issues in earnest, he would frequently ask my advice about his choices or his behavior. This was tricky, because I realized that he was enter-ing a new stage of dependency in his relationship with me, and I wanted to adhere to my policy of not "holding back" with him. However, I wanted him to be able to trust his own judgment, hopefully having internalized my trust of him.

Growth and Change

For over a year, Dan struggled with three parallel tracks: family rela-tionships, dating relationships, and work relationships. Dan's view of men in general gradually started to evolve from that of adversary to group member. No single relationship was more responsible for this than was Dan's relation-ship with his father. The two became good friends, and the resulting change in Dan's level of self-confidence was impressive. His father had apparently grown over the years as well and he no longer felt that masculinity and ex-pressing affection were mutually exclusive. Dan reported that his father's pride and love were evident, and although this did not change the past, it made it far easier for Dan to resolve the emotional trauma that had been associated with it.

In his youth, the relationship Dan had with his older brother was far more problematic than that with his younger brother. This brother had teased Dan, made a point of excluding him socially, and generally behaved cruelly to Dan at every opportunity. In adulthood, Dan saw this brother primarily at family gatherings and holidays. Several years into treatment, Dan decided to confront his brother about the abuse as an initial step in either reconstruct-ing an adult relationship with him and his family or letting go of the rela-tionship altogether. This process went well and resulted in a strong bond developing between Dan and his older brother, his wife, and their two chil-dren. In fact, Dan became quite involved in their lives, taking vacations with them and assuming an active role as "uncle" to the children.

Ironically, it was Dan's younger brother who had in childhood been the least difficult of all of his family members, save perhaps Dan's passive, with-drawn mother. In adulthood, however, this brother had become a "born-again" Christian. Although he and his wife professed to "love" Dan, they also made it clear that they could not "accept his lifestyle." When ultimately Dan developed a long-term relationship, this brother and his wife declined to attend family events where Dan and his partner would be present. To their credit, the family—led by Dan's father—communicated to the youngest brother that they would be missed but that it was their choice, based on their rigidity. Dan's eyes sparkled with tears as he related this to me—not from the standpoint of a competitive sibling, but from the very clear show of support on the part of his father.

Dan's success in dating progressed in direct correlation to his self-confidence. We think of *heterophobia* as a contaminant in social relationships between gay and straight men, but there is reason to suspect that it may also affect relationships that gay men have with other gay men—particularly intimate relationships. Dan's fear of heterosexual men was so strong it generalized to other gay men. It also polluted his self-concept. Given that its origins were in Dan's early life, he convinced himself that if other men knew what he was really like, they would not want to be involved with him. Hence the pattern of 2-week relationships, necessitating an end to the relationship before too much was revealed. As he solidified his relationship with himself, his fear of other men diminished. Not only was he able to date men for longer than 2 weeks, he was more focused on dating men that could be appropriate partners in terms of his interests. After a year of dating, Dan met a man that seemed to be different from anyone else. After having dated for 6 months, Dan announced one day, "I'm in love!" I remarked that through 3 years of therapy, I had seen many emotions—but never such joy. The two had been together for 2.5 years at the end of Dan's therapy, had purchased a home, and were discussing adopting a child.

Dan initially came to therapy to address issues of heterophobia with coworkers. There is a phenomenon I have observed among some gay men that I refer to as "playground ghosts." These are the memories of bullies who engaged in name calling, harassment, physical violence and other threatening behavior, generating fright and shame in the developing psyche of the pregay youngster or adolescent. Years later, it is remarkable how quickly straight men—particularly in groups—can become playground ghosts in the minds of some heterophobic gay men. Dan's work environment was populated with many such ghosts, and he experienced daily anxiety that only escalated as he advanced in his company. As his self-confidence increased through the course of therapy, his fear of male coworkers diminished greatly. He stopped distorting his view of the people with whom he worked, many of whom were reasonable, friendly people whose behavior patterns bore no resemblance to his earlier social trauma. Dan's worry about how he was being perceived at work diminished as well. Finally, when he was obliged to interact with those of his coworkers who told sexist jokes or engaged in other behaviors that made him uncomfortable, he was able to use more effective coping strategies (stay on point, don't attempt to reinforce in an effort to "play along") and ceased feeling embarrassed that he was not "one of the guys."

What were the curative elements in Dan's treatment? There were several: First, it was necessary to exhume some of his early life history to understand what had caused him to develop such strong avoidance reactions toward other men. It was then important for Dan to normalize these responses but to recognize that such emotional protection is no longer necessary—in fact, has negative consequences for his social and romantic relationships. Desensitization and coping strategies were part of his program to develop self-confidence so that he could interact socially with other men. Forgiving his father proved central in Dan's evolving competence in relating to other men. All of these factors helped Dan neutralize much of his heterophobia and to feel more relaxed in the company of other men. It is especially crucial for gay men to feel comfortable with other men, because as Dan's history demonstrated, not only social relationships but also romantic relationships can be disrupted by heterophobia.

Probably the most significant factor in Dan's treatment was the emotionally corrective experiences he had as the result of the therapeutic relationship. Over time, a strong attachment grew between us, such that he was able to truly internalize my support and positive regard for him. More than anything else, this is what he was able to use as an internal frame of reference to transform his relationship with himself. This is why termination with Dan was so emotional. We recognized that, as time went on, more and more of our sessions focused on acknowledging the significant progress Dan had made at work, in his primary relationship, and with his family. After several months of this, we agreed to begin a termination schedule of meeting every other week for several months, then monthly for four sessions, culminating with a termination.

Our termination session was marked by tears on both sides of the relationship. Dan expressed his gratitude for a therapeutic process that had spanned over 5 years. He observed that his increased comfort at work and his relationship with his partner were due to being able to see himself differently. Above all, he stated, "It was you that made the difference. I felt that if you could care for me, knowing what you knew about me, then I could care for myself." For my part, I acknowledged the tremendous affection that I came to feel for Dan. This was partly because I have struggled with heterophobia myself and I felt compassion for him; partly because he reminded me of a younger brother, and I wanted to take care of him; but mostly, because I saw him as a remarkable man, and I felt that he—and others—deserved to have that experience of him as well. In working with Dan, I also grew in the therapeutic process—and came to place a greater value on my own emotional responses to the client.

Heterophobia is a normative consequence of growing up gay in this culture. It is not to be denied, for if it is, its potentially harmful effects cannot be addressed. Nor is it to be enshrined and preserved, for it is limiting and impractical for gay men to attempt to avoid heterosexual people altogether. Rather, it is to be examined, neutralized, and overcome. The ability for gay men to face down the ghosts of the bullies lurking in the schoolyard is the gateway to improved self-confidence, better social relationships with straight men, and more intimate connections with other gay men. This case describes but one variation on this theme. Clearly, the need for research in this area, as well as for more clinical description, is significant.

QUESTIONS FROM THE EDITORS

1. What types of gender-based stereotypes were you aware of in counseling this client? How did that impact your therapy with this client?

The stereotypes that were evident in counseling with Dan were based on his sexual orientation as well as on his gender. As a gender-atypical young-ster, this client experienced a range of threatening behaviors on the part of other boys: verbal harassment, social ostracization, and even physical vio-lence. As a result, Dan developed highly negative views of straight boys in his peer group that he generalized to all heterosexual males. These views were not challenged as he entered adulthood. One of the primary tasks of therapy involved deconstructing this stereotype so that he could relate to heterosexual men as unique individuals, rather than as part of a hostile mob. His views of other gay men were far less negative, but even with them Dan evidenced a reserve that was especially apparent in his intimate relation-ships. Overcoming his fear of men in general enabled him to develop a truly loving relationship with another man.

2. How did your own gender role issues influence your work with the client?

Being gay myself, I understand the challenge that having a somewhat gender-atypical presentation can present—especially for youth. Having been targeted for abuse in my youth by bullies is an experience that I shared with Dan. At the same time, being gay gives gay men the freedom from traditional gender role expectations. Gay men can understand, for example, that it is permissible to show emotion and that achievements are not the only mea-sures of self-worth. In coming out as gay, we have already broken the primary gender role expectation; the rest is up to us in terms of identity construction. Therefore, although it is difficult to thrive lacking the same support our het-erosexual brothers receive, there is also great joy in knowing that we have the freedom to identify and to relate to one another as we choose.

3. Looking back on this case, knowing what you know now, would you change the way you worked with this client?

In retrospect, given the importance of my personal connection with Dan, I would have "opened up" to him a bit sooner. By this, I do not neces-sarily mean that I would have shared more elements of my own life but that I would have more freely shared my emotional responses to him. It was my emotional connection with Dan that in the end proved most helpful in his healing.

4. You mention that gay men share many similarities with heterosexual men in terms of masculinity socialization. Can you expand on this idea and how masculinity and gay identity combine?

All men—gay and straight—are socialized similarly in this culture. Gender role expectations can provide a significant level of stress for all males, gay and straight. Conforming to socially constructed expectations of "toughness" and lack of emotionality can be particularly challenging for gay men or for boys who later come to identify as such. At the same time, it is to other men that we are romantically attracted. More often than not, as previously mentioned, it is the "hypermasculine ideal" that is celebrated in the gay community. What all of this means is that it is essential for gay men to examine their own feelings about, and experiences of, men in general. As Dan's case illustrates, it is possible for heterophobic responses learned from interactions with heterosexual men to be generalized to other gay men, inhibiting intimate relationships. These issues can be submerged away from awareness and can generate automatic avoidant responses. As therapy may help some gay men address and overcome their heterophobia, therapists need to develop an awareness of the phenomenon itself, encouraging research and the development of treatment strategies.

SUGGESTED RESOURCES

D'Augelli, A., & Patterson, C. (Eds.). (1995). *Lesbian, gay, and bisexual identities over the lifespan.* New York: Oxford Press.

Division 44/CLGBC Joint Task Force on Professional Practice Guidelines With Lesbian, Gay, and Bisexual Clients. (2000). Guidelines for psychotherapy with lesbian, gay, and bisexual clients. *American Psychologist, 55,* 1409–1421.

Garnets, L., & Kimmel, D. (Eds.). (2003). *Psychological perspectives on lesbian, gay, and bisexual experiences* (2nd ed.). New York: Harper & Row.

Haldeman, D. C. (2001). Psychotherapy with gay and bisexual men. In G. R. Brooks & G. E. Good (Eds.), *The new handbook of psychotherapy and counseling with men: A comprehensive guide to settings, problems, and treatment approaches* (Vol. 2, pp. 796–815). San Francisco: Jossey-Bass.

Haldeman, D. C., & Brooks, G. R. (2002, Winter). Critical dialogues between gay and straight men [Special edition]. *Society for the Psychological Study of Men and Masculinity Bulletin, 7,* 6, 8.

Haldeman, D. C., & Buhrke, R. (2003). Under a rainbow flag: The diversity of sexual orientation. In J. Robinson & L. James (Eds.), *The tapestry of human diversity* (pp. 145–156). New York: Oxford University Press.

Perez, R., DeBord, K., & Bieschke, K. (Eds.). (2000). *Handbook of counseling and psychotherapy with lesbian, gay, and bisexual clients.* Washington, DC: American Psychological Association.

REFERENCES

American Psychological Association. (1998). Appropriate therapeutic responses to sexual orientation. *American Psychologist, 53*, 934–935.

American Psychological Association. (2000). Guidelines for psychotherapy with lesbian, gay, and bisexual clients. *American Psychologist, 55*, 1440–1451.

Brooks, G. R. (2002). Homophobia, heterophobia: Reflections upon gay–straight dialogue. *Society for the Psychological Study of Men and Masculinity Bulletin, 7*, 3–4.

Cochran, S. (2001). Emerging issues in research on lesbians' and gay men's mental health: Does sexual orientation really matter? *American Psychologist, 56*, 931–947.

Greene, B. (1994). Ethnic minority lesbians and gay men: Mental health and treatment issues. *Journal of Consulting and Clinical Psychology, 62*, 243–251.

Haldeman, D. C. (2002). Don't come any closer: How heterophobia affects friendships and intimate relationships for gay men. *Society for the Psychological Study of Men and Masculinity Bulletin, 7*, 2–3.

Harris, D. (1997). *The rise and fall of gay culture.* New York: Ballantine Books.

Herek, G. (2000). Sexual prejudice and gender: Do heterosexuals' attitudes toward gay men and lesbians differ? *Journal of Social Issues, 56*, 251–256.

Levant, R. F. (2001). Desperately seeking language: Understanding, assessing and treating normative male alexithymia. In G. R. Brooks & G. E. Good (Eds.), *The new handbook of psychotherapy and counseling with men: A comprehensive guide to settings, problems, and treatment approaches* (Vol. 1, pp. 424–443). San Francisco: Jossey-Bass.

Malyon, A. (1982). Psychotherapeutic implications of internalized homophobia in gay men. In J. Gonsiorek (Ed.), *Homosexuality and psychotherapy: A practitioner's handbook of affirmative models* (pp. 59–69). New York: Haworth Press.

Shidlo, A., & Schroeder, M. (2002). Changing sexual orientation: A consumers' report. *Professional Psychology: Research and Practice, 33*, 249–259.

16

A MAN WITH A "WOMAN'S PROBLEM": MALE GENDER AND EATING DISORDERS

REBEKAH SMART

My interests in gender theory, feminist theory, and multicultural counseling have led me to focus on the treatment of eating disorders and body image disturbance. Bordo's (1993) *Unbearable Weight: Feminism, Western Culture, and the Body* was an early, exciting influence, as were works by Peters and Fallon (1994), Striegel-Moore (1995), and others. Working with men and women with eating disorders has opened for me an enduring and fascinating perspective on gender identity and its sociocultural influences. It has also helped me to become a more well-rounded clinician, forced to stretch within and beyond a cultural lens to include a multidimensional perspective on people and treatment. I am grateful for the training opportunities I have had with eating-disorder experts such as Carolyn Costin, Michael Strober, and David Garner.

As a female therapist, I have typically been more drawn to examining the experience of women than of men; however, it is of course impossible to study one gender without considering the other, and working with men has become an equally compelling interest and an invaluable source of growth for me. I have had the privilege of working with Mark Stevens for a number of years and have also been fortunate to collaborate therapeutically with a number of men in both university settings and private practice. Two compilations on a variety of men's issues have been very helpful: *Men's Lives* (Kimmel & Messner, 1992) and the *Handbook of Counseling and Psychotherapy With Men* (Scher, Stevens, Good, & Eichenfield, 1987). In my view, many men who present for therapy are dealing, on some level, with the expectations they and others have of them as representatives of their gender. Most men, I find, struggle against the confines of masculine socialization without necessarily being aware of it. They suffer from trying to handle crises alone; from suppressing feelings; from competing, willingly or otherwise, with other men; from needing to be good providers; and from not understanding how to communicate more effectively with others. Many men struggle to not show emotions or behaviors that would suggest they were weak or feminine.

These "rules" of masculinity exert especially painful consequences on men who romantically and sexually love other men. Gay and bisexual men are often ridiculed as being feminine (whether they exhibit stereotypically feminine traits or not), perhaps because among other reasons, they are viewed as accepting a subordinate position to other men. Many men, especially those of middle-class, European American backgrounds, have been raised with all the privileges and expectations of the dominant culture, while they must negotiate the prejudices, internal and external, inflicted on men who do not conform to those expectations. Working with gay and bisexual men has been especially rewarding to me, from a gender standpoint, given that homophobia is one of the most powerful means of ensuring gender conformity from both sexes. As long as men are supposed to be "masculine" and women are supposed to be "feminine," many people will suffer in their attempts to conform. A homophobic society ensures that men, gay or straight, will try to act "like men." In my view, masculinity and femininity are universal organizing concepts, rather than traits that must directly fit the sex of a person.

The vast majority of research on eating disorders relates to women. A few authors have written about the problem in men (e.g., Anderson, 1992; Anderson, Cohn, & Holbrook, 2000), but the literature is still quite limited. My experience with men experiencing an eating disorder is that much of what is known about treating women also applies to men. However, special attention must be given to the fact that a man has had a different gender socialization and experience and may find himself in the throes of something that is considered in the broader culture to be a "woman's disease." In light of the previously mentioned fear of being feminine, this can be especially threatening. The fact that gay and bisexual men appear to be susceptible to some of the same cultural pressures as women is of course an additional, compelling aspect of the treatment. Young gay men are often in a similar predicament as are straight women: performing for the affections of men, catering to the desires of the socially dominant gender. A number of studies purport that homosexuality is a risk factor in itself for body image problems and eating disorders in men (e.g., Russell & Keel, 2001), although questions remain as to what is in fact most salient about gay men's vulnerability to body and eating problems. A significant segment of gay culture promotes an intense focus on the youth and beauty of its men, with an emphasis on building muscle (Wood, 2004). Wood (2004) states that the two central explanations for this offered in the literature are objectification (like heterosexual women, gay men desire to be attractive to men) and gender nonconformity (as a result of what are perceived to be effeminate traits, gay men desire to be more stereotypically masculine). Many authors also site the HIV/AIDS epidemic, with the painful occurrence of older, wasting men as strong reinforcements for the value of healthy-looking, muscular, young, hairless bodies (Pope, Phillips, & Olivardia, 2000).

I conceptualize client issues from a biopsychosocial framework and use an interpersonal clinical model with most clients. This is essentially an integrative perspective, drawing on attachment theory, relational psychodynamic theory, and family systems theory (e.g., Wachtel, 1993), with a liberal focus on sociocultural influences and work in the here and now. Interpersonal therapy, at its foundation, puts relationships as the primary source of client well-being or lack thereof, and much of the therapeutic focus is on exploring the client's relational history and patterns and then helping the client improve current relationships. By extension, the relationship with the therapist is crucial. My preferred way of working is to use myself and what happens between the client and me in an open way to help both of us learn about the client's relationship to others. This offers a pathway to healing, resolving conflict, and changing behavior.

My work with eating disorders has convinced me of the need for the therapist to be active and assertive at times—more so than with most other issues—and forced me to be, above all, flexible. Wachtel (1993) asserted that psychodynamic therapy can be integrated with cognitive–behavioral and behavioral therapy, and the integration of this concept has freed me considerably in my work. According to Wachtel, many client problems originate early in life but are maintained through cyclical interpersonal patterns created in the present. With this in mind, intervention can often be focused on the present and a number of strategies can be used. This has helped me to expand my approach while feeling theoretically grounded.

In regard to eating disorders treatment, Anderson (1992) recommended a kind of stepped, integrated approach, beginning with psychoeducation, behavioral, and cognitive–behavioral therapy, followed by psychodynamic and existential therapy. Because the client that I am discussing in this chapter presented with an eating disorder, my work with him was even more multidimensional than my basic clinical orientation. In general, depending on the nature of the person and the eating disorder, the avenues of treatment I explore may include an integrated or stepped variety of therapeutic approaches, as well as multidimensional care in collaboration with physicians, dietitians, and psychiatrists. Anyone with an eating disorder should be monitored medically by a physician regularly to assess cardiac and electrolyte problems and more. I find that a good dietitian can be very helpful because he or she can do much of the psychoeducational and behavioral work, leaving me to focus more interpersonally. Many clients are significantly helped by learning some things about nutrition and metabolism. Not only is a team approach often optimal and ethically important, I find that the support that comes with collaborating with other professionals helps me to not become too attached to a client giving up his symptoms right away. The therapist's well-meaning desire for the client to stop starving or vomiting, for example, can drive clients away because it reinforces the client's need to maintain control, thereby increasing the need to maintain the behavior.

A final few thoughts on my methodology regarding eating disorders: In addition to feminist therapeutic strategies (e.g., Fallon, Katzman, & Wooley, 1994), I have found Connors's (1996), Costin's (1999), and Linehan's (1997) work to be exceedingly helpful and practical. Linehan's (1997) recommendation that therapists working with patients diagnosed with borderline personality disorder approach them with an attitude of complete acceptance, while simultaneously helping the clients to see that their behavior has to change, is applicable to people with potentially life-threatening eating disorders as well. This simple formulation has guided me and helped me maintain a consistent and compassionate stance with clients with eating disorder, while minimizing the potential for colluding with the illness. Costin's (1999) delineation of the adaptive functions of eating disorders has been essential in helping me assist clients to relinquish their unhealthy behaviors in favor of healthier ones. The assumption here is that the eating disorder serves a purpose, whether it helps to avoid intimacy, provides structure and predictability, induces a means of numbing or distraction, allows for the discharge of tension and anger, or more. Beginning with the assumption that it is adaptive helps to create and maintain a respectful and empathic stance even when challenging the client to change, and it helps the client to view himself or herself in a new way. Connors's (1996) conceptualization of affect regulation in eating disorders has also been invaluable, and like Costin, she asserts that the eating disorder is adaptive, but further asserts that it is often adaptive specifically in its ability to regulate affect. People with eating disorders often cannot tolerate what comes up for them emotionally if they resist their behaviors; exploring this provides a guide to treatment.

My approach with most men in therapy is to be fairly neutral, to listen carefully, to avoid making broad assertions while staying interactive, and to project warmth but without appearing overly sympathetic (at least initially). In most cases this seems to help the client feel as if I will understand him emotionally and will also be strong enough (or even smart enough) to deal effectively with him. These are not exactly "rules" for working with men, but they are guidelines drawn from my own personality that seem to put most men at ease and give them confidence in both the therapist and the process of therapy. I am aware of what I might portray or model as a woman when seeing clients. I have to acknowledge that I appear as a fairly feminine woman and am perceived as small in size and nonathletic (true) and that these perceptions no doubt play into client transference, particularly around body issues but also around gendered issues of assertiveness, intelligence, and so on. Some male clients prefer to see a female therapist, at least initially, and this is likely due to believing that women will be more nurturing and accepting than men. So the fact that I am a small, feminine woman tends to provide many men with a sense of immediate comfort. I, however, have a different sense of myself internally: I am easily empathic but I also feel quite assertive, and in spite of my ready access to my own emotional states, I often gravitate toward intellectualization. I believe I project a reasonably serious and calm nature, together with a sense of humor, and a strong capacity for empathy. I think that over the years I have unconsciously capitalized on the initial transference to me as a nurturer and have then been able to use that to find a way to challenge and confront male clients in a way they can respect and absorb.

Another central aspect of the therapist in the room with clients who struggle with body image and eating disorders is the therapist's body and look. People with eating disorders are often so self-critical about their appearance that they tend to examine others in the same way (which in turn feeds their belief that others view them in this hypercritical way). My assumption with these clients is that they are quite aware of me physically. They wonder why I do this work, what my connection to it is, and I am quite convinced, are able to track my own minor weight fluctuations. For example, although I consider myself to be at a normal-to-thin weight, some clients have said they see me as having a "perfect" body or a body that obviously has no problems; others have viewed me as overweight or at a weight they could not possibly tolerate. Processing these issues, when possible, is helpful. This has tended to play out more overtly with female clients who may feel a more direct comparison with me. My male clients with eating disorders seem less concerned with me in this way, although I also think I have probably not been as open about processing that with men. I think many of the men are equally preoccupied, but the transference to me as a therapist is different.

THERAPY WITH SCOTT

The following case is based on my work with a client referred to my private practice, although for purposes of privacy and confidentiality I have changed certain identifying traits and have also incorporated elements of two other cases.

The Presenting Problem

Scott was a 22-year-old European American man, soon to graduate from a small college in Southern California, with a degree in French. We met to discuss working together. He was highly anxious, fidgety, had difficulty talking, and was ambivalent, to say the least, about therapy. He planned to use his own, limited funds to pay for treatment, as he did not want his parents to know he was seeking help and so did not want to use insurance. He was planning a move out of state at the end of the summer, so therapy was destined to be short term—approximately 4 months—in nature.

Scott appeared very thin when we met for the first time, as well as anxious and depressed. He opened by saying, "I have a problem with food." I found him immediately likeable and my reaction here, as it often is with people first admitting eating problems, was one of anticipation and energy: I wanted to use myself to the best possible effect to capitalize on the courage that had brought him in. My sense was that he felt so much shame, clearly about the eating problem, but probably about other things too. I responded calmly and empathically, and with no surprise to what he revealed. This seemed to settle him enough to proceed. He explained that the problem had begun about a year previously, when he took a class in optimal fitness for men at a local gym. He had lost about 25 pounds and had begun to exercise obsessively. Now he was feeling irritable and apathetic, with a loss of interest in nearly everything that used to make him happy. Concentration and focus on his schoolwork had been affected and procrastination was a constant problem. As Scott became somewhat more comfortable, he revealed that he worried obsessively about his body, specifically about issues of ageing, amount of body hair, thinness, and physical fitness. He was fidgeting a great deal, was clearly nervous, and I wondered whether he would tell me he was gay. Eventually he stated, "I don't know if I'll ever find love." He explained that he liked men but was not sure about his sexuality and preferred not to identify as gay. "Okay," I said, "What's happened in your love life so far?" He laughed a little and said, "Not a lot," and this was part of the problem. Recently, he had begun to binge, and this is what had driven him to what he considered the desperate act of seeking therapy. Bingeing occurred at least once a day, on large amounts and odd combinations of food. He was exercising and occasionally vomiting to compensate for the binges. Vomiting was an arduous act for him (and was not yet habitual), and the exercise was exhausting, but it was the bingeing that caused the most distress. His own theory was that he might be bingeing and purging in response to stress, as a technique of procrastination, and as a substitute for love.

Scott's History

Scott could not recall much of his childhood initially; it seemed vaguely "okay" to him, without significant trauma. He had been born and raised in Albuquerque, New Mexico. He was the middle child of three, and the only son. The family was of Protestant, European descent; middle class; and educated. His father was a successful businessman and mostly disengaged from family life. His mother was an attorney and worked part time. All three children knew their parents' marriage was not a happy one and wondered whether they would divorce. Scott did not recall yelling or fighting; anger and strain between the parents were felt rather than seen or heard. Scott had ambivalent feelings about his mother; he was closer to her than to his dad, but he also found her more threatening, perceiving her as smart and strong but also as strict and critical. He remembered being anxious as a child but did not know why, and he had occasional trouble sleeping. He had some ritualized obsessive–compulsive behaviors when he was 10 or 11, but they went away in time. He was somewhat overweight as a child, and he remembered being teased about that. When he entered puberty he felt highly self-conscious and out of step with his peers in many ways, but he could not really recall why this was. He said he felt an attraction to other boys quite early. He had two fleeting erotic encounters with another boy, kissing in the locker room after basketball practice, which he described as intense, intoxicating experiences, which were ignored by both participants afterward. As he came into fuller adolescence, his older sister became pregnant and barely completed high school, something that affected his mother greatly. The family destabilized more, and the younger sister got into drugs. Scott, however, was determined to make up for his siblings' missteps, and began to excel academically, athletically, and socially. He had slimmed down and felt empowered by his sports prowess. He became increasingly determined to make both parents proud and be perceived as the perfect son. Among other things, this meant disguising his emerging sexuality.

Initially, Scott had continued to excel in college. He had struggled to maintain good grades and focus on a career path that might allow him to work overseas. However, his parents' marriage worsened, he lost touch with friends from home, he was not close to either sister, and he was increasingly lonely at school. He had a lot of acquaintances to socialize with, and people seemed to be interested in him, but he did not feel close to anyone. He had become more open about his attraction to men, and classmates and acquaintances did not seem to have a problem with this; he had also become more honest about his sexuality with young women who were interested in him. He found himself having excruciating crushes on straight guys, which left him feeling hopeless about love and sex. He had one sexual experience, with a man he met in a bar. He was excited by that but was scared and confused as to how to establish a relationship that might be more enduring. He had recently let his mother know that he was starting to identify as gay, and she had responded somewhat supportively.

Conceptualization and Treatment Plan

My working conceptualization was along the following lines: Scott was suffering from an anxiety disorder, not otherwise specified (NOS; and possible obsessive–compulsive disorder), an eating disorder NOS (a *Diagnostic and Statistical Manual of Mental Disorders* [4th ed.; American Psychiatric Association, 1994] diagnosis of anorexia was difficult because of a lack of specific guidelines for men; additionally, Scott exhibited both anorexic and bulimic symptoms), depression NOS, and possible attention-deficit/hyperactivity disorder. Scott had long-standing anxiety issues, most probably due to family dynamics (e.g., attachment to both parents, sibling stress, parental discord); biological predisposing factors (early overweight, possible predispositions to anxiety and eating problems); and masculine–homophobic socialization (years of feeling different than the prevailing social norm, and the subsequent lack of support for learning about love and connection to other men; the overwhelming, compensatory desire to be "manly"). The family was supportive to a degree (and ultimately fairly accepting of Scott), but non-emotional. Culturally, they had an Anglo American style of repression of overt emotion, extreme reliance on self, and a strong Puritan work ethic. Scott's adaptive strategies included obsessive thoughts and behaviors and a heavy reliance on perfectionism and the pleasing of others, to the point of having little sense of self. Internalized homophobia and sexual identity issues were paramount; cultural emphasis on looks (specifically, gay culture, but dominant culture as well) as a means to power, happiness, love, and sex was instrumental to the development of his eating disorder. In addition, the "failures," as he saw them, at partnering, as well as the fitness class itself, were precipitating factors to the eating disorder and depression. My working hypothesis was that the central adaptive function of the eating disorder behavior was to manage anxiety, particularly around his sexuality and relationships.

The First Stage

My first objectives with anyone with significant weight or eating problems are to establish and maintain rapport, inspire motivation for treatment, and ensure physical (medical) safety. This requires, on the part of the therapist, a somewhat delicate balance of both authoritativeness and attention—that is, attention to the common (and in this case, critical) dynamic of helping the client begin to define his own identity and values, essentially, to find his own voice. Given the short-term nature of the proposed treatment and my own interpersonal bias, my inclination was to explore and acknowledge

Scott's early history but to focus more on the present interpersonal and identity issues.

Scott and I had a fairly immediate rapport. He responded well to my opening style of gathering information, providing information, and reacting without judgment to what he revealed. Exploring the eating behaviors helped to build the rapport because he could tell through my questions that I understood at least something about his experience: "So would you eat the three pizzas by yourself and hide it, or would you kind of block others out of your view and go ahead and eat them in the restaurant?"; "Vomiting sometimes provides a sense of relief and relaxation"; "It's almost like a switch goes off and there's no turning back when you get the idea to binge" Scott would look at me somewhat incredulously, saying, "Yes! That's what it's like."

It did, however, require a number of sessions before I felt that I was beginning to understand more about his internal experience. Scott presented in a chaotic manner—thoughts flying, attention wavering, emotions flowing that were hard to define—and he seemed to both reveal and conceal a lot simultaneously. He censored himself and lost his train of thought frequently. He apologized for much of what he expressed. He was extremely deferential with me. I realized that many principles of feminist therapy (egalitarianism, empowerment) would not be inappropriate here. Scott was a man who did not internally experience many of the privileges routinely assumed by men. I remember also deliberately taking some quiet, deep breaths; I found him endearing but also somewhat overwhelming. I could feel an uncommon (for me) urge to "mother" him, given his deferential, little-boy quality. It seemed important to resist this, as he needed very much to be treated as an equal adult.

It seemed clear that Scott wanted to deal with romantic and sexual issues, but was unable to do so right away. In examining the precipitating factor to the eating disorder—the exercise class—it appeared evident that the culture of the class itself was a rather intense, hypermasculine environment in which the men competed to demonstrate strength, control, and dominance. I wondered whether the class had tapped into Scott's inclination for perfectionism and work ethic and whether it had provided an avenue of distraction for unwanted emotions (anger, sadness, sexual yearnings that he felt he could not express). In any case, he was not ready to talk more about it at the time. My stance was to be calm and empathic and to try to let him know through my questions and responses that I was not coming to any hasty conclusions about who he was. I reflected on much of what he said, while adding the attraction component he was not yet so able to articulate (e.g., "Being around all these men, some of whom you might have been attracted to, must have been kind of confusing and stimulating at the same time").

Responding actively to the health aspects of the eating disorder, in a nonjudgmental but straightforward manner, was also necessary. I could only estimate what his weight was, and he himself was unsure, because he had lost a lot of weight but then had been bingeing recently. I explained in a matter-of-fact way that he had been starving himself for some time, which would set him up physically and emotionally for bingeing, which in turn would increase the desire to purge. Additionally, this had likely affected his mood, hampered his ability to regulate his mood, and increased any tendency he had to engage in obsessive thoughts and behaviors. It was important that he consult with a medical doctor and a dietitian to be stable and safe physically, so that we could focus our energies on the interpersonal underpinnings of his current problems. (I was also concerned about his depression and believed that his mood might to some degree stabilize as his weight did.) His college had a health center where he could see a doctor, which he agreed to do, but it did not provide a dietitian, and the cost of seeing one privately was of concern for him. Early psychoeducation by the medical doctor about the effects of vomiting on his teeth proved to be effective in helping him resist making that an entrenched physical and emotional habit; limiting purging through exercise was more difficult.

Although initially skeptical about therapy, Scott appeared visibly relieved at the end of the first session. Over the next few weeks, I worked to strike that balance between encouraging him to set the pace and process of his recovery, while attending to the critical elements of his disordered eating. One avenue I pursued was to gently but efficiently begin to process our own interpersonal dynamics. For example, in the second session, I brought up the fact that he seemed to agree readily with me on all counts, to the point even of flattery. This began what was to be an enduring theme, and it helped to build our rapport as well as to interfere with one of his central interpersonal problems. It was also crucial as a way of tracking and processing his compliance with treatment recommendations without infantalizing him.

The Working Stage

In the beginning, Scott was consistently late to session, then profusely apologetic, then distressed at not having enough time to talk. By our third meeting, I pressed for a lengthier processing of the issue. One reason for the lateness was Scott's very real problem with attention and focus. However, I also sensed it was indicative of his general interpersonal style, and I gently challenged him to examine this. I said, "I can see you feel really badly about being late and my guess is that even though you feel bad, there's something about it that is necessary for you, or works in some way," and then because he responded well to soft humor, "So do you think we could put aside, just for now, the criticism of being late and talk about it?"

From here, he explored his complex style of eliciting good feelings from others. This involved (a) attempting to do a thing perfectly but "failing" in some way; (b) taking himself to task and expressing self-deprecation to the point where the other person would feel compelled to console him; resulting in (c) good feelings and resolution (of a sort). This left him feeling "superficial" and empty, overwhelmed by worry and guilt. Restricting, bingeing, and purging often followed. Scott and I talked directly about how this pattern might extend to us, and what I represented for him. He said that this relational pattern happened with most people, as he tried rather compulsively to please anyone and everyone. He saw me as an authority figure but had not to any degree examined the impulse to please me. My intention was to be as genuine as possible in an attempt to avoid the patterning of his other relationships and demonstrate something different. I knew it was important to not "console" him but rather to help him examine the interpersonal patterns so that he could choose to change them if he wanted to. Getting it out in the open early on, it turned out, aided me a great deal throughout our time together. Scott responded well, even hungrily, for "real" exchange, and this helped guide the treatment. He sought out ways to interrupt the interpersonal "loop" he created, and he began experimenting in his daily life with being more direct and less self-deprecating. Looking at these kinds of loops is a central component of Wachtel's (1993) theory of "cyclical psychodynamics." My hope was that by helping Scott to understand some about the origins of the patterns and then how they managed to get recreated in daily life, he would experience an increase in insight, emotional processing, and behavior change.

The other fortuitous aspect of Scott's lateness was that it gave me an opportunity to process his ambivalence about treatment. Costin (1999) stated how important this is for building the therapeutic relationship and for putting in place some central means of processing the ups and downs of symptom reduction, emotional and identity issues, and relapse prevention. Because eating disorders are adaptive in some way, they are hard to treat. Even someone miserable from starving and bingeing will be fearful of letting go of the behaviors. So at some point, I said to Scott,

> I wonder too, if you're struggling with whether to really tackle this problem. Most people I know want to get well, but also a part of them wants to keep the eating disorder. It might be really hard to think of being without these behaviors and you might even think that I'm going to insist you give them up.

This was to be an ongoing conversation, but at the time, it seemed to help keep him coming back for therapy.

I had introduced the notion that disordered eating behaviors were rarely about food. Scott knew this was true for him on some level, but making the connections was not easy. In addition, there were aspects of his relationship to food that he was acutely embarrassed about. One was being a man with a "girl's problem." He wanted to know if other men had these issues. Restricting did provide a sense of control and self-worth, but it also felt bad because dieting was such a female thing. He remembered the cruel joking in high school about girls who threw up their food and the media frenzy around young female TV stars who succumbed to eating disorders. Being so concerned about his looks, he said, also made him feel like he was not a man. Further, not wanting to identify as gay while trying to be attractive to men had created a difficult bind. It was complicated, but my sense was that he was also exploring his own ideas and biases regarding gender identity and sexuality, and perhaps testing me on some of them: "Is it okay for me to be like a girl in some ways?" or even "Can I be a man and have these concerns?" My response to much of this was to simply reflect his feelings and help him explore, and to model respect for him, whatever gendered state he was in. I also asked him at times what he thought of gay people, but this surfaced more later. And so these issues arose during our sessions time and again.

Helping Scott focus on and process his feelings about things was challenging. He had difficulty identifying feelings and was clearly overwhelmed by them. Much of our process involved my listening to and reflecting feelings back to him. He was so intellectual in his style that examining feelings came slowly. My sense was that he was also so terrified that his feelings might be "wrong" that even when he could delineate them they were difficult to express. It took time and patience before he could see that it was safe and permissible to do so. I would wait, sometimes for several minutes, while he struggled to express himself. I would gently bring him back to feelings he was quick to dismiss or discount. He told me at one point that his mother never listened to him, that she had her opinions and seemed convinced that she knew what was right for him. And although a part of him trusted her implicitly, there was something about her judgments that "didn't feel good." He liked being able to struggle to put out his thoughts and feelings, without pressure or judgment. He began to recognize thoughts and feelings prior to bingeing, and he was able increasingly to delay bingeing and reduce it. He began to identify anger and the part it played in some of his relationships.

As stated earlier, Scott's long-standing emotional and cognitive connection to pleasing others and "being perfect" required, during our time together, repeated and consistent attention, compassion, and confrontation. He despised himself for being so pleasing in nature, yet he could barely tolerate displeasing anyone. Again, using a here-and-now interpersonal approach, I would regularly ask him about his efforts to please me. We had ample opportunity, given that I was asking him to do things like seeing a medical doctor and a dietitian. With increased rapport, we were able to confront many of his underlying beliefs and thought processes. This allowed us to examine his efforts to please his parents and his belief that he should make up for his sisters' "failures." Even entertaining the notion that these beliefs did not necessarily represent the entire truth about him or his life was new and relieving to him.

As with many people with eating and body image issues, Scott's thought processes were often rigidly fixed. I have found it most helpful to pursue cognitive–behavioral strategies after the therapist–client relationship is more firmly established and the latter has a sense that his feelings will not be labeled as "irrational." Scott responded very positively to a cognitive focus at this point and needed only moderate encouragement to begin examining his thoughts and how they impacted his feelings and actions. He started spontaneously writing down affirmative statements that he or I made in session in order to repeat them during the week. (I supported this, as it was at his instigation and seemed to help him. Later it was to come out that his mother often gave him positive platitudes for "self esteem," a process that tended to make him feel unheard and discounted. But he appeared to benefit from instigating his own affirmations.)

Scott responded well to examining cognitions. He resonated strongly with the idea of "all-or-nothing" thinking and used this concept to look at and interrupt his beliefs about food, body, family, love, and other issues. Early on, only grades of As were acceptable and any deviation from this would send him in a tailspin. In addition, life had to be hard. He was not really working at school if he was not miserable. I mostly just reflected how I saw his thought process, essentially stating that it seemed inhumane to me. Scott began to actively challenge himself to tolerate variations in his achievements academically and would often recognize when he was engaging in a thought process that was self-deprecating and destructive.

Examining thoughts related to food and body provided much grist for the mill. Scott discovered that when he had binged on a food that he liked, he had the thought that he could never have that food again, because it was wrong to eat it in the first place. Recognizing that was what he was thinking at the moment before the binge was important in providing him armor for the next inclination to binge. Changing to a nondeprivation model—one asserting that a human being deserves to have food—helped him assure himself that he could always have that food again and so did not need to eat it all right now. Further exploring of this issue permitted us to examine other ways Scott insisted on depriving himself. We talked about his "puritan work ethic" and related that to his family culture and style. We also explored his use of deprivation to ward off guilt.

At one point, Scott considered trying medicine for attentional difficulties, but he worried that although it would calm his anxiety, it might lessen his ability to burn off calories. In response, I think I said something profound like, "Wow!" I was not reacting in surprise, but attempting to highlight the excessive nature of anorexic thoughts, and Scott began to laugh. Seeing the eating disorder as irrational and antagonistic, rather than the comforting friend, was a huge step. I like to address cognitive issues with clients with eating disorders by suggesting that the eating disorder has a logic of its own and that its goal is to stay alive. I had said to Scott earlier on when addressing his ambivalence about getting well that there was a part of him that wanted to be well and a part of him that did not. Subsequently, I would say, "*You* aren't the eating disorder, it's something that you have and that's claimed a part of you." So when distorted thoughts would surface, my response was often, "Yes, that's the eating disorder talking." And in this case, as we were chuckling over his admission, I said, "Yeah, look at its logic—it's trying to convince you that if you felt calmer and happier and more focused you'd be miserable."

Conscious of wanting to provide a combination of empathy and the sort of practicality Scott seemed to respond to, I at one point introduced the notion of compassion for self, kindness toward oneself. I worked to provide an experience of compassion in the moment, with a logical rationale against the inhumane nature of perfectionism and deprivation, by quietly asking him a series of questions about how he treated himself and how that could be different. I believe it came after he had reported a series of customary harsh internal criticisms as a result of failing to refrain from bingeing. I began with something like,

> You know, many of us grow up thinking we'll be okay if we just ride ourselves hard enough and never let ourselves off the hook. But this is a fundamentally flawed view because most people get exhausted and depleted from this because it's so inhumane.

Scott said he could relate to that but did not know how to make it different. I asked him what he thought had come of it so far, and now that he knows more of what he feels, what he felt about this. "Sad," he said. I asked whether he could imagine treating himself with compassion, the way he might for someone else who was struggling. "Yes, maybe, but probably not," was the gist of the answer, as he became tearful. I remember wondering if this intervention had only served to make him feel even worse about his perfectionism, as perfectionism of a clinical strength can get turned on itself (e.g., "If I can't get rid of perfectionism, I'm not a perfect client"). My hope was that it had the effect of conveying my compassion for him, yet placing the responsibility on him to generate compassion internally as well. Practically, it was crucial that he be able to halt some of the intense criticism if he was going to learn to reduce his unwanted behaviors. So, I pressed through, and in subsequent sessions Scott revisited it, bringing up times when he had success with compassion.

The Last Stage

At this point, we were about two thirds through our allotted time together. Scott was consistently on time for therapy. He had stopped restricting his food intake, and his weight had normalized. He had greatly lessened his bingeing and reported feeling good about his ability to refrain from excessive self-criticism when he did binge. His approach to exercise had significantly altered, and he was not vomiting at all. All this was good news, but in truth assessing "progress" with a person so bent on pleasing others had its own challenges. I had continually confronted his efforts to report only pleasing facts to me, but this gave us more to process. All in all, he indeed looked better, and his mood and focus had improved significantly. He had told his mother about the eating problem and obtained money to help pay for the dietitian and therapy (part of the issue of addressing self-imposed deprivation and asking for what he needed). He still struggled painfully with friends and potential romantic partners, and bingeing continued to be a source of "forbidden" pleasure, although much of that had been demystified. Then there was a lull in the therapy and I was not sure Scott would continue for the remaining five or so sessions. He was busy with his impending relocation and other life changes. I felt good about the strides he had made but regretted the many things left unsaid and unaddressed. I also felt it was very important to spend more time on termination issues but struggled a little with wanting to respect whatever lead he took.

In the next session, however, we began to talk more about gay culture, although still in broad terms. I remarked (again) on the pressures of young gay men to look boyish and toned. Scott responded more enthusiastically than he had in previous sessions, and he began to talk about his fear of aging and finding a man. Most painfully, he stated that the only guys he could get were the guys who reminded him of what he did not like in himself, that is, the "femmie" part. I explored with him his perceptions of who was gay and who was not and how they acted. I was able to press him on his prejudices of gay men, and he resonated to this and seemed to take it in.

Scott came to the next session in a good mood and stated that he wanted to talk more about his concerns about not finding love. We had a lively, somewhat humorous talk about getting a date. At one point we were talking about something and both looked up at the clock on my wall at the same moment; we laughed at this synchronicity and he exclaimed, "This is so cool— you're really tuned in to me!" It was a good moment. More than with most clients, I often had a sense with Scott of simultaneously feeling good about understanding him and concerned that there was so much more to know. Reflecting back, I think I did manage to convey my acceptance of him and to use my confusion to keep an open mind. Given that he was so much in a developmental process of becoming his own person, and had been told so often by others who and what he was, this was probably a good thing. This moment also provided an emotional inroad to termination and continuing treatment. I told him I was going to be sad to say goodbye to him, that I had valued working with him. At that time, Scott just said, "Thanks, thanks a lot," but not much more.

In the remaining few sessions, Scott openly explored the pains and pleasures of getting romantically interested in other men. His acute fear of rejection and low tolerance for conflict were more apparent, and he was entirely inexperienced with the vicissitudes of romantic relationships. We also had more of a chance to look at his body image in relation to being a part of the gay community. His report was striking in its similarity to what women, myself included, say about feeling objectified by men. Of course his experience was unique in its own way too, and I am not sure I could ever fully understand what it is like for him. But he responded favorably to my exploring it with him, and played with the concept of treating himself as a "subject" rather than an "object." There were so many ways in which he was not the subject of his own story. In the end, in such a simple way, this was what seemed to be the greatest gain for him: Talking about himself had made him the protagonist, and he liked that and knew it was good for him.

We had to end, and we were both sad, I think, to be parting midjourney. So much was untapped and unexplored—his relationship with his father, for example—and he had many things yet to conquer, while attempting to nurture that still-fragile recovery from his eating disorder. I had worked hard in the last few sessions to help Scott express what he felt about ending, and his feelings came out somewhat indirectly. His excitement about moving and taking a job on the East Coast was, on the one hand, great, and on the other hand, it was inhibiting my agenda for the processing of termination and dealing more directly with relapse prevention. We had been discussing the possibility of seeking out a gay-identified therapist. At one point Scott said to me, "But how will I know when I meet a new therapist that he will listen to me like you have? I think that might be more important than him being gay." The biggest impact of therapy, he said, was not the behavior change, but that he felt better internally. He related that directly to the freedom of expressing more of himself with me. This opened up space for talking about the difficulty of the transition. In our last session, I did not resist my eyes welling up briefly with tears, and he responded in his typical ingenuous manner, "You really care about me." And we said goodbye.

SUMMARY

The case of Scott highlights an integrative–interpersonal short-term approach to treatment of a young man with an eating disorder. Scott presented in distress over excessive bingeing on food, which was combined with extreme exercise, vomiting, and restriction of food intake. He had long-standing anxiety issues and was now also quite depressed. Scott struggled with his attraction to men, both in terms of his sexual identity and how to create meaningful relationships. I conceptualized the emergence of his issues from a biopsychosocial framework and hypothesized that the eating disorder was serving to help him manage the anxiety of his emerging gay identity and various relational issues, as well as helping to fill a lack of sense of self. Treatment was multidimensional, as Scott was seen for medical monitoring and eventually for nutritional counseling. The therapy was interpersonally focused, even as it incorporated behavioral and cognitive–behavioral elements. Drawing on the work of Costin (1999), Wachtel (1993), and feminist therapists, I worked in a largely here-and-now fashion to help Scott understand his interpersonal processes, internal criticisms, and feeling states and to allow himself to alter his behavior. Toward the end of treatment, Scott had made significant progress in decreasing his eating disorder behaviors. He was experimenting with alternative interpersonal behaviors and had begun to accept himself and his sexual identity more. Although our therapy had to end because of his moving away, he was committed to continuing work with a new therapist.

This case and my approach were fairly typical of how I work with people who have eating disorders. Progress in treatment went somewhat faster than much of the work I do with these issues. I suspect that if I had been able to continue with Scott, I would have seen the reemergence of behaviors and identity issues, and this is why treatment for eating disorders is usually a long-term proposal.

QUESTIONS FROM THE EDITORS

1. *What types of gender-based stereotypes were you aware of in counseling this client? How did that impact your therapy with this client?*

One of the most enjoyable things about Scott was how he seemed to defy stereotypes. Part of this was his chaotic presentation, coupled, from the beginning, with my feeling that I both knew and did not know him. I remember registering some slight surprise, or realignment in my perception, as a result of his rather immediate vulnerability. I think this had to do with the fact that he was male, but my early assumption that he would be reserved and to some degree shut down was quickly cast aside. In fact, my ability to understand his emotionality may have been hampered by an underlying assumption that men are more "contained" than he was with me. I am not aware of that consciously, but I wonder whether it played into some of my feeling confused by him.

Scott did not conform to easy stereotypes in terms of his sexual identity either. Although he objected to parts of himself he considered "femmie," he was someone who could probably "pass" as straight (at least according to the erroneous methods of detecting such things used by people in general). As Scott and I talked more about the eating issues, I was aware of having a stereotype in my mind of young, attractive, gay men who fixate on body and looks and clothes. There is a lot that I appreciate in this culture as fun and joyous; however, after all these years looking at media and societal effects on women, this emphasis for these men on the physical makes me sad. Scott was on the cusp of this, it seemed to me. He was outside looking in, wanting to be a part of that scene. He did not exactly fit this stereotype at the time I saw him, but I wonder whether I shied away from processing it more thoroughly with him because it pained me. I do not believe it is that men should not care about those things (i.e., that it is supposed to be a women's concern); I think it is that in its extreme form, the emphasis on looks is eroding to the soul—anyone's soul—and I do not relish it in men any more than I do in women.

2. *How did your own gender role issues influence your work with this client?*

I am pretty comfortable with my personal sense of gender. I was raised in a somewhat unconventional family that allowed me to work out for myself what my talents and capabilities might be. Specializing in gender issues during graduate school, while in a heterosexual partnership, helped refine at least some of the details. It is an ongoing process, of course, and there are ways in which I conform to a stereotypical female gender role and ways that I do not, and I think that is fine. My expectations of men are inevitably influenced by gender role issues too, and I have less experience confronting that. It takes consistent effort to counteract the pressures of socialization. As I have worked on answering this question, I tried to think if I ever had a moment where I thought, "C'mon, be a man!" I do not recall thinking or feeling this, but these are the sorts of psychically hidden remnants that emerge even when one deliberately works to rid herself of gender role stereotypes, and I am certainly not above it. Scott was interesting because his interpersonal issues were so stereotypically associated with women (e.g., his compulsion to please others, his perfectionism). He was not an effeminate man, but his struggles were utterly familiar to me, given my work with women and my experience of myself. As I reflect, a stereotyped expectation of him as a man was there in subtle form: hence my finding it so poignant that he expressed feelings and worries that many women express. I think this actually helped the process and helped my sense of empathy for him. I believe so strongly that people need more freedom to have "masculinity" and "femininity" mixed into their unique personalities and to make choices that do not conform to these strict categories. I wanted Scott to have this freedom.

3. *Looking back on the case, knowing what you know now, would you change the way you worked with this client?*

I think that for many men, and this client was no exception, issues around masculinity require ongoing exploration. However, after answering the previous question, I believe I could have done more to help Scott process his internal sense of feeling "femmie" and the connection between that and his gender identity and eating behavior. I am thinking in particular about his being overweight as a child and having an early sense of being "different" and how this may have combined to create specific sensitivities around body image.

I also had a twinge of discomfort all the way through that I was not adequately addressing Scott's family issues, not helping him identify and process his relationships with his parents and sisters. I believe this could have been useful, both to illuminate more fully his difficulty regulating affect, and to understand to a greater extent his deeply rooted beliefs about himself. Some of this was dictated by the time limit we had, but I have, in other cases, been able to explore family dynamics more thoroughly within such a time frame. Looking back, I think I went with Anderson's (1992) "stepped" strategy of dealing with present emotional and behavioral issues first, in the hope that the client would then be willing to move on to more psychodynamic and existential issues. However, if I had to do it again, I think I would spend a little more time in this area.

4. How did you communicate to Scott your diagnosis of disordered eating and why did you choose that terminology?

I believe I was quite straightforward about this. I said something like, "From what you're telling me, it sounds like you're struggling with an eating disorder and feelings of depression and anxiety. I'm not sure if you are anorexic, but part of what you're experiencing sounds like a starve-binge-purge cycle that is very painful." I then went on to elaborate about those behaviors and about the need for medical attention and dietary information. Because of the inherent ambivalence about getting well that people with disordered eating often experience, coupled with the need for multidimensional care, I believe it is in everyone's best interest to explicate the diagnosis as soon as possible. I think it may be particularly important with male clients that the therapist not postpone definition and that he or she avoid communicating a sense of surprise that may shame the client. For Scott, it initially provided some relief to have a label for his experience. Then he had to come to terms with all that that meant, and that in turn became part of the therapeutic process.

SUGGESTED RESOURCES

Ball, A. (Director). (2003). *Six feet under: The first season* [Television series]. United States: Home Box Office Video.

Costin, C. (1999). *The eating disorder sourcebook: A comprehensive guide to the causes, treatments, and prevention.* Los Angeles: Lowell House.

Fairburn, C. (1995). *Overcoming binge eating.* New York: Guilford Press.

National Eating Disorders Association. (n.d.). http://www.nationaleatingdisorders.org

Roth, G. (1993). *Feeding the hungry heart: The experience of compulsive eating.* New York: Plume.

REFERENCES

American Psychiatric Association. (1994). *Diagnostic and statistical manual of mental disorders* (4th ed.). Washington, DC: Author.

Anderson, A. E. (1992). Males with eating disorders. In J. Yager, H. E. Gwirtsman, & C. K. Edelstein (Eds.), *Special problems in treating eating disorders* (pp. 87–118). Washington, DC: American Psychiatric Press.

Anderson, A. E., Cohn, L., & Holbrook, T. (2000). *Making weight.* Carlsbad, CA: Gurze Books.

Bordo, S. (1993). *Unbearable weight: Feminism, Western culture, and the body.* Los Angeles: University of California Press.

Connors, M. E. (1996). Developmental vulnerabilities for eating disorders. In L. Smolak, M. P. Levine, & R. Striegel-Moore (Eds.), *The developmental psychopathology of eating disorders: Implications for research, prevention, and treatment.* Mahwah, NJ: Erlbaum.

Costin, C. (1999). *The eating disorder sourcebook: A comprehensive guide to the causes, treatments, and prevention.* Los Angeles: Lowell House.

Fallon, P., Katzman, M. A., & Wooley, S. C. (Eds.). (1994). *Feminist perspectives on eating disorders.* New York: Guilford Press.

Kimmel, M. S., & Messner, M. A. (1992). *Men's lives.* New York: Macmillan.

Linehan, M. M. (1997). Validation and psychotherapy. In A. C. Bohart & L. S. Greenberg (Eds.), *Empathy reconsidered: New directions in psychotherapy* (pp. 353–392). Washington, DC: American Psychological Association.

Peters, L., & Fallon, P. (1994). The journey of recovery: Dimensions of change. In P. Fallon, M. A. Katzman, & S. C. Wooley (Eds.), *Feminist perspectives on eating disorders* (pp. 339–354). New York: Guilford Press.

Pope, H. G., Phillips, K. A., & Olivardia, R. (2000). *The Adonis complex: How to identify, treat, and prevent body obsession in men and boys.* New York: Simon & Schuster.

Russell, C. J., & Keel, P. K. (2001). Homosexuality as a specific risk factor for eating disorders in men. *International Journal of Eating Disorders, 31,* 300–306.

Scher, M., Stevens, M., Good, G. E., & Eichenfield, G. A. (Eds.). (1987). *Handbook of counseling and psychotherapy with men.* Thousand Oaks, CA: Sage.

Striegel-Moore, R. H. (1995). A feminist perspective on the etiology of eating disorders. In K. D. Brownell & C. G. Fairburn (Eds.), *Eating disorders and obesity: A comprehensive handbook.* New York: Guilford Press.

Wachtel, P. L. (1993). *Therapeutic communication: Principles and effective practice.* New York: Guilford Press.

Wood, M. J. (2004). The gay male gaze: Body image disturbance and gender oppression among gay men. *Journal of Gay & Lesbian Social Services, 17,* 43–62.

AUTHOR INDEX

Numbers in italics refer to listings in the references.

Abrahamson, D. J., 279, *282*
Abreu, J. M., 21, *38l*, 215, *221*
Achterberg, J., 211, *222*
Addis, M. E., xviii, *xix*, 14, 16, 26, 28, 31, 37, *38*, 243, 244, 245, 253, *255*
Adler, A., 37, *38*
Akutsu, P., *172*
Alexander, C. M., *171, 221*
Allen, J. O., 180, *195*
Amato, P. R., 26, *38*
American Psychiatric Association, 23, *38*, 326, *337*
American Psychological Association (APA), 5, 6, *10*, 28, 242, *255*, 301, 304, 305, *317*
Anaya, R., 212, 215, 216, *221*
Anderson, A. E., 320, 321, *337, 338*
Andronico, M., xvii, *xix*, 83, 89, 288, *297*
Arrellano, L., 198, *222, 224*
Asian American Psychological Association, *170*
Atkinson, D. R., 152, 155, 156, 157, 162, 163, 167, *171*, 218, *221*
Attenborough, R., 89

Baca-Zinn, M., 197, 200, 206, *221*
Bachelor, A., 32, *38*
Ball, A., *337*
Balswick, J. O., 288, *297*
Banchero, R., 20, *39*, 200, *221*
Baron, A., 21, *47*, 200, *224*
Bartels, K. M., 23, 24, *41*
Barton, E., 88
Baruth, L. G., 21, *38*
Bauserman, R., *xx*
Beck, A., 76, 89, 90
Bem, S. L., 15, 23, *38, 39*
Bergin, A. E., *150, 172*
Bergman, S. J., xviii, *xix*, 101, *107*, 288, *297*
Bernard, J., 6, *11*, 288, *297*
Betcher, R. W., 288, *297*
Betz, N. E., 17, 24, *39*
Bieschke, K., *316*
Billson, J. M., 21, *44*
Blalock, J. A., 24, 40, 178, *195*
Blazina, C., 16, 22, 25, *39*, 46, 279, *282*

Bograd, M., 288, *297*
Bohart, A. C., *338*
Bordo, S., 319, *338*
Borst, T. S., 14, *41*
Bradshaw, R., 26, *38*
Brathwaite, A., 32, *41*
Brannon, R., xvii, *xx*, 17, 26, 39, 40, 52, 67, 79, 81, 90, 288, *297*
Bronstein, P., 26, *39*
Brooking, D. T., 253, *255*
Brooks, G. R., xvii, *xix*, 4, 5, *11*, 13, 15, 31, 33, *39*, 42, 44, 47, 69, 89, 90, *126*, 131, *149*, *172*, 180, *195*, 218, *221*, 239, 243, 244, 253, *255*, 286, 287, 288, 289, 293, 295, *297*, 298, 299, 302, *316, 317*
Broverman, D. M., 6, *11*, 24, *39*
Broverman, I. K., 6, *11*, 24, *39*
Brown, L. S., 5, *11*
Brown, M. T., 218, *221*
Brownell, K. D., *338*
Buhrke, R., *316*

Caldwell, L. D., 29, *39*
Campos, A., 21, *38*, 215, *221*
Cardeña, E., *222*
Carlson, J., 37, *39*
Carlson, N., 287, *297*
Carlstrom, A. H., 21, *47*, 215, *224*
Carpenter, L., 23, *47*
Carrasco, D., 209, *221*
Carrillo, R., *223*
Carter, R. T., *172*
Casas, J. M., 20, 29, *39*, *171, 172, 195*, 197, 200, 212, 215, 217, 218, *221*
Cattell, R. B., 141, *149*
Celentano, E., 43, *282*
Cervantes, J. M., 200, 201, 202, 217, *221, 222*
Chamberlain, K., 26, *40*
Cherry, M., 288, *298*
Chessick, R., 102, *107*
Chin, F., *171*
Chodorow, N., *107, 126*
Chua, P., *171*
Chun, K. M., *172*

Ciarlo, J. A., 14, 46
Clare, A., 6, 11
Clark, C. F., 180, 195
Clarkson, E. E., 6, 11, 24, 39
Cochran, S. V., xvii, 23, 24, 29, 30, 35, 39, 40, 45, 69, 78, 89, 90, 92, 107, 110, 111, 112, 126, 127, 131, 150, 283, 302, 317
Cohane, G. H., 14, 16, 38
Cohn, L., 320, 338
Comstock, D., 46
Connell, R. W., 17, 40
Connors, M. E., 322, 338
Conroy, P., 126
Cook, E. P., 288, 297
Cooper, M., 110, 126
Corey, G., 276, 282
Costanzo, M., 45
Costin, C., 322, 329, 334, 337, 338
Cournoyer, R. J., 23, 40, 288, 298
Courtenay, W. H., 14, 24, 40
Cozza, T., 43, 282
Cromwell, R. E., 197, 215, 222
Cross, W. E., Jr., 185, 195
Cutler, H. C., 131, 149

Dalai Lama, H. H., 131, 149
Danos, K. K., 34, 46
D'Augelli, A., 316
David, D. S., xvii, xx, 26, 39, 40, 79, 81, 90, 288, 297
David, L., 18, 45, 142, 149, 265, 284
Davis, C., xx
Davis, L. E., 43
Davis, S., xx
Davison, D., 275, 283
Deane, F. P, 26, 40
de Beauvoir, S., 15, 40
DeBord, K., 316
DeFranc, W., 288, 298
De la Cancela, V., 215, 222
Dell, D. M., 23, 41, 287, 298
Dennis, W. D., 16, 41
Dewsbury, D. A., xix
Diaz-Guerrero, R., 215, 222
Diemer, M. A., 282
Dillon, M., 24, 41
Division 44/CLGBC Joint Task Force on Professional Practice Guidelines with Lesbian, Gay, and Bisexual Clients, 316
Dovidio, J. F., 26, 46

Doyle, J. A., 17, 40, 288, 297
Duckett, S., 210, 222
Duncan, B., 38
Durrheim, K., 16, 47

Eber, H., 141, 149
Echemendia, R., 173
Edelstein, C. K., 338
Egan, J., 16, 45, 260, 271, 272, 279, 283, 288, 299
Eichenfield, G. A., 171, 224, 288, 297, 298, 300, 320, 338
Eichenfield, M., 47
Eisler, R. M., 15, 17, 23, 24, 40, 47, 178, 195
Englar-Carlson, M., 22, 26, 27, 28, 31, 34, 40, 44
Enns, C. Z., 5, 11
Enright, R. D., 275, 282
Erdoes, R., 201, 222
Erickson, B. M., 69, 83, 89, 90
Eshelman, S, 42
Estrada, A. L., 197, 200, 223

Fagan, J., 282
Fairburn, C., 337, 338
Falicov, C. J., 197, 206, 210, 217, 222
Fallon, P., 319, 322, 338
Faludi, S., 289, 297
Farrell, W. T., 288, 297
Fhagen-Smith, P. E., 185, 195
Fischer, A. F., 23, 34, 40
Fischer, A. R., 289, 297
Fischer, E. B., 23, 47
Fischer, J., xviii, xx
Fishman, D. M., 273, 283
Fitzgerald, L. F., 17, 23, 24, 25, 39, 41, 46, 287, 288, 299
Fitzgibbons, R. P., 275, 282
Ford, D. H., 131, 149
Fouad, N. A., 172
Fragoso, J. M., 197, 222
Franchina, J. J., 23, 40
Franklin, A. J., 21, 41, 182, 195
Freeman, R., 35, 46
Freire, R., 215, 222
Freitas, G., 282
Freud, S., 111, 126
Friedan, B., 80, 90
Friedman, A., 25, 44
Frone, M., 110, 126
Fujino, D. C., 171

Gable, R. K., 18, 45, 142, 149, 265, 284

Gafner, G., 210, *222*
Garfield, S. L., *172*
Garnets, L., 19, *41, 316*
Gergan, K. J., 15, *41*
Gibbons, J. L., 16, *41*
Gilbert, L. A., 14, 22, 28, *41*, 101, *107*, 288, *297, 298*
Gillette, D., 20, *44*, 288, *298*
Gilligan, C., 32, *41*
Gilmore, D., 215, 217, *222*
Gim, R. H., 152, *171*
Glass, S., 89, *90*
Goffman, E., 153, 154, *171*
Goldberg, H., 81, 89, 90, 287, 288, *297, 298*
Gonzales, D. S., 287, 293, *298*
Gonzales, R., 219, *222*
Good, G. E., xvii, *xix*, 4, *11*, 13, 14, 16, 17, 18, 19, 22, 23, 24, 25, 28, 29, 32, 33, 34, 39, 40, *42, 44, 47*, 69, 89, 90, *126*, 131, *149, 171, 172*, 221, *224*, 239, 243, 244, *253, 255*, 259, 283, 287, 288, *297, 298*, 300, *317*, 320, *338*
Good, G. M., 289, *297*
Goodholm, C. R., *239*
Goodyear, R. K., 21, *38*, 215, *221*
Gordon, B., 157, *171*
Gordon, S., 180, *195*
Gosiorek, J., *317*
Gottfried, M., *282*
Gottman, J., 244, *255*
Gowan, M., 197, *222*
Grant, B., 24, *42*
Gray, J., 89,
Green, A., *42*
Greenberg, L. S., *338*
Greenberg, L., 131, *149*
Greene, B., 306, *317*
Grisanti, C., 23, *47*, 263, *284*
Guzman, P., *173*
Gwirtsman, H. E., *338*

Haldeman, D. C., 21, 22, *42*, 303, *316, 317*
Hall, A. S., 22, 23, *42*, 288, *298*
Hamby, B. A., 16, *41*
Hammen, C. L., 26, *42*
Hammond, W. P., 20, *42*
Hanna, E., 24, *42*
Hanson, M. J., 154, 168, *172*
Harris, D., 308, *317*
Hartman, A., 5, *11*
Harway, M., *284*

Hatanaga, H., *172*
Hayes, J. A., 23, 25, *42, 47*
Hays, K. L., 246, *255*
Heesacker, M., 33, 34, *42, 43, 47*, 84, 90, 237, *239, 240*
Helms, B. J., 18, *45*, 142, *149*, 253, 265, *284*
Helms, J. E., 185, 186, *195*, 243, 254, *255*
Hendricks, L. E., 226, *239*
Hendrix, H., 89, *90*
Heppner, P. P., 23, *46*, 287, 293, *298*
Herek, G., 302, *317*
Hersen, M., *41*
Hill, S., *43*, 282
Hirsch, L., *43*
Ho, D. Y., 153, *171*
Holbrook, T., 320, *338*
Holmes, S. E., 19, *45*, 259, *283*
Horne, A. M., *42, 239*, 288, *298*
Horvath, A., 32, *38*
Howard, K. I., 14, *47*
Hoyt, M. F., 36, *42*
Hubble, M., *38*
Hughes, M., *42*
Hurst, M. A., 34, *46*

Imber-Black, E., 210, *222*
Imms, W. D., 16, *42*
Inclan, J. E., *43*
Ipsaro, A. J., 287, 293, *298*
Isaacson, W., 147, *149*
Ivey, A. E., 24, *46, 172*

Jakupcak, M., 15, *42*
James, L., *316*
Jensen, M., *172*
Johnson, N., 89
Jones, J. V., Jr., 131, *149*
Jordan, J. V., 7, *11*, 242, 248, 252, *255*

Kaplan, A. G., 7, *11*
Kashubeck, S., 197, *222*
Katzman, M. A., 322, *338*
Keel, P. K., 321, *338*
Keen, S., 110, *126*, 288, *298*
Keitel, M. A., *255*
Kelley, M. L., 20, *43*
Kellser, R., xvii
Kelly, K. R., 22, 23, *42*, 288, *298*
Kennedy-Moore, E., 35, *42*
Kessler, R., *xx*
Kessler, R. C., 14, *42*
Kilianski, S. E., 22, *42*

Kilmartin, C. T., xvii, *xx*, 6, *11*, 72, 80, 89, 90, 131, *149*, 280, *282*
Kim, E. J., 21, *42*
Kimmel, M., 6, *11*, 15, 16, *42*, *316*, 320, *338*
Kiselica, M. S., xvii, *xx*, 33, *42*, 226, 227, 228, 236, 237, 238, *239*, *240*, 288, 298
Kohut, H., 101, 111, *126*
Kohutian, 102
Komiya, N., 25, 26, *43*
Kopala, M., 255
Kopecky, G., xviii, *xx*, 6, *11*
Krippner, S., 211, *222*
Ku, L. C., 17, *45*
Kupers, T. A., 6, *11*
Kurasaki, K. S., *173*
Kushner, M. G., 26, 27, *43*

Lame Deer, J., 201, *222*
Landers, S., xvii, *xx*
Lara-Cantu, M. A, 206, *222*
Lea, H. D., *283*
Leafgren, F., *44*, *283*
Lee, A., *171*
Lee, C. C., 20, *43*, 180, *195*
Lee, D. B., *171*
Lee, J., 288, *298*
Leibowitz, Z. B., *283*
Lemle, E., 24, *43*
Leong, F. T. L., 157, *171*
Lerner, H., 92, *107*
Levant, R. F., xv, xvi, xvii, xviii, *xix*, *xx*, 4, 5, 6, 7, *11*, 13, 15, 16, 17, 20, 23, 24, 26, 33, 34, 36, 40, *43*, *44–45*, 45, 46, 89, 90, *107*, *126*, *172*, *195*, *223*, 244, 245, 253, 255, 263, 282, *283*, 284, 287–288, 288, 289, 297, 298, 299, 307, *317*
Levine, M. P., *338*
Levitsky, A., 276, *282*
Levy, N. B., *44*, *283*, *299*
Lichtszain, J. L., 215, *222*
Lin, C., 34, *46*
Lin, J., *171*
Linehan, M. M., 332, *338*
Lisak, D., 15, *42*
Liu, W. M., 20, 21, 22, 28–29, *43*, 157, 162, 163, 166, 168, *172*
Locke, B. D., *282*
Loeng, 157
Long, V. O., 220, *223*

Lowe, S. M., 152, 163, *171*
Lowen, A., 111, *126*
Ludlow, L. H., *282*
Lusterman, D.-D., 89, 286, *299*
Lyddon, W. J., 131, *149*
Lynch, E. W., 154, 168, *172*
Lynch, J., xvii, 72, 79–80, 89, 90, 280, *282*
Lynn, S. J., *222*
Lytton, H., 17, *44*

MacEachern, M., *43*, *282*
Madsen, W., 215, *223*
Mahalik, J. R., xviii, *xix*, 14, 16, 22, 23, 25, 26, 27, 28, 29, 30, 31, 36, 37, 38, 40, *42*, *44*, 47, 243, 244, 245, 253, 255, 263, *282*, 288, *298*
Mahoney, M. J., 131, *149*
Majors, R. G., 20, 21, *43*, *44*
Mak, W., 153, 162, *173*
Maler, S., 25, *44*
Malyon, A., 302, *317*
Maniacci, M., 37, 39
Manning, M. L., 21, *38*
Maples, M. R., 148, *149*
Martinez, E. A., 220, *223*
Matovina, T., 203, 209, 210, *223*
Matsushita, Y. J., 156, *171*
Mattis, J. S., 20, *42*
McCann, I. L., 279, *282*
McDavis, R., 21, *45*
McGonagle, K. A., *42*
McIntosh, P., 244, 247, *255*
McNeill, B., 198, *222*, *224*
McRae, J., xvii, *xix*, *xx*
Mejia-Millan, C. M., *239*
Men's Health Network, *171*
Mendoza-Romero, J., 20, 39, 200, *221*
MenWeb, *171*
Messner, M. A., 15, 16, 40, *42*, 288, 298, 320, *338*
Messer, S. B., 32, *44*
Meth, R. L., *11*, 15, 23, *44*, 69, 89, 90, 152, 157, *171*, *172*, *195*, 288, *298*
Miller, J. B., 7, *11*, 92, 105, *107*, 242, *255*
Miller, S., 38
Mintz, L. B., 14, 18, 23, 29, *41*, *44*, 131, *149*, 287, *298*
Minuchin, S., 202, *223*
Mirandé, A., 215, *223*
Mishkind, M. E., 24, *43*
Montoya, J., 201, *223*
Moore, D., *44*, *283*

Moore, R., 20, *44*, 288, *298*
Moore, T. M., 23, *40*
Morgan, R., 80, *90*
Morrell, F. C., 185, *195*
Morris, L. A., 288, *298*
Morten, G., 155, *171*
Moscicki, E., 24, *44*
Muldar, P., 110, *126*
Murry, V., 260, *283*
Mutchler, M. S., 275, *283*
Myers, H., *173*

Nadeau, R. A., 260, 279, *284*
Nadler, A., 25, *44*
Napolitano, J. M., 288, *298*
Nardi, P. M., 288, *298*
National Eating Disorders Association, *337*
Navarro-Arias, R., 206, 222
Negy, C., *221*
Neihardt, J. M., 201, *223*
Nelson, C. B., *42*
Newcomb, M. D., 21, 38, 215, *221*
Niemann, Y. F., 200, *223*
Nutt, E. A., 25, *47*
Nutt, R. L., 89, 286, 288, *298*, *299*

O'Brien, K. M., 25, *46*
O'Brien, S., 236, 237, *240*
O'Connor, E., 200, *223*
Okada, J., *171*
Okazaki, S., *173*
Olivardia, R., 321, *338*
O'Neil, J. M., 14, 16, 17, 18, 19, 21, 22, 34,
    40, *42*, *44*, *45*, 52, 67, 70, 90, 109,
    111, *126*, 142, *149*, 178, *195*, 259,
    260, 263, 264, 265, 270, 271, 272,
    273, 275, 279, *283*, *284*, 288, *299*
Organista, P. B., *172*
Osherson, S., 89, 288, *299*
Oskamp, S., *45*
Owen, S. V., 21, *42*, 260
Owens, R. G., 180, *195*

Paivio, S., 131, *149*
Paniagua, F. A., 21, 33, *45*
Parham, T., 21, *45*, 217, *221*
Park, S., 153, 154, 159, *172*
Pasick, R. S., *11*, *44*, 69, 89, 90, *171*, *172*,
    195, 288, *298*
Patterson, C., *316*
Pedersen, P. B., 6, *11*, 24, *46*
Peñalosa, F., 215, *223*

Perez, R., *316*
Perls, F. S., 111, *126*, 276, *282*
Peters, L., 319, *338*
Peters, S. D., 26, *42*
Phillips, K. A. 321, *338*
Philpot, C. L., 29, *45*, 89, 286, 288, *299*
Pittman, F., 288, 289, 290, *299*
Pleck, E. H., 289, *299*
Pleck, J. H., xv, 15, 16, 17, 18, 19, 20, 21,
    23, *41*, *45*, *47*, 52, 67, 70, 81, 90,
    109, *126*, 157, *172*, 206, 223, 263,
    278, *284*, 288, 289, *299*
Pollack, W. S., xv, xvii, *xix*, 4, *11*, 13, 15,
    16, 20, 24, 26, 29, 32, 33, 36, 40,
    43, *45*, *46*, 89, 90, 92, 101, 102, 106,
    107, 111, *126*, 152, 154, *172*, 186,
    195, 223, 255, *283*, *284*, 288, 289,
    297, *298*, *299*
Pollak, K. I., 200, *223*
Ponce, F. Q., 21, *47*, 200, *224*
Ponterotto, J. G., *171*, *195*, *221*
Pope, H. G., 321, *338*
Pressly, P. K., 33, *47*, 237, *240*
Prichard, S., 34, *42*, 84, *90*
Pytluk, S. D., 215, *221*

Quintero, G. A., 197, 200, *223*

Rabinowitz, F. E., xvii, 23, 24, 29, 35, *39*,
    40, *45*, 69, 78, 89, 90, 92, *107*, 110,
    111, 112, 116, *126*, *127*, 131, *150*
Ramirez, M., III, 200, 201, *223*
Ramirez, O., 200, 201, *221*
Real, T., 23, *45*, 72, 78, 89, 90, 110, *127*
Reich, W., *126*
Reyes, L. I., 215, *222*
Richards, P. S., *150*
Richmond, K., *43*
Riebe-Estrella, G., 203, 209, 210, *223*
Risman, B. J., *46*
Roberts, J., 210, *222*
Roberts-Carroll, M., 288, *299*
Robertson, J. M., 23, 24, 25, 34, 35, *41*, *46*,
    148, *149*, 287, 288, *299*
Robinson, B. E., 226, *240*
Robinson, J., *316*
Rochlen, A. B., 25, 33, 34, 35, 36, *46*, *47*
Rodriguez, L., 197, 215, *221*, *223*
Roemer, L., 15, *42*
Rogers, C. R., 111, *127*, 153, *172*
Rogers, S., 200, *223*
Rohner, R., 37, *46*

Romney, D. M., 17, *44*
Rosen, W. B., *255*
Rosenrantz, D. S., 6, *11*, 24, *39*
Rossello, J., *43*
Roth, G., *337*
Rowan, J., 152, *172*
Rubin, L. B., 32, *46*
Ruiz, R. A., 197, 215, *222*
Ruiz de Esparza, C. A., 29, *39*, 197, *221*
Russell, C. J., 321, *338*
Russell, M., 110, *126*

Sabo, D. F., *40*
Sachs-Ericsson, N., 14, *46*
Sakheim, D. K., 279, *282*
Sapolsky, R. M., 15, *46*
Sargent, A., *67*
Saul, T. T., *171*
Sawyer, J., 289, *299*
Schechtman, K. B., 23, *47*
Scher, M., 4, 5, *11*, 14, 22, 25, 28, 30, 32, *41*, *46*, *47*, 53, *67*, 101, *107*, *171*, 224, 272, 284, 288, 289, 297, 298, 300, 320, *338*
Schreer, G., *xx*
Schroeder, M., 305, *317*
Schwartz, P., *46*, 89
Scott, R. P., *282*
Sharpe, M. J., 23, *46*
Shem, S., 89
Shepard, D. S., 27, 28, 29, 31, 32, 33, 34, *40*, *46*
Shepard, I. L., *282*
Sher, K. J., 26, 27, *43*
Sherrod, N., 24, 25, 33, *41*, *43*
Shidlo, A., 305, *317*
Sibicky, M., 26, *46*
Silverstein, L. B., xvii, *xix*
Simonsen, G., 22, *46*
Skidmore, J. R., 17, *40*, 178, *195*
Skovholt, T. M., 17, *46*
Smiler, A. P., 16, 18, 20, *46*
Smolak, L., *338*
Snell, A. F., 289, *297*
Solberg, S. H., 21, *47*, *224*
Solberg, V., *215*
Solomon, K., *44*, 283, *299*
Sonenstein, F. L., 17, *45*
Steinhorn, L., 182, *195*
Stevens, M., 23, 24, *41*, *171*, 224, 288, 297, 298, 300, 320, *338*
Stiver, I. P., 7, *11*, 92, 105, *107*

Strachey, J., *126*
Striegel-Moore, R. H., 319, *338*
Sturmer, P., 226, *240*
Sue, D., 21, 28, *46*, 152, 154, 166, 168, *172*
Sue, D. W., 21, 24, 28, *46*, 152, 154, 155, 171, *172*
Sue, S., 151, 155, 157, 158, *172*, *173*
Sullivan, H. S., 157, *172*
Surrey, J. L., 7, *11*, 89
Suzuki, L. A., *171*, *221*
Swain, S., 32, *47*
Sweatt, L. I., 200, *222*
Sweet, H., 80, *90*

Tannen, D., 83, 89, *90*, 289, *300*
Tatsuoka, M. M., 141, *149*
Tello, J., 200, 216, *223*
Teyber, E., 153, 154, 156, 160, 161, *172*
Thompson, E. H., 16, 17, 23, *47*, 206, *223*, 263, *284*
Thomson, D. A., 32, *41*
Toerien, M., 16, *47*
Tokar, D. M., 289, *297*
Torres, J. B., 3, 21, *47*, 200, 215, 216, 217, 223, *224*
Trachtenberg, J., 275, *283*
Trevino, M., 197, *222*
Turner, J. A., 29, *39*, 197, *221*

Uba, L., 152, 153, 155, 168, *172*
Unger, R., *41*

Valdez, L. F., 21, *47*, 200, *224*
Vandiver, B. J., 26, *40*, 185, *195*
Vasquez, M. J. T., 246, *255*
Velasquez, R., 198, *222*, *224*
Veneziano, R., 37, *46*
Vessey, J. T., 14, *47*
Vogel, D. L., *240*
Vogel, S. R., 6, *11*, 24, 33, *39*, *47*, 237, *239*

Wachtel, P. L., 217, *224*, 321, 329, 334, *338*
Wade, J. C., 21, *47*, 178, 179, 183, 186, *195*
Wagenheim, B. R., 20, *39*, 200, *221*
Wainrib, B., 283, *299*
Walker, L. E. A., 29, *47*
Walker, M., 242, 243, 244, 248, 249, *255*, 255
Wallace, D. L., 14, *41*
Walsh, F., *222*
Wampold, B. E., 32, *44*
Watkins, C. E., 22, *46*, 279, *282*

Watkins, C. E., Jr., 23, 25, *39*
Watkins, P. L., 23, *47*
Watson, J. C., 35, *42*
Watts, R. E., 37, *39*
Wentzel, J. T., *239*
Wester, S. R., 33, 35, *47*, 237, *239, 240*
White, J. L., 29, *39*
Whitely, S., 152, *171*
Whiting, R. A., 210, *222*
Whitley, B. E., 23, *47*
Wisch, A. F., 25, *47*
Wohlford, P., *173*
Wong, J. Y., 33, 34, 35, 36, *47*
Wood, M. J., 321, *338*
Wood, P. K., 25, *41*

Woodford, J., 34, *46*
Wooley, S. C., 322, *338*
Wrightsman, L. S., 18, *45*, 142, *149*, 265, *284*

Yager, J., *338*
Yalom, I. D., *107*, 111, *127*
Yarber, W., *xx*
Yeh, M., 153, *173*
Young, K., 155, *172*

Zane, N. W. S., 151, 153, 154, 155, 157, 158, 159, 162, *172, 173*, 218, *221*
Zhao, S., *42*
Zilbergeld, B., 288, *300*

SUBJECT INDEX

Abuse in family background
    in case study (Bill), 115, 116
    in case study (Dan and brother), 312
    in case study (Jack Smith), 267–268
    in case study (John), 156
    in case study (Joshua), 143, 148
Action
    men's solutions through, 288
    vs. uncomfortable emotions, 75
Action empathy, 32–33
Action intimacy, for father and son, 37
Action mode, 122–123
Action plan, 130, 146
    in case study (Joshua), 141
Adam (case study), 289–295
    questions on, 295–296
Adolescent parents. *See* Teenage fathers;
    Teenage parents
African American boys, 20
African American men. *See* Black men
Ageism, in gay community, 306
Aggressiveness and aggression
    and behavioral patterns of gender role
        conflict, 264
    in case study (Brent), 99, 105
    and gender role socialization, 17
Alcohol abuse
    by Black men (clinicians' response), 178
    in case study (George), 181, 186, 188–
        189, 191
    in case study (Jack Smith), 267
    in case study (John), 155
    in case study (Juan), 202, 205, 206, 207,
        208, 212
Alcoholics Anonymous (AA), in case study
    (Juan), 208, 213
Alexithymia, xviii, 34, 236–237, 287
    among gay men, 307
    normative, 34–35
Ambiguity, therapist's reducing of, 170
American Indians, maleness for, 201
American Psychological Association
    (APA)
    APA Ethics Code on treatment of LGB
        individuals, 305
    Division 29, Psychotherapy, xvi

Division 51, the Society for the Psycho-
    logical Study of Men and Masculin-
    ity, xvii, 6, 286, 287
gay client's question on work with, 309
new multidivisional task force of, xix
Anger
    in case study (Adam), 293
    in case study (Bill), 115, 116, 119
    in case study (Brent), 93
    in case study (Carlos), 235
    in case study (Dan), 310–311
    in case study (George), 181–182, 182,
        183, 184, 185, 186, 186–187, 188,
        189, 190–191, 192
    in case study (Jack Smith), 262, 265,
        266, 267, 268, 269, 271, 275
    in case study (John), 156, 161
    in case study (Len), 112
    in case study (Mike), 249, 250, 251
    in case study (Scott), 327
    dysfunctional machismo as, 216
    and eating disorders, 322
    and loss experiences, 111–112
    as mask, 288
    in men, 192
        as able to express, 180
    sadness shown through, 83
    and women, 92
"Angry Black man," 182, 194
Anorexia
    in case study (Scott), 326
    See also Eating disorder
Antisocial personality disorders, of men, xvii
Anxiety
    and behavioral patterns of gender role
        conflict, 264
    in case study (Adam), 291
    in case study (John), 155, 157, 159, 162,
        164
    in case study (Joshua), 141
    in case study (Scott), 326, 331, 334
    in case study (Paul), 54, 56, 59, 60, 65
    and loss experiences, 111–112
APA Ethics Code, on treatment of LGB in-
    dividuals, 305
Arrogance, in case study (Mike), 248, 253

347

Asian American man, 21
    author as, 151
    building blocks in work with, 154
    case study of (John), 154–170
    and masculinity, 154
    new definition of, 152
Asian culture, core elements of, 170
Assumptions, on LGBT persons, 307
Attribution of failure, by women vs. men, 245
Authoritarian family role, in case study (Joshua), 137

Behavioral patterns of gender role conflict, 264
Behavioral therapy
    in case study (Scott), 334
    psychodynamic therapy integrated with, 321
Being and doing, 112
Bias, antigay, 303
Bibliotherapy, 83
"Big boys don't cry," 91
Big wheel, 17, 30, 84
Bill (case study), 113–123
    questions on, 123
Biopsychosocial framework, 321
Birth order, in case study (Adam), 291
Bisexual men, 21–22. See also Gay or bisexual men; Lesbian, gay, bisexual and transgender (LGBT) clients
Black Elk, 201
Black (African American) boys, 20
Black men (African American men), 191–192
    case study of (George), 181–194
    and father–son relationship, 178
    ignored influences on, 178
    masculinity of, 20–21, 193–194
    stereotype of, 182, 194
Black racial identity theory, 185
"Blueprint for manhood," 17
Bodywork, for men, 124
Boxing metaphor, in case study (Adam), 294
Bradshaw, Terry, xix
Brent (case study), 93–105
    questions on, 105–106

Bridging Separate Gender Worlds: How Men and Women Clash and How Therapists CAN Bring Them Together (Philpot, Brooks, Lusterman, & Nutt), 286
Brooks, Gary, 286

Bulimia
    in case study (Scott), 326
    See also Eating disorder
Bullies
    in case study (Dan), 313, 315
    as "playground ghosts," 313, 314
Bush, George W., xviii

Cancer, in case study (Bill), 118–119, 120
Carlos (case study), 229–236
    questions on, 236–239
Chicano, 198. See also Mexican American men
Child abuse. See Abuse in family background
Child molestation, fear of committing (case study of Paul), 55, 58, 65
Cleansing ceremony, in case study (Juan), 210–211
Clinical application, absence of in psychology of men, 8
Clinical considerations
    and men's concerns about psychotherapy, 27–28
    in psychotherapy with men, 28–35
Clinician–person, 52–53
Clinton, Bill, xviii
"Clone" movement, 307
Cochran, Sam, 110
Code of masculinity, xvii–xviii
Cognitions about masculinity, 263
Cognitive–behavioral approach
    in case study (John), 159
    in case study (Scott), 334
    after establishment of relationship, 330–331
    for male clients, 71, 83
    of men, 180
    psychodynamic therapy integrated with, 321
Communication, in case study (Jack Smith), 265
Communication style, of Blacks vs. Whites, 184
Compartmentalization
    and case study (Jim), 76, 77, 86
    as defense, 74
Competition
    in CRCS, 19, 142
    vs. intimacy, 288
    in male-client–male-therapist pairing, 293
    and masculine socialization, 29–30

Confidentiality
    in case study (John), 161
    in case study (Joshua), 138
    inquiries about, 148
Conflict
    between approach and avoidance ten-
        dencies, 26
    in family background (case study of Jack
        Smith), 261
    in gay or bisexual men, 22
    gender role, 18, 178, 260
        behavioral patterns of, 264
        in case study (George), 186
        in case study (Jack Smith), 262, 262–
            263, 270, 281
        in gay or bisexual men, 22
        and homophobia, 282
        masculine, 19, 34
        in men of color, 21
        personal experiences of, 264
        and restrictive emotionality, 25
    partners' avoidance of, 113–114
Conflicts Between Work and Family Rela-
    tions, in GRCS, 19
Confrontation, need to avoid, 130
Constructivism, 16, 131
    in case study (Joshua), 146
Contracts, on child-care responsibilities (case
    study of Carlos), 234
Control
    in case study (Adam), 291, 292
    and case study (Jack Smith), 262, 272,
        273, 274, 276, 279
        in therapy sessions, 269, 270, 281
    and case study (Joshua), 132
    and case study (Paul), 55, 58, 59, 66,
        67
Conversion therapy, 304, 305, 308, 309
Coping strategies, in case study (Dan), 314
Costin, Carolyn, 319
Countertransference, 81
    in case study (George), 185
    in case study (Jack Smith), 271–272,
        281
    in case study (Jim), 71
    and case study (John), 169
    in case study (Mike), 254–255
        negative, 247
    exploration of (female therapist), 82
    and therapeutic decisions, 249
Couples counseling
    in case study (Adam), 292

in case study (Bill), 113–114, 124
    in case study (Jim), 72, 76–77, 87
Credibility
    and Asian American clients, 152, 154,
        168, 170
        in case study (John), 157, 158, 159
    of Asian male psychologist, 151
Crisis of connection, between men and
    women, xvi
Critic, introjected, in case study (Bill), 119
Cultural ambivalence, in case study (John),
    157
Cultural considerations, in treatment plan,
    192
Cultural differences, and case study (Carlos),
    238
Cultural diversity, xvi
    new awareness of, 28
    See also Diversity; Multicultural coun-
        seling
Cultural expectations of masculinity, failure
    to meet, 24
Cultural identity, in case study (John), 160–
    163
Cultural messages. listening for, 180
Culture
    Asian, 170
    in author's work with clients, 169–170
    and masculinities, 16
    of Mexican and Mexican American
        men, 215–216
    and teenage fathers, 228
    and therapeutic relationship with Mexi-
        can American client, 206–207
    See also Diversity
Culture of psychotherapy, and masculine
    socialization, 32
Cyclical psychodynamics, 329

Dalai Lama, 131
Dan (case study), 308–315
    questions on, 315–316
Dean, Howard, xix
Deconstructing
    of client's success, 36
    of traditional masculinity, 188–191, 192
Deepening therapy approach, 110–112
    and case study (Len), 112–113
    preparation or cleansing for, 210
Defenses, 260
Dependence
    in case study (Dan), 312

and deepening approach, 111
inability to tolerate, xviii
and reference group, 179
Depression
    and behavioral patterns of gender role
        conflict, 264
    in case study (Adam), 293
    in case study (Dan), 308
    in case study (George), 181, 189
    in case study (Jack Smith), 266, 267,
        269, 274
    in case study (Jim), 72, 75–76, 78, 79,
        87
    in case study (Joshua), 135–136, 141,
        143, 145
    in case study (Juan), 205, 206, 208
    in case study (Mike), 246, 248
    in case study (Scott), 324, 334
    and loss experiences, 111–112
    in men, 23, 72
    and sadness, 105 (see also Sadness)
Desensitization, in case study (Dan), 314
Developmental notions, in case study
    (Joshua), 146
Diagnoses, and case study (Joshua), 139
Diagnostic schema, 259, 260, 263. See also
    Gender role conflict diagnostic
    schema
Diagnostic and Statistical Manual of Mental
    Disorders (4th ed.)
    and depression in men, 23
    and eating disorder, 326
Dialogues, internal (case study of Jack
    Smith), 272
Disclosure, therapist. See Self-disclosure
Discrepancy strain, 18
Distress, psychological, 131
    men's rates of symptoms of, xvii
Diversity
    among gay men, 21–22, 307
    and masculinity, 20–22
    See also Asian American man; Black
        men; Fundamentalism; Gay men;
        Mexican American men
Divorce
    in case study (Adam), 289, 292, 293
    in case study (Bill), 116, 118
    in case study (Jack Smith), 262
    and case study (Jim), 70, 72, 74
    of client's parents (case study of Paul),
        63–64
    and female therapist as preferred, 293

"Doing gender," 101
Drug and alcohol abuse
    by Black men (clinicians' response), 178
    in case study (George), 181, 186, 188–
        189, 191
    in case study (Juan), 209
    See also Alcohol abuse
Drumbeat, in case study (Juan), 211, 213
Dysfunctional strain, 18

Eagleton, Thomas, xix
Eating disorder
    as adaptive, 329
    case study on (Scott), 323–337
    critical attitude with, 323
    and food, 329
    and gay or bisexual men, 320–321
    treatment of, 321–322
Ellis, 302
Emotional awareness
    in case study (Jack Smith), 264–265
    in gender role conflict diagnostic
        schema, 263
Emotional expressivity, valuing of 86
Emotional intimacy. See Intimacy
Emotional support, in case study (Joshua),
    140–141
Emotional vocabulary, 122
Emotions
    and bodywork, 124
    in case study (Adam), 294
    in case study (John), 165, 168
    in case study (Joshua), 144
    in case study (Mike), 250
    as clinical consideration, 33–35
    males' difficulty in expressing, 236–237
    masculine-congruent interpretations of,
        130, 146
        as tools, 144
    men's resistance to, 82
    See also Feelings
Empathy
    action, 32–33
    and self-empathy, 248
Empty chair technique
    in case study (Bill), 115
    in case study (Jack Smith), 276
    in case study (John), 167
Ending of psychotherapy sessions. See Ter-
    mination
Essentialist position on differences between
    men and women, 14

Ethnic identity development, 162
    in case study (John), 155, 157
Evidence-based practice, 29
Expectations. *See* Cultural expectations of
    masculinity; Gender role expecta-
    tions, male

"Face"
    and Asian Americans, 153, 154
        in case study (John), 155, 158, 162
        in work with Asian American men,
            170
    in Asian male–male relationships, 168
Family, in case study (Paul), 63–65, 67
Family counseling approach, in case study
    (Carlos), 238
Farrell, Warren, 286
Fasting, in case study (Juan), 213–214
Fatherhood, 36–37
    and teenage fathers, 227
        in case study (Carlos), 233
        in case study (Joshua), 143
        in case study (Mike), 250
Father–son relationship, and Black men, 178
Fears of emotions, in case study (Jack Smith),
    264–265
Feelings
    and alexithymia, 287 (*see also* Alexi-
        thymia)
    in case study (Jim), 79
    vs. cognitive–behavioral approach, 180
    and male vs. female clients (female
        therapist), 85
    men's view of, 25–26, 80
    See also Emotions
Female gender role specialization, 289
Female therapists (clinicians), 69–70, 80, 84
    and male clients' disrespect toward
        women, 83, 296
    and male clients' exploration of painful
        feelings, 86
    male clients' preference for, 293, 323
    and men's experiences, 84
    sexualizing encounters with, xviii
    women of color as, 241–244
Feminine Mystique, The (Friedan), 80
Feminine qualities, in case study (Jack
    Smith), 282
Femininity
    in case study (Jack Smith), 265
    fear of, 19
    as organizing concept, 320

in personality mixture, 336
stereotypes of, 260
Feminism, 80
Feminist principles, in therapeutic approach,
    259–260, 327
Feminist psychotherapists, on traditional psy-
    chotherapy, xvii
Feminist relational–cultural perspective, 242
Feminist scholars, and new psychology of
    women, xv
Feminist therapeutic strategies, for eating
    disorders, 322
"Fishing," in emotional depths, 123
"Fishing expedition," in case study (Jim), 75
Fitzgerald, Louise, 130
Forgiveness, 275
    in case study (Jack Smith), 275, 276
Forty-Nine Percent Majority, The (David &
    Brannon), 81
Franklin, Benjamin, 147
Friendships, male, 32
Fundamentalism, 132, 147. *See also* Joshua
    (case study)

Gange, Sam, 52
Garner, David, 319
Gay men, 303
    of color, 306
    and conversion therapy, 304, 305, 308,
        309
    Dan as case study of, 308–316
    and hegemonic masculinity, 17
    psychotherapy with, 304–308
    See also Homosexual orientation; Les-
        bian, gay, bisexual and transgender
        (LGBT) clients
Gay or bisexual men, 320
    conflict in, 20
    diversity among, 21–22
    and eating disorder, 320–321
        case study on (Scott), 323–337
    and hegemonic masculinity, 17
Gender, 14
    new awareness of, 28
    vs. sex, 14
    social construction of, 252
Gender-aware therapy, 29
Gender-based stereotypes
    in case study (Adam), 295–296
    in case study (Bill), 123
    in case study (Brent), 105–106
    in case study (Carlos), 236–237

in case study (Dan), 315
in case study (George), 192
in case study (Jack Smith), 280–281
in case study (Jim), 84–85
in case study (John), 168–169
in case study (Joshua), 147
in case study (Juan), 218–219
in case study (Mike), 253
in case study (Scott), 335–336
Gender gap, in symptoms, xvii
Gender identity, in case study (Scott), 330
Gender ideologies, 16–17
Gender role(s), 15
    androgynous, 228
    in case study (Adam), 296
    in case study (Bill), 123–124
    in case study (Brent), 106
    in case study (Carlos), 237
    in case study (Dan), 315
    in case study (George), 193
    in case study (Jack Smith), 281
    and case study (Jim), 85–86
    in case study (John), 169
    in case study (Joshua), 142–143, 147
    in case study (Juan), 219
    in case study (Mike), 253
    and case study (Paul), 66
    and case study (Scott), 336
    and culture or context, 20
    dimensionality of, 16–17
    disadvantageous system of, 81
    and distress, 131
    as learned, 15, 131
    masculine (male), 23, 25, 26, 289
      in case study (George), 191
      and help seeking, 25
      stigma from failing to live up to, 26
      traditional, 119, 125, 289
    and multicultural counseling, 5–6
    and psychotherapy with men, 28
    for reference group dependent status, 179
    and religious teachings, 148 (*see also* Joshua)
    vs. sex roles, 15
    understanding of men and women through, 6
Gender role analysis, as clinical consideration, 31
Gender role conflict, 18, 19, 178, 260
    behavioral patterns of, 264
    in case study (George), 186

in case study (Jack Smith), 262, 262–263, 270, 272, 281
    in gay or bisexual men, 22
    and homophobia, 282
    masculine, 19
    in men of color, 21
    personal experiences of, 264
    and restrictive emotionality, 25
Gender role conflict diagnostic schema, 263–264
    in case study (Jack Smith), 264–278, 279
Gender Role Conflict Checklist, 265
Gender Role Conflict Scale (GRCS), 19
    in case study (Joshua), 142
Gender role expectations, male, 288–289
    and gay men, 315, 316
    stress from, 315
Gender role journey, 288
Gender role norms
    and Black male-to-male expression of closeness, 194
    exploration of regarding treatment, 79
    traditional masculine (and loss), 105
Gender role schema, 15–16, 279
Gender role self-concept, 179
Gender role socialization, 14–16, 259–260
    development restricted by, 285
    female, 289
    male (masculine), xv, 22, 28, 29–30, 31–32
      in case study) (Adam), 295
      in case study (Bill), 121
      in case study (Brent), 96
      in case study (George), 191
      as clinical consideration, 29–30
      and depression, 23–24
      development restricted by, 285
      exploration of, 31
      and mental health, 24
      positive attributes of, 35–37
      struggle against, 320
      traditional, xviii, 17, 19, 109, 112 (*see also* Traditional male socialization and conceptions of masculinity)
Gender role strain, 16–17, 18
Gender role stress, masculine, 178–179
Gender role transitions, 260
    in case study (Jack Smith), 275, 279
Gender role traumas, male, 260, 278–279
George (case study), 181–192
    questions on, 192–194

Getting the Love You Want (Hendrix), 74
"Gift giving" (immediate symptom reduction), 158, 170
"Give 'em hell," 17
Goldberg, Herb, 286
Good, Glenn, 52, 130, 131, 286
Grief, 105
    in case study (Dan), 310–311
    in case study (Bill), 114, 124
    in case study (Brent), 104
    and deepening approach, 111
    See also Loss experiences
Guided imagery, 47
    in case study (Paul), 65
Guidelines on Multicultural Education, Training, Research, Practice, and Organizational Change for Psychologists (APA), 242
Guidelines for Psychological Practice With Girls and Women (APA), 5
Guidelines for Psychotherapy With Lesbian, Gay and Bisexual Clients (APA), 304
Guilt
    in case study (George), 188, 190
    in case study (John), 156, 164
    in case study (Juan), 212, 214
    in case study (Scott), 328–329, 331

Hazards of Being Male, The (Goldberg), 81
Healing environments, 213–214
Hegemonic masculinity, 17, 20, 22
    and depression, 23–24
    in gay or bisexual men, 22
    and help seeking, 25
    See also Traditional male socialization and conceptions of masculinity
Help seeking
    factors in, xviii
    and fears about psychotherapy, 24–28
    and fear of appearing gay, 27
    therapists' need to understand, 30
Hendricks, Leo, 226, 230
Heroic men, exploration of work of, 37
Heterophobia, 302–303, 314, 316
    in case study (Dan), 309, 310, 313, 314, 315
Hispanic men
    and masculinity, 21
    See also Chicano; Latino men; Mexican American men
HIV/AIDS epidemic, 321

Homework
    in case study (Jim), 72, 74
    in case study (John), 159, 168
    in case study (Juan), 213
Homophobia
    in case study (Jack Smith), 281–282
    and case study (Paul), 62
    coining of term, 302
    and encounters with male therapists, xviii
    internalized, 22, 302
    in masculine ideology, 22
Homosexual orientation
    attempts to change, 303 (*see also* Conversion therapy)
    and masculinity, 307
    See also Gay men; Lesbian, gay, bisexual, and transgender (LGBT) clients
Honor, in working with Asian American men, 170
Horne, Andy, 286
Hostility
    toward women, 296
    See also Anger
Humor, 33, 85
Hypermasculine ideal, 316
Hypermasculinity, in exercise class, 327

"Ice Man," 109–110
    and Bill (case study), 113, 116, 117, 119, 121
    and deepening therapy approach, 110–113
Identity
    cultural (case study of John), 160–163
    gender (case study of Scott), 330
    masculine (case study of Brent), 98
    masculine (case study of George), 189
Ideology(ies)
    gender, 16–17
    gender role, 143
    masculine, 17–18, 245–246
        in case study (George), 189
        in case study (Jack Smith), 264, 266
        in case study (Joshua), 142
        in gender role conflict diagnostic schema, 263
    as varying, 20
Immersion stage of racial identity, 164, 166–167, 185, 186

Indiana Council on Adolescent Pregnancy, 226

Internal dialogue (case study of Jack Smith), 272

Interpersonal interaction experiment (case study of Paul), 60–63

Interpersonal process approach or therapy, 153–154, 165, 167, 321

Intimacy
    action (father and son), 37
    in case study (Dan), 309, 310, 311–312, 315, 316
    in case study (Jack Smith), 265, 266, 267, 275, 278, 279
    in case study (Jim), 72, 73, 74, 75, 87, 88
        and female therapist, 77, 79, 85–86
    by doing, 37
    eating disorders for avoidance of, 322
    and female therapist, 88
    and heterophobia, 316
    in-session (case study of Brent), 100, 102, 106
    and male lives, 32, 80
    men's difficulty with, xviii
    in men's group (case study of Bill), 122
    and men in therapy, 69, 111
    with other men, 288
    and psychotherapeutic relationship, 33
    and sex role strain, 70
    sexualization of, 82, 88

Introjected critic, in case study (Bill), 119

Investigation, in psychotherapy with gay men, 305–307

Invisibility syndrome, 21

"Invisible male chorus," 290

Jack Smith (case study), 259, 261–263, 278–280
    and gender role conflict diagnostic schema, 263–278, 279
    questions on, 280–282

Jim (case study), 70–80
    questions on, 84–88

John (case study), 154–168
    questions on, 168–170

Joshua (case study), 131–146
    questions on, 147–149

Juan (case study), 202–215, 216–218
    questions on, 218–221

Kiselica, Marak, 286

Lame Deer, 201

Language, of men, 83

Latina woman, as psychotherapist, 241–244, 253

Latino men, 197
    drumbeat as tool for, 211
    healing environments for, 213–214
    machismo for, 215–216
    masculine ideology among, 21
    selection of psychotherapist by, 33
    working with, 206, 218
    See also Chicano; Mexican American men

Len (case study), 112–113

Lesbian, gay, bisexual, and transgender (LGBT) clients, 301–302
    social attitudes toward, 303–304
    special high school for, 306

Levant, Ron, 286

Lewis, C. S., 78

"Little boy inside the adult man" (case study of Jack Smith), 272

"Load" metaphor, in case study (Brent), 96, 103, 105

Loss experiences, 91, 92
    in case study (Bill), 120
    in case study (Brent), 96, 104, 105
    and deepening approach, 111
    and gender role norms, 105
    unexpressed, 111–112

Love, psychological effects of, 116

Lusterman, Don-David, 286

Machismo (macho), 21, 197, 200, 215–216, 217
    and case study (Juan), 216–217, 220–221
    dysfunctional, 216

"Macho man syndrome," 209, 211–212, 215

"Male chorus, invisible," 290

Male clients, 13
    arrival of
        appreciation shown for, 111
        welcoming environment for, 71, 81–82
    with attitudes demeaning women, 83, 296
    author's approach to, 322–323
    author's life enriched by, 123
    cognitive–behavioral approach for, 71, 83
    and competition with male therapist, 293

deconstructing success of, 36
difficulties of in entering psychotherapy, 4, 7
with eating disorders, 323
exploration of masculinity for, 336
female author's approach to, 71
and female therapists
    and disrespect toward women, 296
    and exploration of painful feelings, 86
    preference for, 293, 323
initial approach of, 148
in initial encounter, 3–4
    recognition of strengths at, 125
nonpathological problems of 177
restricted emotionality of, 34
safe therapeutic environment for, 9
self-definition of as man, 112
and sex role norms, 69
and testing period, 125
therapeutic approach and structure for, 27–28, 287–289
transference of (female therapist), 82–83
See also Asian American man; Black men; Fundamentalism; Gay men; Mexican American men; Psychotherapy for men (males)
"Male-friendly psychotherapeutic process," 228
Male gender role. *See* Masculine gender role
Male gender role expectations. *See* Gender role expectations, male
Male (masculine) gender role socialization, xv, 22, 28, 29–30, 31–32
    in case study (Adam), 295
    in case study (Bill), 121
    in case study (Brent), 96
    in case study (George), 191
    as clinical consideration, 29–30
    and depression, 23–24
    development restricted by, 285
    exploration of, 31
    and mental health, 24
    positive attributes of, 35–37
    struggle against, 320
    traditional, xviii, 17, 19, 109, 112 (*see also* Traditional male socialization and conceptions of masculinity)
Male gender role trauma, 260, 278–279
Male identity. *See* Masculine identity
Male ideology. *See* Masculine ideology

Maleness, in case study (Juan), 214
Male reference group identity, 179–180, 189
Male resistance, 125, 244, 287–288
    in case study (Jack Smith), 268, 270, 271
    as therapeutic assumption, 260
Male role. *See* Masculine gender role
Male sexuality, 106
Male therapists, experience of homophobia with, xviii
"Manhood"
    for Latino men, 206 (*see also* Machismo)
    rules of, 110
Manhood meaning, among African American men, 20–21
Marlboro Man, 86
Marriage
    gay marriage movement, 305
    LGBT persons' opinions of, 307
    men's liking of, 291, 294
Masculine conformity, in gender role conflict diagnostic schema, 263
Masculine (male) gender role, 23, 25, 26, 289
    in case study (George), 191
    and help seeking, 25
    stigma from failing to live up to, 26
    traditional
        in case study of Adam, 289
        in case study of Bill, 119
        positive aspects of, 125
Masculine gender role norms, traditional, 105
Masculine gender role socialization. *See* Male gender role socialization
Masculine gender role stress, 178–179
Masculine identity
    in case study (Brent), 98
    in case study (George), 189
Masculine ideology, 17–18, 245–246
    in case study (George), 189
    in case study (Jack Smith), 264, 266
    in case study (Joshua), 142
    in gender role conflict diagnostic schema, 263
    as varying, 20
Masculine norms, in gender role conflict diagnostic schema, 263
Masculine self, fragile, 279
Masculine socialization. *See* Male gender role socialization
Masculine stereotypes. *See* Stereotypes
Masculinities, xvi, 16, 29, 193
    of African American men, 194

and culture, 20
and male reference group identity theory, 180
and psychological relatedness to other males, 179
Masculinity, 14–15
achievement as validating, 123
and Asian American clients, 152, 154, 168
of Black men, 20–21, 193–194
in case study (Jack Smith), 264, 279
in case study (John), 157, 166, 168
and therapist, 167
in case study (Mike), 249
changing view of, 6–7
code of, xvii–xviii
and cultural admonitions, 91
and dimensionality of gender roles, 16–17
and diversity, 20–22
female therapists' view of, 83–84
hegemonic, 17, 20, 22
and depression, 23–24
in gay or bisexual men, 22
and help seeking, 25
and homosexuality, 307–308
and gay identity, 316
Korean American author's perception of, 153
and Latino men, 206 (see also Latino men; Mexican American men)
in man's experience of psychotherapy, 7, 13
and mental health, 22–28
and new psychology of men, 6
and new psychotherapy, 4–5
normative, 22
as organizing concept, 320
in personality mixture, 336
and physical health, 24
as problematic construct, xv
rules of, 320
reluctance to question, 51
and sadness, 92
self-definition of, 112
and sex roles vs. gender roles, 15–16
stereotypic, 260
and therapy, 170
and teenage fathers, 227
traditional, 17, 20, 22–23, 180 (see also Traditional male socialization and conceptions of masculinity)
and case study (George), 186

deconstructing of, 188–191, 192
fixation on as neglect of estimable characteristics, 22
Masculinity crisis, xvi
Masculinity mystique model, 17, 18
Masculinity prescriptions or scripts, 192
McGovern, George, xix
McGuire, Mark, xix
Men
bodywork as help to, 124
cognitive and behavioral approach of, 180
connections between discouraged, 252–253
and crisis of connection, xvi
dependence of scorned, 69
differences of from women, 14
emotional intimacy as sexual for, 82, 88
female therapists' experience with, 84
fear or dislike, 83
female therapists' need to understand, 84
gay, 303, 304–16, 320 (see also Gay or bisexual men)
gender roles and biological differences in understanding of, 6
language of, 83
psychology of (and unwillingness to participate in therapy), 24–28
sadness and anger in, 77
safe interactions among, 163
socialized characteristics of, 18 (see also Male gender role socialization)
therapy resisted by, 125, 244, 287–288
in case study (Jack Smith), 268, 270, 271
factors in, xviii
as therapeutic assumption, 260
Men of color
Asian American, 21, 151, 154 (see also John (case study))
Black, 178, 182, 191–192, 193–194 (see also George [case study])
challenges in working with, 151–152
gay, 306
and masculinity, 20–21
See also Latino men; Mexican American men
Men's issues
author's involvement with, 285–287
and women's issues, 285–286
Men's Lives (Kimmel & Messner), 320

Men's psychotherapy groups, 37, 83
    in case study (Bill), 115–117, 122, 123
    in case study (Paul), 65
Men's studies
    and masculinity as problematic con-
        struct, xv–xvi
    need for, 84
Mental health, and masculinity, 22–28
Me-search, 51–52
"Mestizo," 201
Mexican American men, 21
    and author's life, 198–202
    and case study of Juan, 202–215, 216–
        221
    cultural oppression of, 201
    and machismo, 21, 197, 200, 215–216,
        217
        and case study (Juan), 216–217,
            220–221
        dysfunctional, 216
    relational hierarchy established by, 206
Mexican American/Chicano mainstream
        identity, 218
Mike (case study), 244–252
    questions on, 253–255
Mind games
    in case study (Jack Smith), 265
    fear of (case study of Carlos), 230
Minuchin, S., 202
Modeling, in case study (John), 159, 160, 167
Montoya, J., 201
Mother blame, in case study (Jack Smith),
        267–268
Mourning, 105. See also Loss experiences
Multicultural counseling, 5–6, 169–170
    in case study (John), 167–168
    in case study (Mike), 254
    guidelines for, 28
Multicultural diversity, xvi
Multiple identities, 20
Muscular armoring, 124
Muskie, Ed, xviii–xix
Myth of Masculinity, The (Pleck), 81

Native American men, 21
New psychology of men (males), xv, 6, 13
    and emotional expression, 33
"No physical contact" policy, 310
No reference group status, 179
Normative masculinity, 22

Objectification

and gay men, 321
    in case study (Scott), 333–334
of women, 333–334
See also "Success object"
O'Neil, Jim, 286
Openness
    in men, xviii–xix
    in therapy process, 122
Osherson, Sam, 286

Pack on back metaphor, 96, 103, 105
Pain paradigm, 271
Patriarchy, and men's problems, 259–260
Paul (case study), 53–66
    questions on, 66–67
Perfectionism
    in case study (Joshua), 141
    in case study (Scott), 326, 331, 332, 336
Perls, 302
Persona
    of client in case study (Jim), 72, 78, 80
    of Ice Man, 119 (see also "Ice Man")
Personal experiences of gender role conflict,
        264
Personalismo, 33, 238
Personality disorders, of men, xvii
Personality variables, in case study (Joshua),
        141–142
Philpot, Carol, 286
Physical contact, policy against, 310
Physical health, and masculinity, 24
Pittman, Frank, 286
"Playground ghosts," 313, 314
Pleck, Joseph, 286
Pollack, Bill, 286
Postnatal counseling, in case study (Carlos),
        234–235
Power
    in case study (Jack Smith), 273–274
    in CRCS, 19, 142
    as therapy issue with men, 268
Power balance, and anxious client (Paul), 54,
        58
Prayer, in case study (Juan), 214
Prenatal counseling, in case study (Carlos),
        231–234
Presenting concerns, and masculinity, 7
Problem solving
    in case study (Jim), 84–85, 87
    men's approach to, 180
    psychotherapy presented as, 129
Projective question, 164

Psychodynamic therapy, cognitive–behavioral and behavioral therapy integrated with, 321
Psychoeducational approach
    in case study (Paul), 55–56
    cognitive–behavioral therapy as, 83
Psychological distress, 131
    men's rates of symptoms of, xvii
Psychological practice guidelines, as task force goal, xix
Psychological research, males as focal point of, xv
Psychology (Western)
    and Asian cultures, 152
    and religion, 146
Psychology of men, and unwillingness to participate in therapy, 24–28
Psychology of Men and Masculinity (journal), 286
Psychotherapy
    and choice of therapist as reflecting status, 293
    culture of, 32
    as inpatient treatment, 185
    stepped strategy in, 337
Psychotherapy: Theory, Research, Practice, Training (journal), xvii
Psychotherapy for men (males), xvi, 38
    advent of, xvi–xvii
    for boys, 227–228
    clinical considerations in, 28–35
    and cross-cultural process, xviii
    fear of seeking help in, 24–28
        and fear of appearing gay, 27
    feminist principles in, 259–260
    framework for relationship in, 154
    with gay men, 304–308
    growth of, 7–8
    larger context of, 177
    little known about, 5
    men see selves as pushed into, 4
    need for, xvii
    new approaches in, xviii
    and positive aspects of masculinity, 36
    power as issue in, 268
    resistance to, 125, 244, 287–288 (*see also* Resistance, male)
    strategies for conducting, 129–130, 146
    theoretical perspectives on, 29
    traditional practice of, xvii
    See also Asian American man; Black men; Fundamentalism; Gay men;

Male clients; Mexican American men
Psychotherapy groups, men's, 37, 83
    in case study (Bill), 115–117, 122, 123

Questioning of assumptions, about LGBT persons, 307

Race, and case study (Carlos), 238
Race-based (racial) stereotypes
    in case study (George), 192
    in case study (Mike), 253
Racial identity, immersion stage of, 164, 166–167, 185, 186
Racial identity theory, White, 186
Racism
    and African American men, 21
    and Black teen fathers, 228
    and case study (George), 184
    in case study (Juan), 219, 220
    in mental health system, 183
    toward Mexican Americans, 199
    and personality development, 201
Rapport building, in case study (Paul), 54–58
RCT (relational–cultural theory), 242, 243, 252
Reconstruction, in case study (Joshua), 140
Reconstruction metaphor, 111
Reference group dependent status, 179, 189
Reference group identity, male, 179–180, 189
Reference group nondependent status, 179–180
Reframing, in case study (Joshua), 141
Relapse prevention, in case study (Scott), 334
Relational–cultural theory (RCT), 242, 243, 252
Relationships, as clinical considerations, 31–33
Relaxation response or process
    in case study (John), 159
    in case study (Juan), 211, 213
    in case study (Paul), 56, 57, 65
Religion
    in case study (Juan), 203, 209–210, 211, 220
        cleansing ceremony, 210–211
    in counseling with Latinos, 217
    and fundamentalist client (Joshua), 131–149
    and machismo, 216

and psychology, 146

Religious men, 148–149. *See also* Joshua (case study)

Resistance, male, 125, 244, 287–288
    in case study (Jack Smith), 268, 270, 271
    as therapeutic assumption, 260

Respect, in psychotherapy with gay men, 304–305

Restrictive Affection Behavior Between Men, in GRCS, 19, 142

Restrictive emotionality, 34–35, 264
    in case study (Jack Smith), 262, 264, 265, 266, 270, 271
    in case study (Jim), 79
    in GRCS, 19, 142
    and reluctance to seek psychological help, 25

Revenge fantasies, 294

Ritual, 217
    as preparation, 210

Robinson, Bryan, 226

Rogerian counseling, 181, 302

Role norms, gender
    and Black male-to-male expression of closeness, 194
    exploration of regarding treatment, 79
    traditional masculine (and loss), 105

"Rules of manhood," 110

Sadness, 105
    and action mode, 123
    in case study (Adam), 290, 293
    in case study (Bill), 115, 117
    in case study (Brent), 97, 100, 102, 104, 105
    in case study (John), 154
    in case study (Len), 112
    and gender role socialization, 17
    hitting as release of, 124–125
    in men clients, 91–92
        prohibition on expressing, 111
    as shown through anger, 83
    underestimation of, 84

Safety, in psychotherapy with gay men, 304

Sage burning
    in case study (Juan), 210, 213
    in psychotherapy, 210

"Saving face." *See* "Face"

Schema, gender role, 15–16, 279

Schematic structure, in case study (Joshua), 140

Scher, Murray, 286

Schwartzkopf, Norman, xviii

Scott (case study), 323–335
    multidimensional therapy with, 321, 334, 337
    questions on, 335–337

Scripts, masculinity, 192

Self, masculine, 279

Self-concept, gender role, 179

Self-destructive dynamic
    in case study (Brent), 100, 102, 103, 104
    in case study (Juan), 212
    in case study (Mike), 247, 251–252
    from traditional male gender role, 23

Self-disclosure
    in case study (John), 163–164
    in case study (Joshua), 136–137
    in case study (Juan), 217
    in case study (Paul), 61, 66
    as clinical consideration, 33
    in male-friendly process, 228
    therapeutic decisions on, 249

Self-esteem, in case study (Scott), 331

Self-sufficiency, requirement for, xviii

Sex, 14
    vs. gender, 14

Sex differences, in emotionality, 33–34

Sexism
    in case study (Jack Smith), 267–268, 278, 281
    and female therapists' view of men, 84
    and homophobia, 282
    as women's issue, 260

Sex role differences, misunderstandings from (case study of Jim), 77

Sex role norms
    and male clients, 69
    positive attributes of, 83–84

Sex roles, vs. gender roles, 15

Sex role strain, 70, 81

Sexual involvement, in case study (Jack Smith), 265–266, 274–275, 277

Sexuality, in case study (Scott), 330

Sexuality, male, 106

Sexualization of intimacy, 82, 88

Shadowlands (film), 74, 78

Shaking hands, in case study (Brent), 100

Shame
    in case study (Dan), 310
    in case study (John), 155, 162, 165, 166
    in case study (Joshua), 139
    in case study (Mike), 249

vs. face, 153
and RCT model, 243
underestimation of, 84
in working with Asian American men, 170
Silence, in therapy session (Paul), 58–59, 63
Sisterhood Is Powerful (Morgan), 80
16 Personality Factors (16PF), inventory, in case study (Joshua), 141
Smith, Jack. *See* Jack Smith
Social class
    and case study (Carlos), 238
    and masculine experience, 22
Social construction. *See* Constructivism
Social interest, 37
Socialization, 15
    as accounting for male–female differences, 288
    expectations derived from, 295
    of gay and bisexual men, 22, 316
    gender role, 14–16, 17, 259–260
        development restricted by, 285
        of women, 82, 84, 85, 253, 289
    male (masculine gender role), xv, 22, 28, 29–30, 31–32
        in case study (Adam), 295
        in case study (Bill), 121
        in case study (Brent), 96
        in case study (George), 191
        as clinical consideration, 29–30
        and depression, 23–24
        development restricted by, 285
        exploration of, 31
        and mental health, 24
        positive attributes of, 35–37
        struggle against, 320
        traditional, xviii, 17, 19, 109, 112
            (*see also* Traditional male socialization and conceptions of masculinity)
    need to counteract, 336
Society for the Psychological Study of Men and Masculinity (Division 51), xvii, 6, 286, 287
Stepped strategy, 337
Stereotypes
    of angry Black man, 182, 194
    of client's professional standing (case study of Juan), 220, 220–221
    about emotionally restricted boys, 236–237
    of femininity, 260

of gay men, 307
gender-based
    in case study of Adam, 295
    in case study of Bill, 123
    in case study of Brent, 105–106
    in case study of Carlos, 236–237
    in case study of Dan, 315
    in case study of George, 192
    in case study of Jack Smith, 270, 280–281
    in case study of Jim, 84–85
    in case study of John, 168–169
    in case study of Joshua, 147
    in case study of Juan, 218–219
    in case study of Mike, 253
    in case study of Scott, 335
    dispelling of, 125
gender roles defined by, 18
of machismo, 215
of male partner superiority, 295
of masculinity, 260, 270
and Mexican American males, 217
race-based or racial, 192, 253
of relationships of men and of women, 291
of teenage fathers, 226
of White male, 252
of women (case study of Scott), 336
Stevens, Mark, 319–320
Stoplight metaphor, for emotional expression, 35
Storytelling, as therapeutic tool, 207
Strain, gender role, 16, 18
    masculine, 16–17
Strength(s)
    in case study (Joshua), 138
        need for control as, 132
    emotional expressiveness as, 144
    emphasis on, 36
        in case study of Jack Smith, 279
    perceived weakness redefined as, 129–130
    recognition of at first encounter, 125
    seeking help as sign of, 269
    structures to use, 260
Stress, gender role, 178–179
    and behavioral patterns of gender role conflict, 264
Strober, Michael, 319
"Sturdy oak" trait, xviii, 17, 26, 79, 84
Substance abuse, by men, xvii. *See also* Alcohol abuse; Drug and alcohol abuse
Success

in case study (Joshua), 142
in CRCS, 19, 142
outcome-based definition of, 169
and traditional gender roles, 289
"Success object," client (Adam) seen as, 291, 294
Sue, Stanley, 153
Suicides, male–female ratios of, xvii
Surrogate partner, female therapist (author) seen as, 88

Talk therapy, feminine norms in, 69
Task Force on Men's Roles and Psychotherapy (APA), xvi–xvii
Team approach, for eating disorders, 322
Teenage fathers, 225–226
agenda of, 230
author's regard for, 239
and male-friendly psychotherapy, 227–228
See also Carlos (case study)
Teenage Fathers (Robinson), 226
Teenage parents, 225
families' relations to each other, 232
Termination (ending of therapeutic relationship), 145
in case study (Adam), 292
in case study (Brent), 103–104, 106
in case study (Carlos), 235
in case study (Dan), 314
in case study (George, discharge from hospital), 191
in case study (Jack Smith), 278
in case study (John), 166–167
in case study (Joshua), 145–146
in case study (Juan), 214
in case study (Mike), 251–252
in case study (Paul), 65–66
in case study (Scott), 333, 334
Testing period in therapy, 125
Theoretical perspectives on treating men, 29
Therapeutic alliance
in case study (Jim), 85
and first session, 71
and therapeutic outcome, 32
Therapeutic approach, 287–289
Therapeutic assumptions, in therapy with men, 259–260
Therapeutic environment, 9
and men's concerns about psychotherapy, 27–28

as welcoming, 71, 81–82
Therapeutic relationship
and action empathy, 32
and ambivalence about treatment, 329
with Asian American men, 152
in case study (John), 157
in case study (Juan) 220
and culture, 207
in interpersonal therapy, 321
with Latino males, 218
types of (minority and White), 243
Therapist disclosure. *See* Self-disclosure
Therapy process, 122
testing period in, 125
Three Approaches to Psychotherapy (film), 302
Traditional male socialization and conceptions of masculinity, 17, 19, 20, 20–23, 109–110, 112
in case studies, 119, 186, 289
deconstructing of, 188–191, 192
and male reference group identity, 180
and men's reluctance to seek health care, xviii
positive aspects of, 22, 35–37, 83–84, 125
and sadness, 17, 105
Trance state, in case study (Juan), 211
Transference, 66
in case study (Brent), 98–99
in case study (Dan), 311
in case study (John), 158–159, 160
in case study (Paul), 67
good feeling from, 57–58
with therapist author, 323
Transgendered men, 22. *See also* Lesbian, gay, bisexual and transgender (LGBT) clients
Treatment fears, 24–28
and fear of appearing gay, 27
Treatment plan, cultural considerations in, 192

Unbearable Weight: Feminism, Western Culture, and the Body (Bordo), 319

Videotherapy, 83
Volunteer work, men's social interest enhanced by, 37
Vulnerability
in case study (Jack Smith), 265, 269, 270, 282
in case study (Jim), 74–75, 85
in case study (John), 166

in case study (Juan), 204, 208
in case study (Mike), 248, 251
in case study (Paul), 66
and gender role socialization, 17
and male resistance, 125
in therapy relationship, 111
women's understanding of, 86

Wallace, Mike, xix
"White Privilege," 244, 247
*White Privilege: Unpacking the Invisible Knap-
    sack* (McIntosh), 244
White racial identity theory, 186
"Woman's perspective," 293
Women
    and anger, 92
    changes in roles of, xvi
    and close connection, 86
    differences of from men, 14
    gender roles and biological differences
        in understanding of, 6
    and men's feelings, 79–80, 82
    sexism as problem for, 260
    socialization of, 82, 84, 85, 253, 289
    traditional therapy designed to treat,
        xvii, xviii, 5
    See also at Female; Feminine
Women of color, as psychotherapists, 241–
    244
Women's issues, and men's issues, 285–286
Women's movement
    psychotherapy critiqued by, 5, 6
    See also Feminism
Women's studies, and understanding of gen-
    der roles, 70
Work related challenges, in case study
    (Mike), 246–247
Wounded Knee incident, 200

You Just Don't Understand (Tannen), 83, 291

ABOUT THE EDITORS

Matt Englar-Carlson, PhD, is assistant professor of counseling at California State University, Fullerton. He received his doctorate in counseling psychology from Pennsylvania State University in 2001. His clinical and research interests focus on two aspects of diversity: men's issues and social class. In reference to men, he is interested in training issues related to assisting practitioners in understanding how masculinity influences well-being, interpersonal relationships, and self-identity. This exploration extends to how men ask for and receive assistance from the mental health field. He serves on the editorial review boards for *Psychology of Men and Masculinity* and *The Family Journal*. Dr. Englar-Carlson resides in Huntington Beach, California, with his wife, Alison, and son, Jackson.

Mark A. Stevens, PhD, is the director of University Counseling Services at California State University, Northridge. Prior to his present position, he was the coordinator of training and assistant director of Student Counseling Services at the University of Southern California. He received his doctorate in clinical psychology from the California School of Professional Psychology, San Diego, in 1982. Dr. Stevens has been active in developing and facilitating programs for college men on antiviolence and other men's issues since 1981. He is an editor of the *Handbook of Counseling and Psychotherapy With Men* (1987) and is the featured therapist in the *Psychotherapy With Men* two-part videotape series (2003) produced by the American Psychological Association (APA). Dr. Stevens is an active member and president-elect of APA's Division 51 (Society for the Psychological Study of Men and Masculinity) and an APA fellow.